FOUNDATIONS in DRAWING

The Affordable Way to Learn Professional Skills

MARCO BUCCI

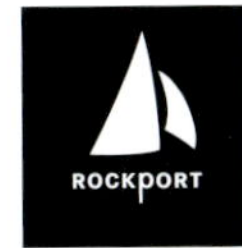

To Renée, and to my parents,
who support me unflinchingly in everything I do.

Quarto.com

© 2025 Quarto Publishing Group USA Inc.

Text, Photos, Illustrations © 2025 Marco Bucci

First published in 2025 by Rockport Publishers, an imprint of The Quarto Group,

100 Cummings Center, Suite 265-D, Beverly, MA 01915, USA.

T (978) 282-9590 F (978) 283-2742

Rockport Publishers titles are also available at discount for retail, wholesale, promotional, and bulk purchase. For details, contact the Special Sales Manager by email at specialsales@quarto.com or by mail at The Quarto Group, Attn: Special Sales Manager, 100 Cummings Center, Suite 265-D, Beverly, MA 01915, USA.

10 9 8 7 6 5 4 3 2

ISBN: 978-0-7603-9160-0

Digital edition published in 2025

eISBN: 978-0-7603-9161-7

Library of Congress Cataloging-in-Publication Data

Names: Bucci, Marco, author.
Title: Debt free art degree : foundations in drawing : the affordable way to learn professional skills / Marco Bucci.
Other titles: Foundations in drawing
Description: Beverly, MA : Rockport Publishers, 2025. | Includes index.
Identifiers: LCCN 2024016299 (print) | LCCN 2024016300 (ebook) | ISBN 9780760391600 (trade paperback) | ISBN 9780760391617 (ebook)
Subjects: LCSH: Drawing--Technique.
Classification: LCC NC730 .B77 2025 (print) | LCC NC730 (ebook) | DDC 741.2--dc23/eng/20240620
LC record available at https://lccn.loc.gov/2024016299
LC ebook record available at https://lccn.loc.gov/2024016300

Design: Sporto

Page Layout: Sporto

Photography and illustration: Marco Bucci, except Rachel Bradley on pages 42 (right), 45 (left), 46 (top left), 47 (top left), 48 (top right), 52 (top right), 53 (top left), 87 (both; poses), 88 (both; poses), 89 (both; poses), 91 (top left), 92 (top right), 93 (top left; pose), 110 (top), and 114 (top left); Unsplash on page 49; Brian Wong on pages 111 (top, bottom left, bottom right) and 113 (top right)

Printed in China

Acknowledgments

As any artist will attest, you can't learn art in a vacuum. While I have structured and assembled these lessons myself over the years, many of the core concepts found in this book (and beyond), I have learned from others who have been kind enough to pass them on to me. The list of names here could fill its own book, but I would be remiss if I did not mention at least a few standouts.

First, thank you to Nick Kilislian, the person who taught me how to see like an artist (and an amazing artist in his own right). If I hadn't walked into his studio in 2001, I don't know that I'd be where I am today.

Thank you to Morgan Weistling and Scott Christensen, both prodigious, excellent fine artists, and generous teachers. Without their lessons and in-person tutelage, I almost certainly would not be as passionate about, or as familiar with, many of these fundamentals.

Thank you to Mark Behm, the first artist who ever selflessly responded to one of my emails asking for help with the drawing and painting process.

CONTENTS

Introduction: How Did I Get Here? ... 6

1

The 2D World of Shapes ... 10

What Are Simple Shapes? ... 12

Drawing Is Design ... 14

Tangents? Bad. T-Connections and Overlaps? Good. ... 16

Guide to Thoughtful Shape Design ... 19

Differences in Art Styles ... 24

Assignments ... 25

2

Abstract Art Plays a Part: Gesture Drawing ... 26

Gesture Is All about Rhythm ... 28

Capturing Body Language ... 29

The Stick Figure ... 32

A More Dynamic Gesture ... 36

Landmarking Major Elements ... 38

Rhythms Capture Physicality ... 42

Let's Draw Gestures! ... 45

Assignments ... 55

3

The 3D World of Form and Space ... 56

Understanding the Horizon Line ... 58

Ellipses Are Foreshortened Circles ... 60

Blocking Out 3D Space with a Perspective Grid ... 62

Why Freehand Is Important ... 68

Twisting, Bending, and Folding Forms ... 69

Assignments ... 73

4

Building the Figure ... 74

Basic Forms of the Body ... 76

The Torso and Hips Relationship ... 77

Overlapping Forms: The Accordion Effect ... 81

Legs and Arms ... 84

Hands and Feet ... 86

Trace Over Studies ... 87

Figure Construction Studies ... 90

Draw, Draw, Draw ... 94

Assignments ... 95

5

Capturing Poses, Shapes, and Character ... 96

"Character" Is the Key Word ... 98

Silhouette ... 100

Guide to Thoughtful Shape Design, Part II ... 104

Weight, Balance, and Movement ... 110

Designing Your Drawing ... 111

Assignments ... 115

6

Constructing the Head ... 116

The Head Is a Box ... 118

Building the Facial Features ... 120

General Proportions ... 130

Adding Features onto Framework ... 135

Assignments ... 137

7

Shading and Lighting ... 138

Light and Shadow: Neighbors That Don't Get Along ... 140

Good News: You Only Need to Know Six Values! ... 142

Our First Two Tones: Average Light and Average Shadow ... 144

Form Shadows and Cast Shadows Act Together ... 146

Halftone: The Bridge between Light and Shadow ... 147

Reflected Light Illuminates the Shadows ... 148

Highlights: Your Lightest Value ... 150

Dark Accent/Ambient Occlusion: The Anti-Highlight ... 152

Applying the Value System to More Complex Subjects ... 154

Assignments ... 157

8

Color Doesn't Have to Be Scary! ... 158

Color Temperature: The All-in-One Color Theory ... 160

The Easiest Way to Move from Warm to Cool and Back ... 162

Light and Shadow Colors: The Bully Principle ... 165

Grays Are Powerful (And Another Way to Shift Temperature) ... 168

Assignments ... 172

Final Note ... 173

About the Author ... 174

Index ... 174

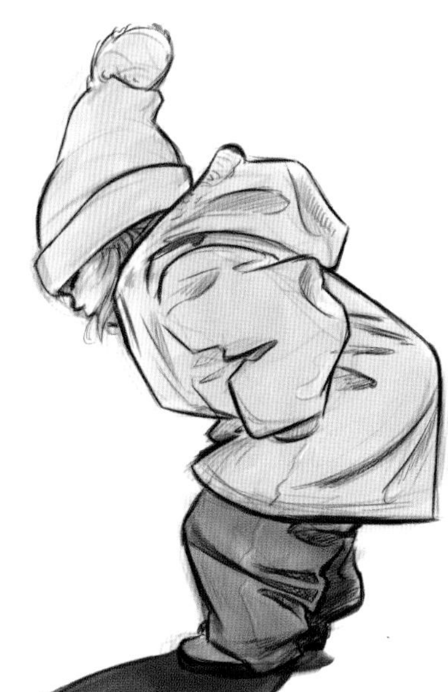

Introduction:
How Did I Get Here?

I was nineteen years old when I decided to give this whole "drawing" thing a go. I started from the bottom. No art talent, no skill. Why did I wait so long? Well, like many people, I thought you had to be born with the ability to draw.

A high school classmate posed for this drawing for a figure drawing assignment, circa 1999. Proof that I'm not some savant.

But I was always fascinated by art, especially animation. When I was nineteen, computer animation had just achieved liftoff with Pixar's *Toy Story*, and I wanted to be a CG animator. It was a perfect plan, I thought, because using the computer would circumvent the need to draw! But, that's when I found out that many Pixar animators were also good at drawing and had the portfolios to show for it. This was a punch to the gut.

Until I came across one Pixar animator's blog. He had all these recommendations for how I could, get this, *learn to draw*. Learn to draw? My first thought was that it couldn't be real. Talent was in-born, not made. People who were good at drawing were always good at drawing . . . right?

Wrong. I learned that many animators honed their craft by learning to draw the human figure, and this was broken down into simple lessons. After picking up my brain fragments off the floor, I began to seek out local life drawing classes. As luck would have it, I met an animator who happened to be offering such classes out of a studio nearby. He taught me that learning to draw is largely a matter of learning to *see*. Or, the way I think of it now, reprogramming *how* you see.

Under his tutelage, I began noticing improvements immediately. This stuff was for real. It worked, and I was hooked.

I became a certified "professional artist" (which is to say I got my first paying job) in 2004, about three years after I began my studies. By that time I had hundreds of figure drawings with which to build a portfolio. I chose just my best ones—drawings that demonstrated an aptitude for the quick sketch, as well as more thorough studies, complete with form, light, and construction. I had also experimented with various mediums, such as

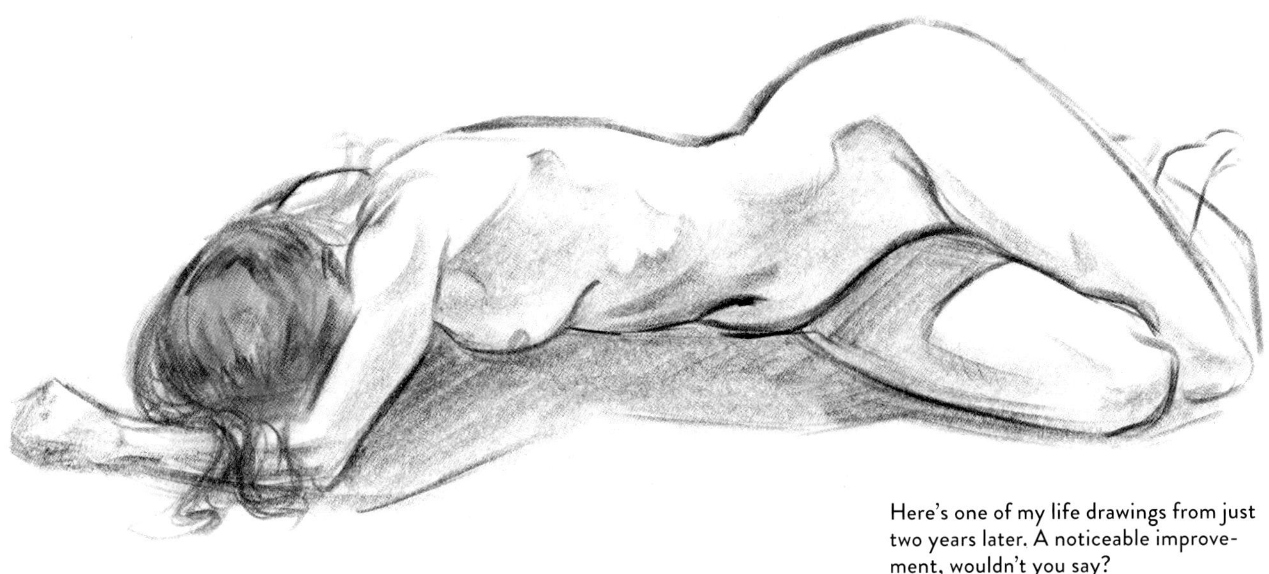

Here's one of my life drawings from just two years later. A noticeable improvement, wouldn't you say?

pencil, pen and ink, watercolor, gouache, oils, and digital, which helped give my portfolio a breadth that art directors always like to see, and I got hired by a Toronto studio that was crewing up for a kids' animated TV show. So I had a standard 9 to 5 job . . . but as an artist in an animation studio! My work wasn't done yet, though. Being surrounded by other professional artists, I took it upon myself to learn from them. I watched what they did and how they did it. I tried to soak in as much as I could, from everyone around me.

Fast forward about twenty years and here I am today. I've learned and grown a lot in that time. I've worked as a professional artist and continue to learn in my spare time. I also still remember where I came from and what it felt like to *not* know any of this stuff.

I'm here to give you the information that changed my life.

Learning how to draw is a lot like learning a new language. It's helpful to first become familiar with common words and phrases. From there you build in grammar and syntax to structure your communication. After that, it's extremely helpful to immerse yourself in that language, so that you're actively hearing *and* putting what you've learned to use.

The Debt-Free Art Degree series is designed to be your guide to learning the visual language of drawing and painting.

In time, it can take you from beginner to fluent. In this first book, we'll go over the fundamental building blocks of drawing and begin to tie them together as part of an overall, structured process, bringing our skills to an intermediate, and even advanced level.

Debt-Free Art Degree is modeled after a college curriculum. Yes, you can read it all in one sitting, but it will be best to absorb the information slowly, returning to various chapters with each new level you reach.

Consider this book your definitive guide as you become immersed in the visual language of drawing.

HOW TO STUDY FROM THIS BOOK

Every chapter in this volume (except for Chapter 4: Building the Figure, which combines all previous chapters) covers its own separate drawing fundamental, and you can study it separately. But the fundamentals are not intended to be used separately. They *must* work together to make good drawings. It is possible, however, to *learn* the fundamentals separately, and *focus* on them separately and bring them together later down the line.

By compartmentalizing fundamentals, your brain becomes a sort of hotel for art. Need to capture life in a pose? Well, that's over in this room. Need to shade something realistically? That's down the hall. The hotel occupants start as strangers, but

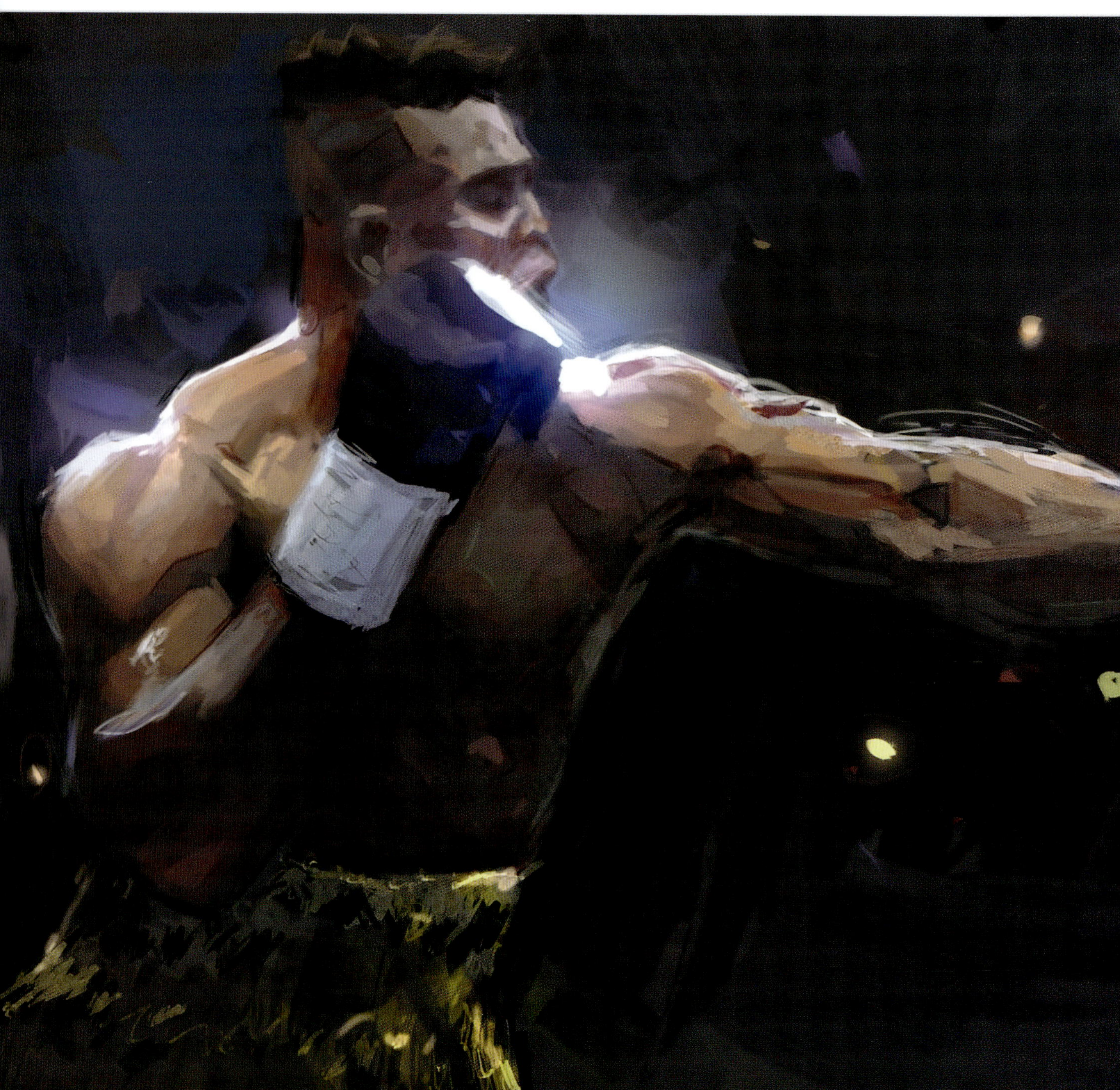

eventually they'll comingle in the party room, and that's where the real party (and art) happens.

In this book, we're building that art hotel from the ground up. That means we're shaping your fundamentals, sharpening your observational skills, and ultimately constructing the framework that you will use in the future for any drawing you do.

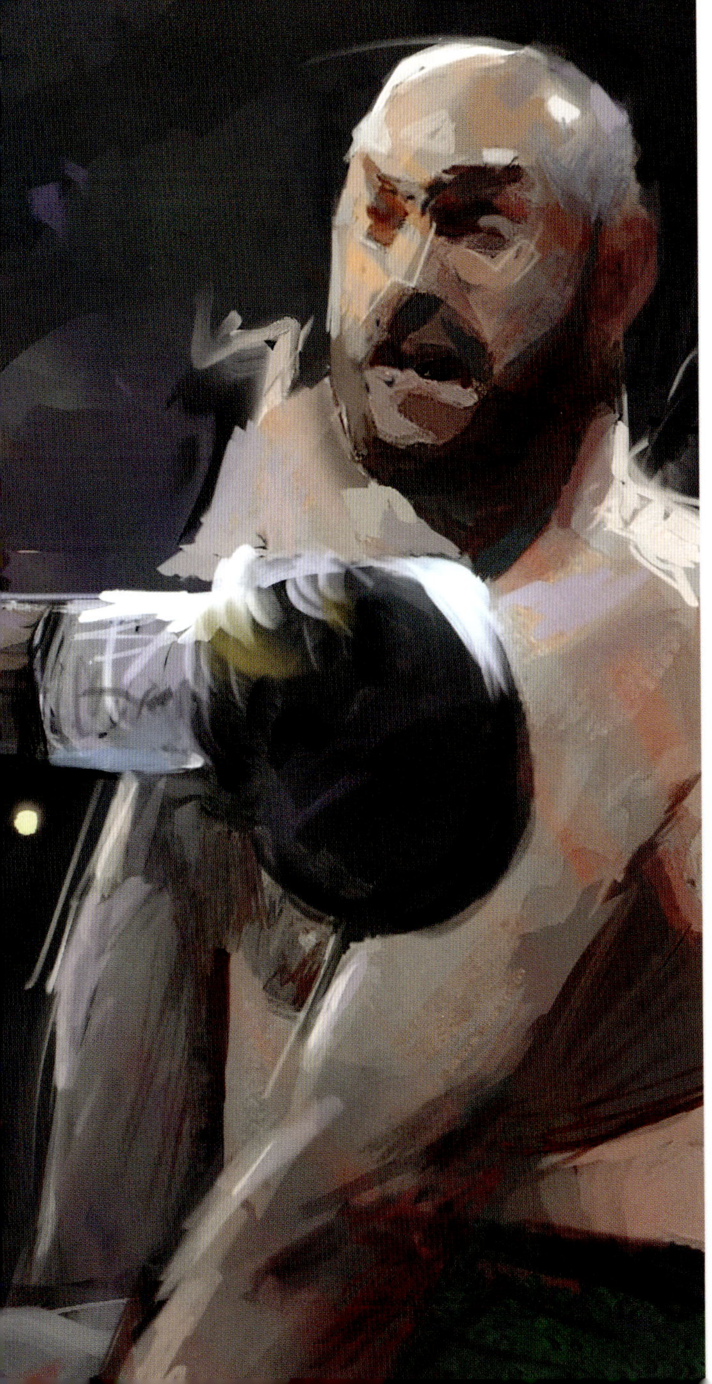

With a few exceptions, we will not be making *finished drawings* in this book. Finished *studies* yes, but not finished, portfolio-ready art. Instead, we are focusing on something I argue is far more important.

This book largely centers around the figure—the many ways to understand it, break it down, and ultimately, draw it. The figure has been the focus of artists since art's beginning, and for good reason: If you can draw the figure, you can apply those skills to everything else. The figure has equal parts emotion, composition, and structure. It encompasses both the whimsical and the concrete. We are so familiar with the figure—every proportion, shape, intricacy, change in posture—that we instantly register and react to it, artist or not.

You don't even need to be a practicing artist to study from this book. It will take you from the very first steps of your art journey, and propel you down a path that, if you continue to follow it, can take you to wherever you want to go, be it a proficient hobbyist, a professional, and beyond.

Finally, understand that learning how to draw takes two things above all else: *time* and *persistence*. Both of which neither I, nor any teacher, can give you. You need to bring that to the table yourself. But if you bring that, I will meet you halfway.

Let's get started.

A more recent digital sketch, which was informed by all of the techniques and tools I share in this book.

1

The 2D World
of Shapes

Circles, squares, and triangles are three shapes I'm certain you can easily draw. I'll bet you can draw them without any instruction, and probably nail them every time. What if I told you that creating appealing drawings is fundamentally no different than filling that page with those simple shapes? It's true, I swear!

A drawing is just a series of 2D shapes sitting next to, over, on top of, or behind another. Realistically, a drawing or painting can contain hundreds, perhaps even thousands, of shapes, which the human eye sees as a picture that can look complex. But here's a little art secret: That complexity is an illusion!

Think of a juggler. Give that juggler two bowling pins, and their movements are simple enough to understand. Give the juggler eight bowling pins, and the performance appears far more complex. But the complexity is simply due to the scale increase. The actual movements are fundamentally the same.

In this analogy, the shapes in your drawing are the bowling pins. The skill of drawing isn't the ability to create an intricate piece with layers upon layers of complexity. The skill of drawing is keeping *all your shapes simple and clear, all the time.*

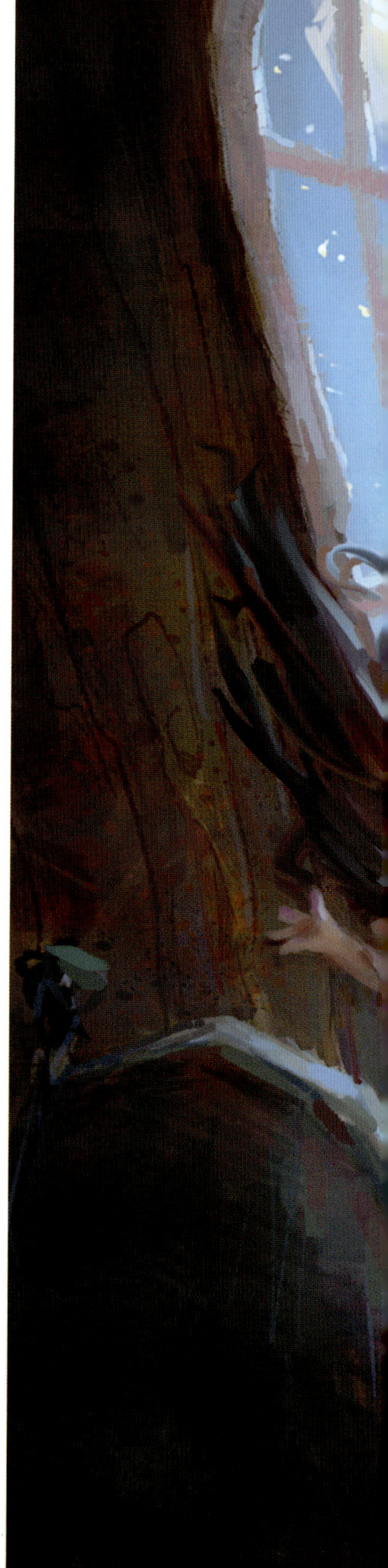

Green Monster is a circle that's been offset in symmetry and slightly elongated but he's still a circle!

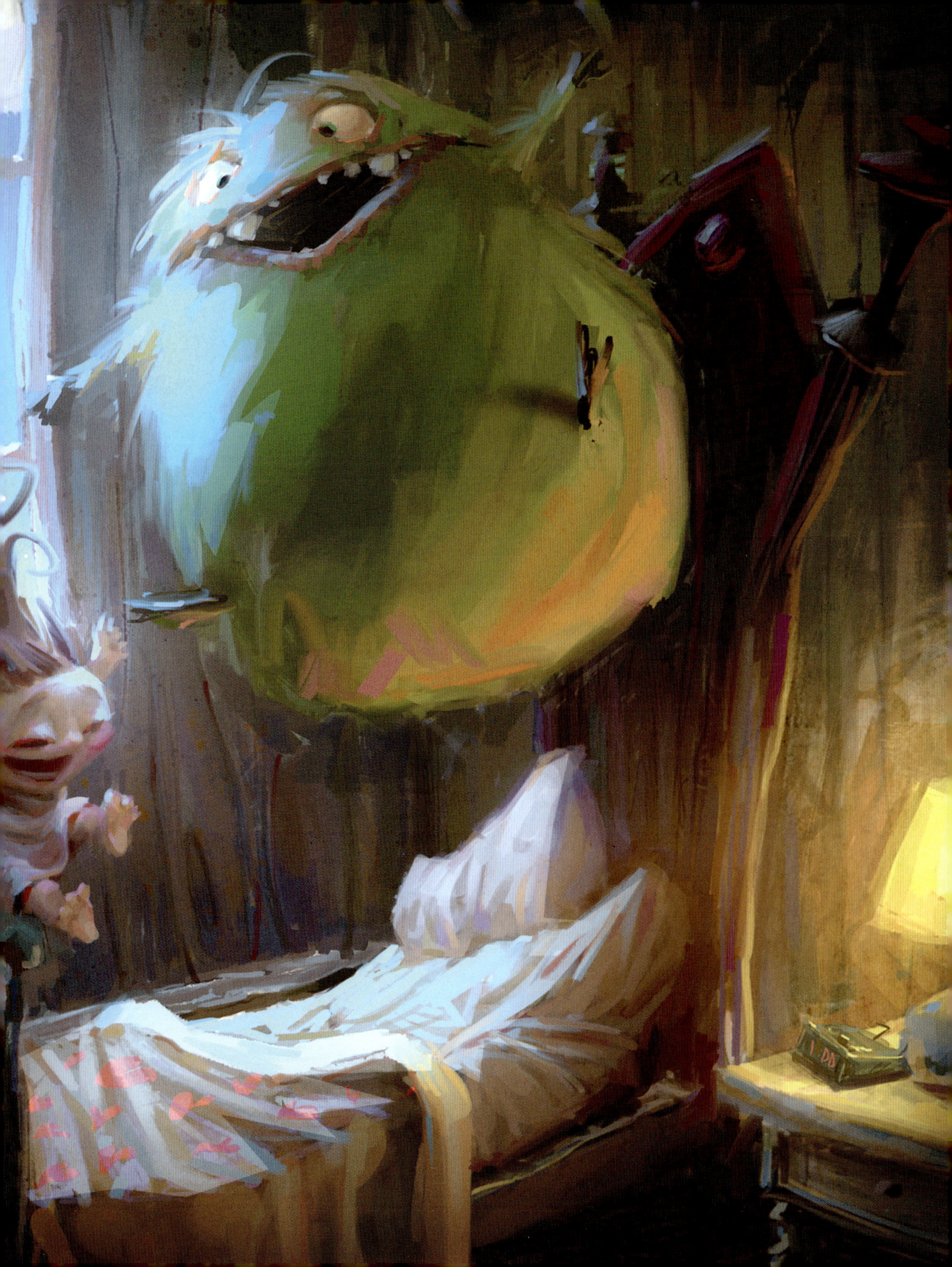

What Are **Simple Shapes**?

A simple shape is drawn with the minimal contours. The circle, square, and triangle's contours are irreducible. You *cannot* remove a contour from those shapes and have it read as the same shape. This is the mindset you need when designing your shapes.

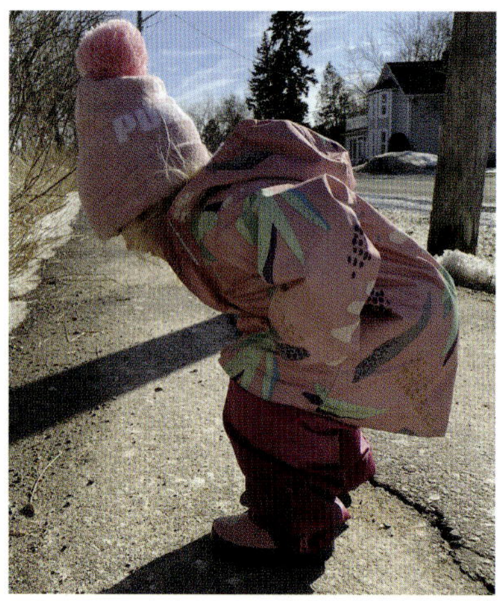

A photo of my daughter, bending down to examine a caterpillar, and the accompanying drawing.

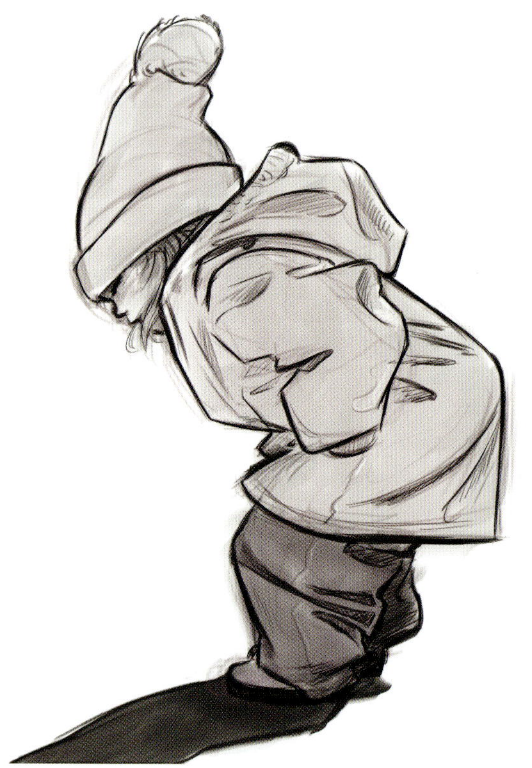

IRREDUCIBLE SIMPLICITY

You can make virtually any shape following the guideline of *irreducible simplicity*. There is no limit to the number of sides a shape can have, or the number of lines used to create a shape. However, the more lines or sides you use, the more careful you have to be. Make sure that every piece of the shape, including every change in contour, has a reason. This is easy to read, but hard to do consistently.

This drawing of my daughter is an example of a complex subject made simple and easily readable as a result of mindfully drawing with simple shapes. There are nearly one hundred unique shapes in this drawing, all of which I gave the same care and attention. I'm juggling those bowling pins!

On the opposite page, I've isolated various shapes from my drawing. I've also scaled each shape to be similar in size. Some shapes you may recognize out of context, like the winter hat, and some shapes you may not. Seeing shapes removed from their context like this helps you gain insight into and appreciation of their simple design. Simple designs are easy to draw.

Ideally, there is no such thing as a less important or more important shape. Every shape is equally important. After all, the juggler can't afford to consider one bowling pin less important than the others, or the whole act comes crashing down!

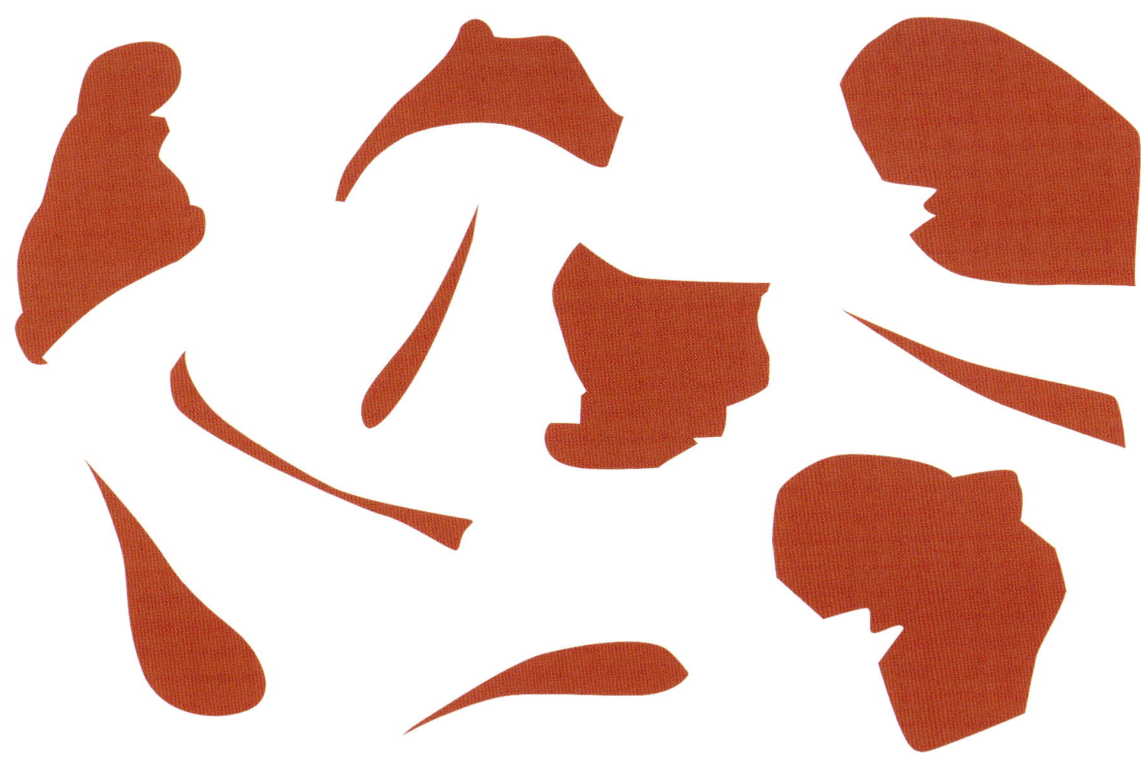

Isolated shapes from the drawing of my daughter. Each change in contour adds to the identity or character of the shapes. The goal is to waste no lines.

IMPORTANT AREAS VERSUS LESS IMPORTANT AREAS

An important area of this drawing is my daughter's winter hat as it comprises a nice bit of the silhouette of the figure. It's a natural fit to make that shape *more interesting* than, say, a fold in the jacket, which can be kept more basic.

A more interesting shape still needs to be fundamentally simple in its design. It just may include more changes in direction, more lines, more undulations, and so on. But despite the winter hat being a more interesting *area* of the drawing than the jacket fold, both of those shapes are given equal consideration as to how they're designed. Again, you can tell when a shape is well designed by how easy it is to draw.

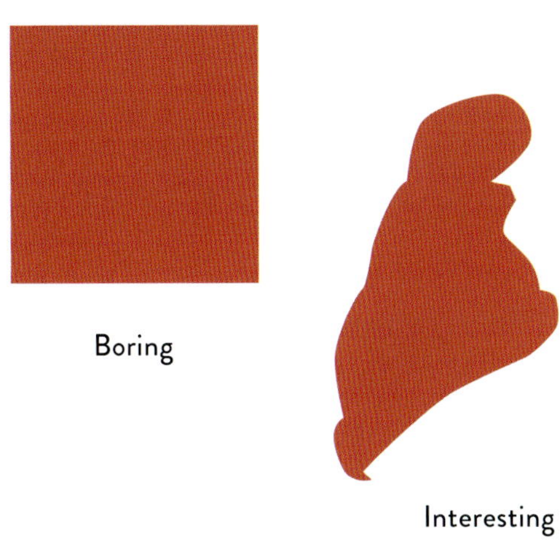

Having shapes that are more complex looking versus less complex looking is good for variety. Just make sure to keep them all simply designed!

Drawing Is Design

There are only **three types** of lines: C-curves, S-curves, and Straights.

A C-curve doesn't have to be a perfect letter c. It can have variety, like this:

An S-curve doesn't have to be a perfect letter s, either. It can also have variety:

A Straight can be a perfectly straight line, or something very close to that:

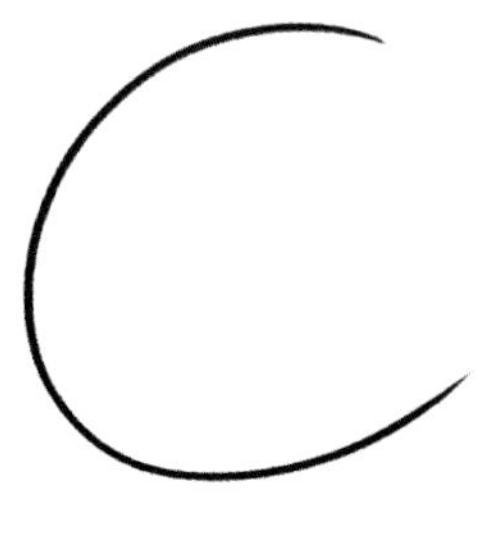

A C-curve.

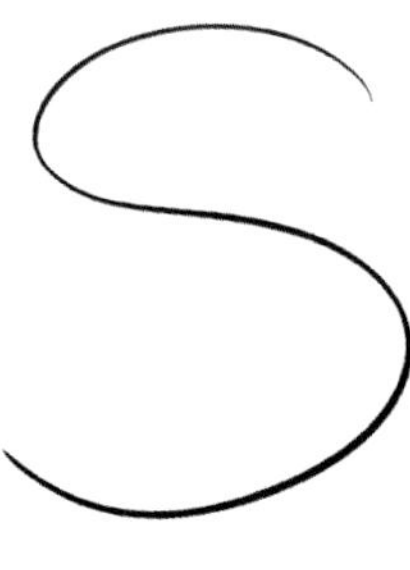

An S-curve.

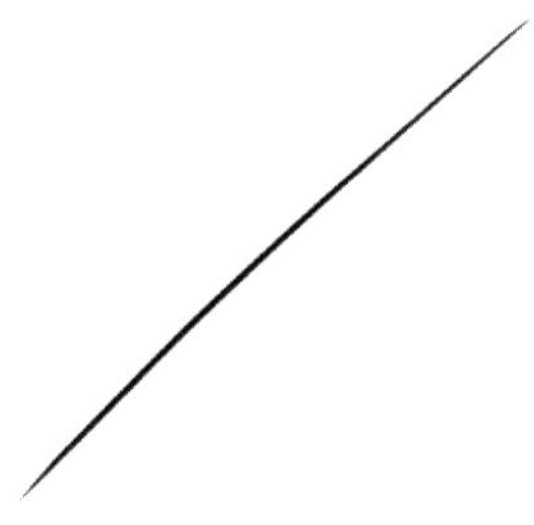

A Straight.

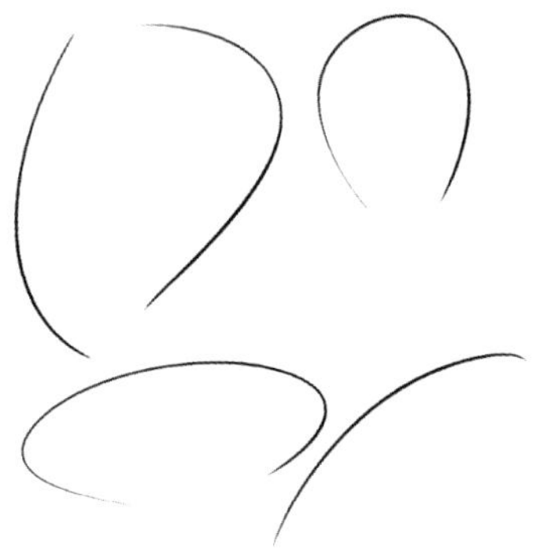

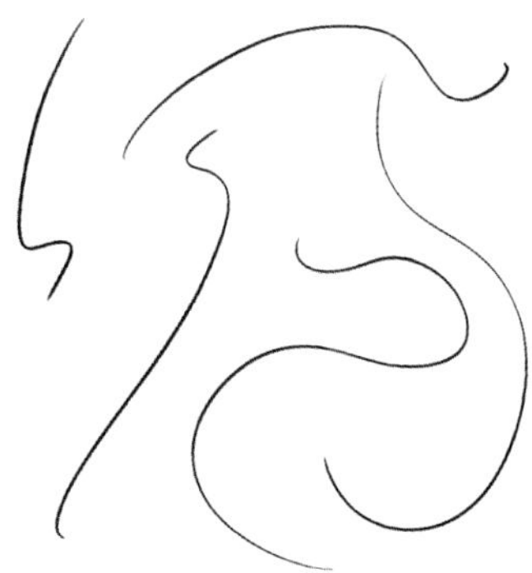

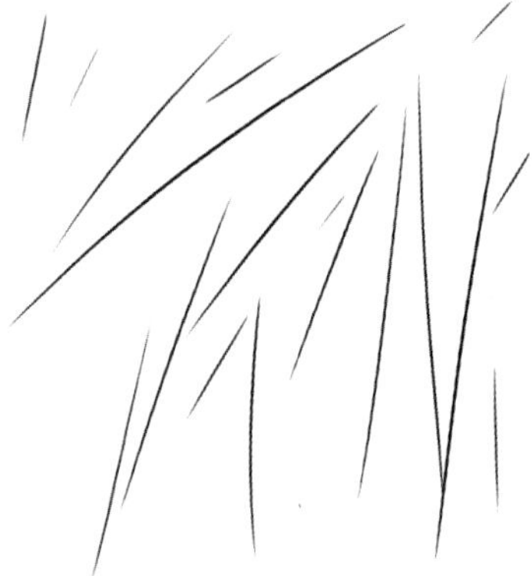

And that's it. Those three types of line are all you'll ever have to think about when drawing a shape! That's good news, right? When you use those lines consciously, that is called *designing*.

UNDERSTANDING THE DESIGN OF YOUR SHAPES

We need to build awareness of what shape design entails. So, let's break down one of the shapes from the previous drawing. Here's what I was thinking design-wise when I drew it.

Here's another shape from the drawing. It's a long C-curve flanked by two Straights:

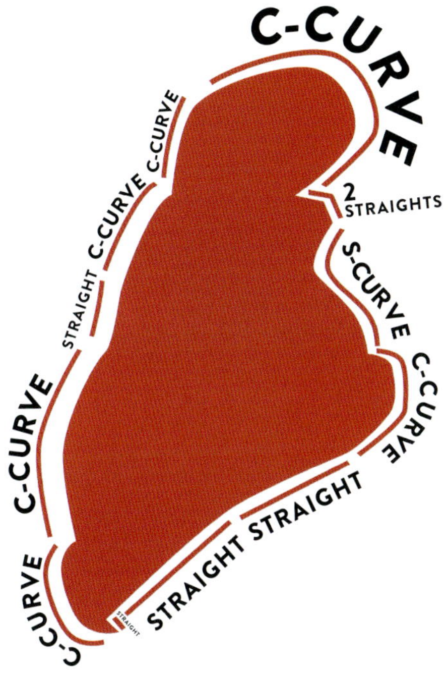

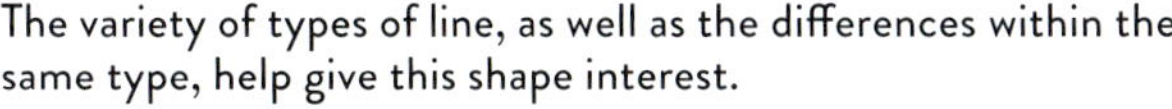

The variety of types of line, as well as the differences within the same type, help give this shape interest.

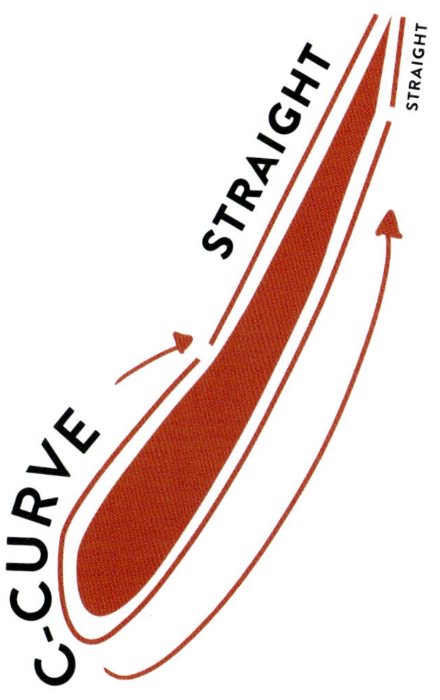

The different lengths of each type of line help give this shape interest.

When somebody laments, "I just can't draw!" what they probably mean is that they're unable to design shapes. Nobody is born good at this. Not even gifted young artists. Designing shapes always takes a conscious effort and lots of back and forth, even for the pros!

Tangents? Bad.
T-Connections and Overlaps? Good.

Tangent is a term that refers to a shape whose edge or contour perfectly aligns with an adjoining shape's edge or contour. For example:

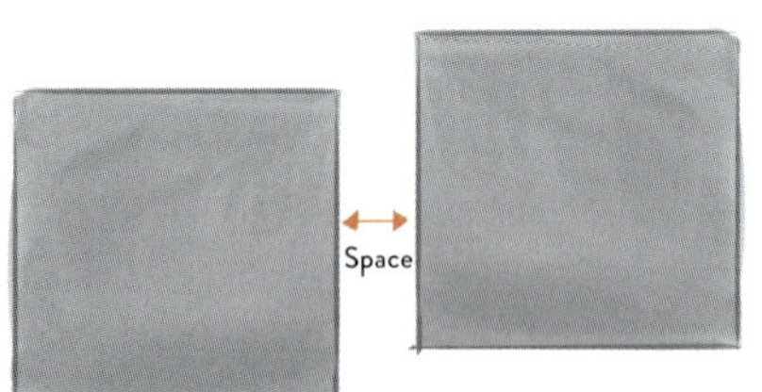

No tangent here, due to the space between shapes.

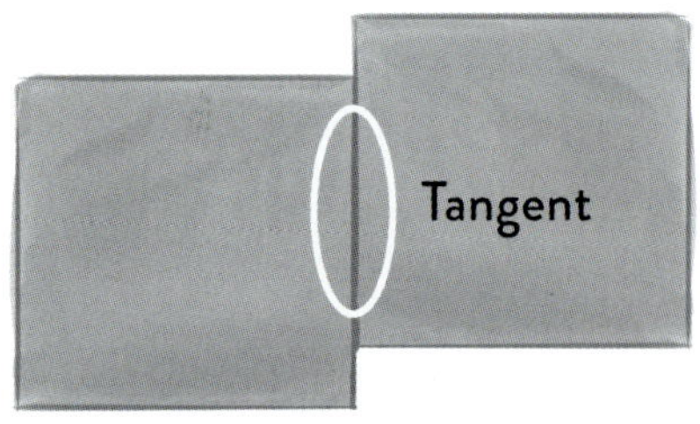

The two shapes' contours are "kissing" each other in the circled area, causing a tangent.

Tangents can occur at single points, as well:

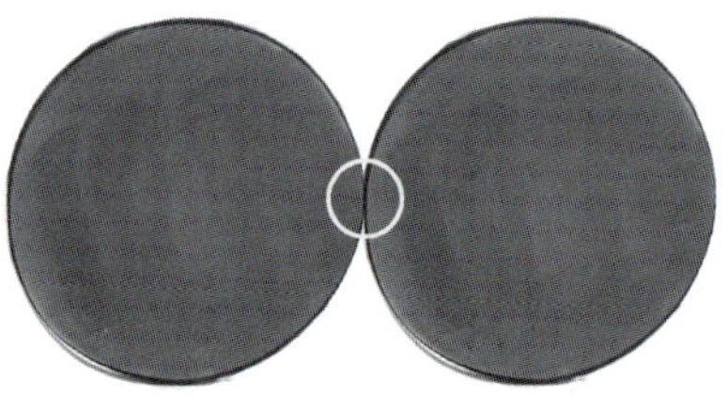

The two circles "kiss" at a single point. That point is the tangent.

Tangents flatten or compromise depth, and are generally not desirable in a drawing. Think of it this way, if our goal with drawing is to create a believable world, one pillar of that is making sure the relationship between shapes is clear. That not only involves a shape's design, but *where* the shapes are in relation to each other. Is one shape in front of another shape? Behind it? Flush with it? A tangent makes that very difficult to determine. Here's another example:

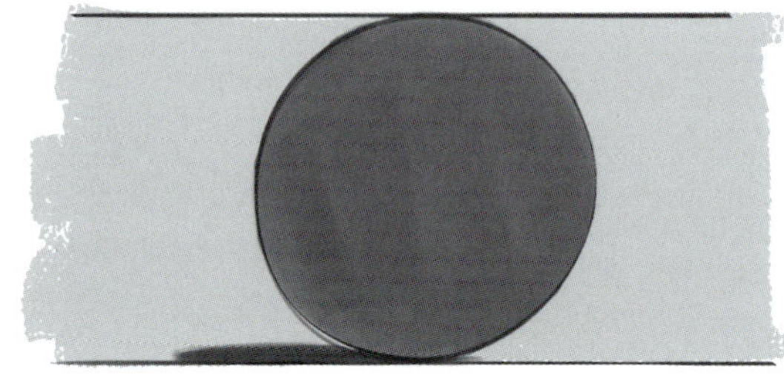

The tangents have robbed this drawing of depth.

This is supposed to be a ball sitting on a table. But it doesn't really read that way, does it? There are two bad tangents here. One at the top of the ball, and one at the bottom. Both are single points just "kissing" the rectangular table shape. Simply changing the position of the circle solves this problem:

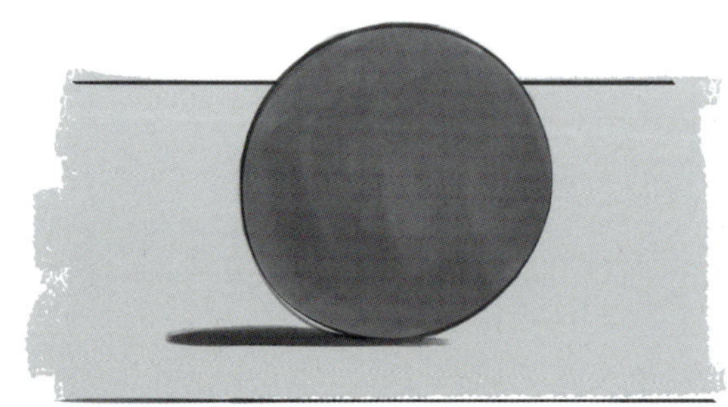

Notice how the illusion of depth is restored by removing the tangents. That's the (destructive) power of tangents!

Here are a few ways to fix a tangent in your drawing. Remember that tangents tend to happen by
accident, so it's up to you to spot them as they
pop up and fix them before they cause further
damage.

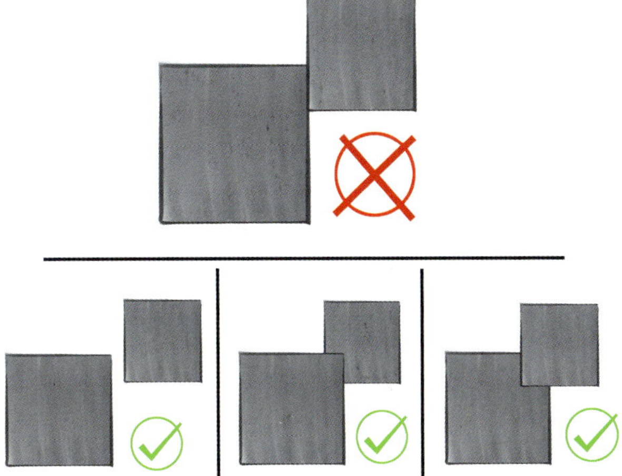

A few ideas for fixing tangents. Simply
create a space between shapes (left) or
overlap the shapes (middle and right).

T-CONNECTIONS AND OVERLAP

A T-connection is a principle that will help you
avoid tangents. It's the idea that whenever you
have a shape intersecting another shape, that
intersection resembles the letter *T*. It looks like
the image at right.

The function of the T-connection is to show the
overlap between two shapes. It puts one thing
clearly in front of or behind the other clarifying
depth. This principle is so ingrained in my day-
to-day work that I've learned to even edit my
photo references to put T-connections in where
they may not appear. Yes, photographs can have
tangents too, and good photographers also learn
to avoid them for the same reasons!

Remember that a tangent *cannot* occur in real life,
because real life is a three-dimensional space, and
our eyes and brain decipher depth entirely differ-
ently. A tangent is strictly a two-dimensional
artifact that can crop up when we attempt to
represent a three-dimensional space.

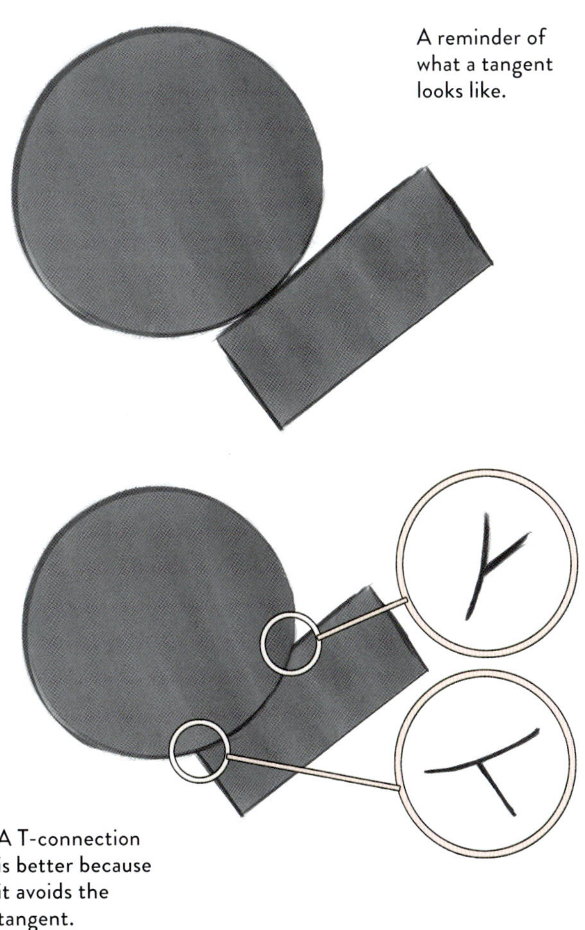

A reminder of
what a tangent
looks like.

A T-connection
is better because
it avoids the
tangent.

T-CONNECTIONS EVERYWHERE!

At right is a drawing that features lots of *stuff*. But underneath all that, I wanted to create depth and the feeling of a cozy little room. This meant that I had to pack things closely together with a lot of overlap.

The bed overlaps the girl and the monster, the pillow overlaps the headboard, the lampshade overlaps the picture frame, which is overlapped by the pile of books.

To keep all those overlaps manageable and not confusing to the viewer, there are T-connections all over the picture. In some areas I made the conscious decision to *not* overlap things such as between the monster and the girl. When I did that, I was sure to leave a clear space (or negative shape) between the objects to *not* create near-tangents.

The T-connection is not a formula. It isn't something that will betray your art by looking repetitive, or "cheap" to the viewer. Even if you use a hundred T-connections in a drawing, your audience won't ever have an awareness of them. But, they will better understand the depth you are conveying and appreciate your work all the more for it!

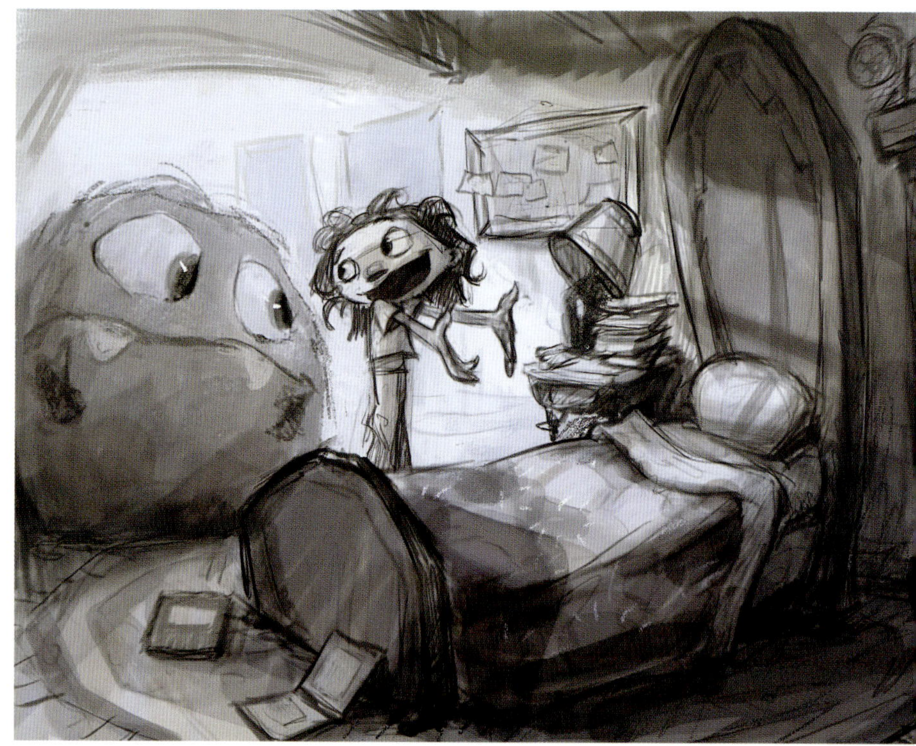

A sketch from a personal project I never finished. The T-connections are circled in red in the image below.

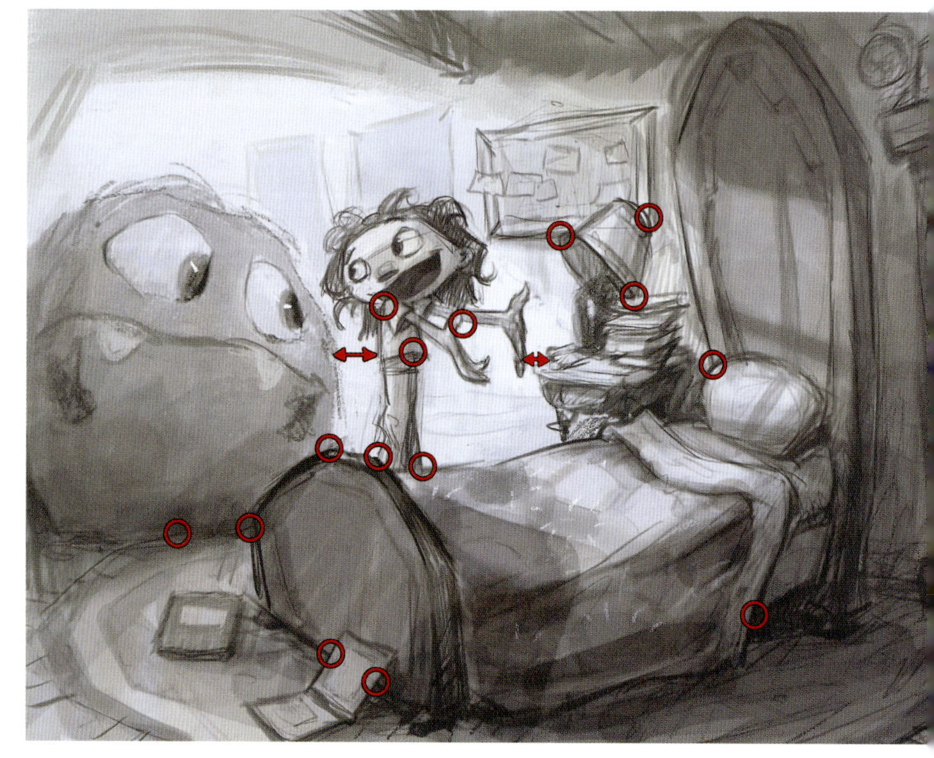

Guide to Thoughtful **Shape** Design

We now have some parameters around how to keep shapes simple . . . but that is only the first step to thoughtful (or good) design. While I do firmly believe that a well-designed shape is a simple one, the risk you run in the pursuit of keeping shapes simple is you also make them *boring*.

Allow me to start with a comparison we looked at earlier.

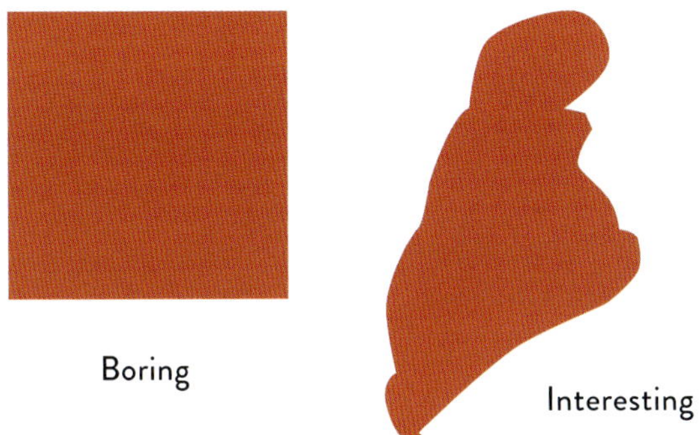

Boring

Do you agree?

Interesting

Both shapes pass the "simple" test. But the square just isn't all that interesting to look at. So, just because a shape is simple, that doesn't mean it'll make for compelling drawing.

But this isn't to say that you can never have "boring" shapes! By populating less important areas of your drawing with less interesting shapes you reserve the most interesting shapes for the most important areas, and that's a recipe that tends to work. You could do the inverse of this, too. The contrast of shape designs is what the viewer responds to.

What we need is methodology for taking a "boring" shape and sprucing it up. Here are some ideas!

OFFSET SYMMETRY

This is one of my favorite ways to give a mundane shape a bit of an edge. Let's use a square. Squares are symmetrical both horizontally and vertically. It tends to not be very interesting, because symmetry is by its very nature redundant, and redundancy can sow the seeds of boringness.

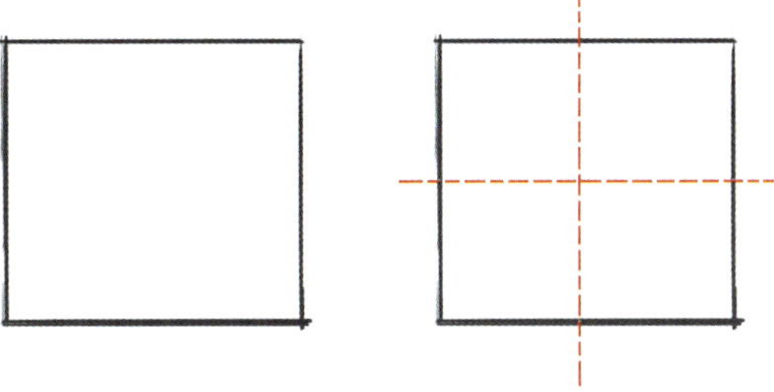

Let's try preserving the basic identity of the shape (keep it square-ish) but pick an axis and slide it *out* of symmetry:

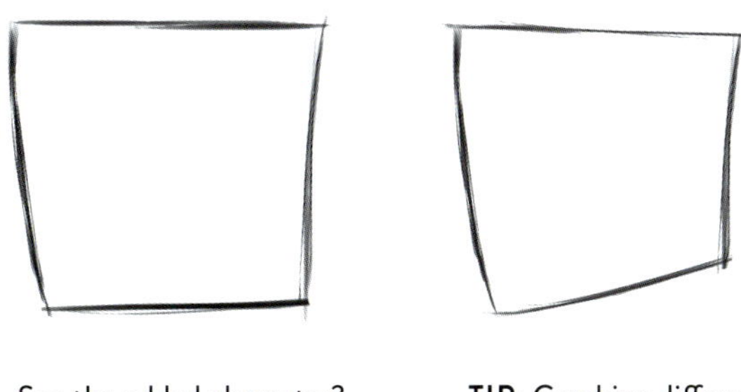

See the added character?

TIP: Combine different types of lines for even more interest.

Nothing's stopping us from offsetting the symmetry on both axes.

VARY SIZE AND SPACING

This one comes in handy when you have multiple shapes of a similar size seen in close proximity. Again, the idea here is to *avoid* redundancy.

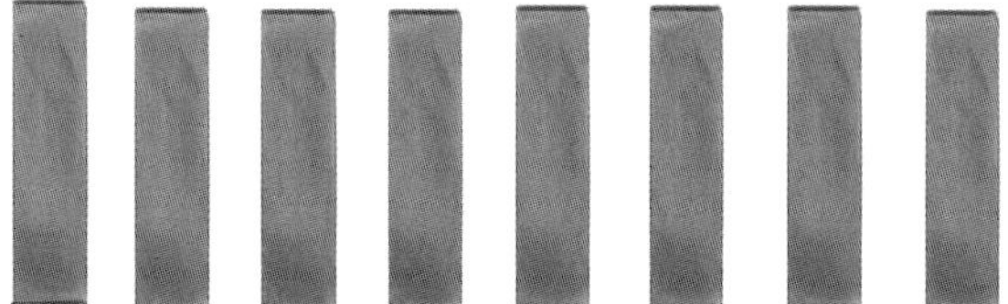

Same size and spacing causes obvious repetition, which isn't all that engaging to look at.

To avoid this, your first plan of attack could be to adjust the spacing between the shapes (which also varies the negative shapes):

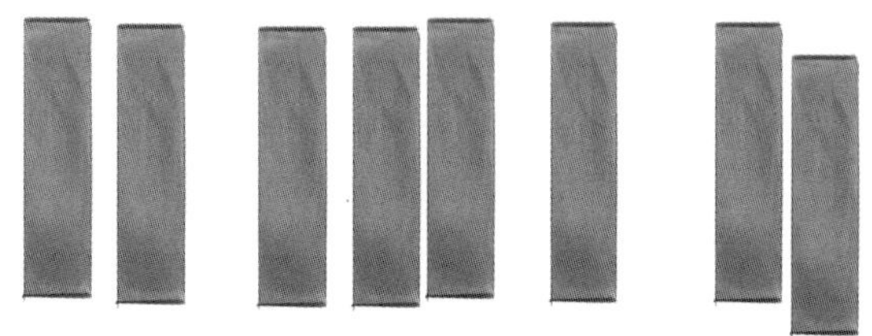

See the horizontal adjustments in the spacing, and smaller vertical adjustments, too.

You may also try varying the sizes of the shapes themselves.

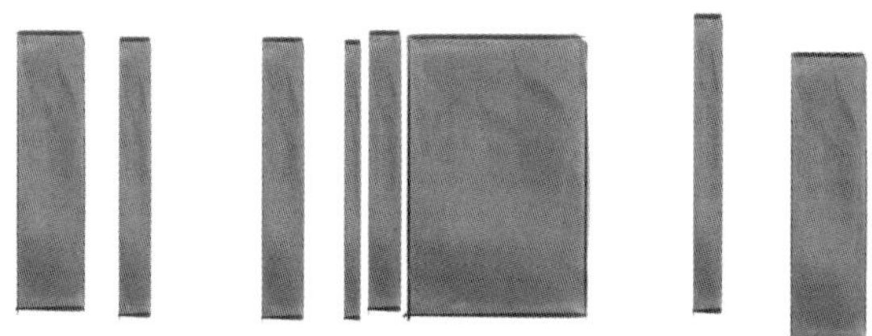

You might ask why I'm so against redundancy. There's a time and place for redundancy in shapes, but students tend to make shapes repetitive and redundant by default, and I want you to break free from that.

TAKE A BITE OUT OF IT

This solution works great when your shapes have a lot of uninterrupted edges. Consider the squaroid shape we ended up with a couple pages ago:

Now take a bite out of it. You can take multiple bites if you want, and you can use all three types of line to draw those bites. Here are some examples:

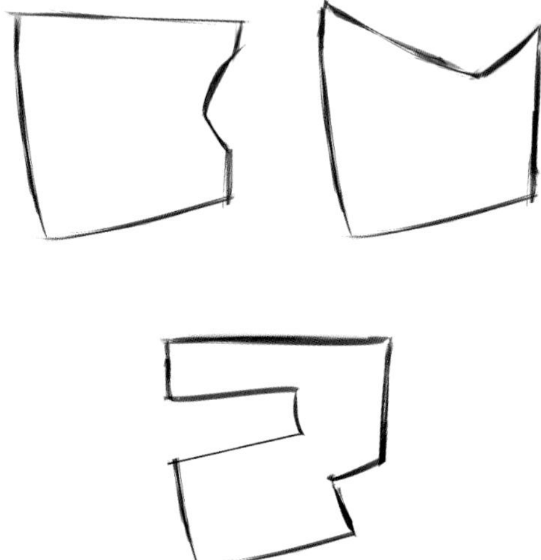

I often use this principle in reverse. When drawing an already-interesting shape with lots of "bites" in it from the start, I'll ask myself, "What is the underlying, super simple shape here?"

Looking at the example on the next page, the yellow part of the baby dragon's belly is defined by an interesting shape. You can see many bites have been taken out of it. I look at the shape I'm creating and make sure it's still traceable to basic foundational shapes. Sometimes it helps if it reminds you of a real object. This one reminds me of a chicken drumstick:

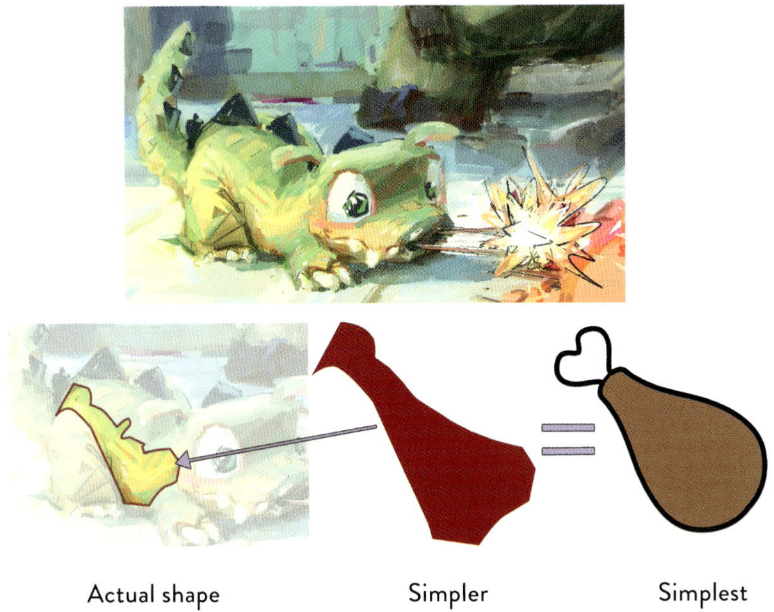

Actual shape   Simpler   Simplest

You might wonder why I felt the need to make the shape as complex as I did. Why not just use the shape in the middle? The answer is simple: I think this shape looks better and fits the "fun" feeling of the piece more. But to connect it with the fundamentals in this chapter, the multiple sides and lines in this shape all contribute something valuable. I believe it still falls into the "simple" category, and therefore it's good to go.

BEND IT, TWIST IT

Another good way to combat redundancy in your shapes is to give them a bend or twist. Pretend your shape has a spine and is doing a little dance. In other words, add movement!

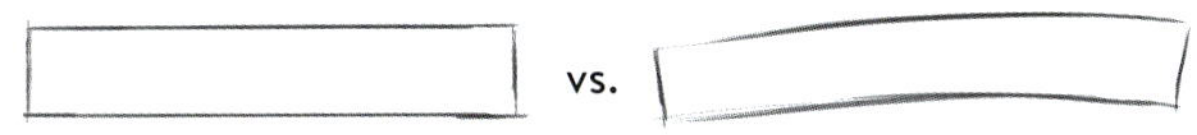

The shape on the right looks more alive to me.

You could combine this with a bit of *asymmetry*, too.

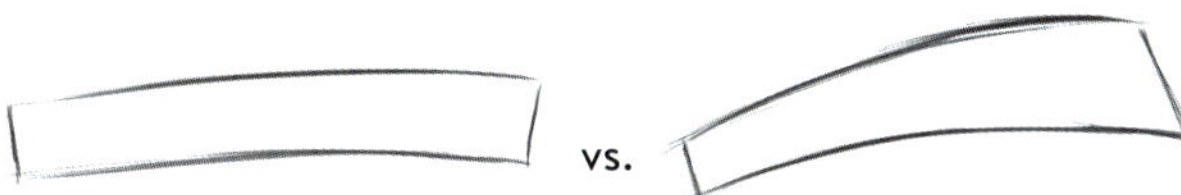

The shape you use depends on the mood and style of the drawing.

This isn't me being fanciful. Nature designs these shapes all the time! It's all over human anatomy. Consider this drawing of a hand.

Every finger there has a little bend or twist to it. It's perhaps most noticeable on the thumb and index finger indicated by the isolated red lines.

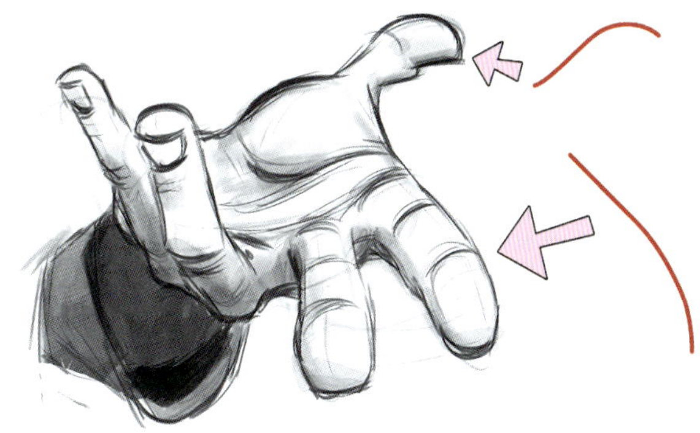

WHAT'S TRENDING?

This one's related to the chicken drumstick. It's useful to recognize an overall design, or idea, that your shape is trending toward. The chicken drumstick was a literal interpretation, but sometimes it can be more abstract.

Navigating your way through shapes while continuously analyzing them helps keep them under control. Remember, it's not unusual for a drawing to have lots and lots of shapes in it, so any tool you can train to help stay in control is worth your time!

You could use those examples of underlying shapes verbatim. After all, they're simple, and therefore can work well. But let's take them and build slightly more interesting shapes based on them. This will help you see the power of the underlying shape when it comes to creating more complex shape designs.

Below are some examples of possible underlying shapes, with descriptions of what they trend toward:

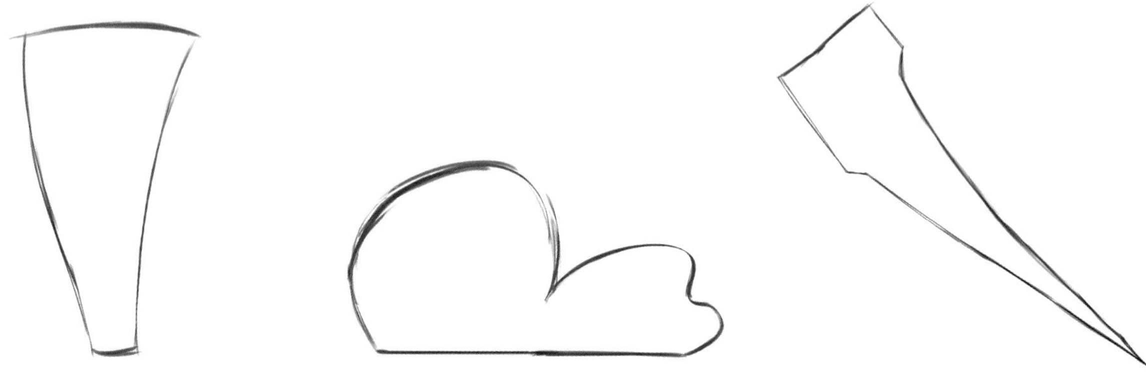

Narrow at the bottom, widens as it goes upward (no literal object here).

Straight lines on bottom, curves on top (cloudlike).

Pointy and on a diagonal (lightninglike).

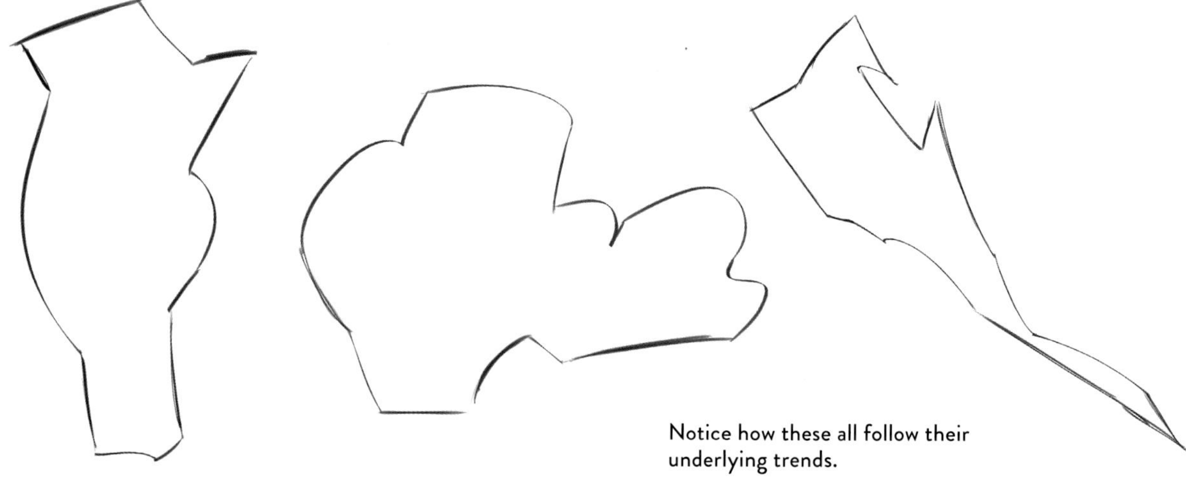

Notice how these all follow their underlying trends.

Pros use this idea to create "thematic shapes" in their work. For example, the movie *Lilo & Stitch* is full of shapes that are wider at the bottom, and narrower at the top. Look at the characters' limbs for example. The average viewer probably doesn't notice this, but it helps tie the art style of that movie together in a way the audience can *feel*.

Other times you can use underlying shapes as the basis for your entire art style. This can be a natural fit if your arm or hand muscles are more inclined toward making a certain type of shape. Maybe you like to draw more straight lines than curves. Herding your shapes this way can be a powerful force that binds your art together in a signature way.

FIXING A POORLY DESIGNED SHAPE

You can also use this "trending" method to re-design bad shapes. The shape shown below *isn't* mindfully designed, and wouldn't fit well in a majority of circumstances.

To rein in the shape, notice how it trends. A "line of best fit" through the shape's many undulations helps clean it up.

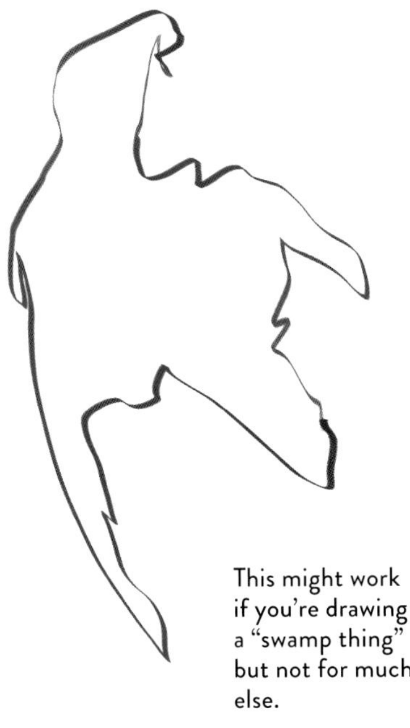

This might work if you're drawing a "swamp thing" but not for much else.

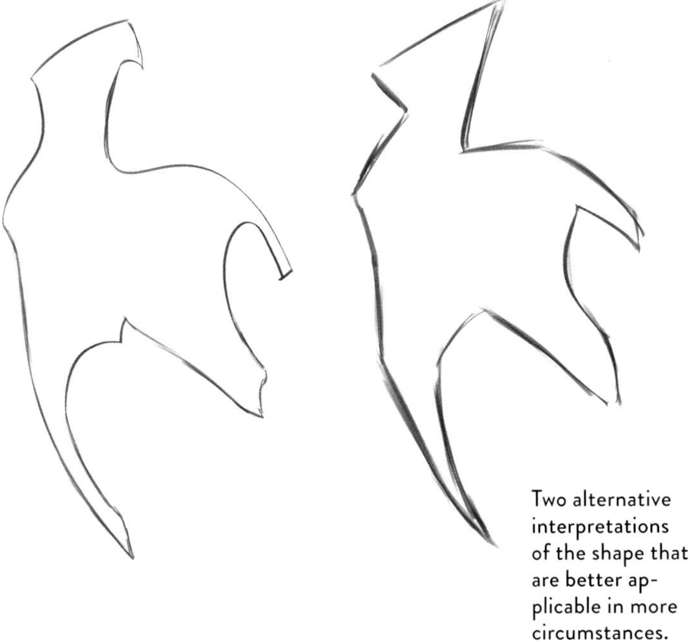

Two alternative interpretations of the shape that are better applicable in more circumstances.

Differences in Art Styles

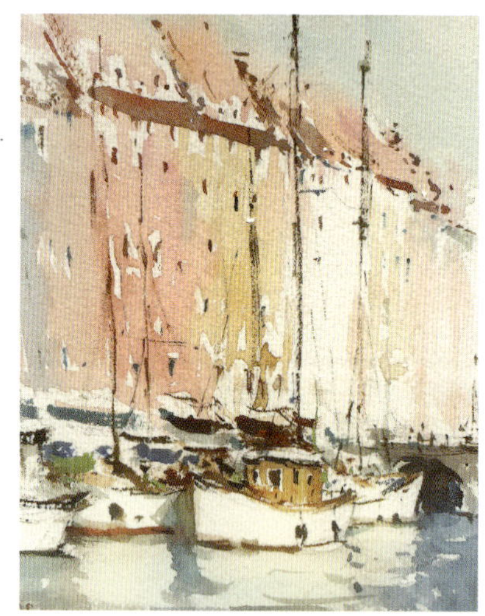
Sketch from life, watercolor.

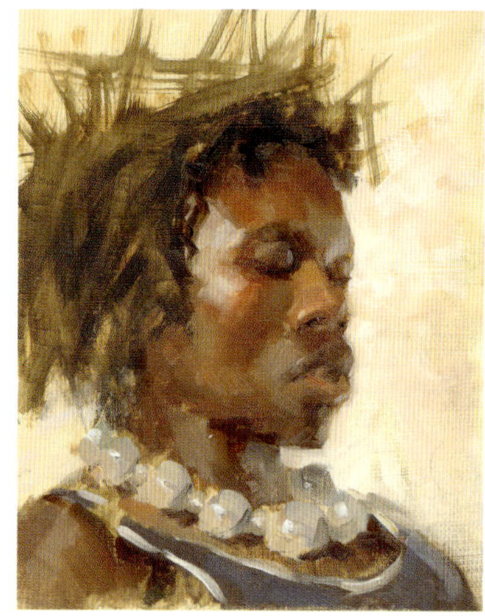
Portrait quick sketch from life, oil on board.

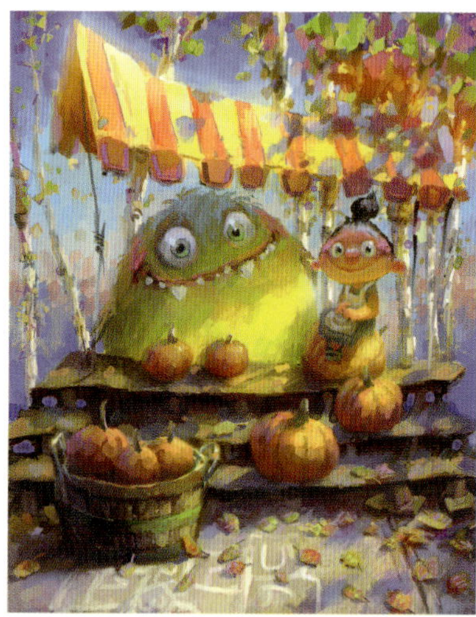
Cartoony illustration, digital

The nice thing about fundamentals is that they tend to remain steadfast, regardless of the art style you're working in. Art fundamentals are pillars that hold up a larger structure. The structure itself could be in whatever style you like, but without fundamentals in place, it will fall.

A cartoonist uses shapes in exactly the same way as a fine artist does. While minor differences in *application* may exist between styles, one is *not* categorically more skilled with shapes than the other.

Personally and professionally I've dedicated serious study and time to many different art styles. I've seen the throughline that shapes provide, and they've allowed me to wade in and out of all kinds of stylistic pursuits.

Below are some shapes that I plucked out of the pictures above. I bet you can't easily tell which shape is from which picture. And that's the point! There is no material difference in shape design between styles! Down at the shape level, there is no such thing as style.

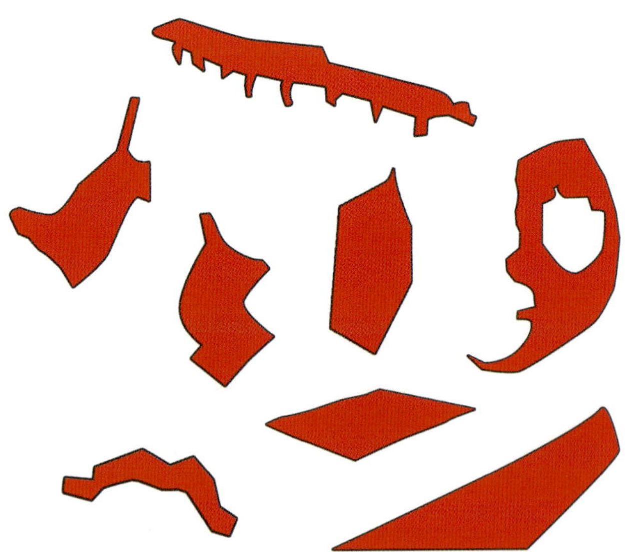

ASSIGNMENTS

In two words: *Make shapes*! But, to expand . . .

ASSIGNMENT #1

Look at art you like and see if you can find new appreciation in the artistry behind the shape design. Don't worry about drawing anything. Simply study by looking. You can do this with real life too, although be careful. Real life does not necessarily give you well-designed shapes, as the real world isn't an art piece. I do recommend looking at people's silhouettes, as the human figure is chock-full of good shapes.

ASSIGNMENT #2

Choose shapes that you think are designed well and copy them. As you make the replica shape, be very deliberate with the type of line you're using at each point in the drawing. It may even help to say the name and nature of the lines aloud as you draw: Straight. C-curve. C-curve into a Straight. Long S-curve. The goal is to establish a connection to each shape you draw.

ASSIGNMENT #3

Take a basic shape like a circle or a square. Draw it as uncreatively as possible. Then, right beside it, try to spice up the shape by adding asymmetry, offset symmetry, take bites out of it, and so on. Try ten different versions of the shape. No matter how many differences you try, then make sure it is still identifiable as that original shape. If it drifts too far away, try to bring it back!

ASSIGNMENT #4

In a small sketchbook (or a low-resolution digital canvas), draw yourself a little frame. Inside that frame, build an abstract composition made exclusively of simple shapes. Because you are now dealing with multiple shapes, be on guard against tangents! Don't allow them anywhere. Use T-connections, overlaps, and negative space throughout the frame rather than in just one area.

2

Abstract Art Plays a Part: Gesture Drawing

One of the most common questions I get fom students is, "What's the best way to improve at drawing poses?" My answer? Gesture drawing.

Gesture is the single most important type of drawing I ever learned. I say type of drawing because the goal of a gesture is to capture the *feeling* or *attitude* of a pose, rather than a finished picture.

To draw gestures well, you first need to reframe what it is you're looking at and looking *for*. In one word: movement. To capture a sense of movement, use big, sweeping lines, and strokes. These should ideally flow through *and* between body parts, connecting them rhythmically.

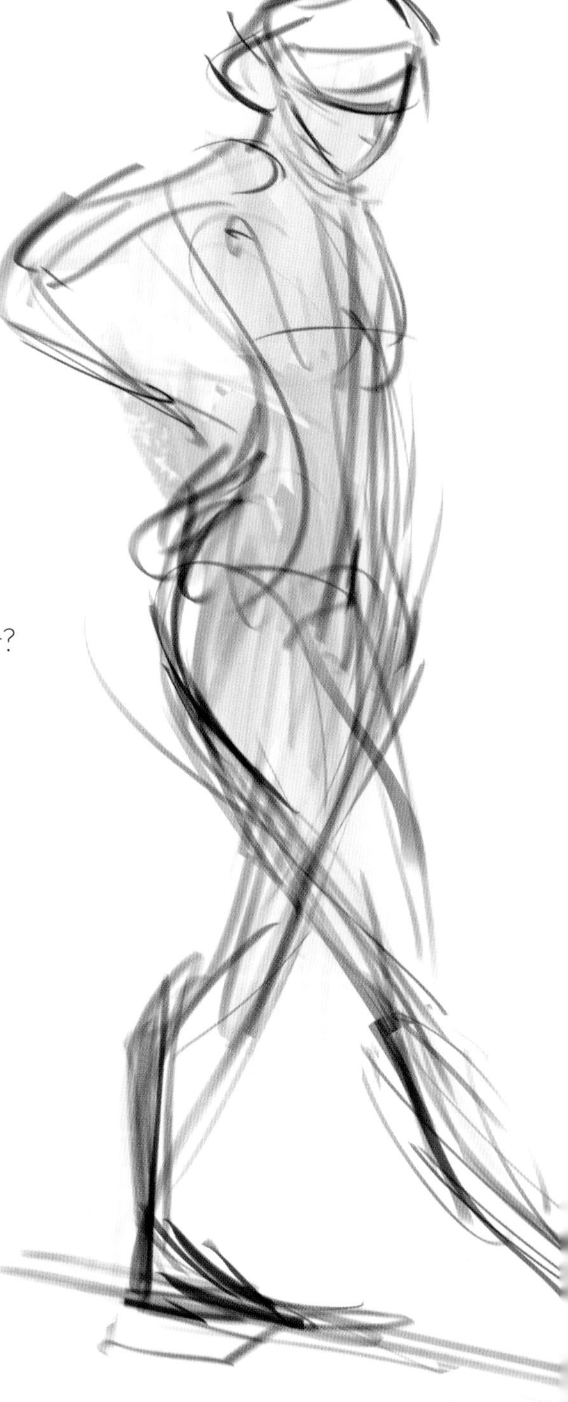

A gesture drawing communicates a very specific feeling, without final lines, or any detail whatsoever. Due to their simplicity they can be drawn quickly, making them indispensable for creating poses, figures, and characters.

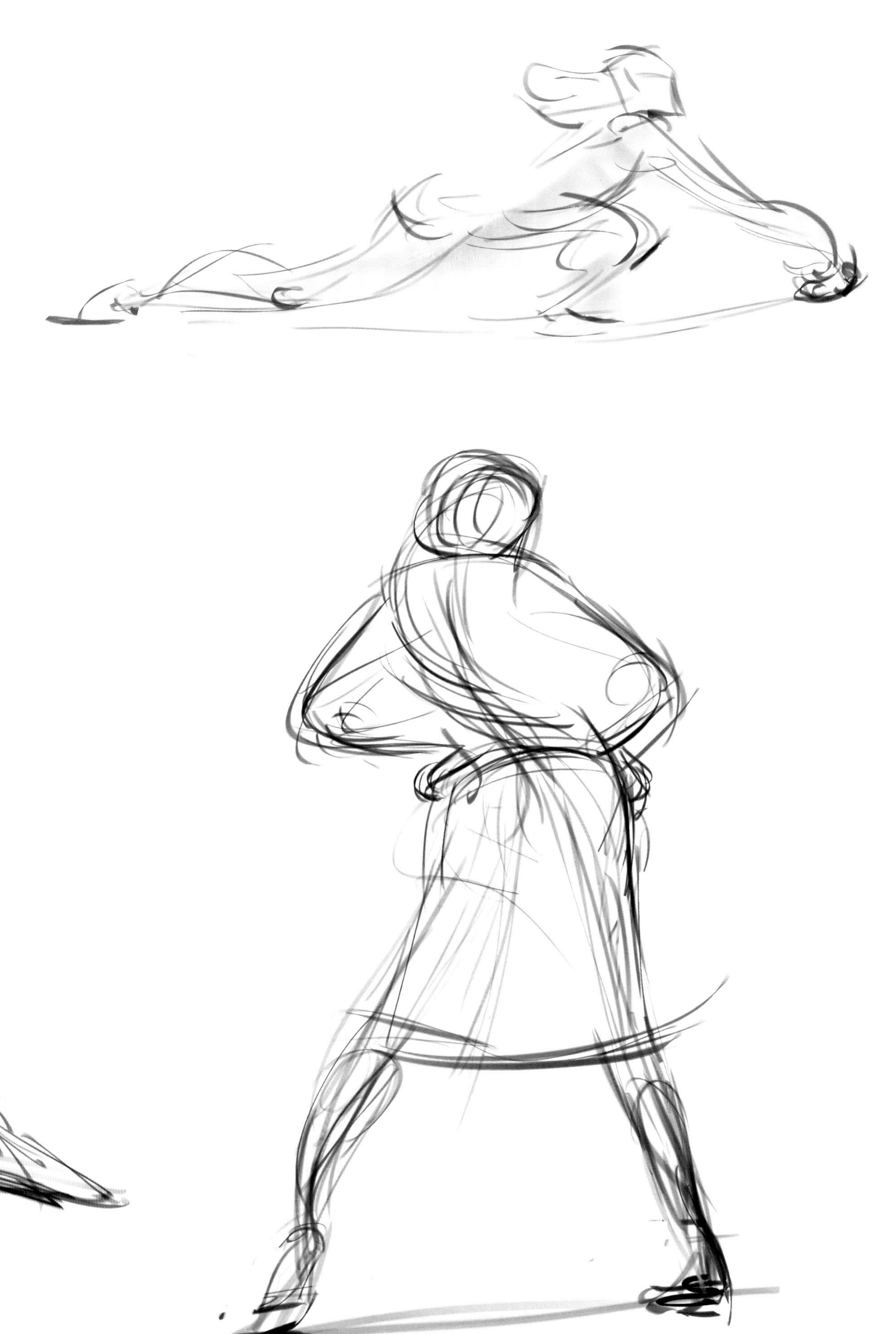

Gesture Is All about Rhythm

Much like how the beat of a song is like an undercurrent that carries you through the music, rhythm in a gesture drawing carries the forms and features through the piece, making the drawing easy to follow.

Just like musical rhythm follows a time signature, visual rhythm follows lines—either C-curves, S-curves, or Straights, just like we saw with shape design!

It's important to identify what a drawing of *rhythm* looks like. The exact method will vary from person to person, but generally rhythmic strokes are flowy lines, and feel like they were drawn with big sweeping motions.

These are the literal "broad strokes" of a picture. Sometimes it helps to draw gestures with thicker media (I often used a China marker in my life drawing classes) to avoid literal interpretations of the reference.

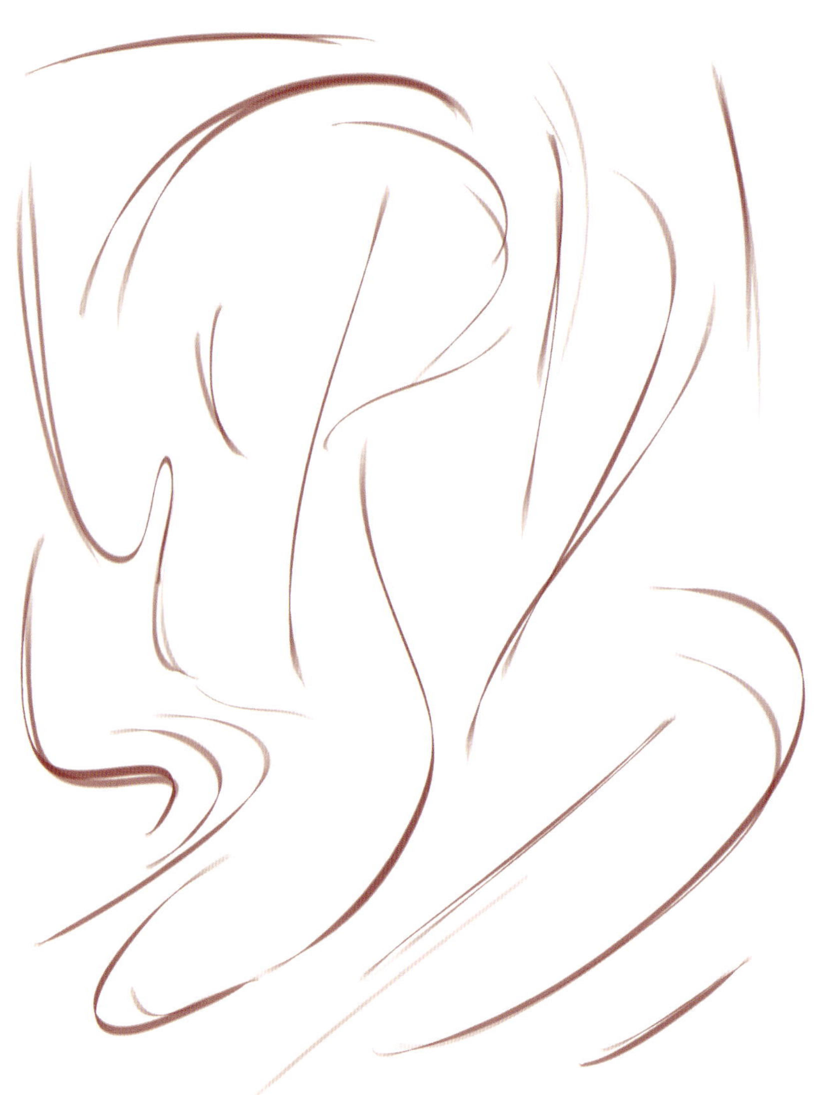

Capturing **Body Language**

The first rhythm to notice is the one that defines the entire pose. This is rarely a straight line. It can be a C-curve, an S-curve, or perhaps a series of opposing Straights. The human body's range of movement is magnificent, and gesture is the tool to harness that potential in your drawings.

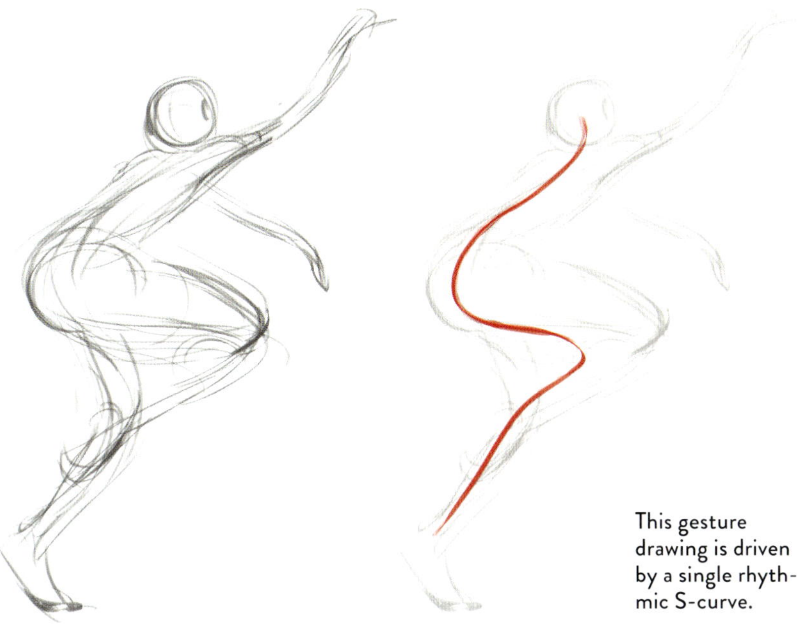

This gesture drawing is driven by a single rhythmic S-curve.

Gestures are *not* meant to be finished drawings. Gesture is a *stage* of drawing. It's the exploration stage. You are *supposed* to make very sketchy marks, because you are actively searching for rhythm, movement, emotion, weight, balance, and attitude. It's a very intuitive method of drawing.

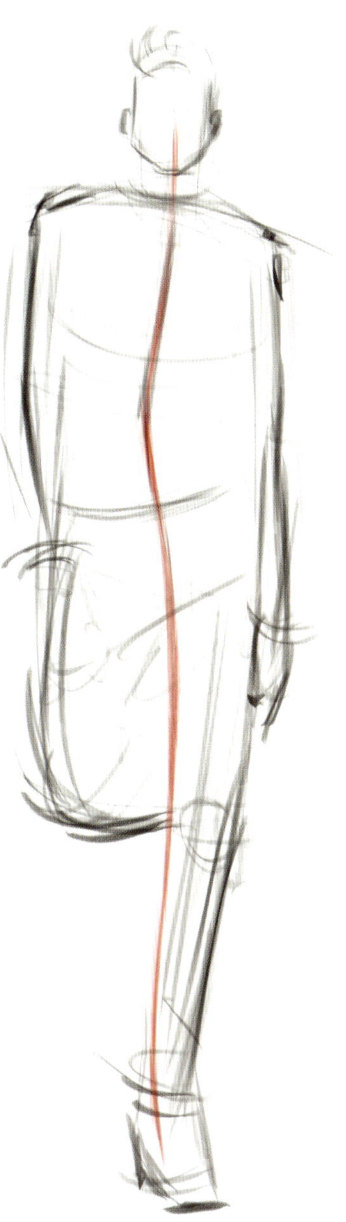

Even "straight up and down" poses often contain subtle rhythms through the body.

We've all met people who have a natural artistic
talent. You may be one of them! However, I've
never met a student who is naturally gifted at
gesture drawing. It's such a departure from how
drawing is intuitively understood that it takes a
focused effort to reprogram your eyes to disre-
gard finished outlines in favor of the underlying
rhythms, and to get to the point where you can
do it quickly!

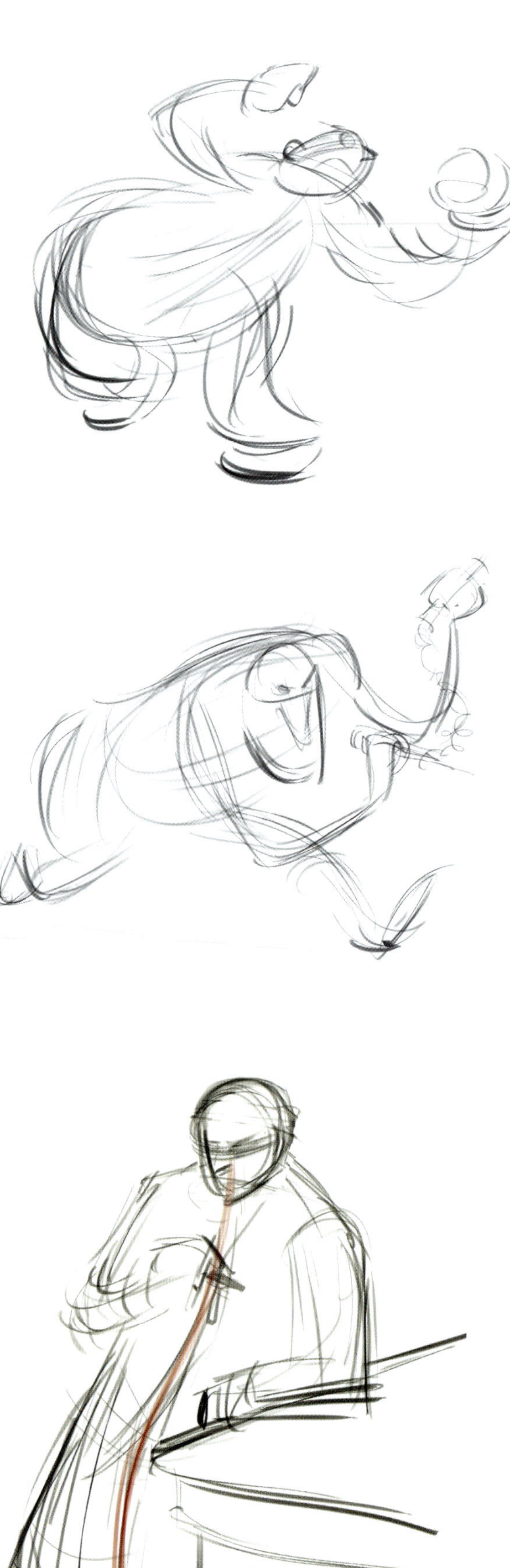

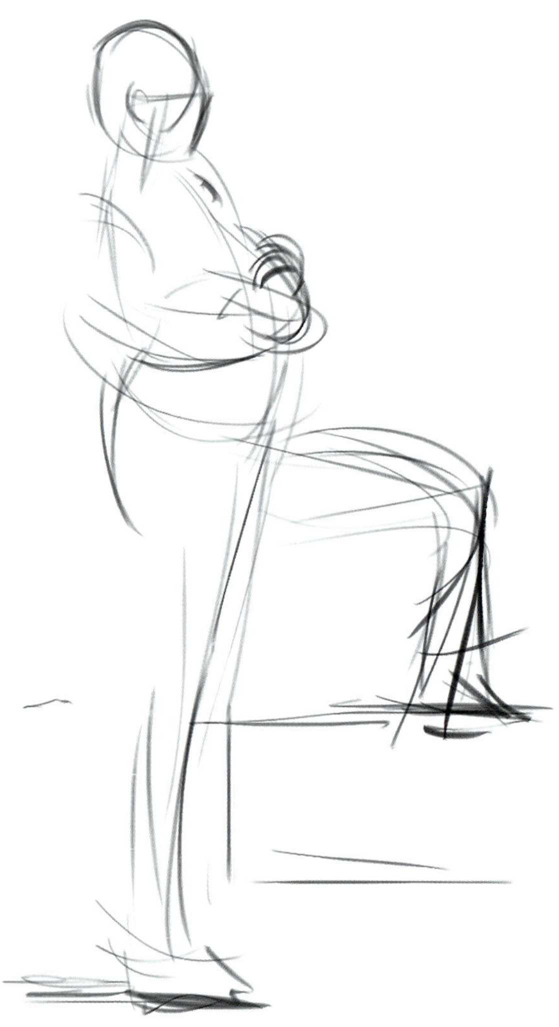

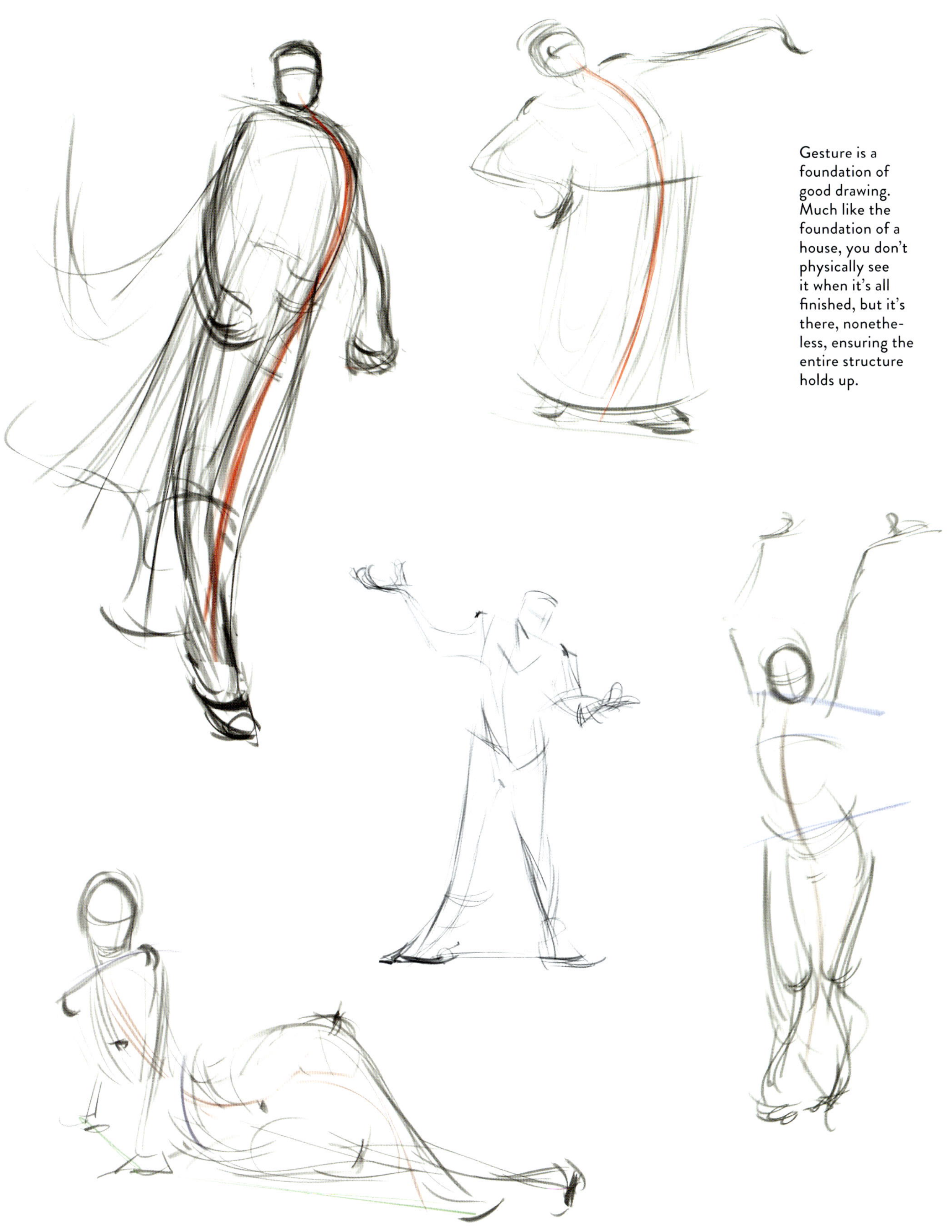

Gesture is a foundation of good drawing. Much like the foundation of a house, you don't physically see it when it's all finished, but it's there, nonetheless, ensuring the entire structure holds up.

The **Stick Figure**

Believe it or not, there *is* a place for the classic stick figure in good drawing. It's just perhaps not quite drawn the way you may be accustomed to.

That stick figure isn't useful because it resembles a real figure on only the most superficial of levels. For it to be useful, it needs anatomy like a neck, shoulders, and hips.

We now have a stick figure with essentially the same major joint-articulation as a real figure, which means we can pose it!

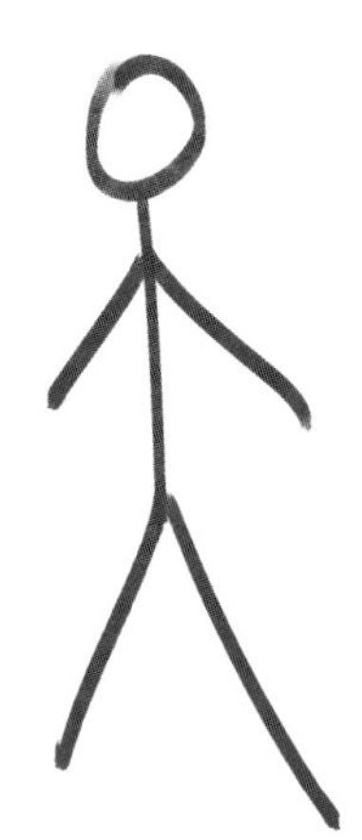

The classic stick figure.

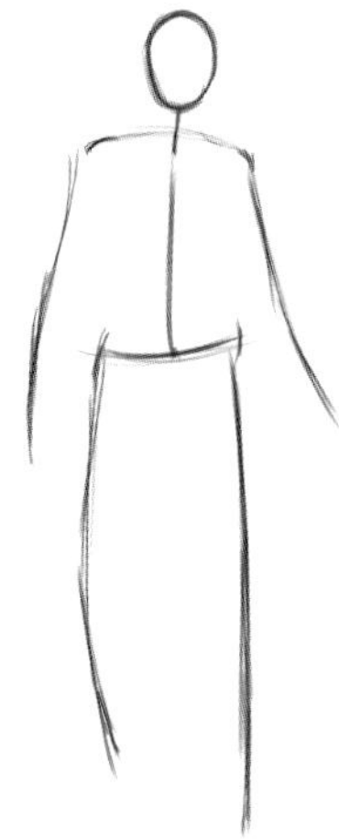

A more anatomical stick figure.

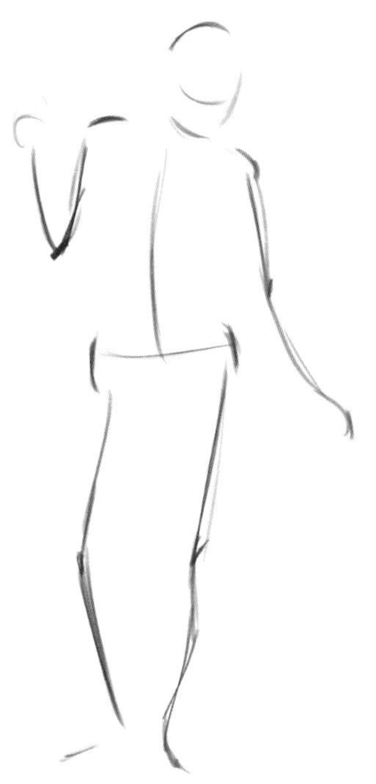

Our upgraded stick figure can assume lifelike poses.

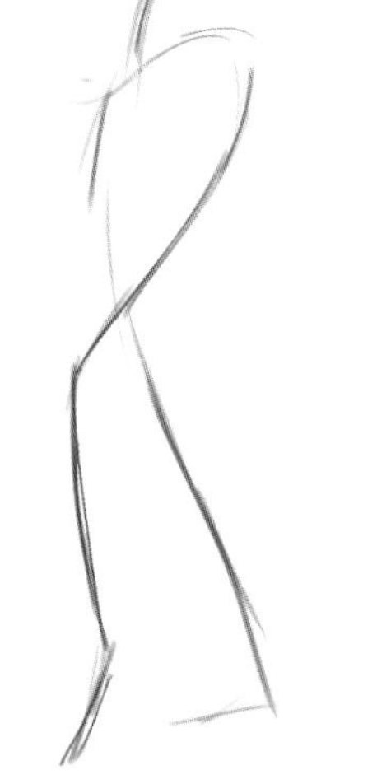

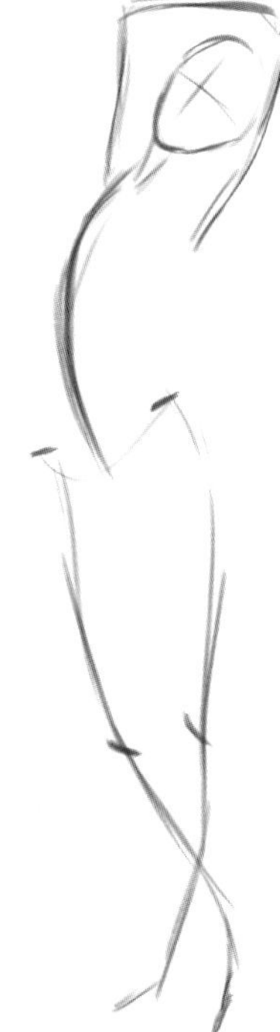

SHOULDERS AND HIPS

We communicate a lot of body language with our shoulders and hips. They are always moving, providing balance, energy, and momentum. Getting them right is essential to a good gesture drawing. What we're looking for first is simply their relative angles. *Relative* is the key word. A simple line through the shoulders and hips will be enough to visualize this.

It's easy to spot the shoulders, as they're often part of the silhouette, and of course it's where the arms begin. The hips can be a bit trickier. You're looking for the hips' pivot points also known as the iliac crest, which is the very top of our large bowl-shaped hip bone.

Another handy method to visualize the hips is to imagine the belt-line.

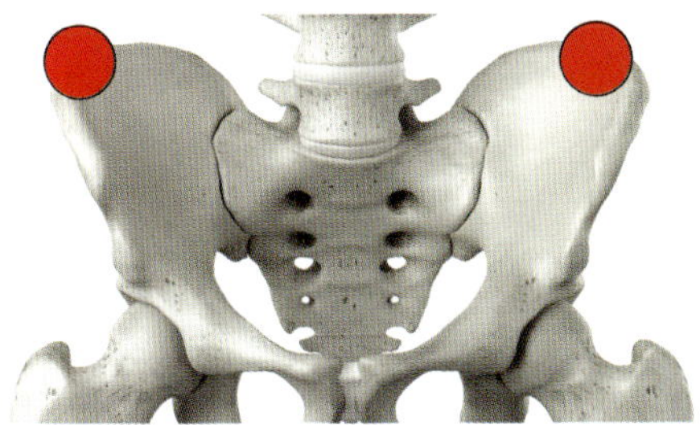

The red dots mark the iliac crest. This part of the hip bone touches the skin, making it easy to feel and see.

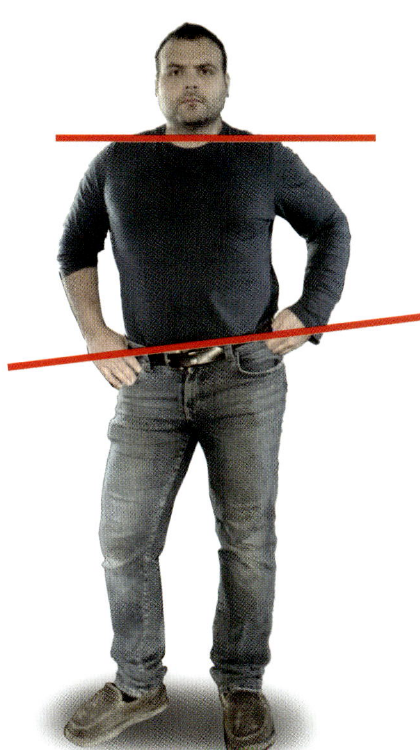

It's essential to notice the relationship of angle between these lines. This pose would fool a lot of people into making the hips and shoulder lines parallel. A quick look at your reference will often reveal a nonparallel relationship.

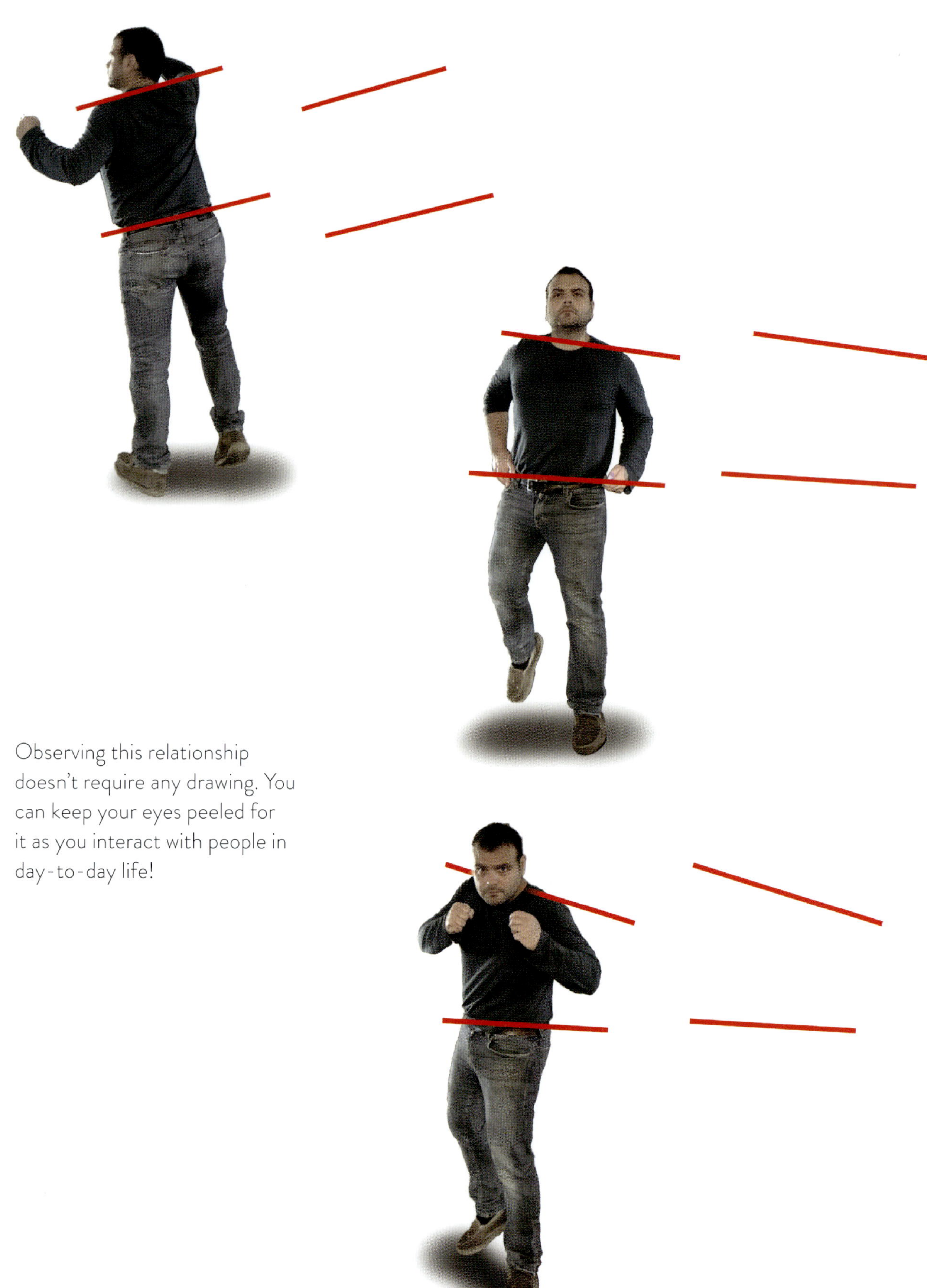

Observing this relationship doesn't require any drawing. You can keep your eyes peeled for it as you interact with people in day-to-day life!

A gesture drawing can be as simple as aligning
that stick figure to the hips and shoulder lines and
drawing the limbs using the sticks as middle-lines.
Let's try it with this reference:

Draw an oval for the head (ignore the crosshairs
for now), plot lines for the shoulders and hips,
and make simple marks to represent how wide
they are in proportion to the head.

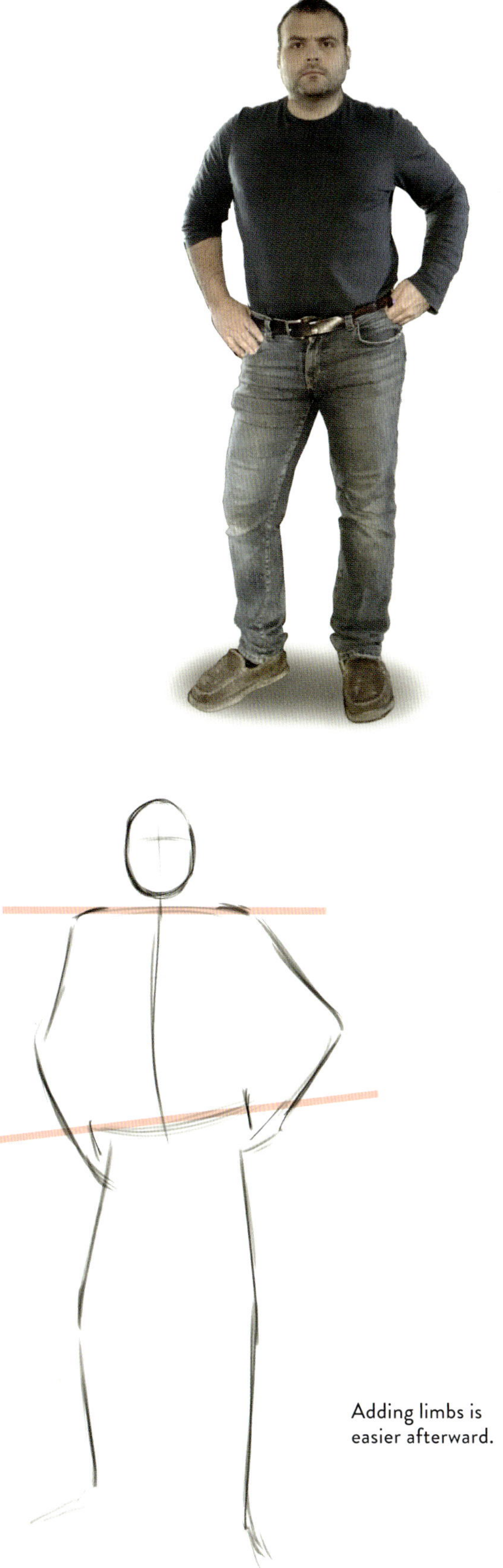

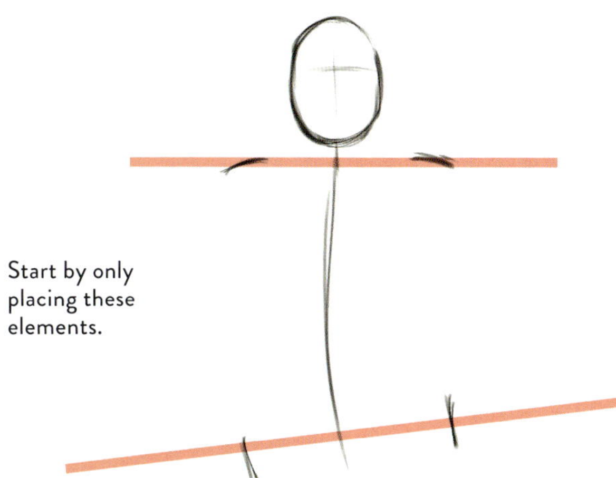

**Start by only
placing these
elements.**

**Adding limbs is
easier afterward.**

A **More Dynamic** Gesture

Using the stick figure is a great starting point, but you will likely outgrow it quickly.
Consider this gesture drawing:

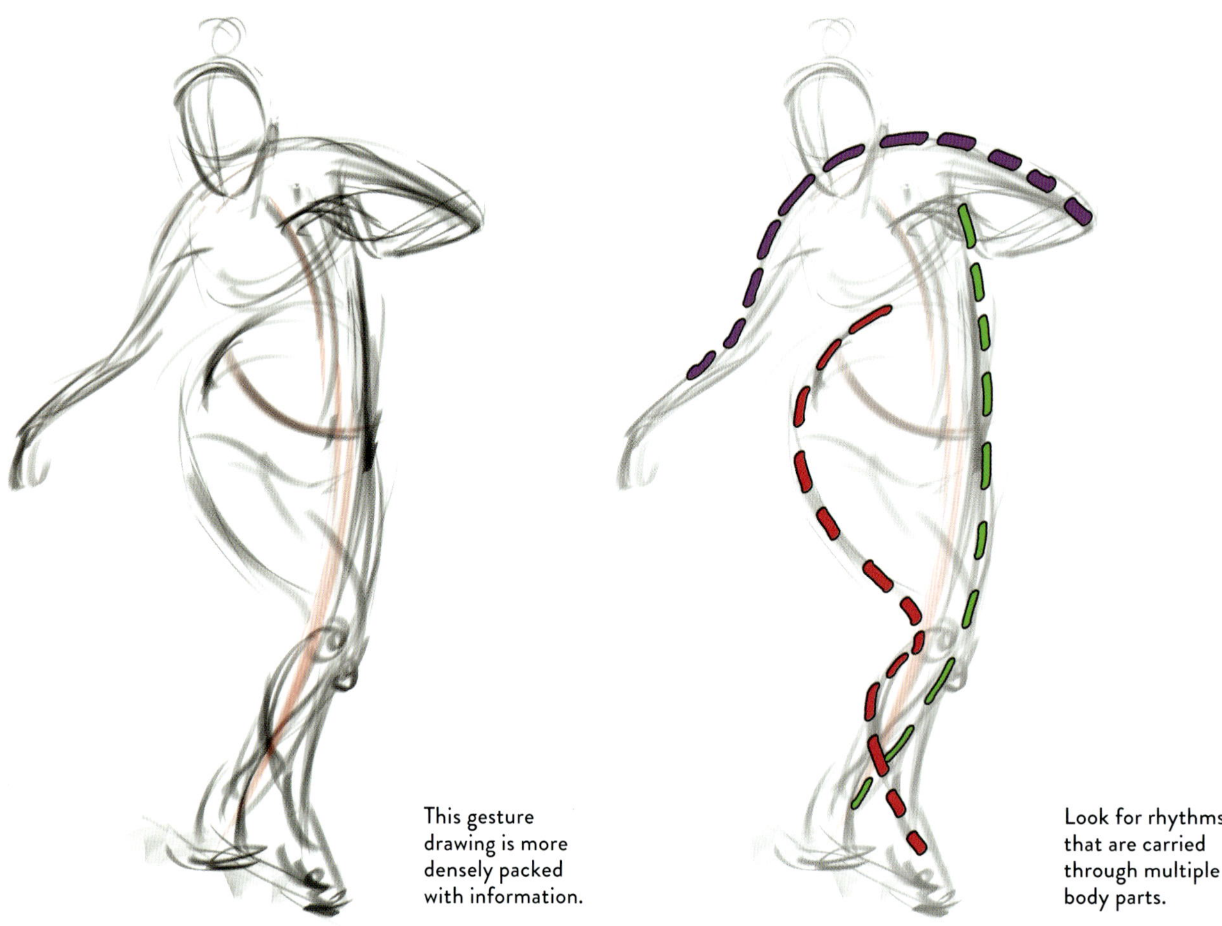

This gesture
drawing is more
densely packed
with information.

Look for rhythms
that are carried
through multiple
body parts.

This application of gesture drawing captures the same information as the stick figure, but also includes a stronger sense of rhythm, weight, and balance. This gesture drawing not only captures the position of things, but also captures the *feel* of the pose. This is achieved by paying closer attention to the inherent rhythms each part of the body presents, both on its own, and in relation to other parts of the pose.

This figure appears to be in motion, perhaps dancing, or doing some other kind of elegant movement. You can tell the weight is on the back leg, and that the body is moving toward page-right. You can also tell that the weight is in the act of shifting forward, and the pose that comes next will undoubtedly be the front leg planting itself on the ground to catch the weight.

Over the years, I've learned to double-up my strokes so that a gestural statement never happens with just one line.

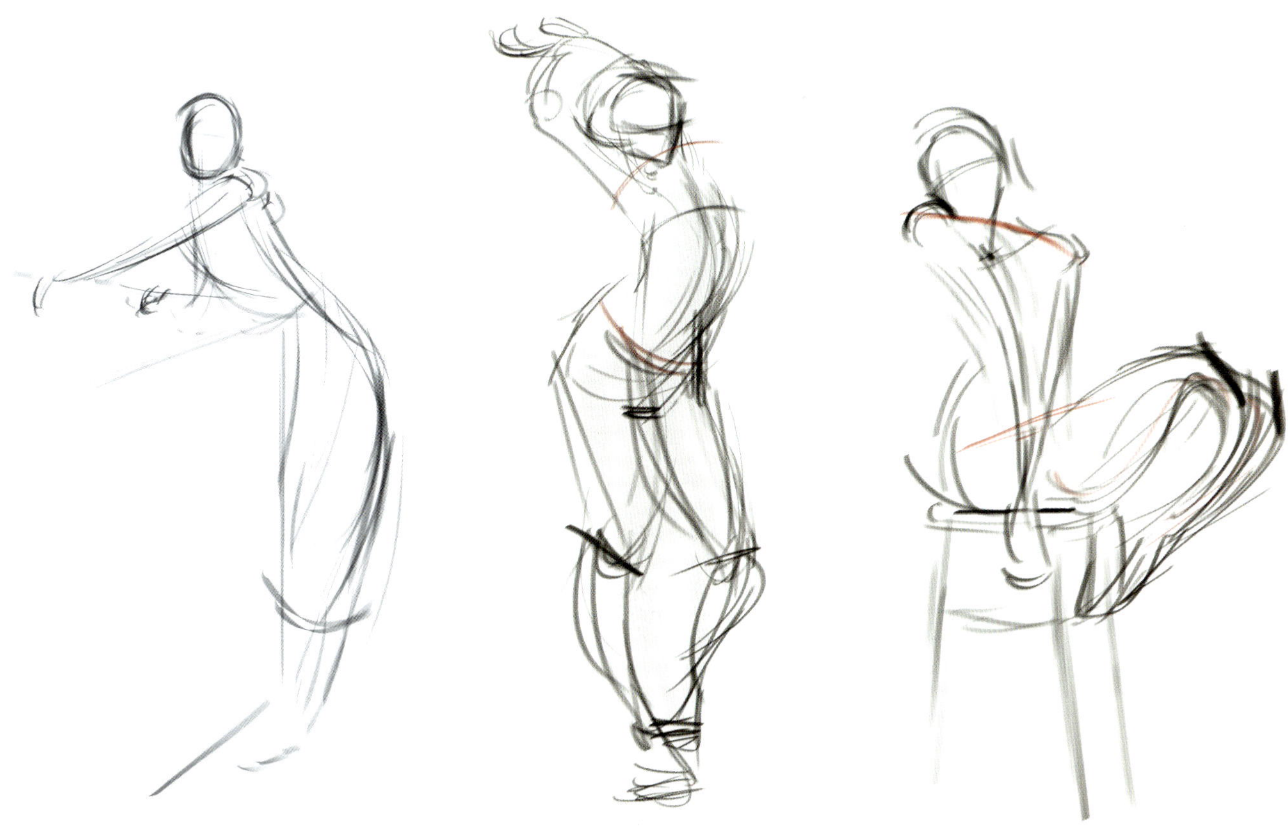

Instead of this . . .

. . . it's this. Using multiple strokes.

Doing this is more of a physical preference than anything aesthetic. Putting down multiple lines helps me feel the energy and movement in my own body, which, in turn, feeds back into the gesture drawing itself, imbuing it with more life. You can also use this sequence of strokes to hone in on the rhythm or actively search for it on the page.

Landmarking **Major** Elements

Because gesture drawing can be an emotional outpouring, it's easy to let those strokes wander too far off the mark. Landmarking is a type of measuring tool you can use to set start and end points to your strokes, which helps to contain or guide them.

Place two dots or marks. One for the start of the stroke, and one for the end.

You can connect the points using however many strokes you'd like and whatever type of rhythmic strokes you need for the gesture.

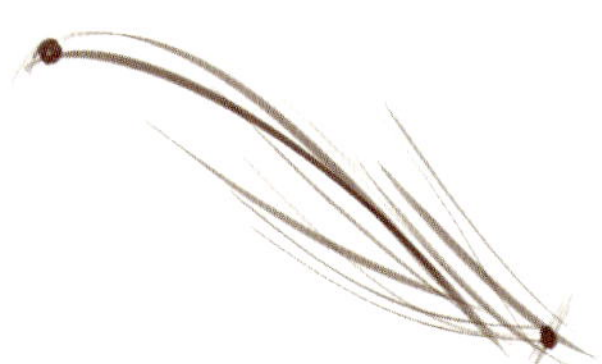

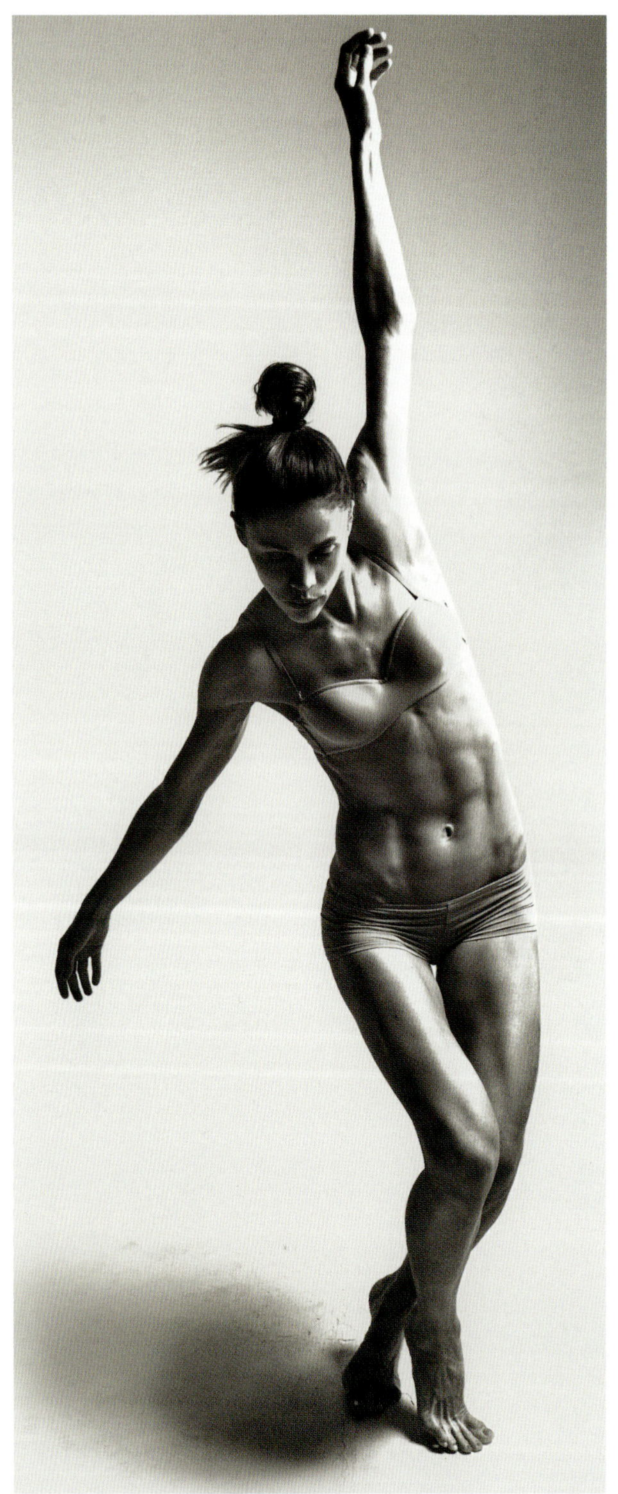

A pose with many elements working together.

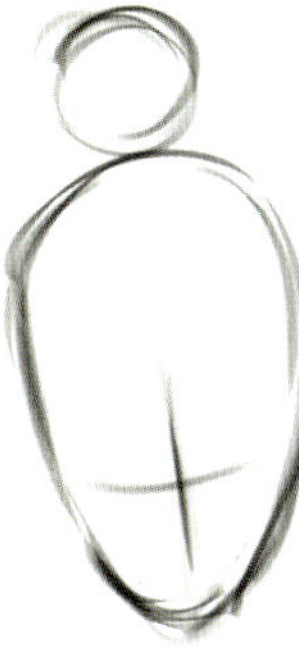

The crosshairs tell me where the eyeline is as well as where the middle of the face is. In this case, the bun is also useful to indicate the direction of the head.

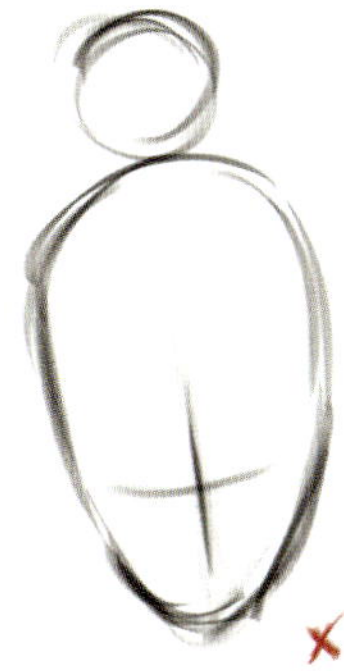

Make a dot or X to denote the location of the area you're landmarking. In this case, it's the pit of the neck.

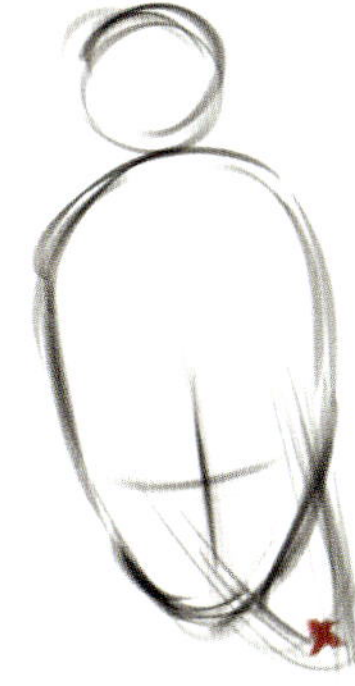

Put down gestural lines to connect the head and neck. Notice I'm drawing right through the head. This is okay and even encouraged at this stage to help you feel out those rhythms.

Using landmarks, you can break the pose into smaller sections.

I like to make an oval shape for the head first and base all my measurements off that.

The easiest measurements to make are the smallest ones. You can use any body part you like as a landmark. I commonly use the pit of the neck. Being very close to the head, it makes for the easiest measurement. It's also a good candidate because it's generally where the head/neck ends and the torso begins.

The next major pair of land-marks is what we've already looked at, the shoulder and hips relationship. I jot them down with quick lines, making my best guess at the relationship between the two angles, as well as the distance between the shoulders and hips.

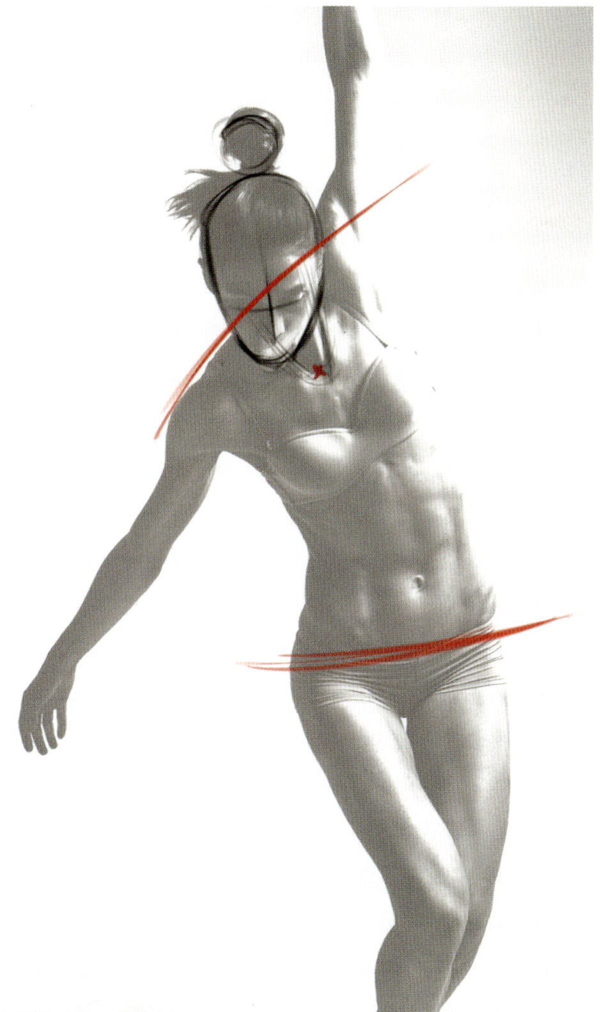

TIP: Many artists learn to measure things in head-lengths. It's another good reason to start with the head.

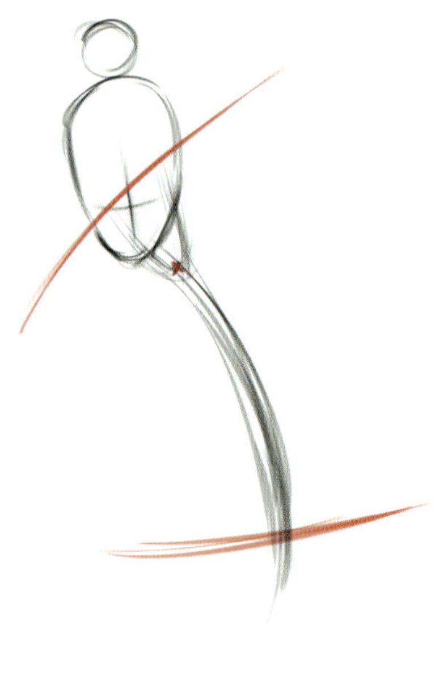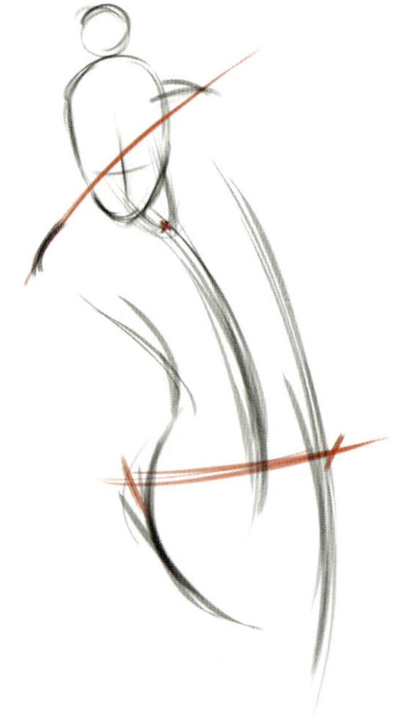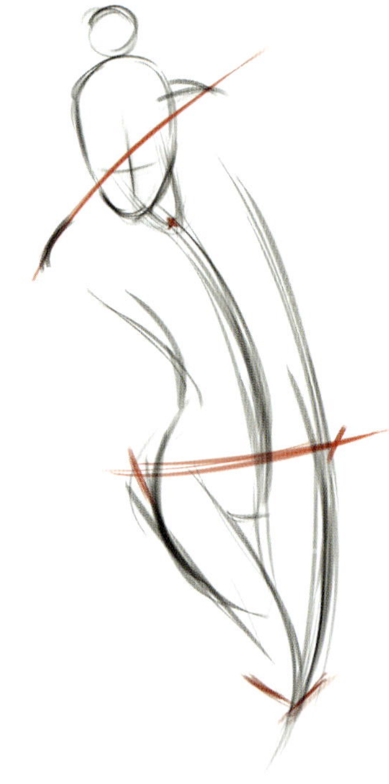

I am using multiple strokes to capture one C-curve rhythm.

Now I can find two more rhythms, one for either side of the torso. On the left is an S-curve, and on the right is a C-curve, but it's a straighter C-curve than what goes down the middle of the body. Note that I am *not* attempting the torso's final shape, nor do I care if the width is accurate at this stage!

Sometimes I like to indicate an angle for the knees, often made visible by the top of the kneecap.

From here, I like to gesture down from the pit of the neck, which lies at the middle of the torso, down to the middle of the hips. There will only be one rhythm here. In this case, it's a medium-wide C-curve.

Because the body is more complex than just a middle line, I like to also landmark the iliac crest, or corners of the hips, as well as the shoulders. These points should be somewhat easy to measure, as they'll exist on the hip and shoulder lines that are already landmarked.

Notice how capturing the sides of the torso gives me some rhythms to feed into the legs. I like to build the leg gesture off the iliac crest point on either side. Because the legs are long, the likelihood of making a proportional error is higher. So, I like to cut them in half and first landmark the knees. You can do this with a single line, or with one mark per knee. Then simply gesture down to that landmark.

Repeat the process for the feet, measuring from the knees. Because the feet can take on many different angles, I always indicate that with my landmark.

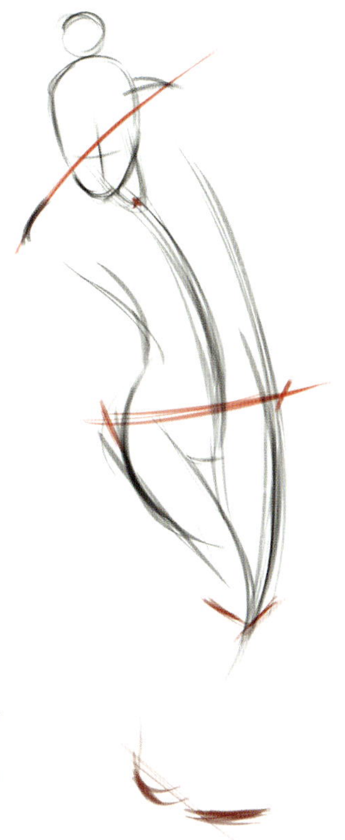

Now I can gesture down to the feet. Much like the torso, I try to find the rhythm on either side of the leg.

To place the arms, I start by locating the hands. Because you have the body in place at this point, you can measure the hands using plumb lines. Plumb lines shoot a straight horizontal or vertical measurement to see where the hands line up with the body.

Think of the hands as an extension of the arm's rhythm. Note that there is quite often a break in direction at the wrist, as you can see on this model's right.

Note the landmarks, but also the straight line connecting them. This line helps solve basic perspective, which can cause the feet to appear in different locations vertically on the page.

TIP: The tibia, or the shinbone, is a straight bone that often makes for a straight-ish rhythm at the front of the leg, complimented by a curvier rhythm courtesy of the rounded calf muscle at the back of the leg.

Be very clear where the feet contact the ground!

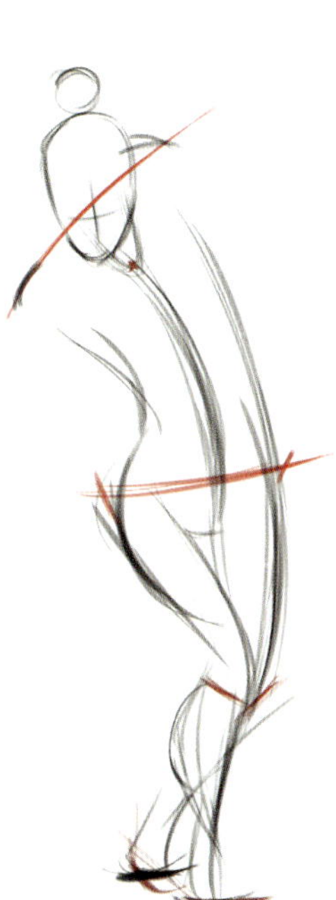

You are free to physically draw these plumb lines or visualize them with your mind's eye.

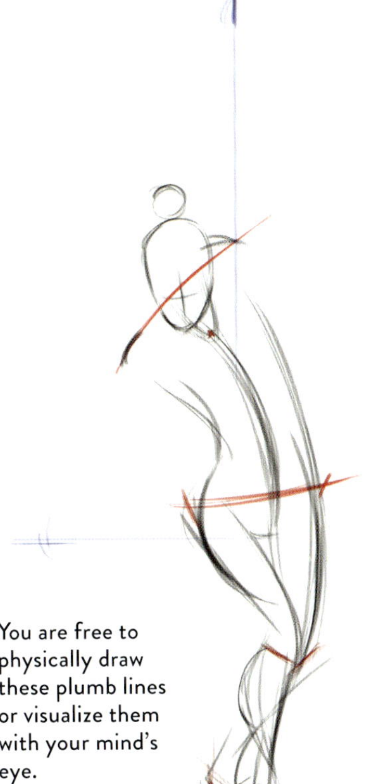

The finished gesture drawing.

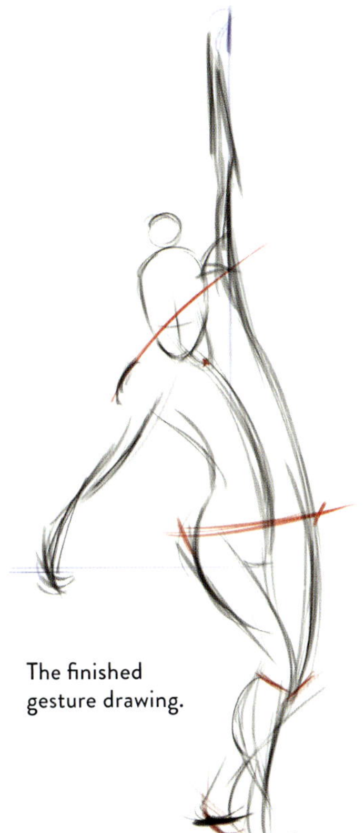

Rhythms Capture Physicality

Let's try another gesture that uses various rhythms to capture the pose and establish the feel of movement and weight. Here's the reference:

Certain rhythms are more likely to invoke different physical actions or phenomena. For example, let's look at a curvy rhythm versus a straight one.

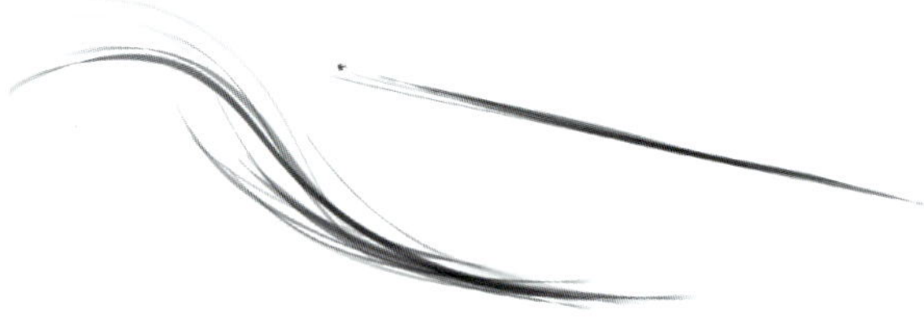

A curve generally tends to possess more elegance or flow, while the straight gains more speed, solidity, or energy.

In our finished gesture drawing on the previous page, look at the straight rhythms used to indicate the model's left arm shooting up into the air with force and speed versus the model's right arm, which drapes downward in a more fluid motion.

It's also important to consider the *amount* of curve you're observing.

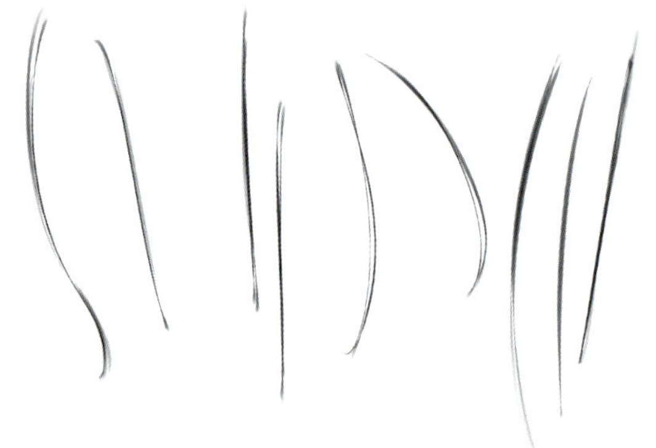

Each of these present slightly different feels and rhythms. Learning to select which suits your needs is part of the skills you are building with gesture drawing.

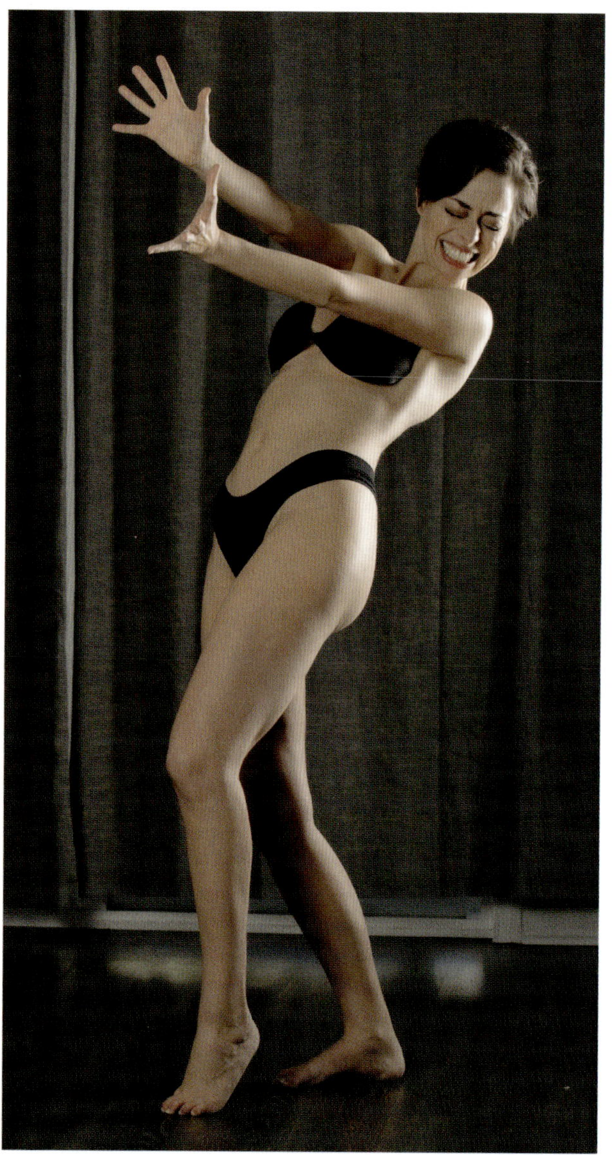

Before drawing anything, try to establish where you might use curves versus where straights might be better.

Here is what I am thinking to myself before drawing a single line:

The outstretched arms are thrusting a lot of
energy outward. I can use Straights there to show
that. Bolding and thickening my lines can emphasize it. The whole pose is an unbroken C-curve,
which is a nice contrast for the Straights in the
arms. Two opposing rhythms add contrast and
therefore interest. The weight appears to rest
entirely on the back leg and since weight is best
communicated with Straights, I want to use more
Straights in the back leg and more C-curves and
S-curves in the front.

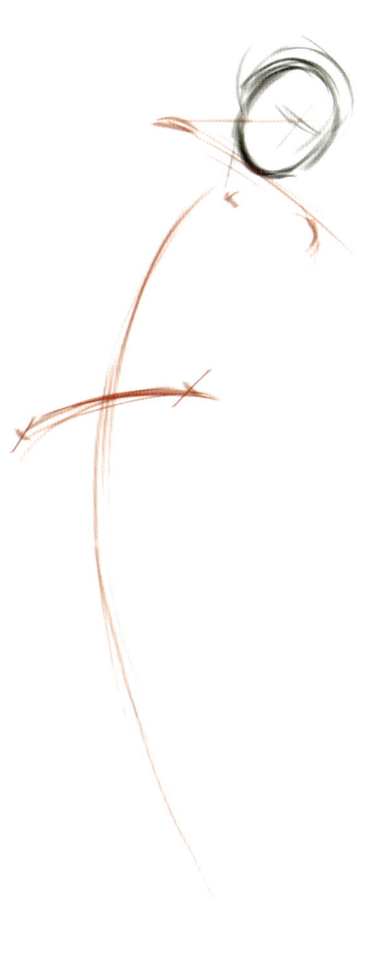

I begin with the head and three landmarks, the pit of the neck,
the shoulder line, and the hip line. In this pose, the shoulders
and hips create heavily opposing angles, which adds dynamics to
the pose.

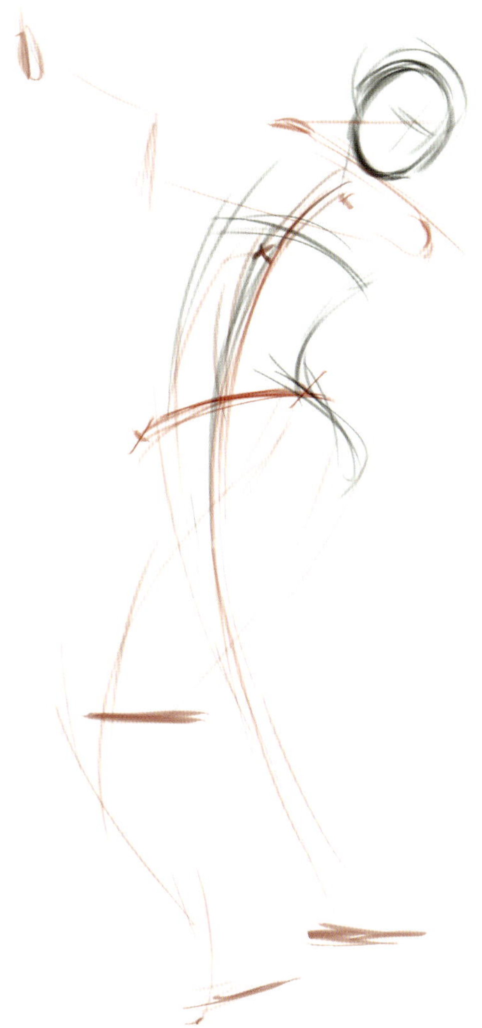

Here I've added the rest of the landmarks, the knees position,
feet position, and hands position. There is another landmark
here that is sometimes useful, the sternum. The sternum
is about halfway between the pit of the neck and the hips.
Subdividing lengths with reliable points always helps because
it's easier to measure shorter distances than longer ones. The
sternum isn't always visible, however, so you should be used to
working without it as well.

Here I've added those bold Straights to capture the thrust-out arms. See how Straights help capture that sense of motion and energy? When I drew them, I literally pulled my pencil or stylus across those lines five or six times, just to ensure I'm feeling that energy in my own body. I also capture the various rhythms at either side of the torso, a C-curve on the left, and an S-curve on the right, culminating at the hipline.

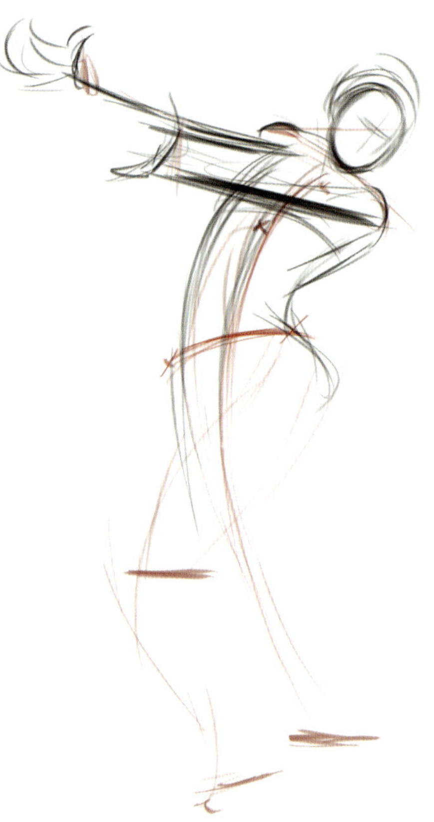

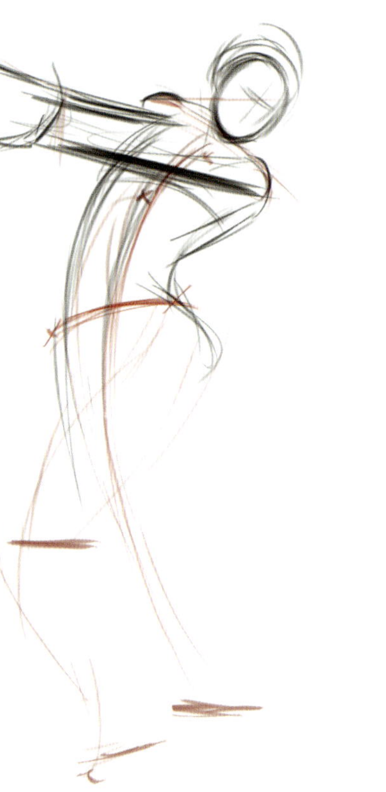

The finished gesture drawing. Note the addition of a line establishing the basic perspective of the feet on the ground, as well as tapered lay-ins for the feet themselves, which are continuous with the legs' rhythms.

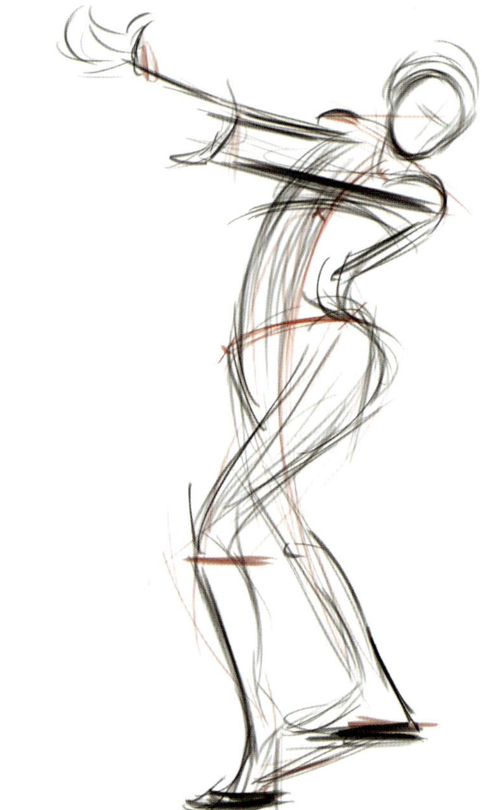

Connecting rhythms from one landmark to another. In this case, the hips' relationship with the knees is established, noting that either leg uses a different rhythm. I also firmly establish where the feet land. Because the back leg contains the weight, I draw it first, knowing that the non-weight-bearing leg can be wherever.

TIP: You'll often find that your initial landmarks are off. If I placed the feet incorrectly, this is where I'd notice and correct it.

Scan to watch a tutorial.

Let's **Draw Gestures!**

A gesture drawing session should involve lots of quick drawings, each one lasting no more than two to three minutes. If you find yourself needing more time than that, it is likely you're trying to focus on the actual contours, rather than rhythm and flow. In a contour drawing you can have "wrong" lines, but in a gesture there are no wrong lines, only lines that search for the desired feeling. If you fail to capture that desired feeling, you've only spent two to three minutes, and can just go to the next one or try again.

All right, enough words, let's draw!

In this one, the torso follows a clear C-curve rhythm. The back leg feels like a subtle S-curve, and the front leg a more pronounced C-curve. The arms are also C-curves, save for the strong Straight line in the left upper arm.

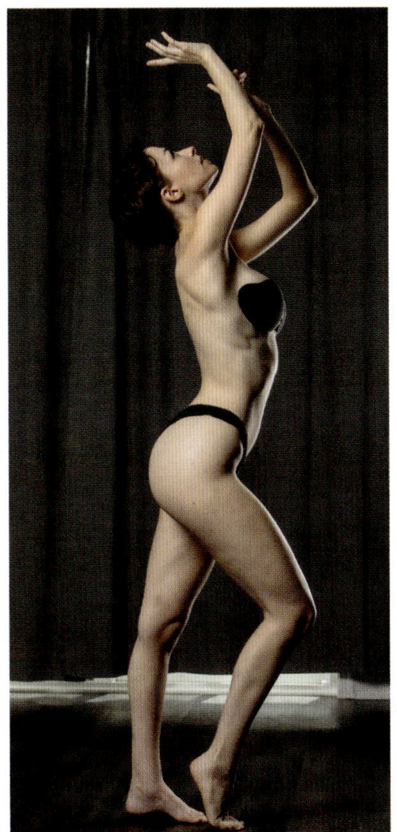

Scan to watch a tutorial.

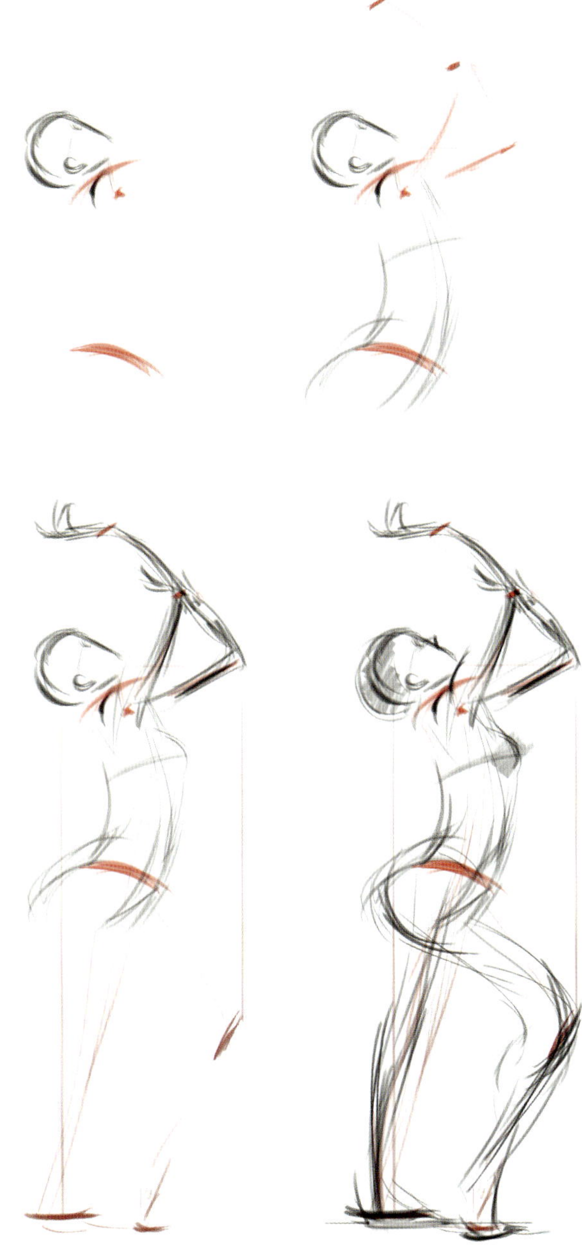

There's a lovely sense of movement created when a shoulder
bumps up against the head
like that. Shoulder lines, when
angled as they often are, can be
very expressive parts of a pose
and gesture drawing. Look out
for a subtle difference of angles
between the shoulders and hips
here. They're not parallel!

Scan to watch a tutorial.

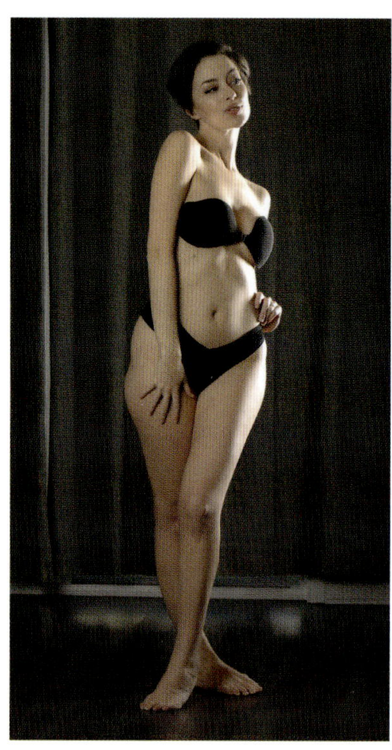

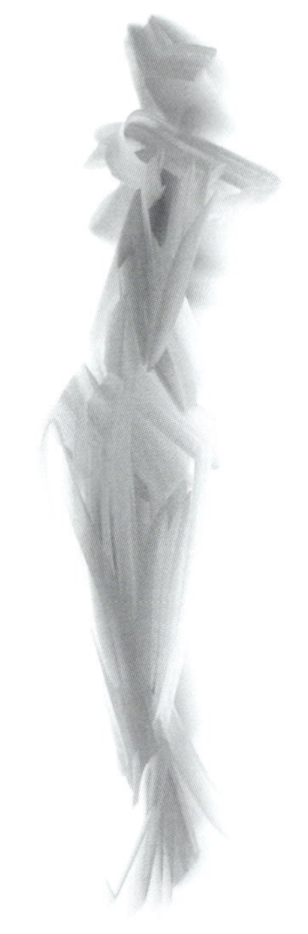

Starting the gesture by smudging some tone around, but in an overall S-curve rhythm.
We would do this sometimes with charcoal during life drawing class and work out of it.

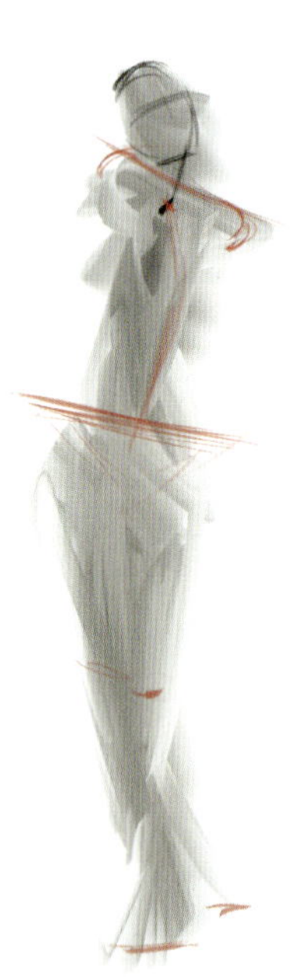

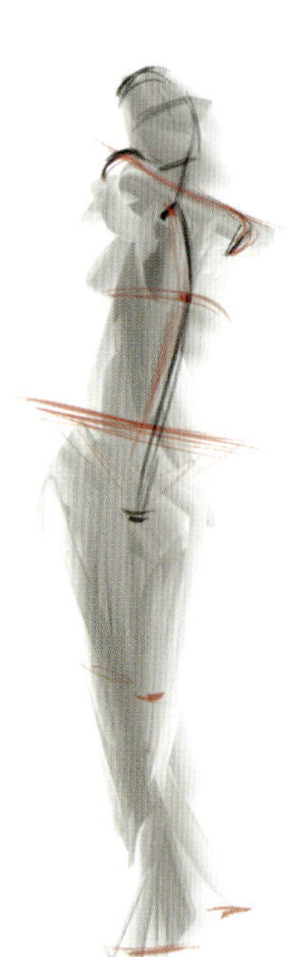

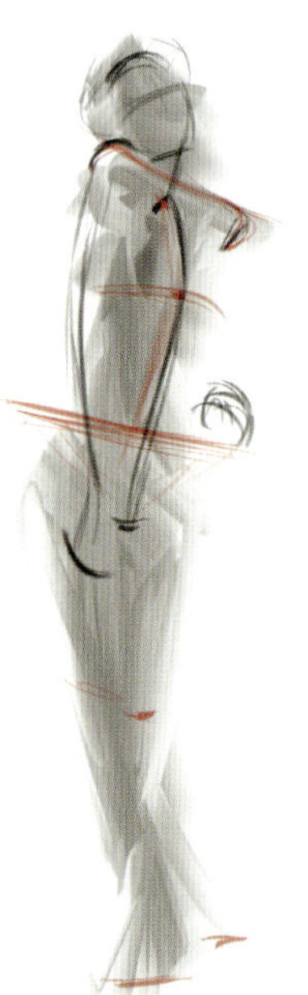

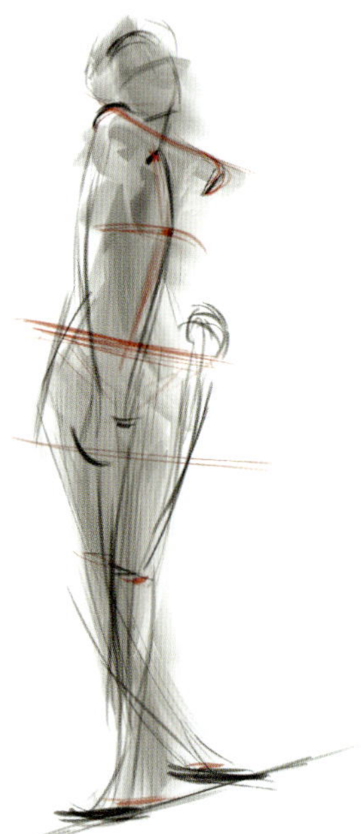

Notice that the initial C-curve flows through the whole pose, but it's the left leg that carries it through to the ground, while the right leg is doing its own rhythmic thing. Often this will happen with one or both legs stopping the flow at the hips and segmenting off into their own rhythms. With this one I had an uninterrupted rhythm all the way through, and those are always fun poses to gesture out.

Scan to watch a tutorial.

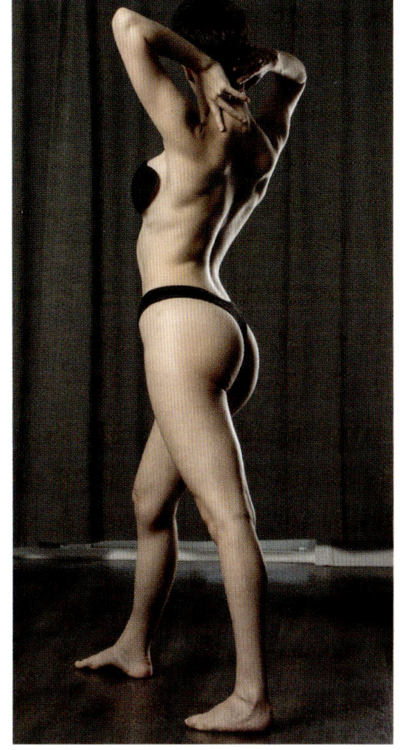

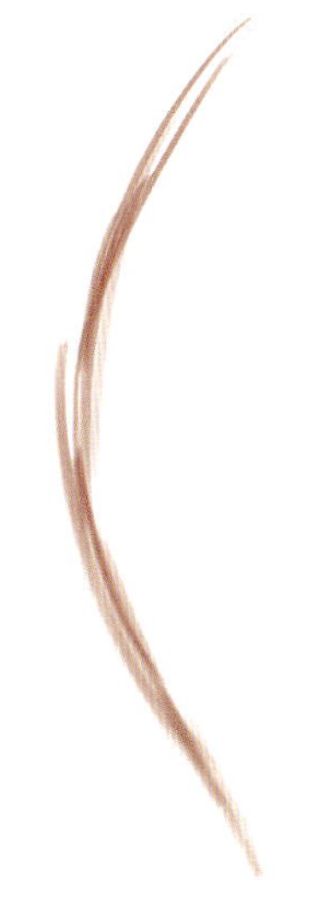

A big C-curve anchors this pose, so I start with that.

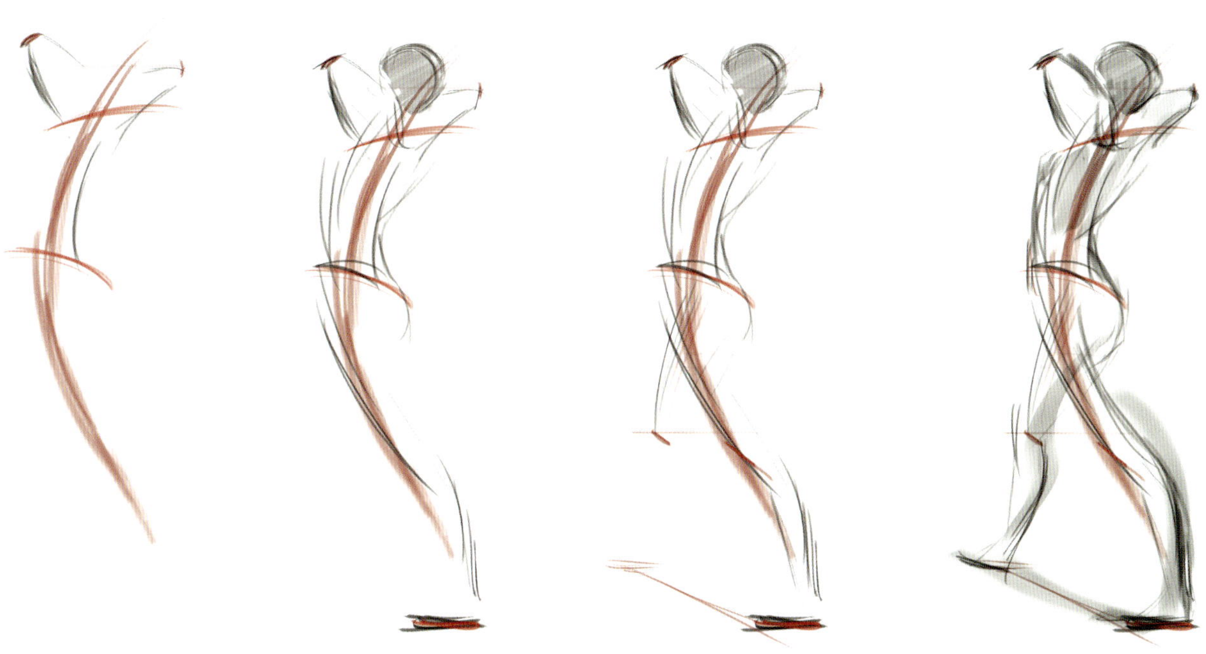

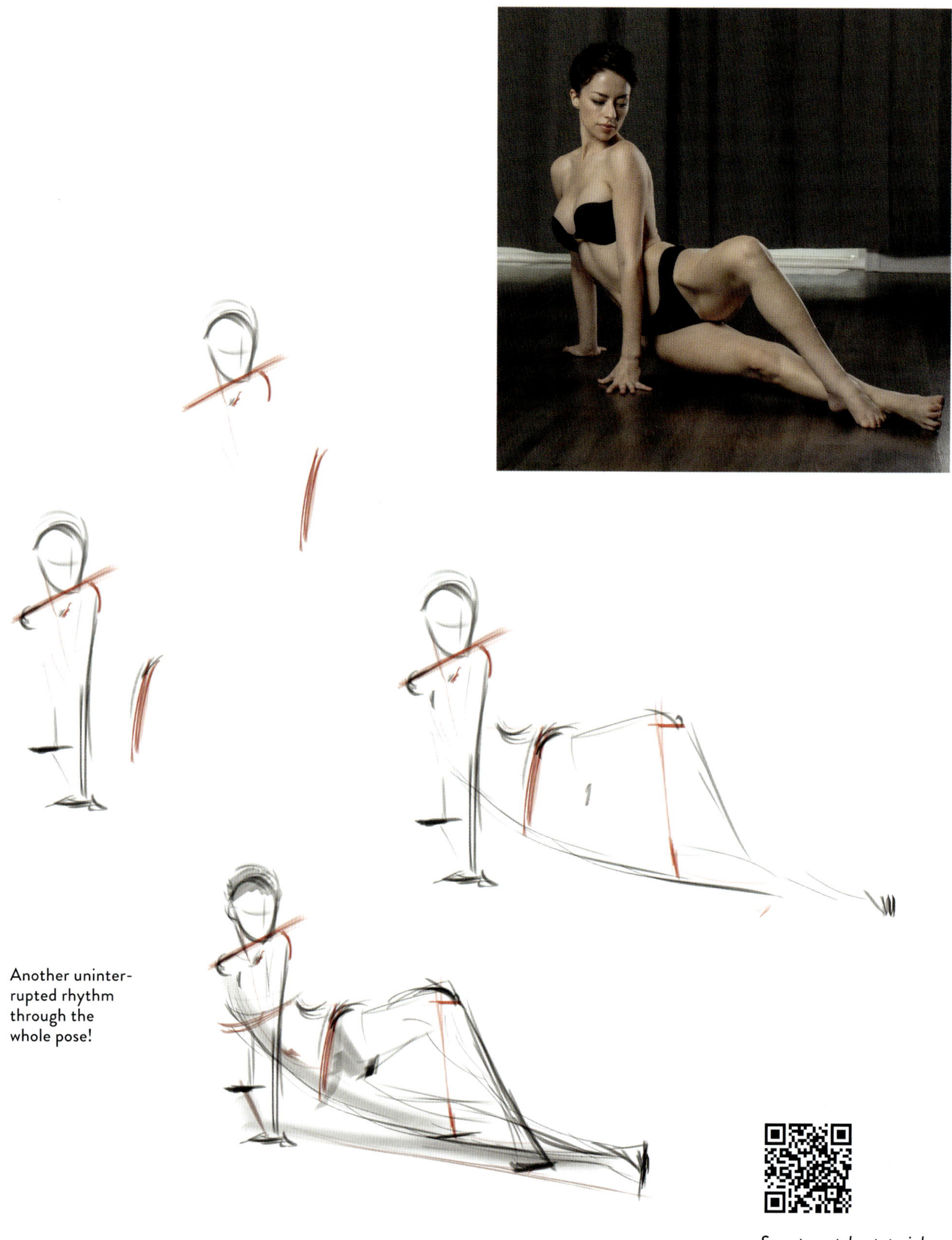

Another uninter-
rupted rhythm
through the
whole pose!

Scan to watch a tutorial.

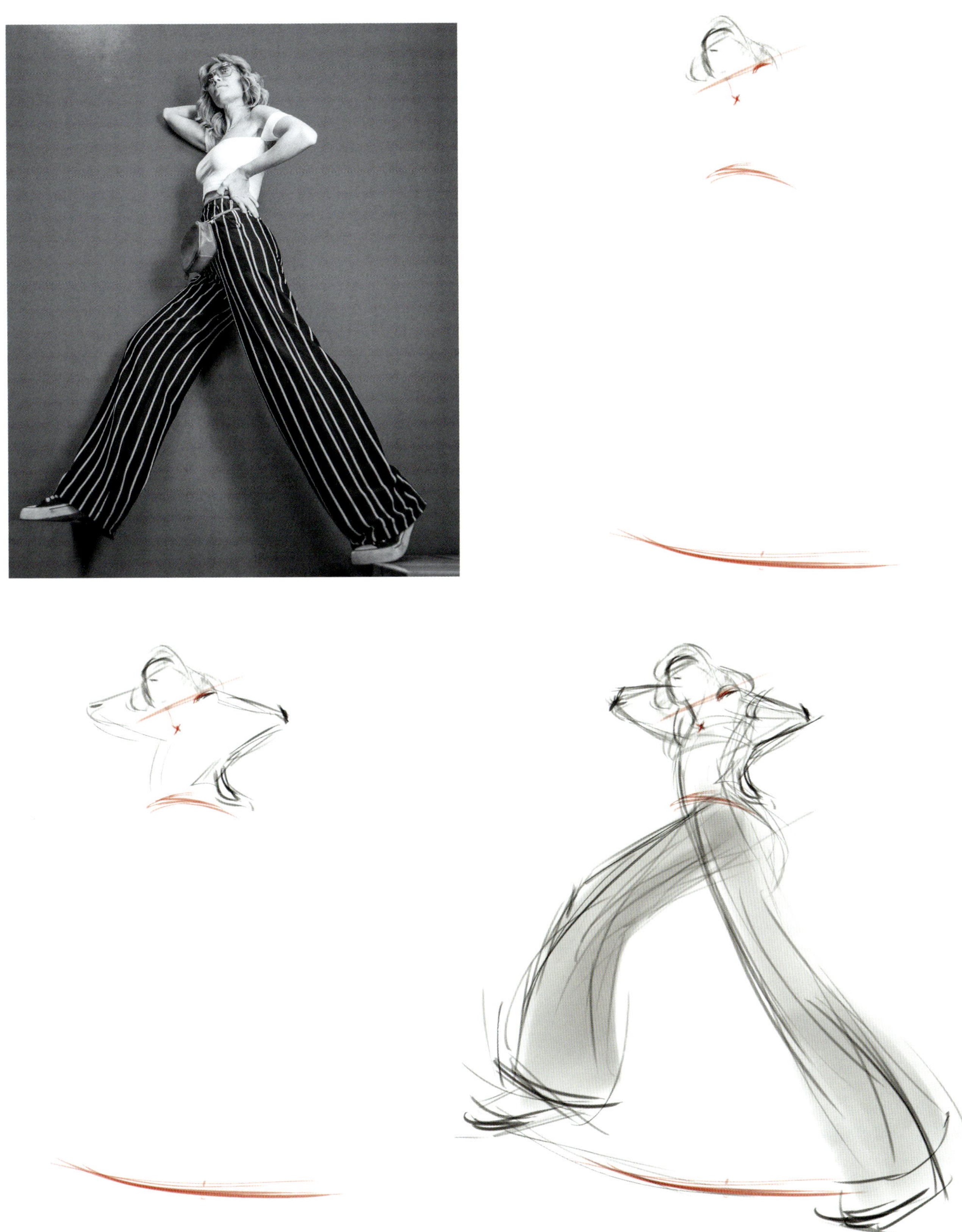

Using landmarks, we can begin to map out the forced perspective on this one.

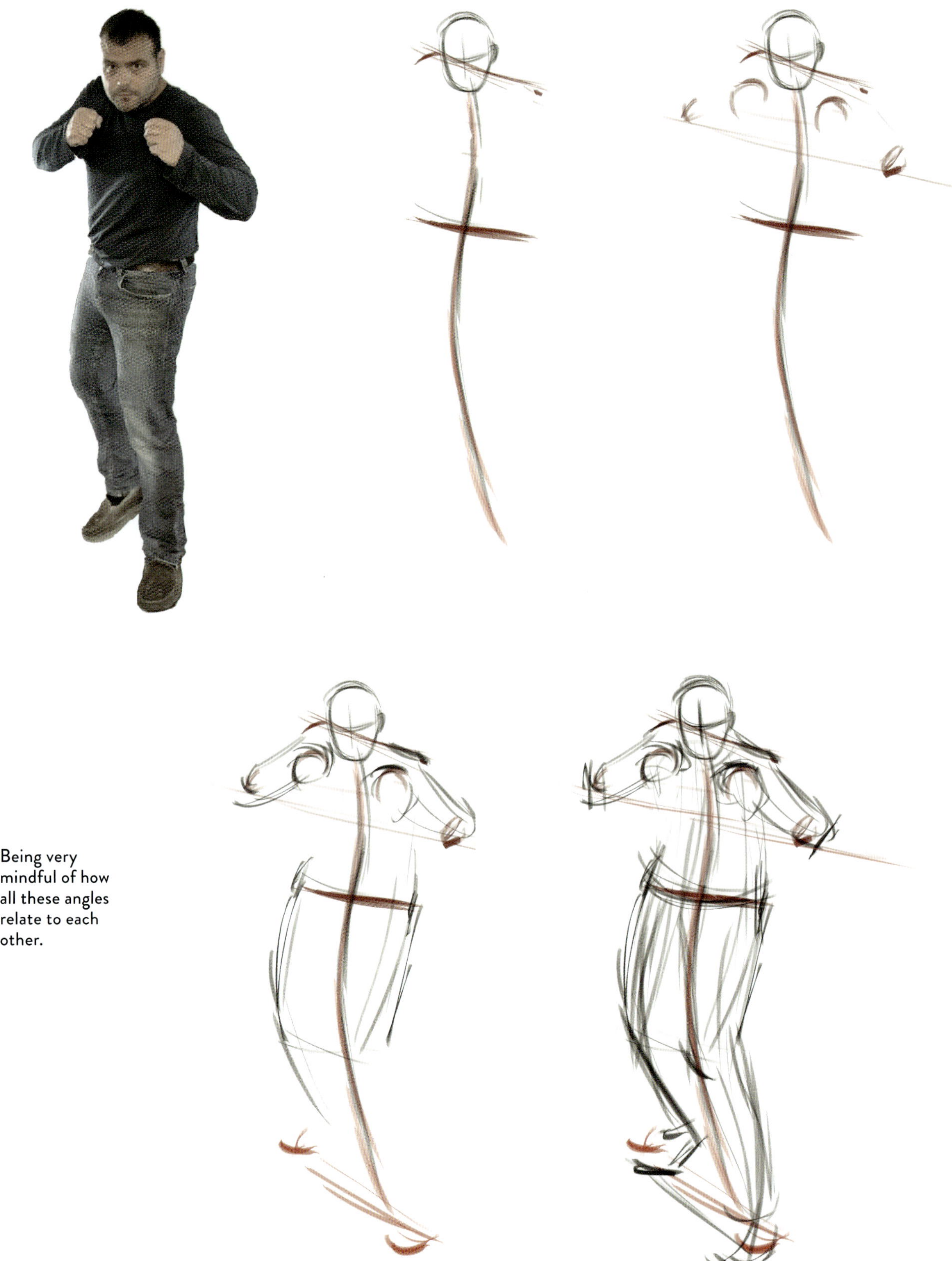

Being very mindful of how all these angles relate to each other.

Let's try that same pose, same rhythms, but from a different angle!

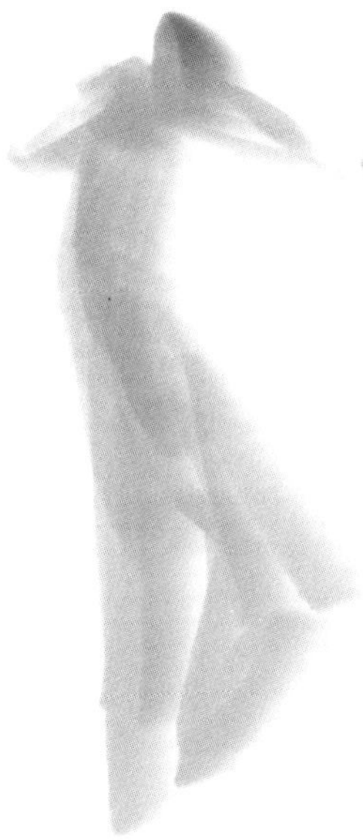

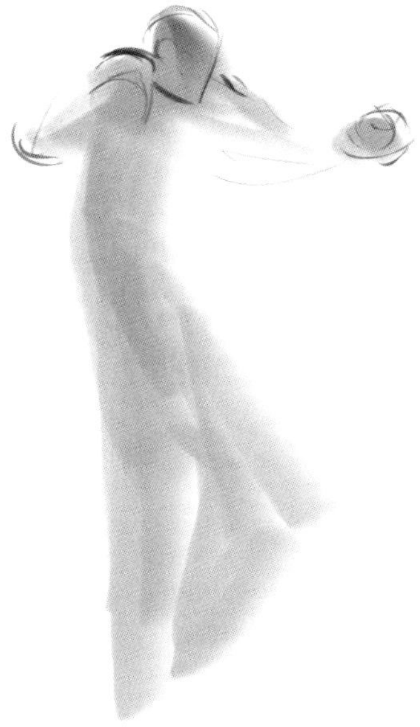

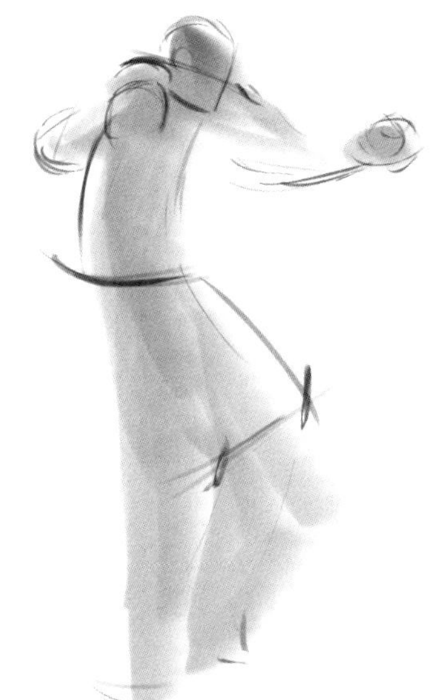

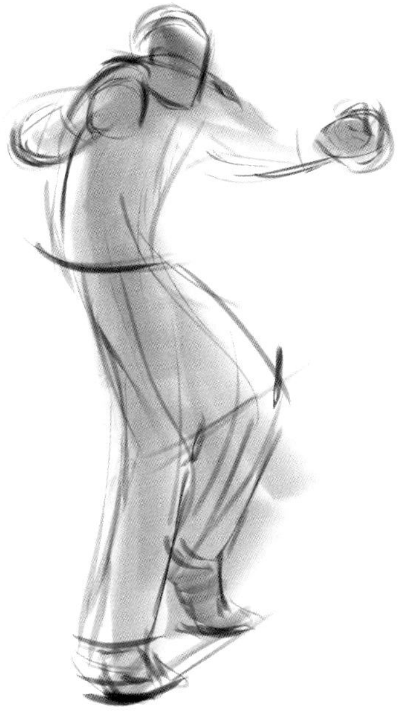

Scan to watch a tutorial.

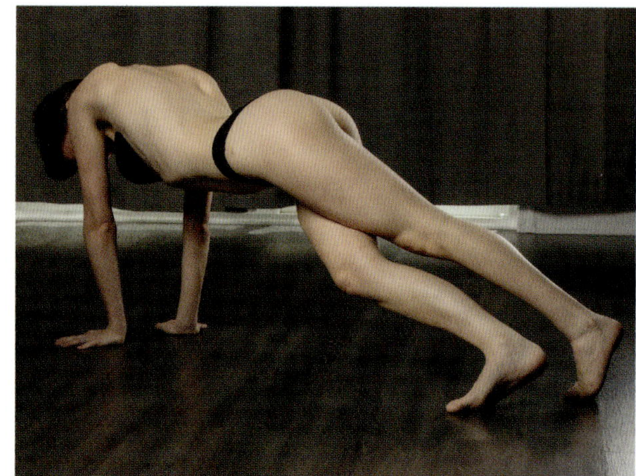

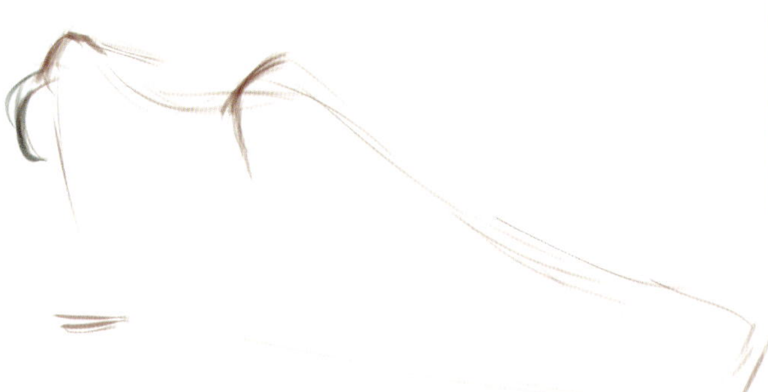

Notice the use of
Straights here to show the
arms bearing the weight.

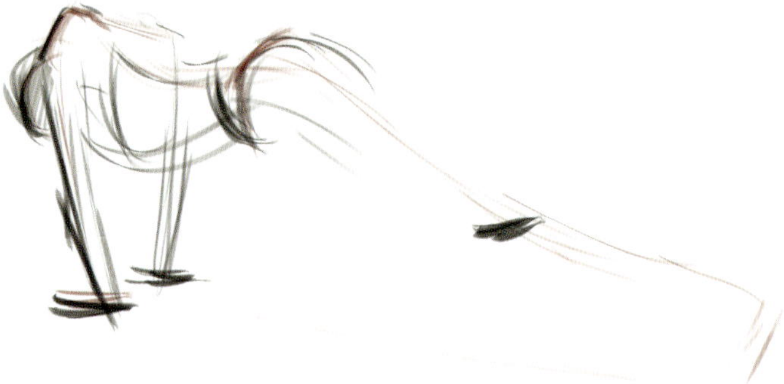

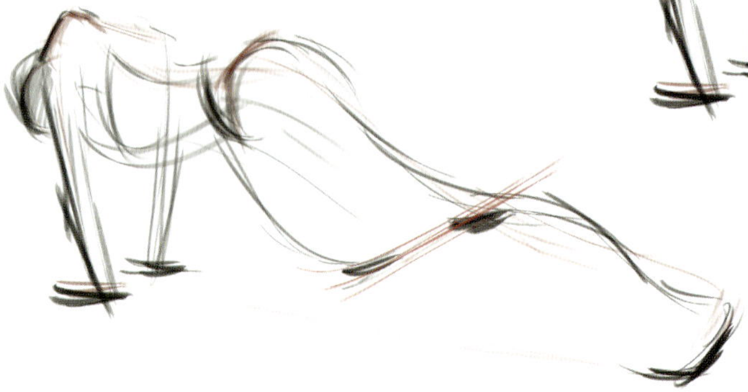

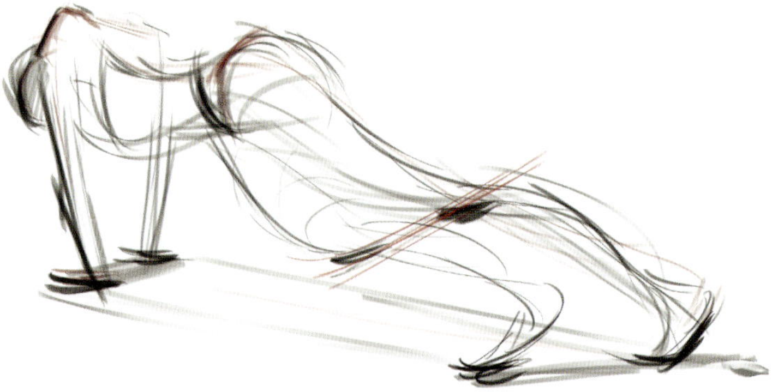

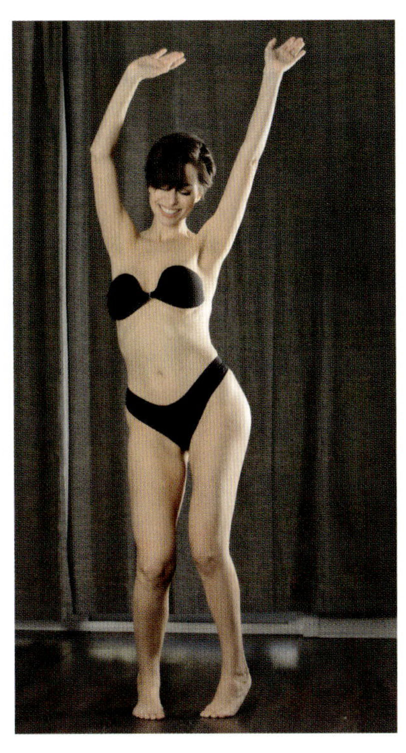

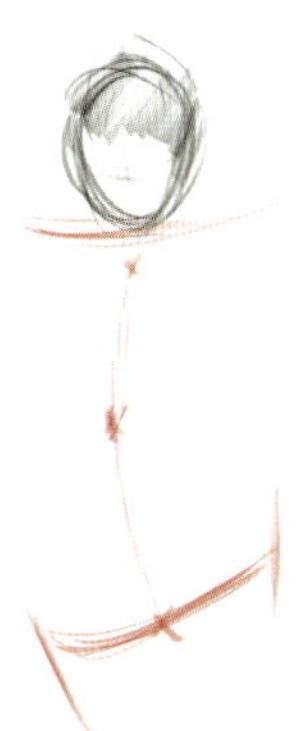

Scan to watch a tutorial.

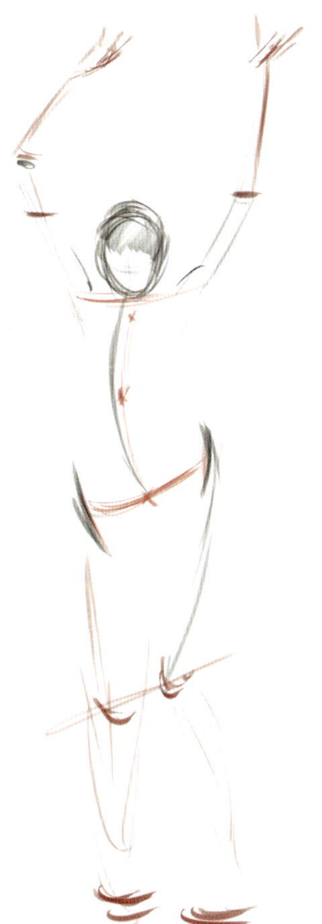

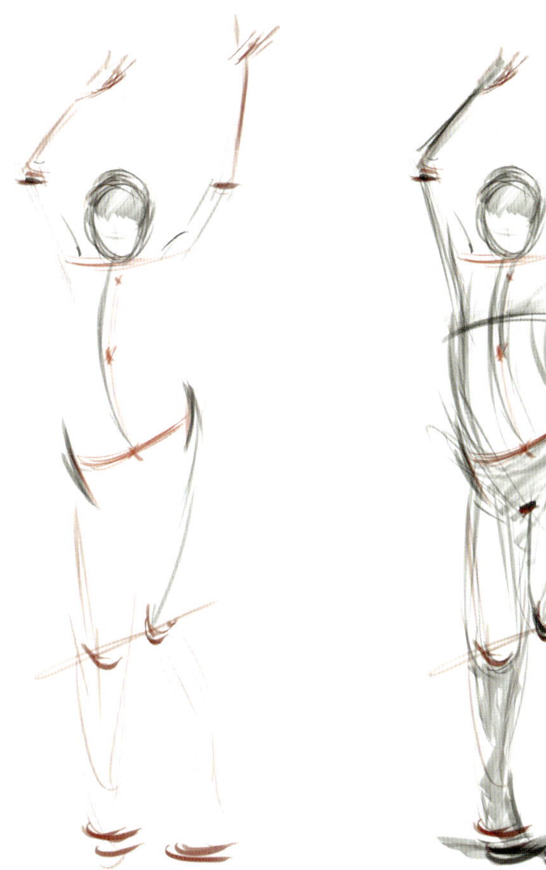

The arms were way too long before!

Fill your sketchbook with gestures. Do them from photos or from life. Make ones of your kids or your pets. Anything that inspires you!

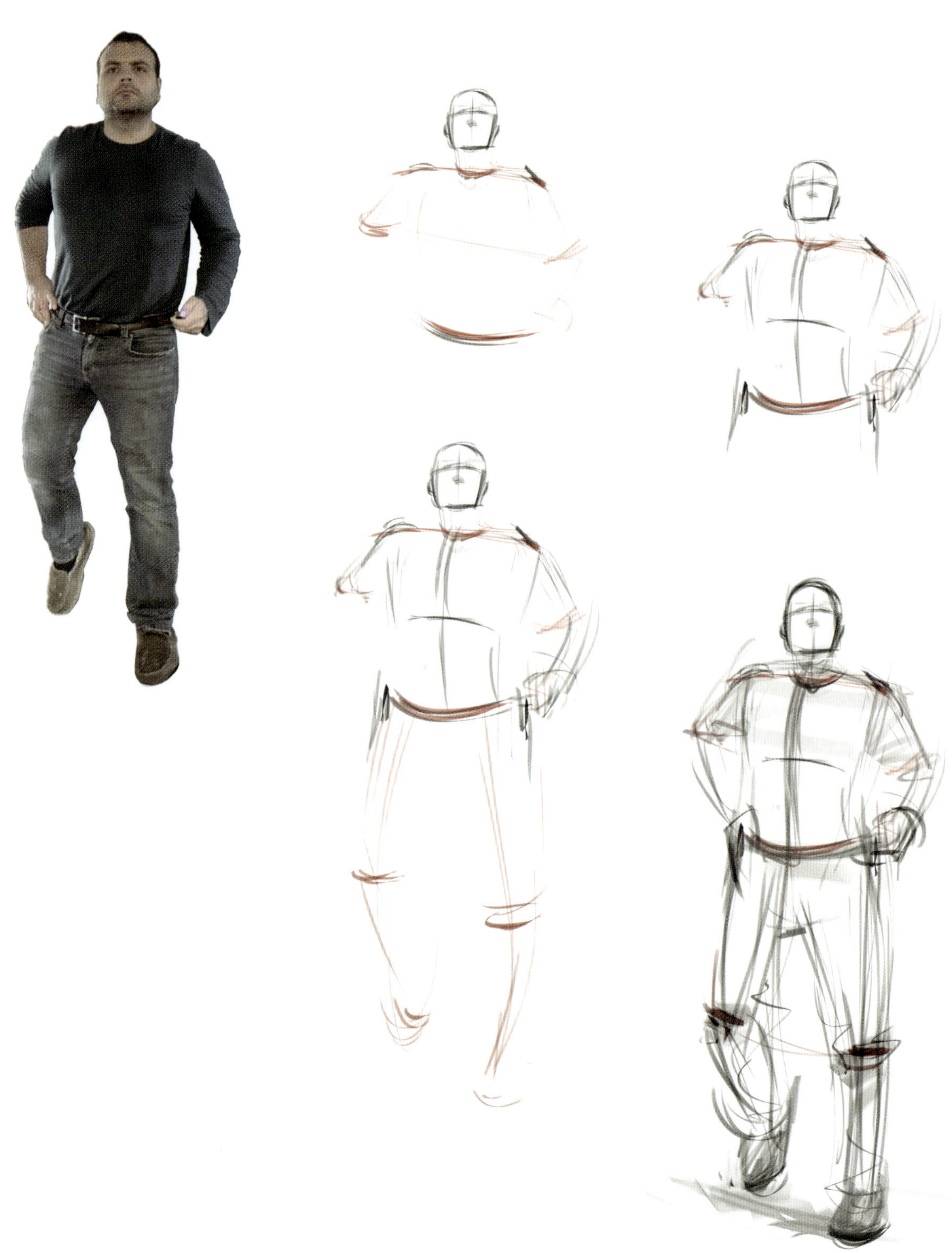

ASSIGNMENTS

These assignments encourage you to try out some of the tools from this chapter.
Overall, remember this: these are all just tools. Only use them when you need them,
and you do not need to use all of them on every drawing!

ASSIGNMENT #1

Using a free online source, collect several photos of a model posing. Load them up in
your digital painting app of choice (or print them out and lay a sheet of vellum over the
photos), and with a digital brush or big Sharpie, map out the common landmarks outlined in this chapter. From here, study the 2D relationship of these points and notice
how they change with each pose and vantage point.

ASSIGNMENT #2

Advance your landmark studies from assignment #1 by turning them into the "anatomical" stick-figure style of gesture. Follow the steps outlined in this chapter to produce
a simple drawing that looks like it's assuming the pose in the reference, with hints of
weight and movement where present. Remember that you're not trying to replicate
exact contours here.

ASSIGNMENT #3

Using the same set of landmarks, complete a more fleshed-out gesture drawing by
searching for the right rhythms to connect those landmarks. Work from one landmark to another, finding the rhythms that connect them. If you change your mind
mid-stroke, complete the stroke, then simply overlay another one. With each rhythm
or line you make, try to consciously think about what category it falls into: a straight,
C-curve, or S-curve.

ASSIGNMENT #4

Try some gesture drawings where you first begin with an overall rhythm that captures
the entire pose (sometimes called a *line of action.*) Then, apply your landmarks onto
that rhythm, and build out the gesture drawing as you did in assignment #3.

3

The ## 3D World of Form and Space

When a new artist imagines "drawing," the ability to turn the flat page into a convincing three-dimensional illusion is typically what comes to mind. Creating that illusion is indeed a hallmark of good drawing, and something we should strive toward in our learning.

A quick word of caution before we proceed, however. As an art teacher for over a decade, I've noticed the 3D form and space tends to suck up a lot of oxygen in the room. In the pursuit of three-dimensional drawings, it's easy to forget about the more abstract things like shape and gesture. Do not fall into this trap. The abstract brings life to the work, while the 3D form and space brings solidity. You need both!

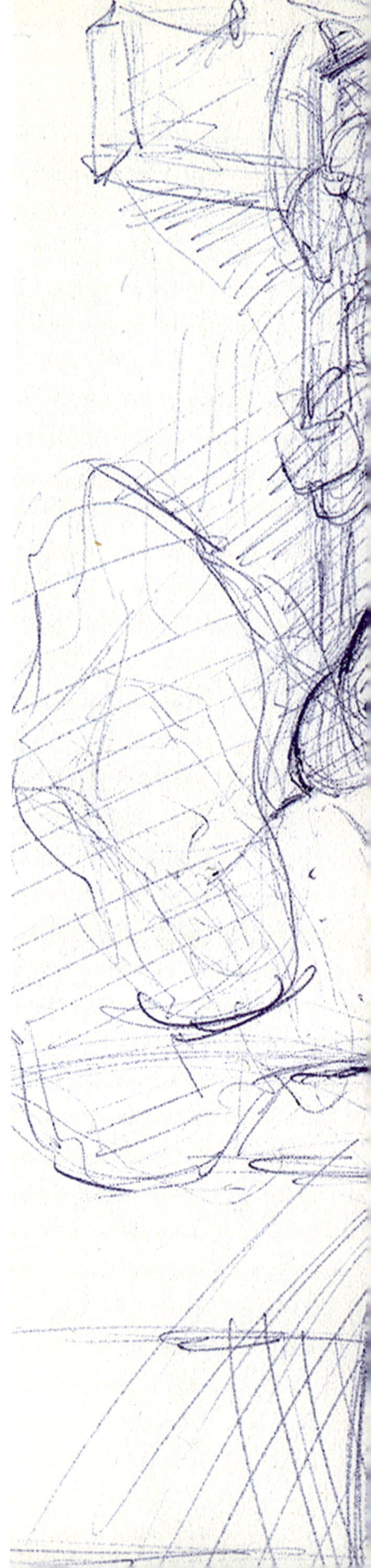

A pen sketch (2006) that freely combines various drawing fundamentals, but with the illusion of 3D form and space at its core.

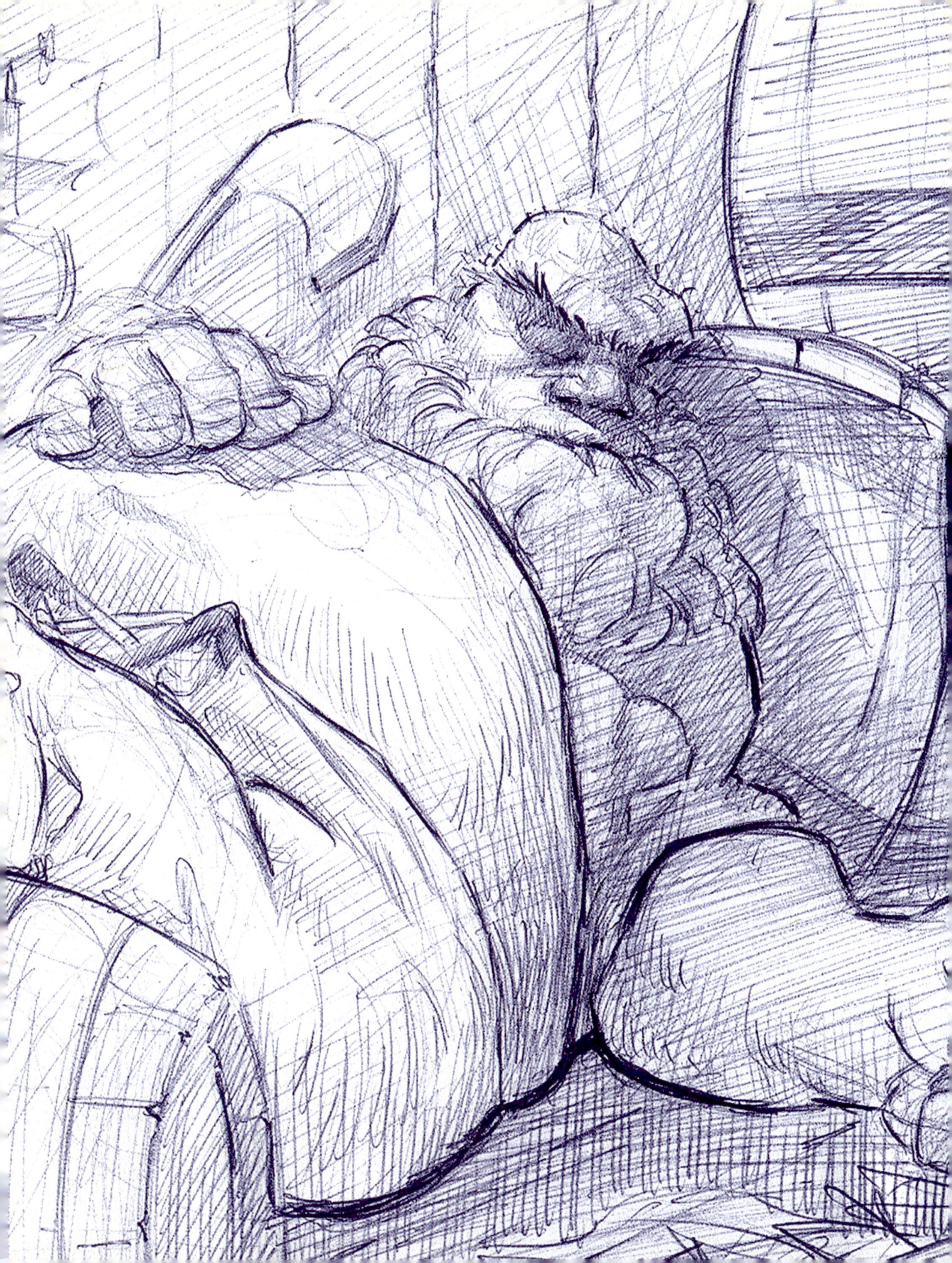

Understanding the Horizon Line

The horizon line is the first key to drawing a convincing sense of space on a flat page.

First, I'll tell you what the horizon line isn't. The horizon line is *not* the horizon. Counterintuitive, I know. So, what is the horizon line, then? Well, it's all tied to the viewer's eyeline.

The viewer refers to the point we see the scene. You can also think of it as a camera shooting a scene. The red line is the horizon line, and it is always exactly in line with the viewer's eyes or camera's lens.

Here's a simple truth: The horizon line moves *with* the viewer.

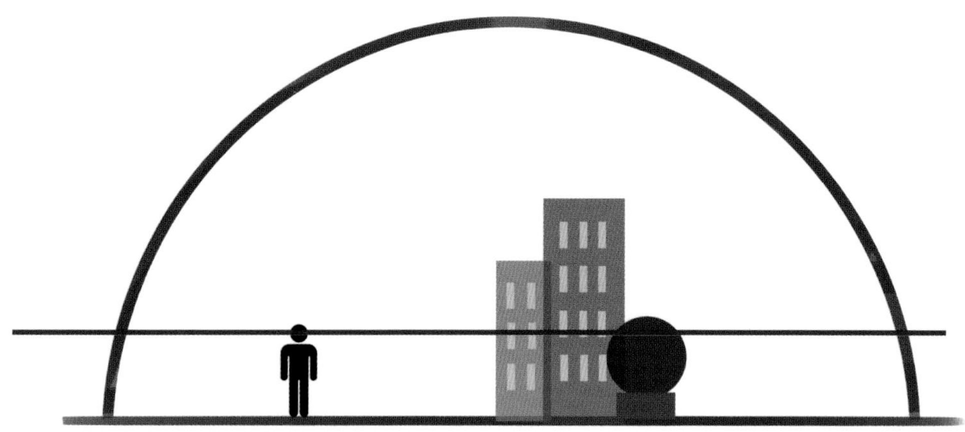

The figure is the proverbial viewer. The red line is the horizon line, or eyeline.

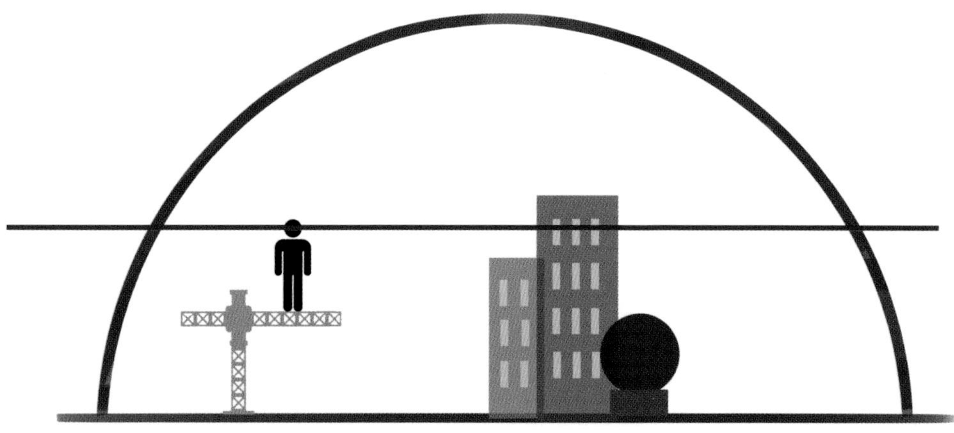

The horizon line's position changes with the viewer's position relative to the scene.

WHAT'S ABOVE, WHAT'S BELOW?

The main thing a horizon line does is determine what is *below* the viewer's eyeline, and what is *above* the viewer's eyeline. This dramatically alters how a form is drawn in 3D space, because we will see different sides of that form.

It stands to reason that if an object is above the viewer's eyes or horizon line, we will see the underside of that object. Conversely, if an object is below the viewer's eyes, we will see its topside.

Before drawing any form, ask yourself, is it above or below the horizon line?

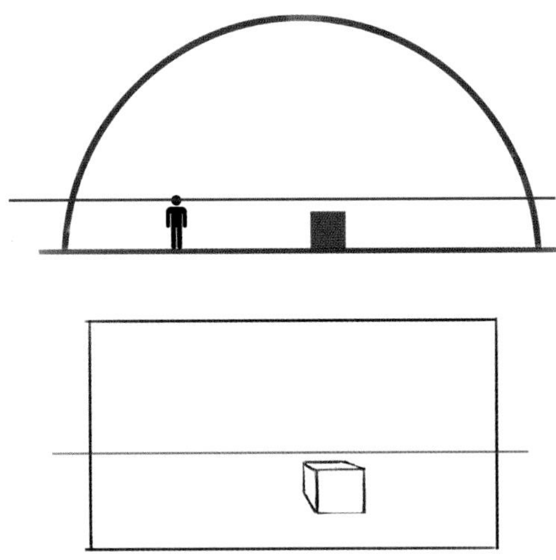

Top image: Our viewer is looking at a box that sits below the horizon or eyeline.

Bottom image: How that box form would be drawn in three dimensions. Note that we see the top side of the box.

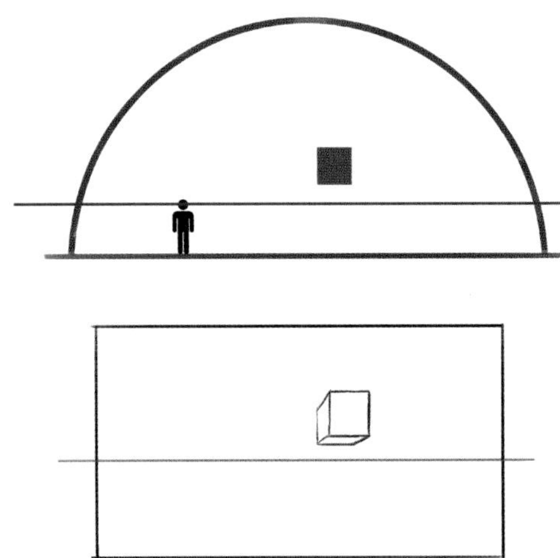

This time the box sits above the eyeline. When drawing it in three dimensions, we no longer see the topside of the box. Instead we see the underside.

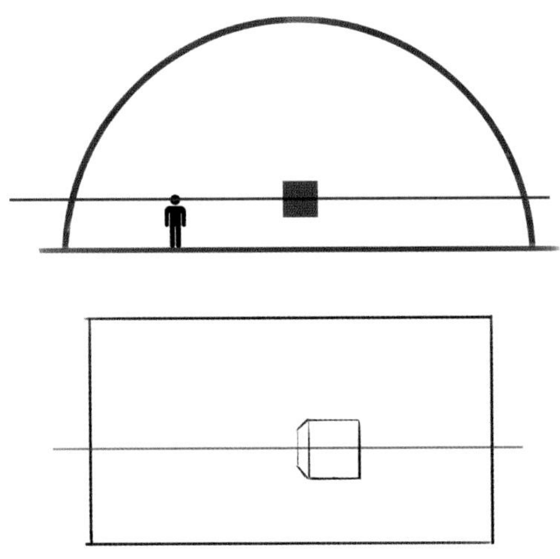

When an object crosses the eyeline, we see neither the top nor bottom sides.

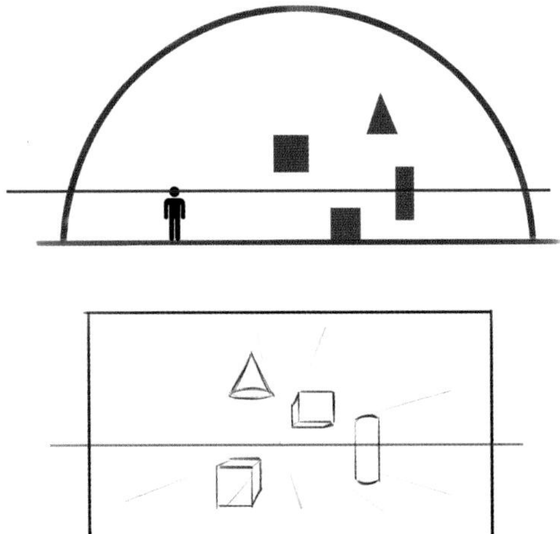

The rule applies to all forms.

Ellipses
Are Foreshortened Circles

Foreshortening is often seen as intimidating, but it's mostly just misunderstood.

Foreshortening is when you see a whole or partial 3D object from an oblique angle, which skews or shortens its 2D shape. It's how we produce the illusion of three dimensions on a flat surface.

When you draw forms in space, something will always be foreshortened since it's impossible to see every side of a 3D object straight on. To get a basic grasp on this, we'll use a circle.

A circle seen straight on. The grid is to indicate the presence of a 3D space.

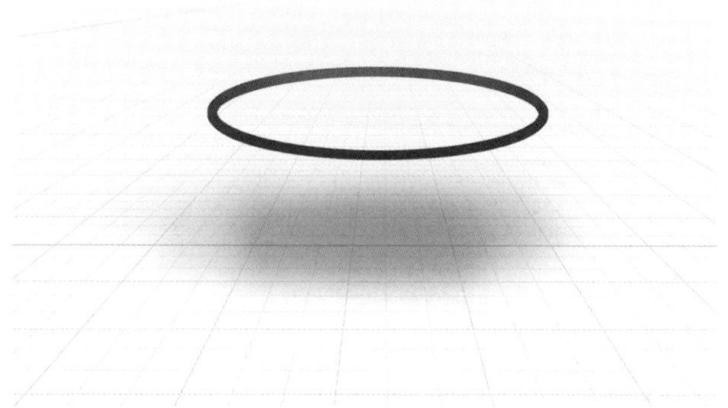

In any non-straight orientation, the circle shape gets foreshortened into an ellipse. We understand this as a circle seen in perspective.

FORESHORTENING AND THE HORIZON LINE

Foreshortening is directly related to the horizon line. These examples show how a circle's fore-shortening increases the closer it is to the horizon line. Conversely, the farther away it is from the horizon line, the closer it is to a pure circle shape.

The same is true for the vertical axis. The green dotted line represents the exact middle of the

view, such as right between the viewer's eyes, or in the middle of the camera's lens. The circle's fore-shortened shape changes based on its distance from that.

The exact same principle applies to squares in perspective.

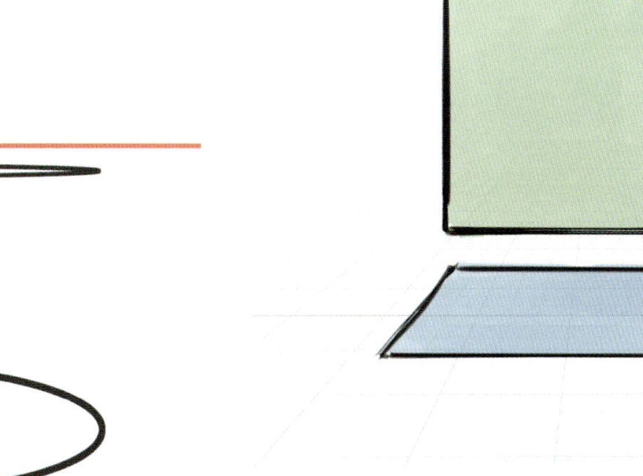

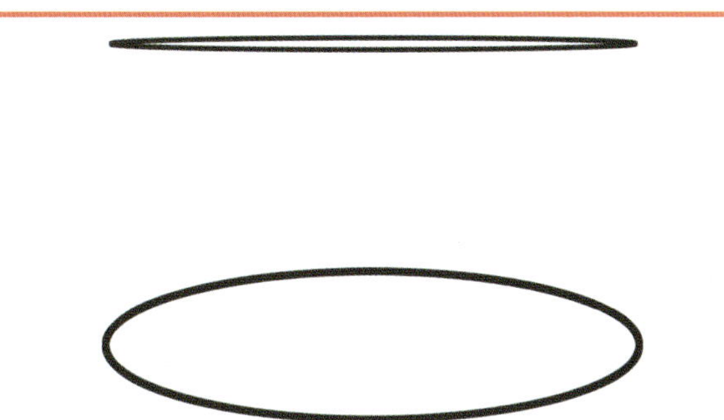

The red line is the horizon line/eyeline.

The green square is seen straight on while the blue square is rotated 90 degrees, and therefore foreshortened. We still understand this as a square, viewed in perspective.

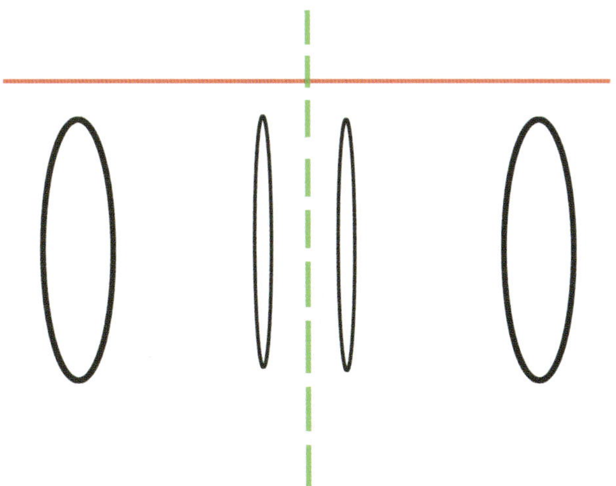

Interestingly, if the circle were seen dead in the middle of the view along the green dotted line, or along the horizon line, it would be 100 percent foreshortened, and would appear as a single line, rather than a shape.

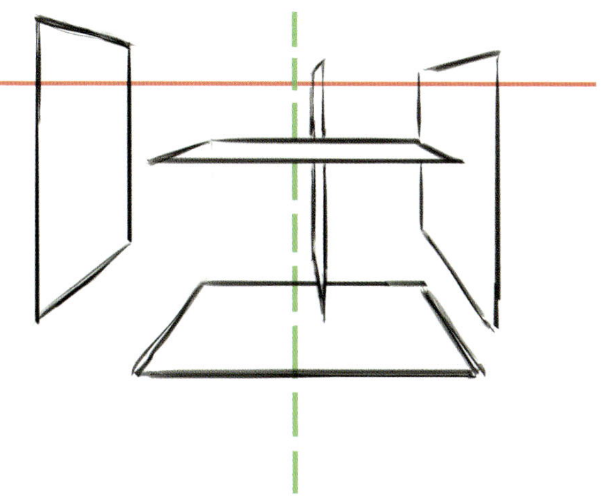

Like we saw with the circle, the amount of foreshortening of the square is dictated by its distance from the horizon line, or vertical midline.

Blocking Out 3D Space with a
Perspective Grid

It's useful to know how to build a basic perspective grid, which aids in understanding how the angle of a line changes based on where it is in space. In this exercise we'll make what's called a one-point perspective grid.

First, place a horizon line anywhere in the frame.

Next, place a point on the horizon line. It doesn't matter where. This is called a vanishing point. It's where the Z-axis lines responsible for depth converge to a single point in the infinite distance.

Next, draw Straight lines emanating from the vanishing point.

In one-point perspective, lines running perpendicular to the Z axis are parallel with the horizon line. Feel free to put a few of them in.

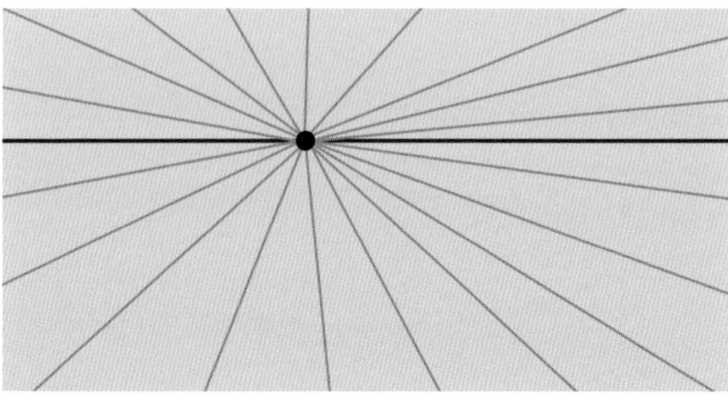

This is the time to get technical. Break out the straight edge, or digital line tool!

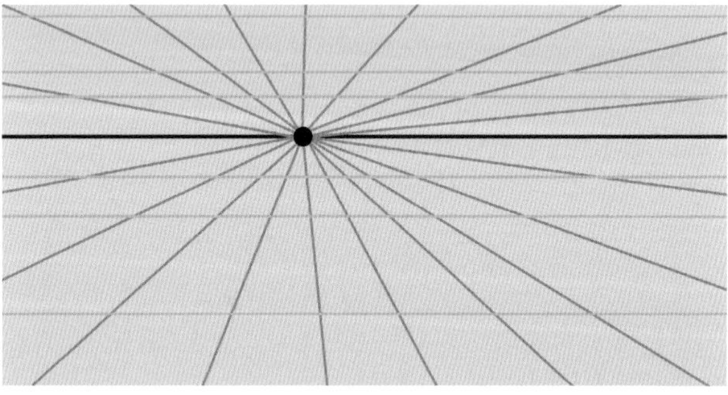

I like to put a few faded parallel lines, as it helps me further feel the space.

We're only placing one point, hence why this is a one-point perspective grid.

DRAWING IN SPACE

Now that you have a 3D space in front of you, go ahead and populate it with some basic forms! Try boxes to start.

The most important thing to note is how the angles of the Z-axis lines change based on their relationship to the vanishing point.

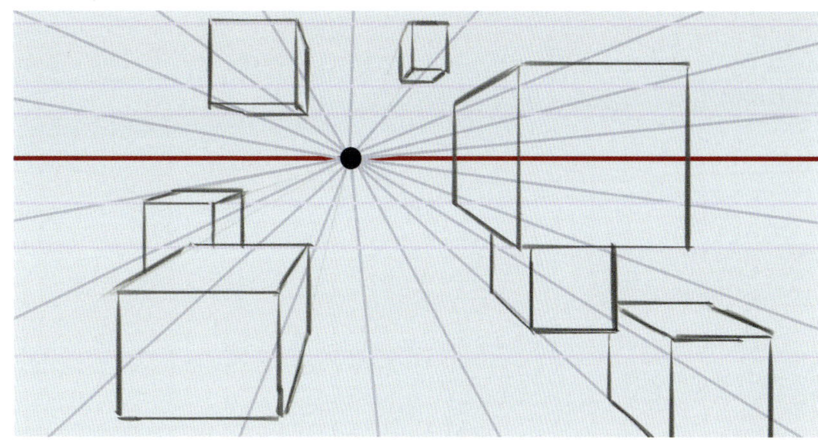

Try putting boxes in front of and behind other boxes and above and below the horizon line.

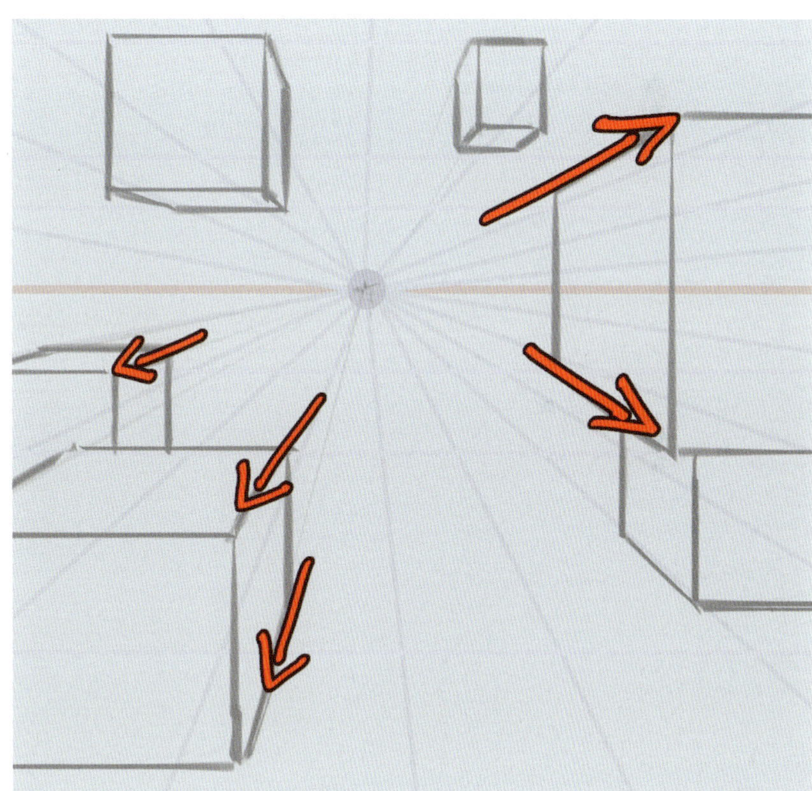

Scan to watch a tutorial.

This relationship is pretty easy to understand: The lines flow back to the vanishing point. This skewing also happens to circles. It's easy to miss this.

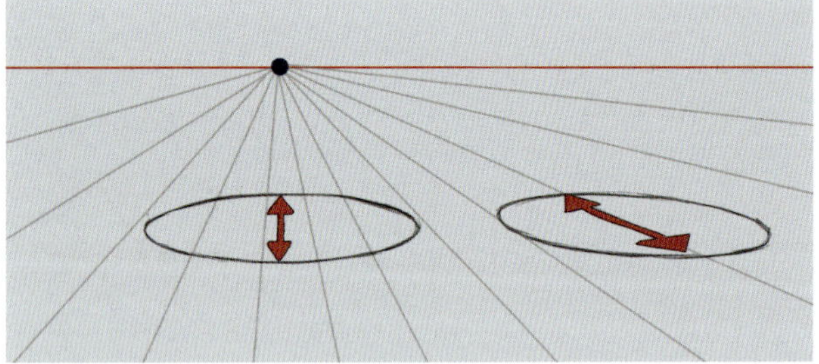

The arrows point to the "high points" of the ellipses. Notice how they follow the perspective grid lines.

To draw a cylinder place two ellipses in space and connect the ends with straight lines. Play with positioning them around a 3D space!

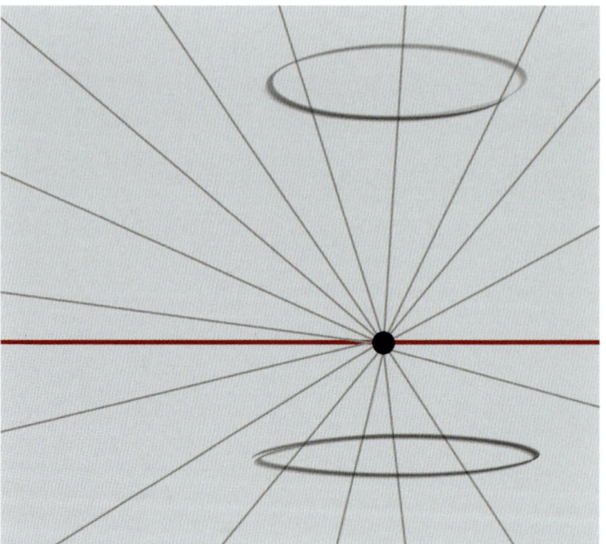

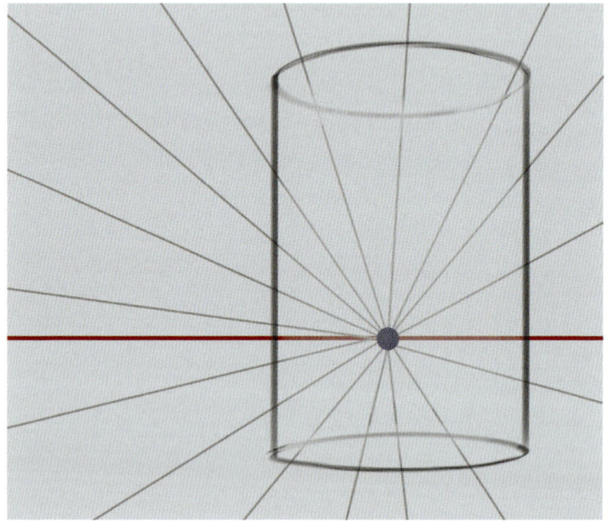

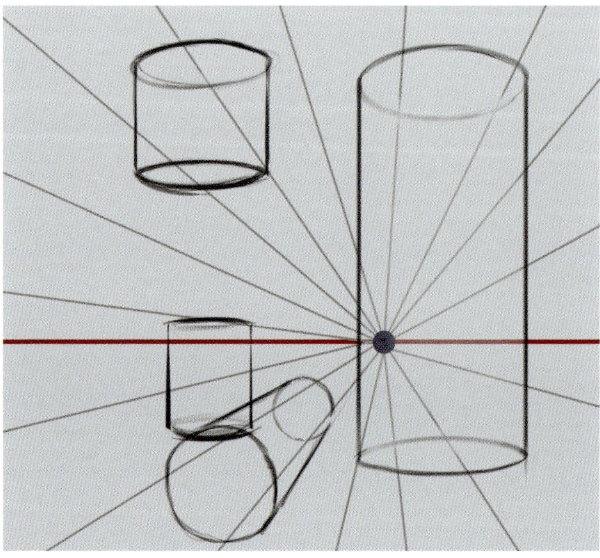

Scan to watch a tutorial.

BALLPARKING IT

Next we want to get used to ballparking these lines with some degree of accuracy, *without* a grid!

Ballparking is a crucial skill to develop when it comes to drawing forms in space. You don't want to be stuck needing grids for everything, and many things just don't conform to grids, as we'll see.

Here's a drawing done by only *thinking about* the horizon line, vanishing point, and grid, rather than physically drawing them.

And now for the honesty test!

As you can see, I'm pretty close. The margin of error is small enough to be acceptable to the naked eye. There *is* one thing that I'd consider too far beyond the margin of error, however. Can you spot it?

Because the horizon line is so important, I consider this a mistake. Remember: It's okay to make mistakes. The skill is to notice them and know how to fix them!

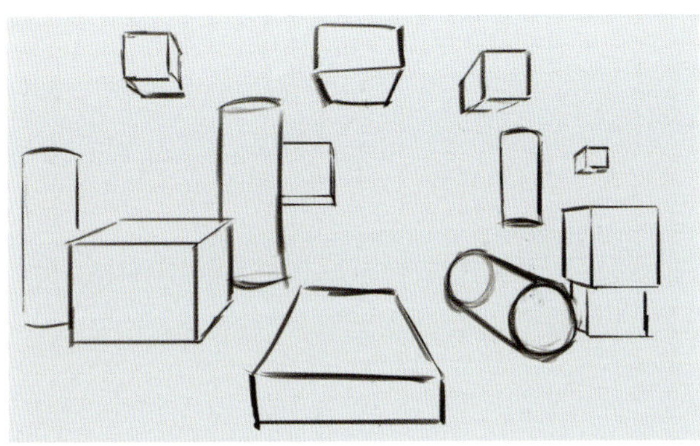

Does it look passable? I think so!

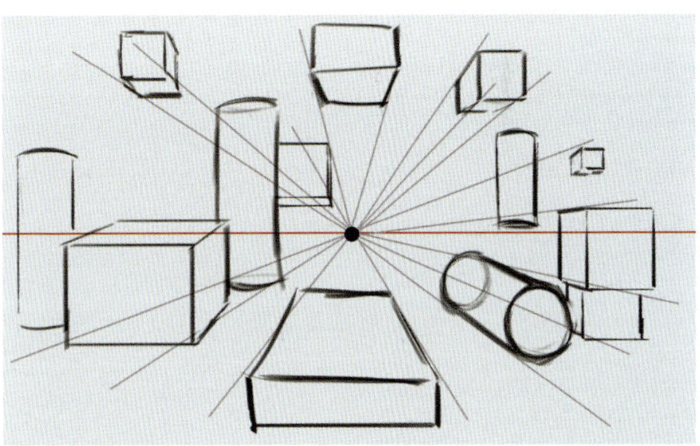

I've added in the horizon line, vanishing point, and grid lines after the fact to reveal the margin of error.

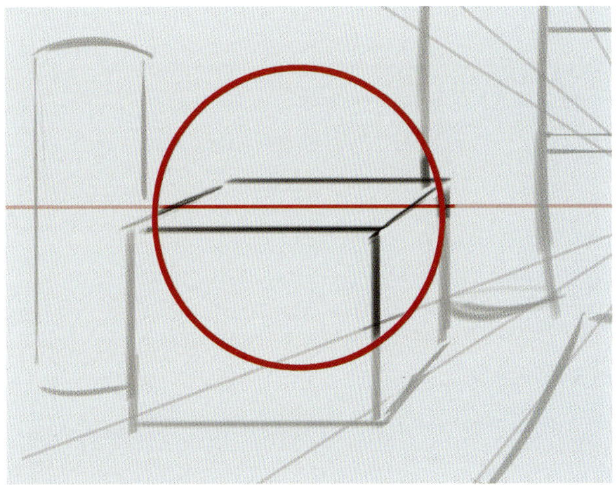

This box's topside should not be visible since it's above the horizon line.

TWO-POINT PERSPECTIVE

As the name implies, a two-point perspective grid simply involves adding one more vanishing point.

The added complexity with two-point perspective involves the distance between the vanishing points. The grid you see below is rare. It mimics an extremely wide lens.

The wider apart your vanishing points are, the longer the lens. The closer together the vanishing points, the wider the lens.

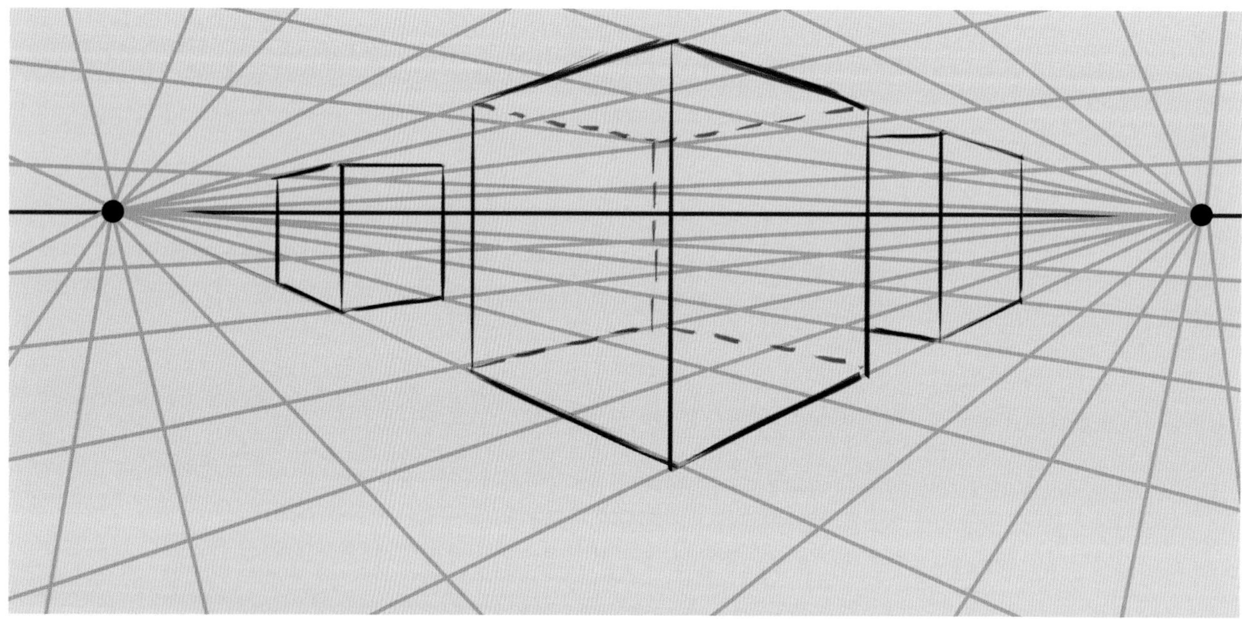

There are no parallel lines in this grid. The lines that were parallel in a one-point perspective grid now also converge at a point.

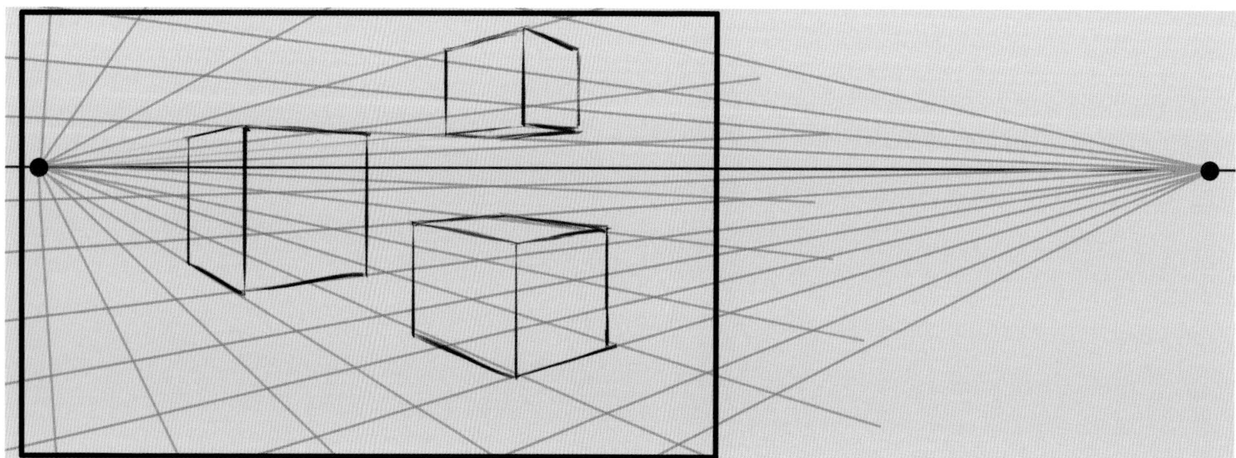

Typically one of the vanishing points lies far out of frame but still on the horizon line!

COMBINING GRIDS

You can freely mix one-point and two-point perspective grids. The top image shows a simple object adhering to a one-point perspective.

But if we add a second box and rotate it off-axis (bottom), more vanishing points are needed on the horizon line to rotate the object correctly and within the same space.

So here we have a combination of one-point and two-point perspective in the same drawing. You'd add even more pairs of vanishing points if you added a third cube in a different orientation.

Again, it's extremely common with a two-point perspective for one vanishing point to be located off frame.

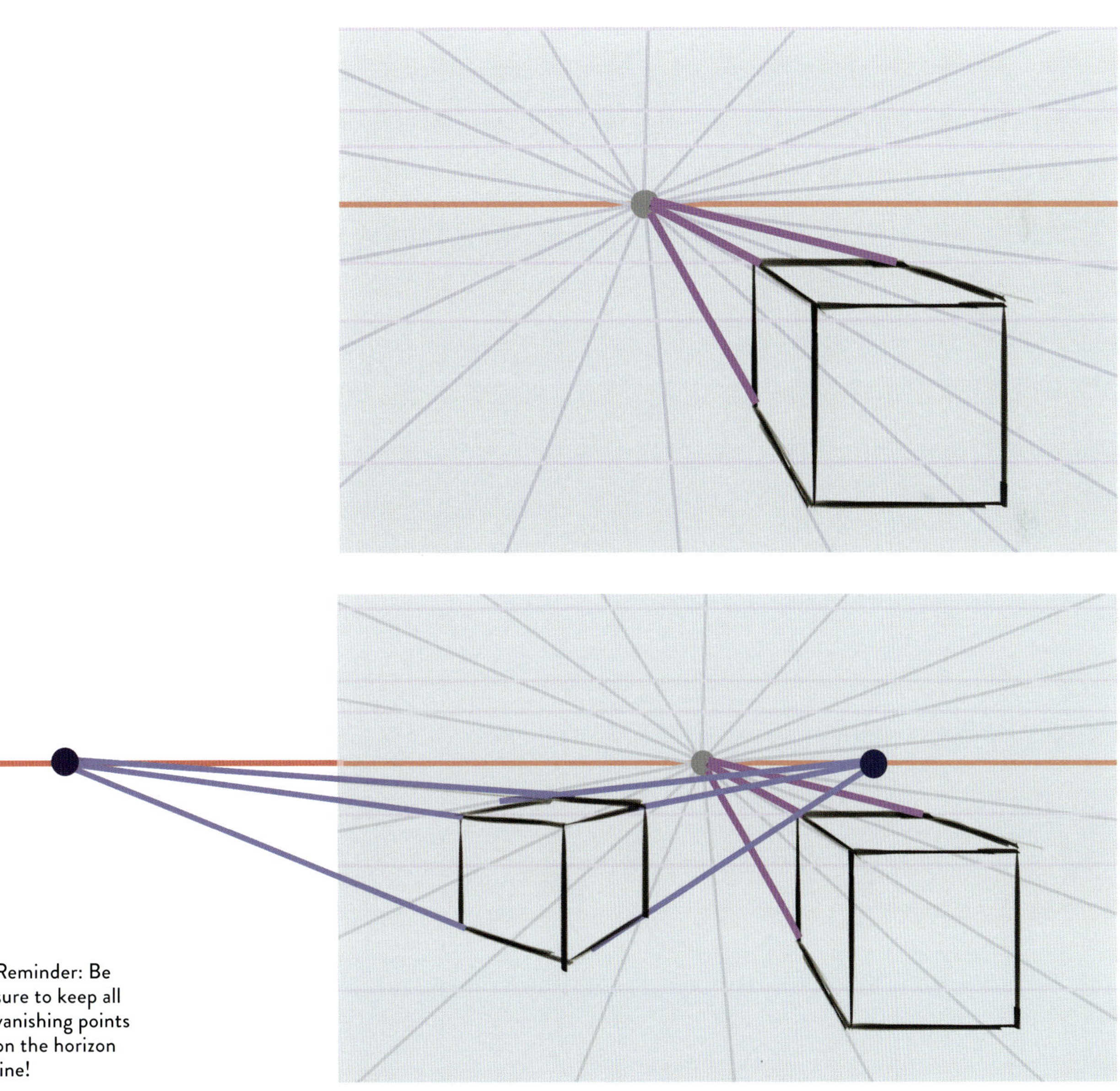

Reminder: Be sure to keep all vanishing points on the horizon line!

Why **Freehand** Is Important

At this point you can begin to see why drawing perspective freehand (or, ballparking it) is a great skill to have. You simply don't want to be bogged down by vanishing points and grids all the time. I tend to make several practice strokes when I draw this way, feeling my way from or to an invisible vanishing point on an invisible horizon line, before physically committing to the line.

CROSS-CONTOURS AND THE MIDLINE

What are those red lines, anyway? They might be one of the most important tools in this book. A cross-contour is simply a line that travels over the form. Think of it like an elastic band wrapping around the object, defining its topology. Often a cross-contour is most useful going through the *middle* of a form, as the middle tends to be important for construction, as we'll see in the next chapter.

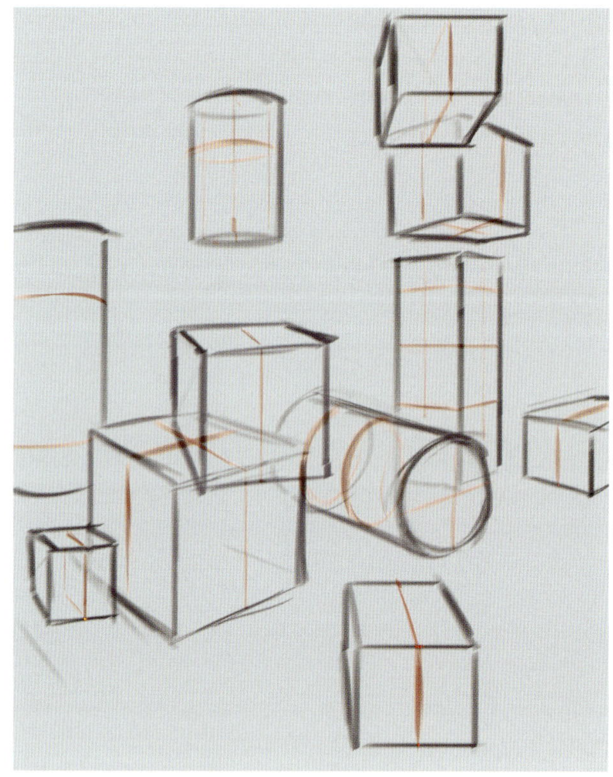

If you have trouble doing this freehand, flesh it out with a perspective grid then come back and try it freehand again!

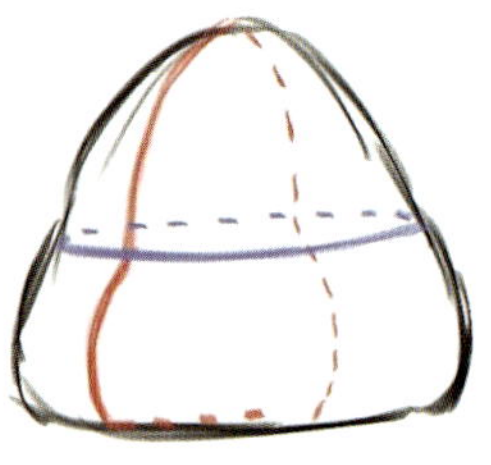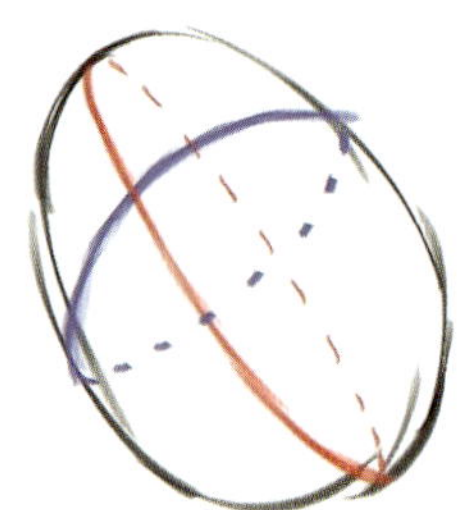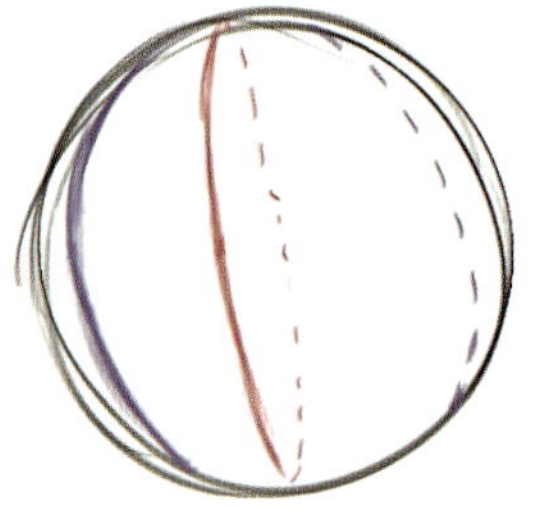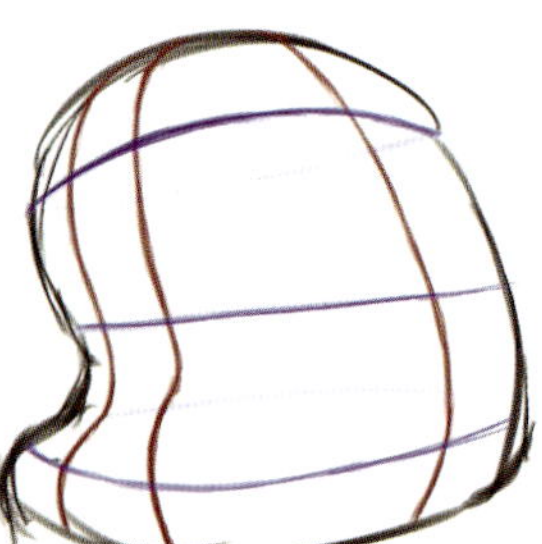

Any form, rigid or organic, can be further described with cross-contours and midlines. Get into the discipline of drawing cross-contours as they travel around to the back side of the object, as well.

Twisting, Bending, and Folding **Forms**

A huge part of drawing, especially for people or characters of any kind, is visualizing how something might twist, bend, or move in an organic way.

Now we're getting into character! To start practicing, first draw a rigid square in a 3D space.

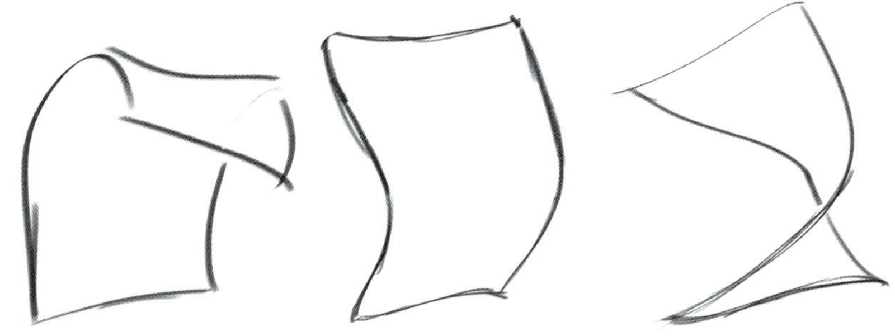

This is where the perspective grid goes right out the window.

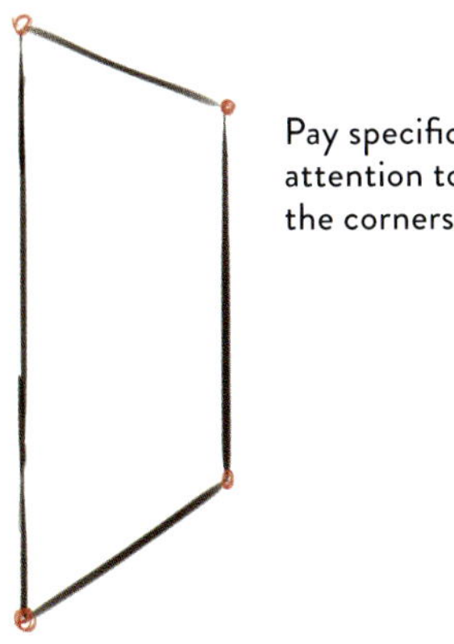

Pay specific attention to the corners.

Now plot those four corners in a less rigid way and connect them. Try to use curvy lines here, like the shape has a spine. When you're done, trace a line down the middle of the form, feeling out the new topology you've created.

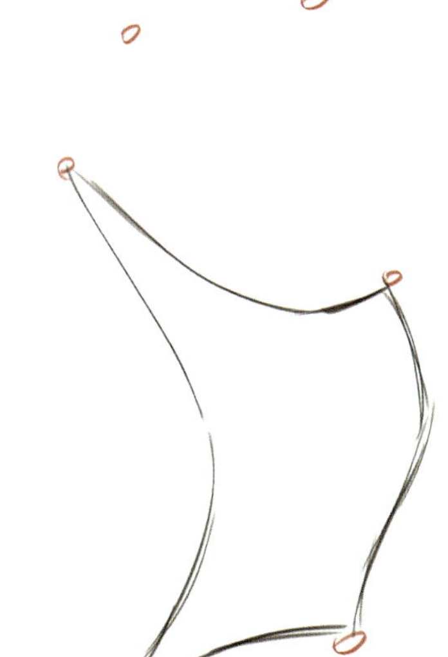

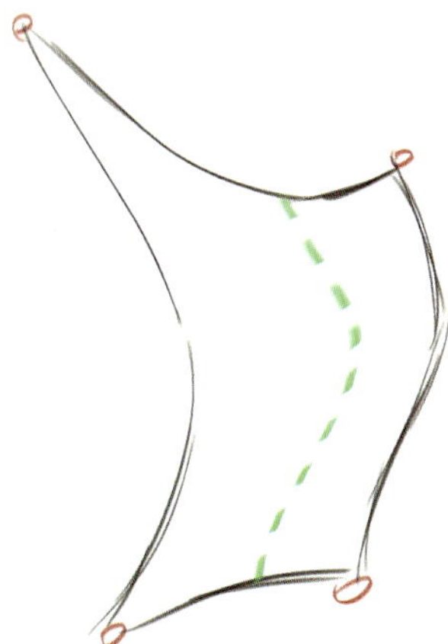

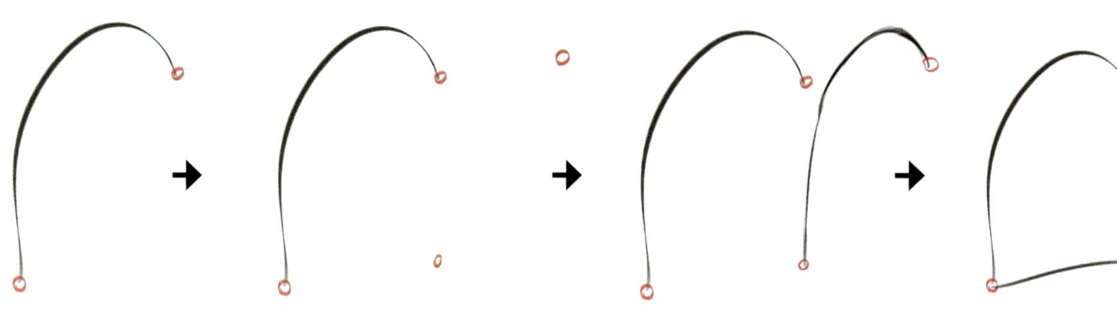

Folding a form involves the shape overlapping itself. Thinking of a bendy rectangle in perspective,
start with just the front side. Then plot out the
two points defining the far side of the shape. Then
draw the far side, using a similar bendy curve.

Now connect the top and bottom points. You'll
also need to draw a third line, showing where the
top of the fold is.

It's always a good idea to "ghost out" the lines that
are not actually visible in this view. This ensures
you stay accountable to where they are in space,
which is a very good habit to develop.

This is one of my favorite exercises for training
your brain to see the 2D page as a 3D space. You
can use the idea of the horizon line to help position the object.

I'm imagining the back half of this shape just below
the horizon line, but because it's bending upward,
its front half is above the horizon line, and therefore it's very easy to see the underside.

At right is the same pose except I've put the
whole thing well below the horizon line. In other
words, we're looking down at it. So even though
the form is bending upward, it's so far below the
eyeline that much of the underside is still hidden
from view.

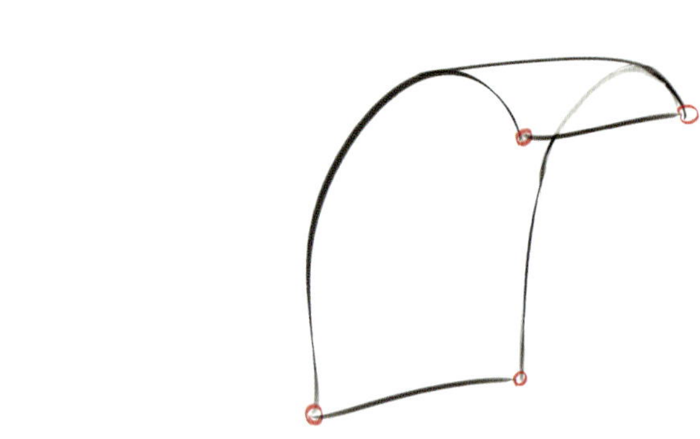

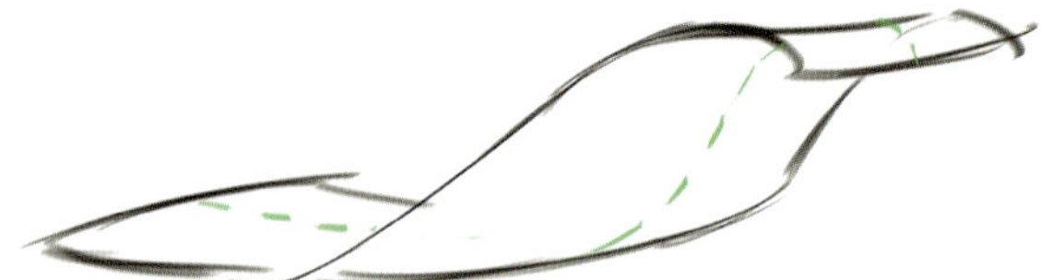

The dotted green line is the midline, which is always helpful to visualize.

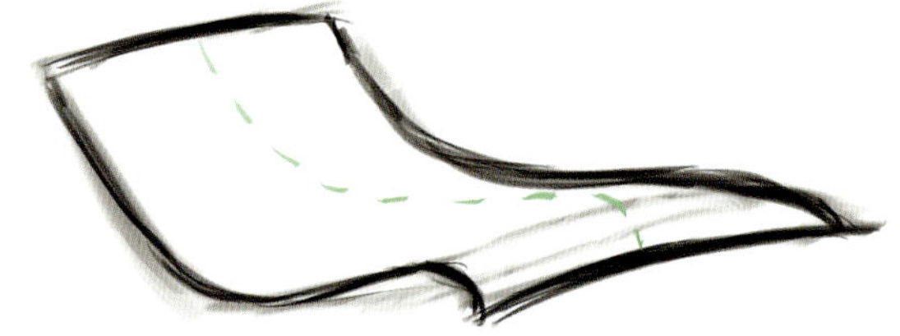

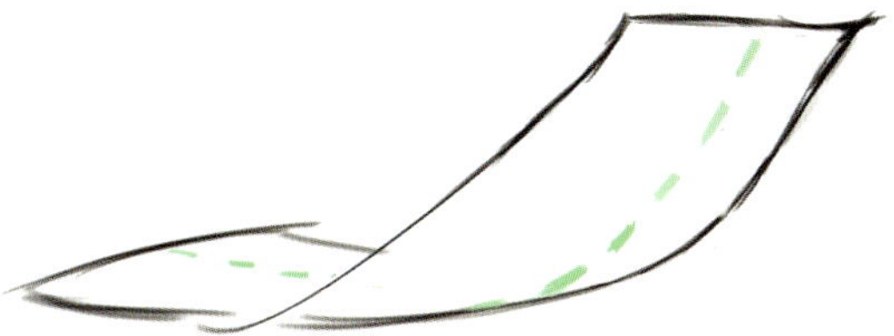

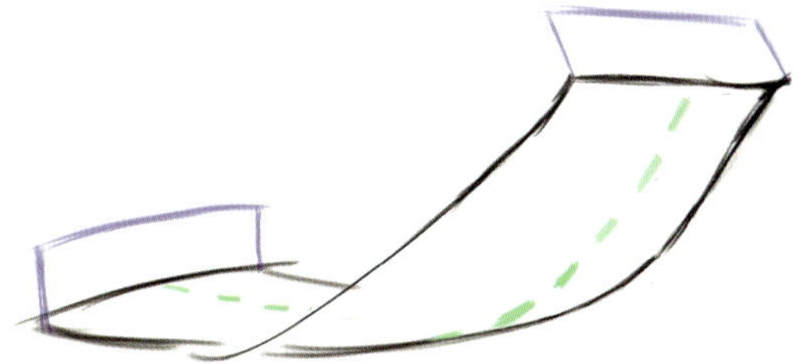

Now let's try adding the third dimension to our object. We'll start here with the shape above.

I recommend using a box form, because it's straightforward to push our flat plane upward at all four corners, and then connect them.

From here, we can continue our practice with rotating and twisting the form.

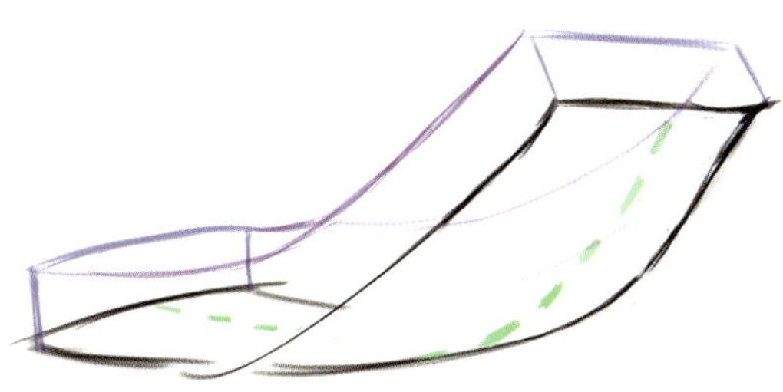

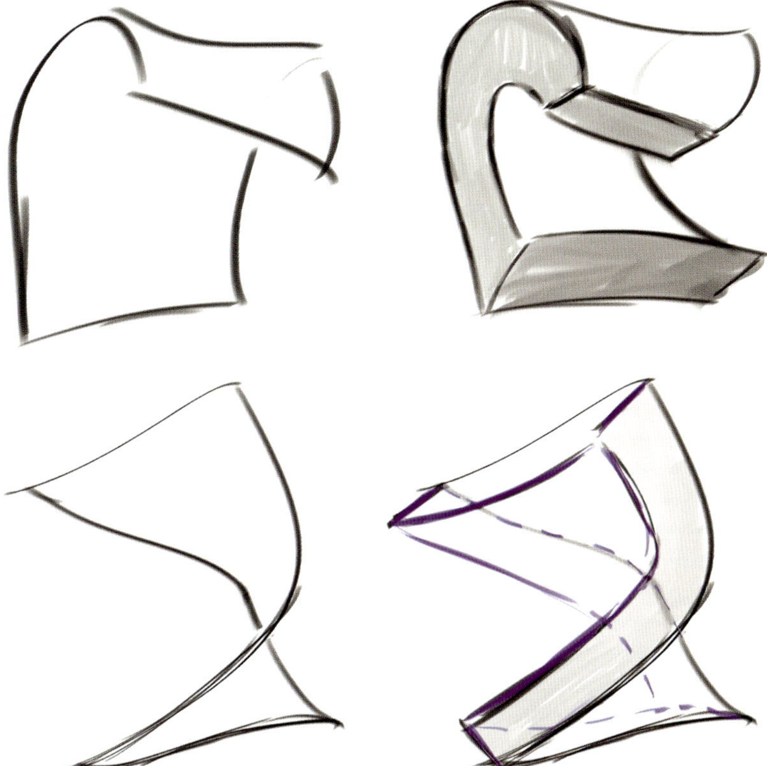

It's a good idea to begin with the flat plane, then add three dimensions to it. Remember to draw behind the form to help visualize it all the way around. Don't forget the cross-contours, either!

THE HALF-FILLED FLOUR SACK EXERCISE

This exercise was developed by Disney animators nearly a century ago, to aid in visualizing and maintaining form through their drawings, as well as injecting a sense of character.

The flour sack is essentially a rounded box, with a little more volume at the bottom half. Even if you aren't interested in animation, this exercise is invaluable for honing your drawing ability, and will pay off massively when you draw figures and characters. The best part is, you can get through one of these drawings quickly, allowing you to do a lot of them. Fill your sketchbook with flour sacks!

While this introductory chapter ends here, we are certainly not finished with 3D form. In the next chapter we'll apply these principles specifically to building the figure.

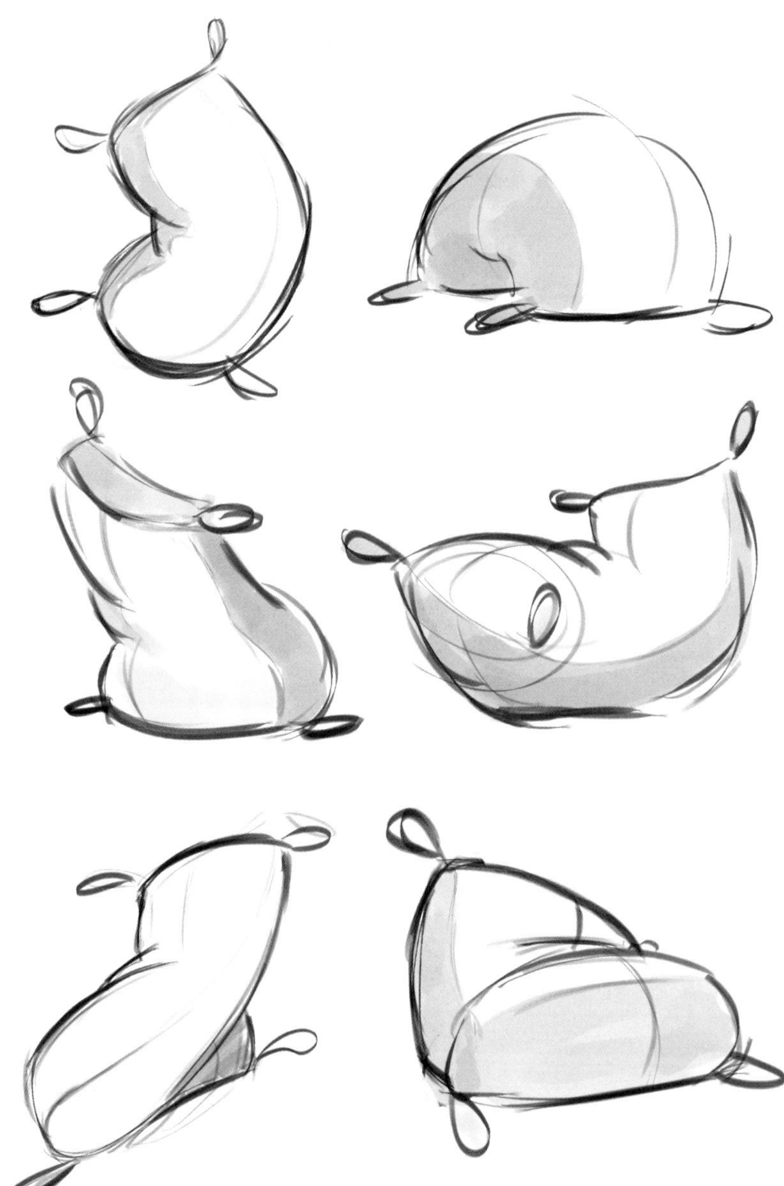

Ideally, the flour sack should appear to have a consistent volume from drawing to drawing. Note the use of cross-contours to help understand the volume.

Scan to watch a tutorial.

ASSIGNMENTS

Perspective is not just an abstract concept. Practicing it will give your drawings a hefty dose of realism.

ASSIGNMENT #1

Construct a one-point perspective grid. Feel free to use straight-edges to help keep these lines technical and accurate. Start with a horizon line, then simply place the vanishing point anywhere you like on the horizon line. Work out the grid from there, adding parallel horizontal lines at the end.

ASSIGNMENT #2

Construct a two-point perspective grid. Remember that with two-point perspective, both of your vanishing points may be off the page entirely, with one of those points being *far* off the page. Play with the positioning of these points, and map out simple cubes in the space to see what the resulting images look like.

ASSIGNMENT #3

Find simple objects in your home: cylindrical things like mugs and paper towel rolls and square things like your TV or boxes. Take photos of these things together, looking into the scene straight-on (as if you're looking directly down a city street.) Be sure to capture at least three vantage points: one from above, another in the middle of the objects, and another below the scene (if possible), or placed at ground-level. Bring these photos into your digital app of choice or print them and work on a sheet of vellum over top. Place your horizon line, then map out your perspective grid and watch how it aligns with your forms.

ASSIGNMENT #4

Freehand everything! Working from imagination now, construct a perspective grid of your choosing, and simply draw basic forms within it! Try to keep your forms basic: boxes, spheres, cylinders.

4

Building
the Figure

If you can draw a box, you can draw the figure.
Seriously!

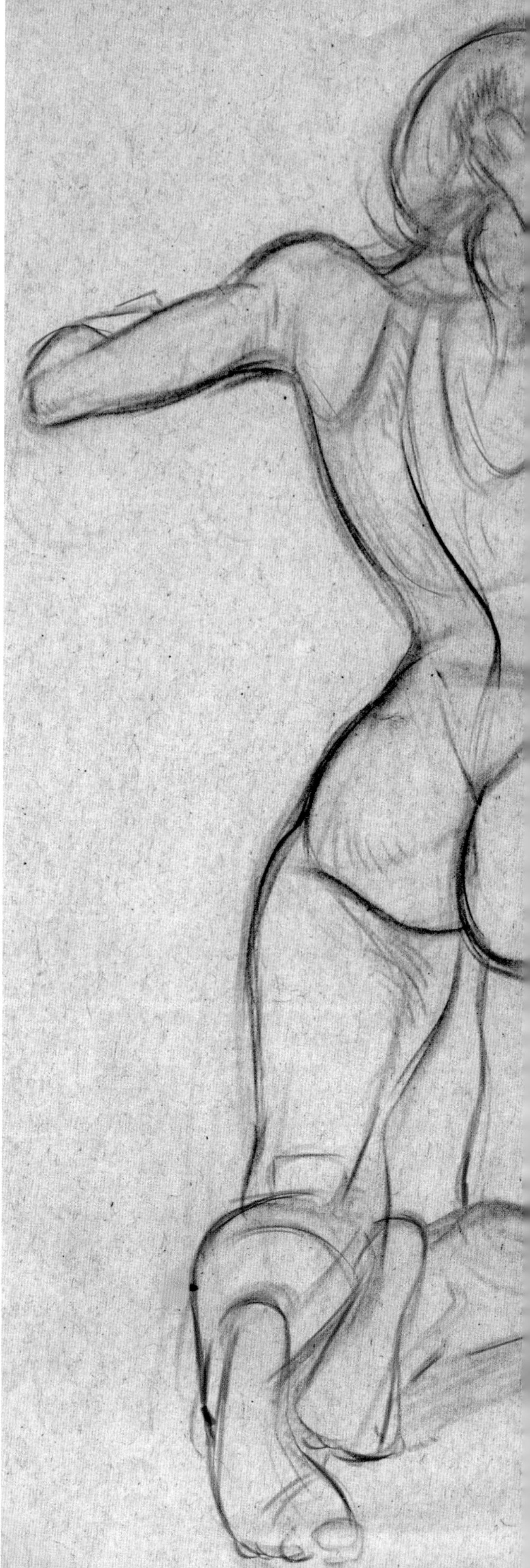

A life drawing I did in my earlier student days. I remember this
being a watershed moment for me in terms of using basic 3D
forms to build the figure, and then apply shapes over it. Circa
2003. (For reference: I began my studies in 2001.)

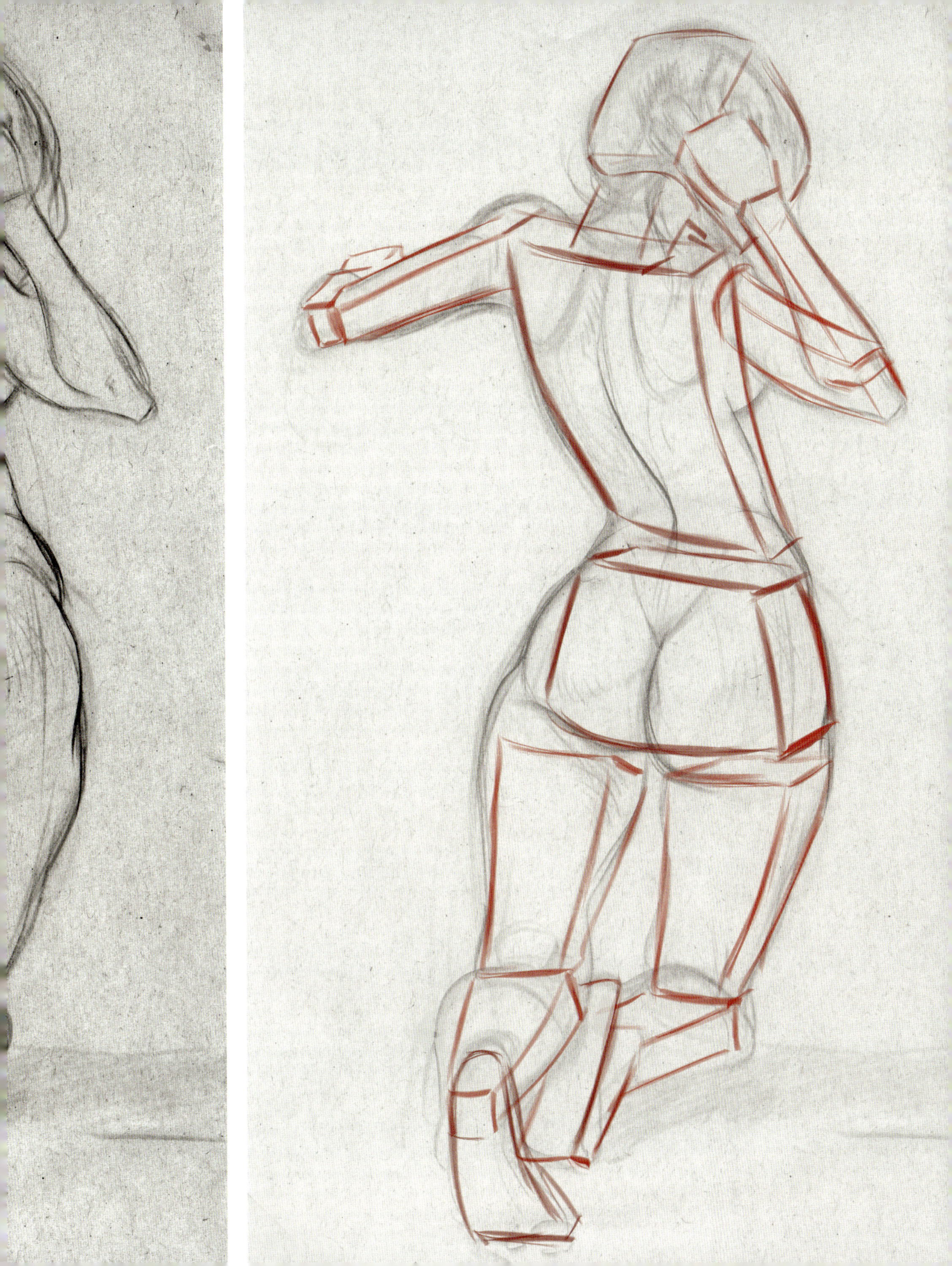

Basic Forms of the Body

A box is the ideal form to simplify things down to, for one very good reason: A box has clear planes.

A plane is a face that has a specific orientation in 3D space. So, a box has six planes, each one pointing 90 degrees from its neighbor.

Master the box, and you are well on your way to mastering draftsmanship.

Draftsmanship is similar to craftsmanship except it refers specifically to sound foundational drawing. Establishing good draftsmanship should be your first goal on the road to bringing your creations to life with your art.

OTHER FORMS YOU'LL NEED

It's helpful to have a few other forms under your belt like cylinders, which we saw in the last chapter, and spheres. Luckily, spheres may be the easiest form to draw, as their silhouette does not change, no matter where it is in space, or which angle you see it from.

A sphere's silhouette is always just a circle. What changes, as far as draftsmanship is concerned, is where the midline is located as it travels through space relative to the viewer.

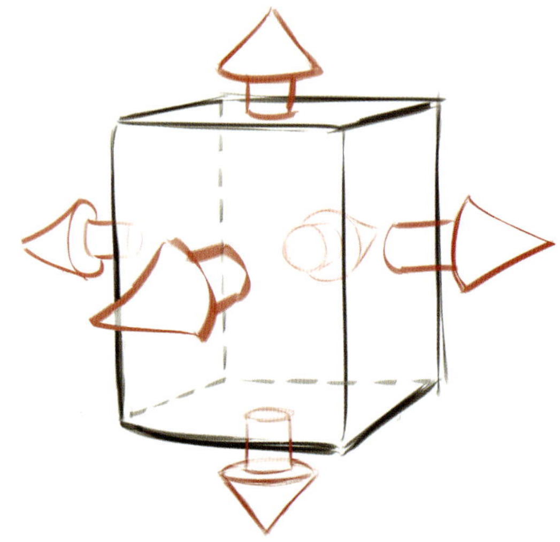

3D arrows show the direction each plane of the box faces in 3D space.

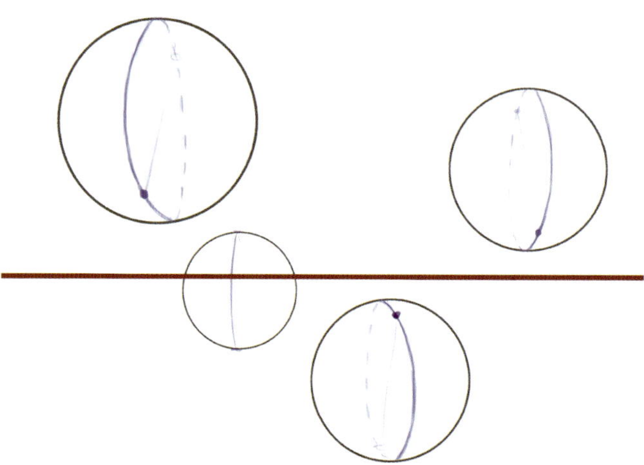

I've placed dots at the top and bottom poles, which also helps visualize their orientation in space. For the technically minded, a sphere's silhouette can change if you think of it being seen through a camera's lens.

The **Torso** and **Hips** Relationship

We saw with the gesture drawing chapter how important it is to capture the relationship between the shoulders and hips. Of course, between the shoulders and hips lies the volume of the torso itself, which becomes quite important when we add 3D forms to the body. In gesture drawing, we also never accounted for the volume of the hips. The time for all that is now.

The two boxes at right represent the torso and hips. As you can see, they have different volumes: The upper (torso) box is taller, and the lower (hips) box shorter.

Seeing it on an actual person, the forms should land in these areas:

Notice how the torso box leaves a space before the hips box starts. That space is due to the fleshy stomach area, whose shape can vary dramatically. The upper torso's form is mostly dictated by the rib cage, and the hips by the hip bone. These bones don't change from person to person and can be simplified down to these forms, regardless of your subject's stature.

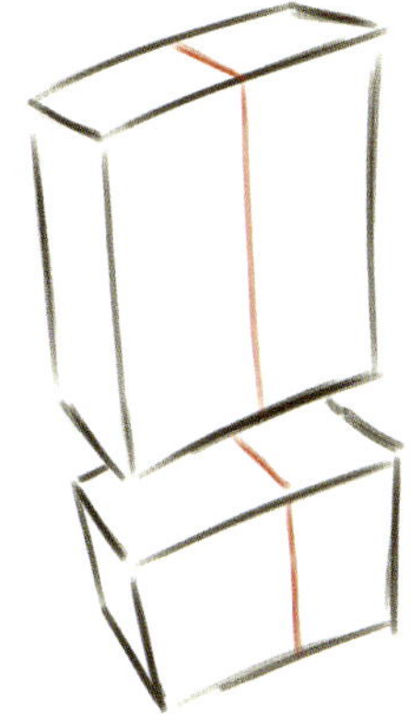

Two boxes can say a lot about the figure.

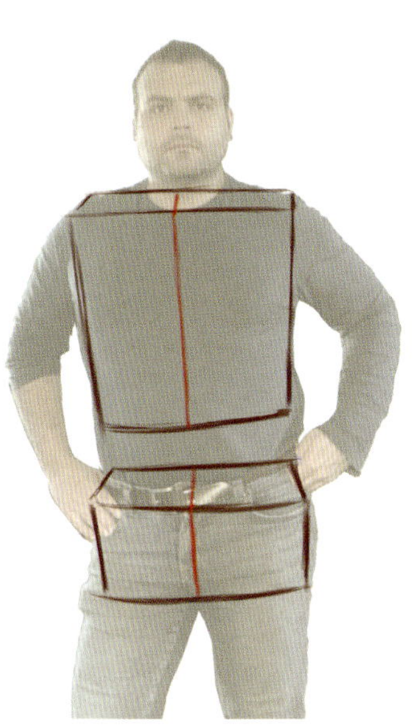

Remember that the red lines are midlines and help invoke a perspective grid.

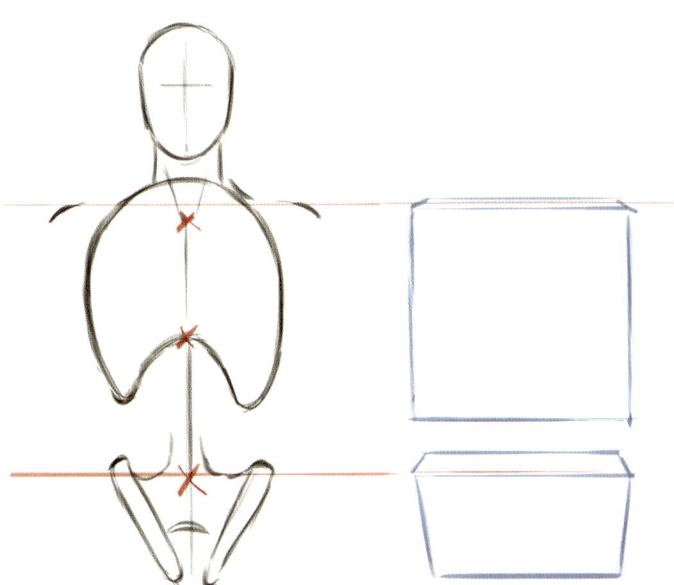

The basic anatomy we're representing with boxes. Red marks show the areas we were landmarking in our gesture drawings: shoulder line, hips line, pit of the neck, sternum, and middle of hips.

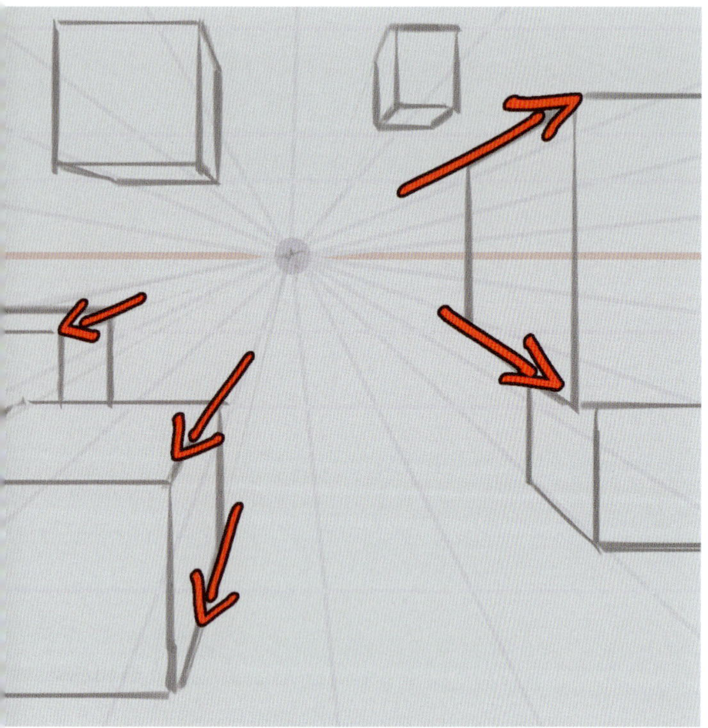

Remember this diagram from Chapter 3? It shows how the lines we use to draw boxes have different angles based on where they are in relation to the perspective grid.

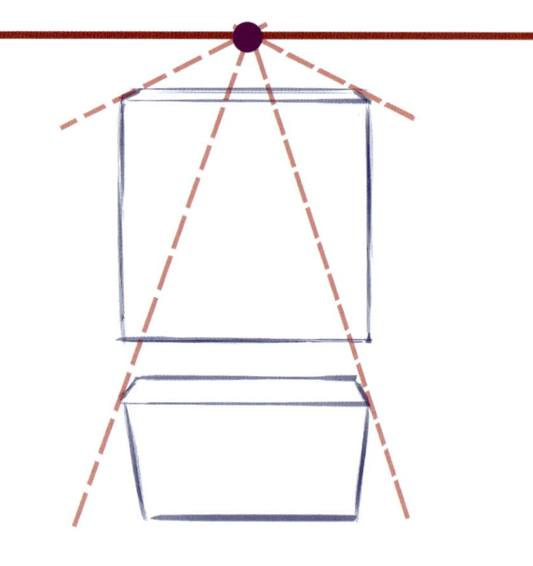

In this case, the top box (top of the shoulders) sits just below the eyeline, making its angles open and wide. By comparison, the hips are far below the eyeline, and therefore receive much narrower angles as that box's angles still need to converge at the same vanishing point on the horizon line.

There is something both basic and important to notice about the figure. It takes up space. Especially vertical space. That means the boxes we're using to simplify it need to correspond with a perspective grid.

Therefore our simplified figure boxes also correspond to that same perspective information. To determine exactly how, recalling Chapter 3, we start by identifying the horizon line, or eyeline, and work from there.

Determining the location of the eyeline is easy when you're working from life. Project an invisible line straight outward from your own eyes, and where it collides with the figure in front of you is where your horizon line is. For example, if you're sitting on the ground and the model is standing on a podium, your eyes might collide with the model at their ankles, and that becomes your horizon line. If you're standing and the model is sitting, the entire model could be below your horizon line, and therefore you'll see the top planes of everything.

Figuring this out from a photograph is more difficult because you really have no way of knowing exactly where the camera's lens is in relation to the figure. Thankfully, though, it isn't too difficult to make an educated visual guess. Let's try it!

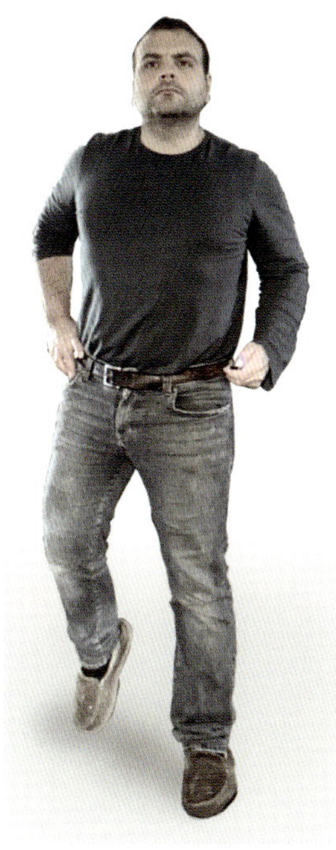

Vertically, where does the camera's lens line up with the subject in this photo? Take a guess.

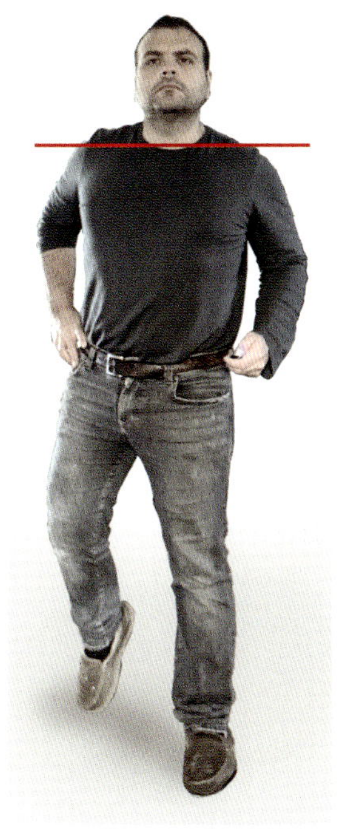

The lens was even with the pit of my neck. Did you guess right? Don't worry if you didn't get it exactly. All you really need to be is in the ballpark.

Because this is a photo of me I took with my camera on a tripod, I can tell you exactly where the horizon line is.

That means that the shoulders, neck, and head, are above the horizon line, while the rest of the body is below the horizon line. So, the boxes on this figure look like this:

Notice how we can see the top plane of the hips-box, but we can't see the top plane of the torso-box. The reason should be obvious by now. The upper plane of the torso box sits *above* the horizon line, and the upper plane of the hips box sits *below*. Also notice the cylinder and corresponding ellipses I've made for the head. The ellipses curve upward, meaning we can see their bottom planes because they are *above* the horizon line. The head

is tilted slightly upward in this pose, which makes the curvature of the ellipse more pronounced.

Remember that the goal with these solid forms is to not only approximate the dimensionality of the figure, but also to capture its movement. The torso and hips can move independently of each other, which makes these two boxes ideal, as you can move, rotate, and orient them independently also.

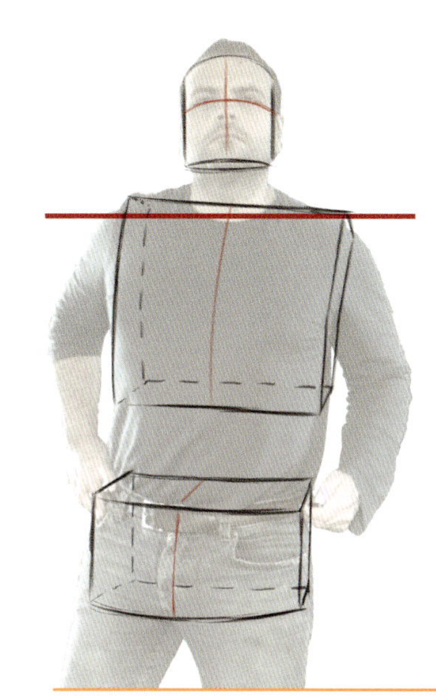

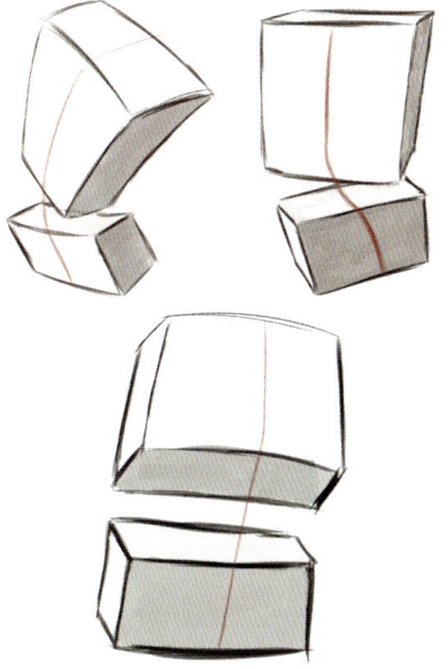

These drawings are now beginning to resemble actual poses!

TIP: To apply some simple shading, pick a direction and shade all planes that face that direction.

YOU CAN DO THE TWIST . . . BUT YOUR HIPS CAN'T

Remember that the forms aren't necessarily rigid. The torso box is quite elastic!

The reason the torso box can twist is that this box covers three distinct areas: the shoulders, the rib cage, and the fleshy stomach area. The ribcage and shoulders are attached so when one rotates, so must the other. But when the shoulders move, the hips do not necessarily need to follow. They can stay planted, or even rotate the opposite way, making for dynamic poses full of life.

The hips box itself, however, cannot twist or bend. It remains rigid. That's because it represents the large bowl-like hip bone itself, which is solid all the way through. The combination of the two boxes allows for a huge range of motion.

THE MIDLINE IS IMPORTANT

The midline shown in red is a useful landmarking tool. From the front view, it passes through the navel, keeping the middle blank area between boxes consistent. Think of it as a tool for binding these boxes and preventing them from drifting away from each other. Running it through the middle of the form will help keep things aligned on either side, too!

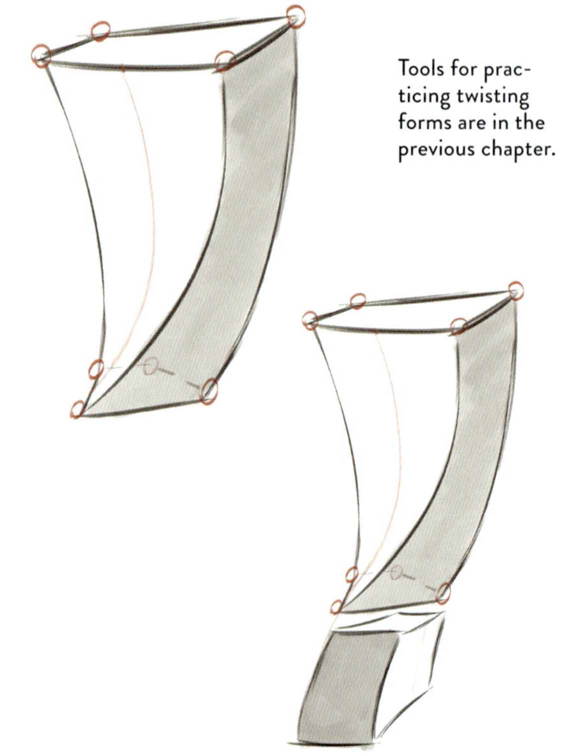

Tools for practicing twisting forms are in the previous chapter.

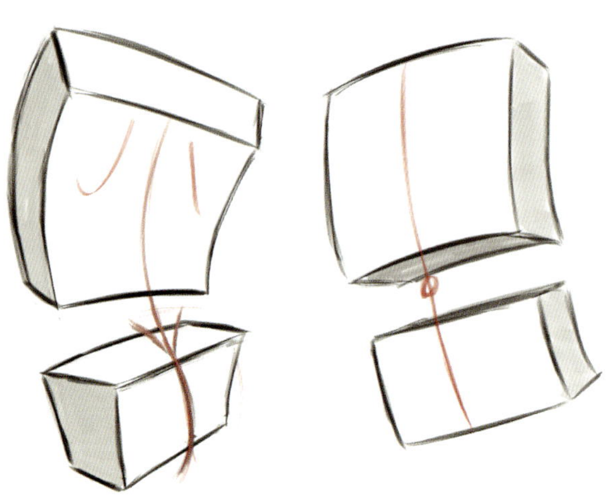

If drawing a back view (left), the red line represents the bendy spinal cord, passing through the tailbone and linking up with the middle of the buttocks. In a front view (right), the midline passes through the navel or belly button.

Overlapping Forms:
The Accordion Effect

Because the body can bend and twist, you will often run into situations where the skin on one side of the body is stretched, while squished on the other side. Imagine these two forms as a preliminary under drawing.

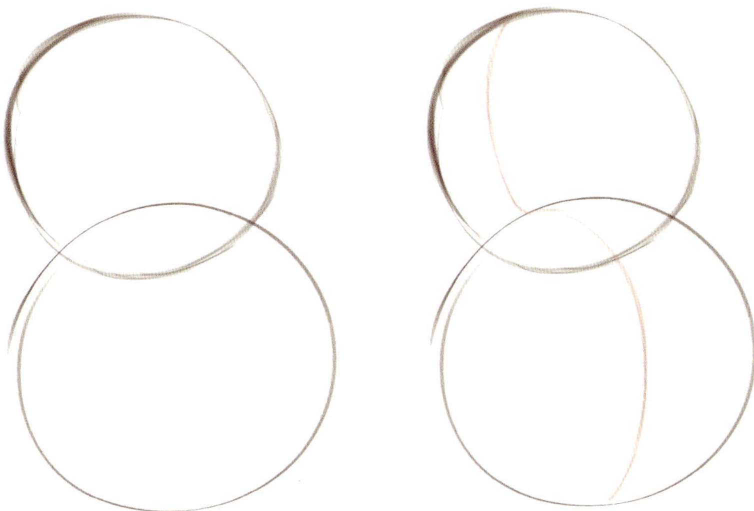

Just to shake things up, I'm using spherical forms to represent the torso, instead of boxes. There are no rules. Use whatever tool helps you most!

Now imagine drawing "final" contours over this. If you did it like this, you'd lose the depth:

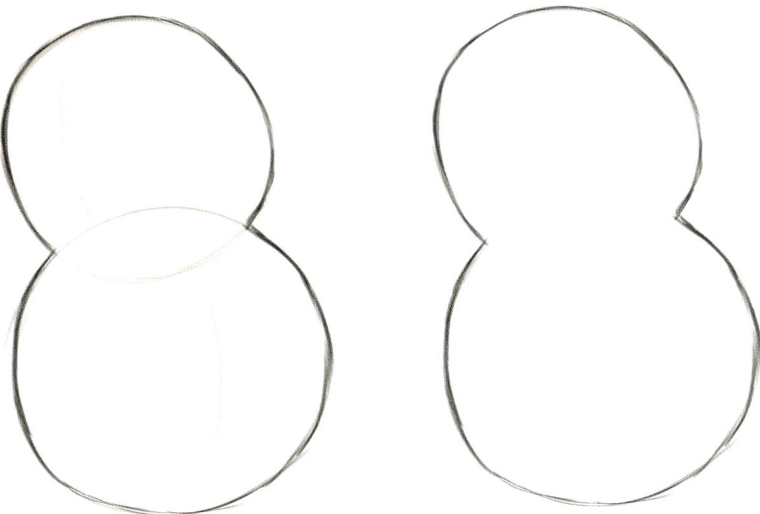

The drawing on the right loses all depth without the under drawing present. How do you fix this?

Consider where and how your shapes are overlapping. Also imagine, or observe directly, if using reference, which side of the form is being stretched, and which is squished.

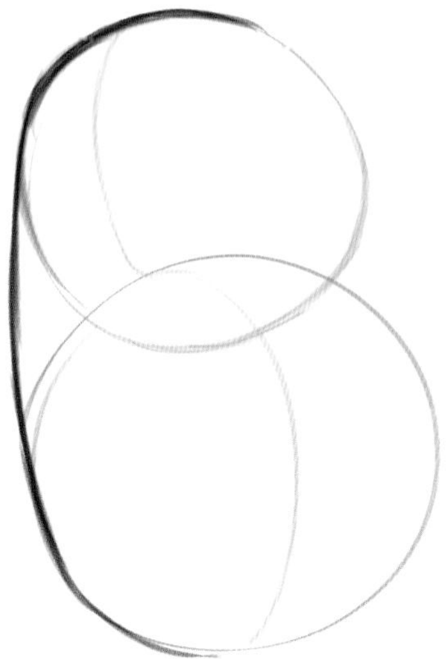

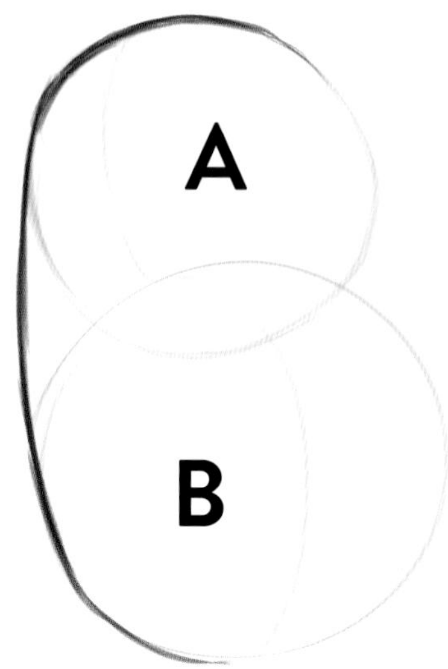

Here I've determined that the left side is the stretching side. So, I draw a very tight C-curve to connect the two forms.

Now I'm observing that form B is in front of form A in space. In other words, form A is overlapped by form B. This is crucial in informing the next step of the drawing.

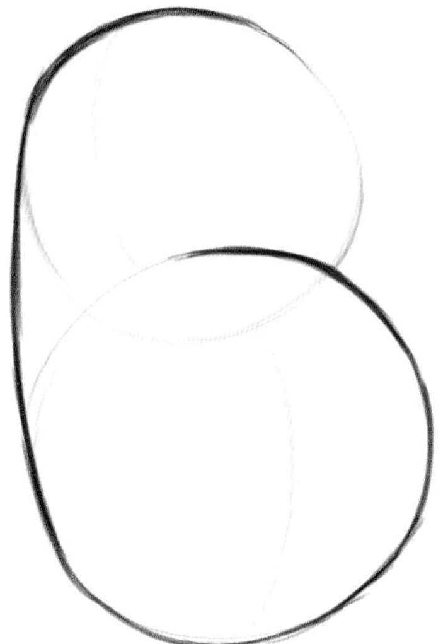

Because I know that form B is the one in front, I can allow its contour to partially overlap that of form A whose contour gets cut off by form B.

Scan to watch a tutorial.

I call this the accordion effect.
That squishy, doubled-up set of
lines tell the viewer all they need
to know about form and space
and they maintain a clean shape
design without needing an
under drawing to communicate
dimension. In my experience,
this is the single principle that
gets the most mileage in my
drawings.

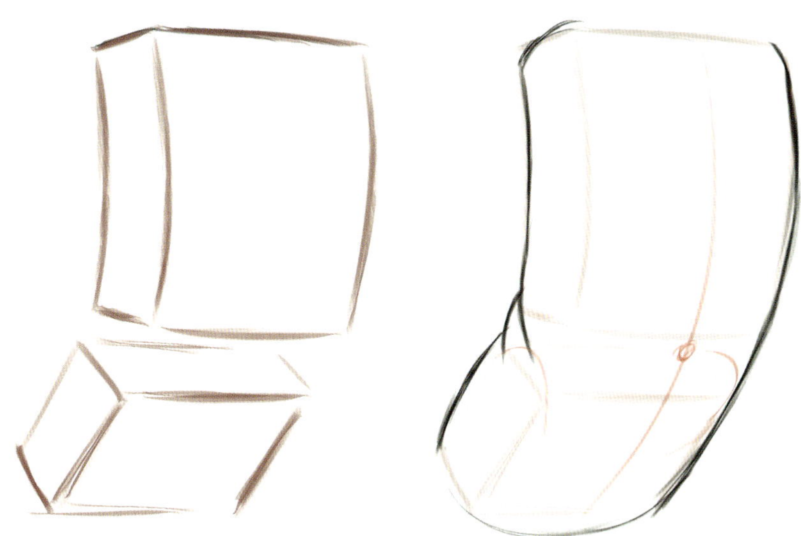

In the drawing on the right, the iliac crest (the pivot plane of hips) is indicated in red, as is the navel.

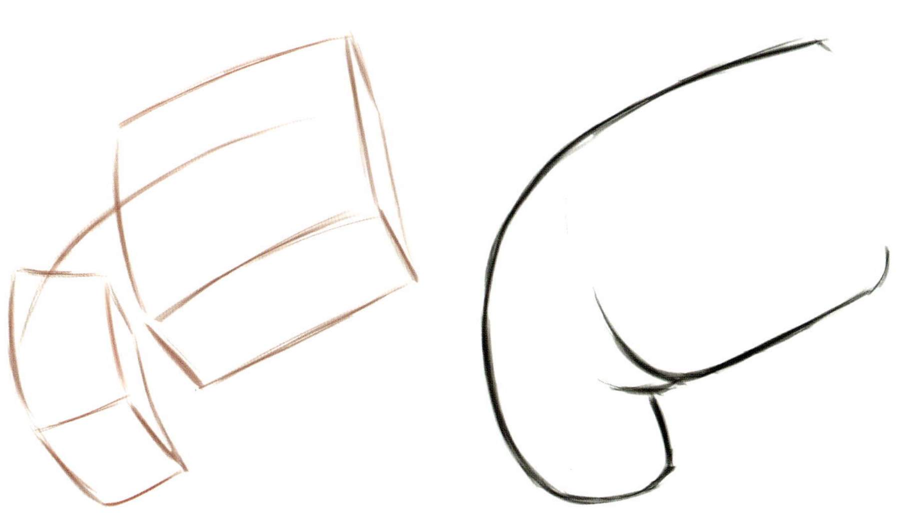

Legs and Arms

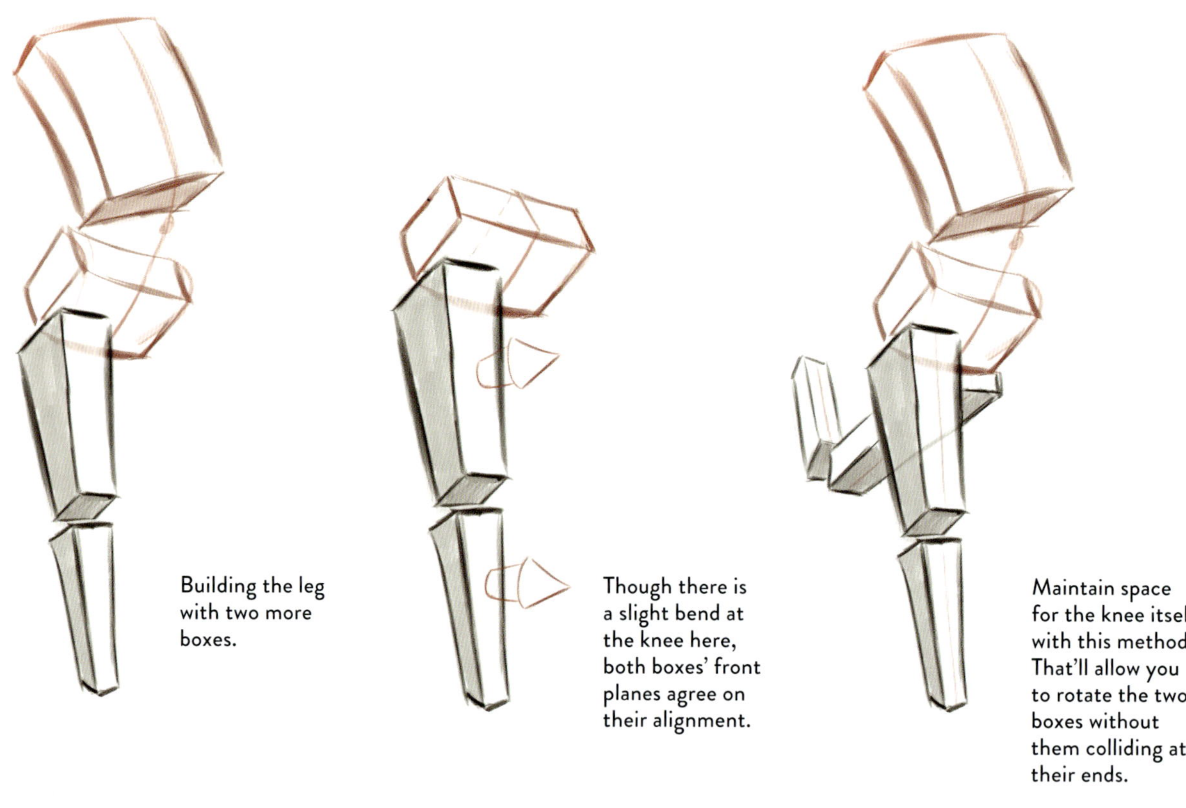

Building the leg with two more boxes.

Though there is a slight bend at the knee here, both boxes' front planes agree on their alignment.

Maintain space for the knee itself with this method. That'll allow you to rotate the two boxes without them colliding at their ends.

Of course, we need to attach legs and arms to our hips and torsos. The good news is that these are much easier, as they're more rigid elements. Our arm and leg bones don't allow for a ton of elasticity. Instead, they hinge at the elbow and knee joints. That hinge motion means we'll need two boxes for each limb: one for the upper arm or leg, and one for the lower arm or leg.

Notice how both leg boxes' orientation is the same, relative to each other, meaning their front planes are both facing equally to the front.

This is because the leg isn't built to twist like the torso is. If your shin is facing a different way than your quads, you are having a very bad day.

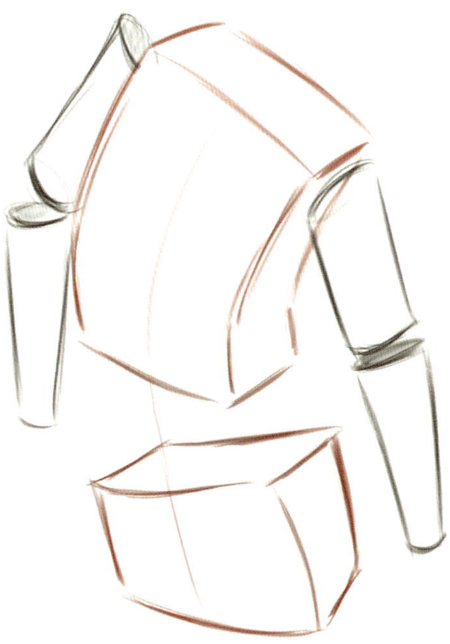

Because the wrist is so much thinner than the top of the arm, it's wise to taper the forms as they travel along the arm especially between the elbow and wrist.

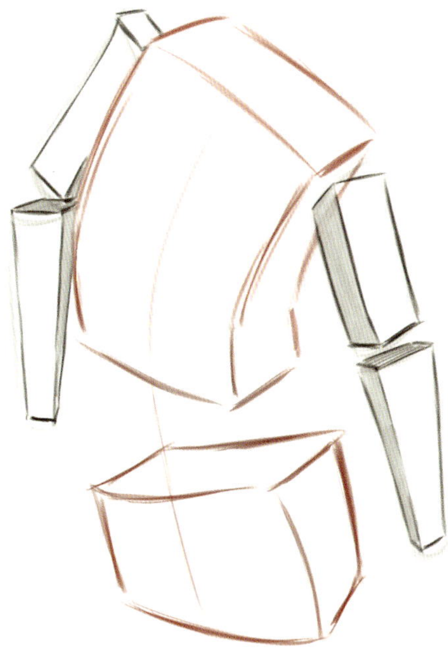

The same drawing with boxes for arms instead of cylinders.

Arms branch off the upper torso. Similar to the knee, we leave a bit of a gap between the torso box and the upper arm, to leave room for the shoulder that fits in there.

Notice I've used cylinders for the arms. There isn't a significant benefit or difference between using cylinders or boxes. Use whatever forms you're comfortable with most. These arms could just as easily be represented as boxes.

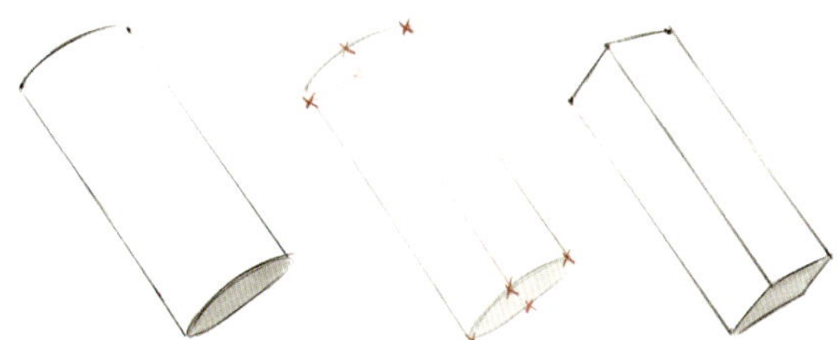

The process of converting a cylinder to a box. I usually prefer using boxes for form simplification, because the planes are easier to see and therefore easier to throw some simple shading on. But it's up to you!

Hands and Feet

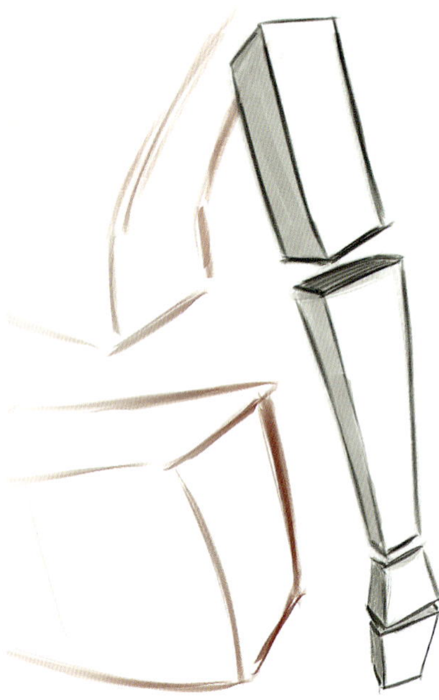

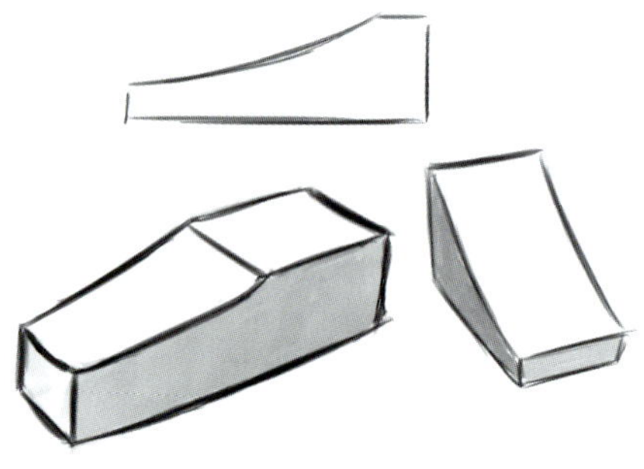

Think of hands as two box forms. One is for the palmar or dorsal area with the thumb grouped in ending at the knuckles, and the other the fingers.

For the feet use one box modified into a wedge or doorstop shape. Create a box with the top face tapered toward the toes. Any variation does the job.

Trace Over Studies

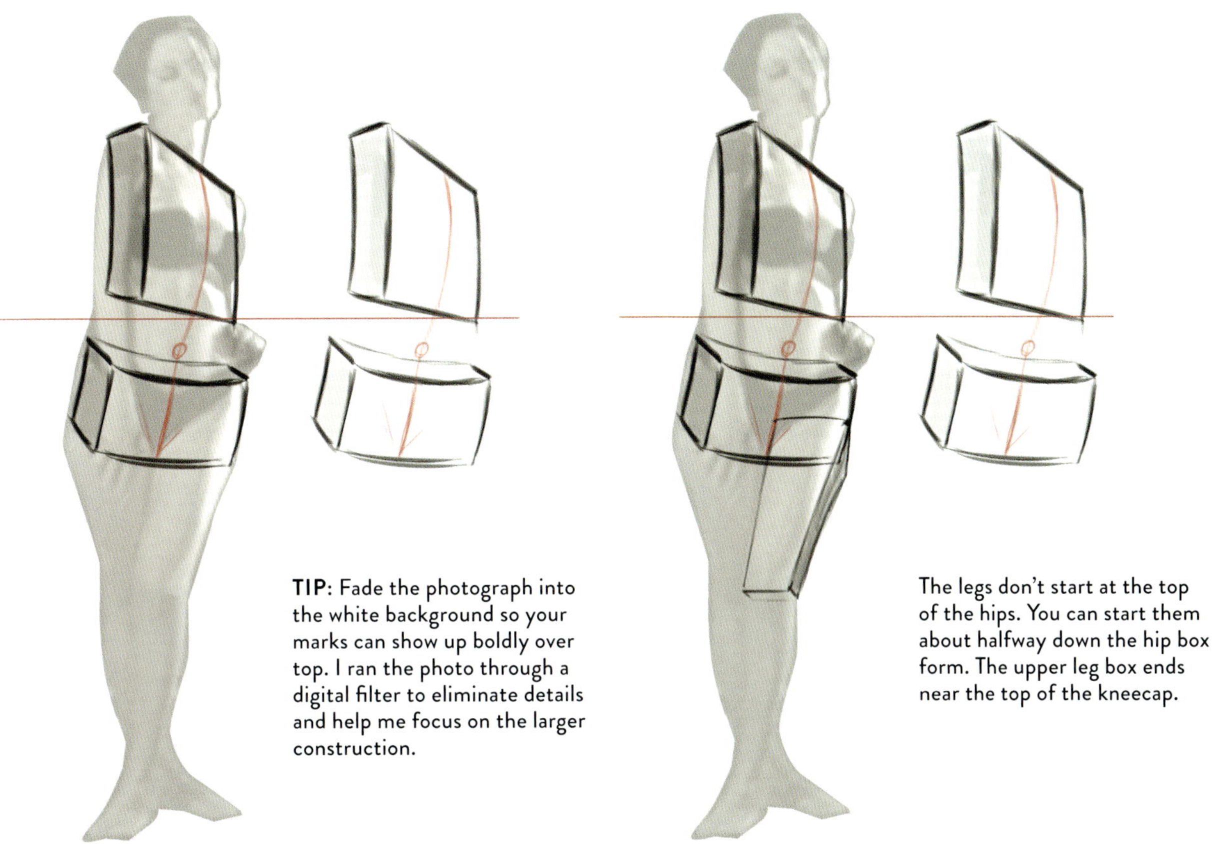

TIP: Fade the photograph into the white background so your marks can show up boldly over top. I ran the photo through a digital filter to eliminate details and help me focus on the larger construction.

The legs don't start at the top of the hips. You can start them about halfway down the hip box form. The upper leg box ends near the top of the kneecap.

Tracing gets a bad rap, but it has a place in your learning as you aren't copying! In this exercise, we take a photograph of the figure and build our simplified forms on top of it. To stay consistent, we'll work in the order we've been exploring so far, starting with the torso and hips and their relationship to the horizon line.

I've added my guess at the horizon line's position. This seems to match the perspective of the figure best. It's tricky as that torso box's bottom plane is just above the horizon line on the left side and even with it on the right. That means we're able to see the bottom plane, but just barely!

There is a slight twist to this pose, which is easily captured with these tools. Remember that the midline starts at the pit of the neck, passes through the sternum, then passes through the navel, connecting the middle of the torso with the middle of the hips. When tracing over the figure, this should be very easy to see, hence why this exercise is useful!

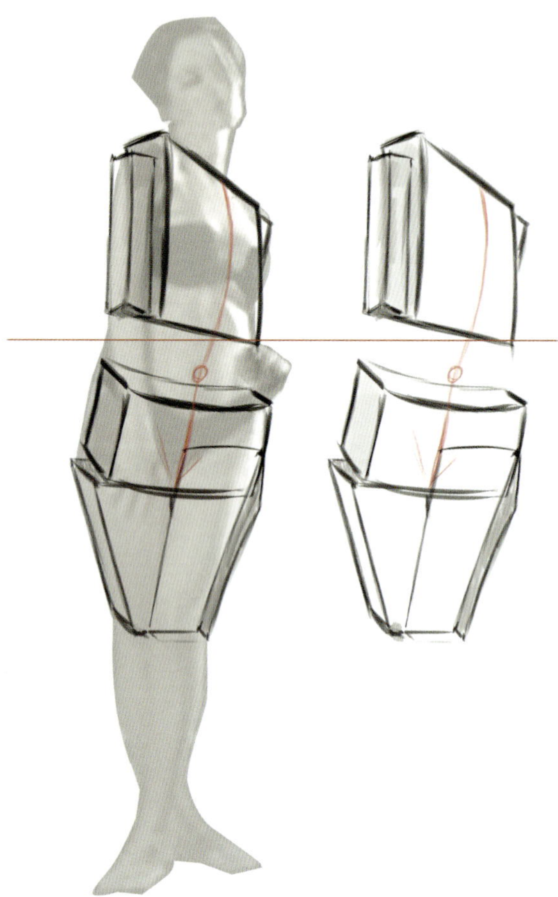

Filling in the upper limbs, both arms, and legs. The arms' upper box will end around the middle of the elbow.

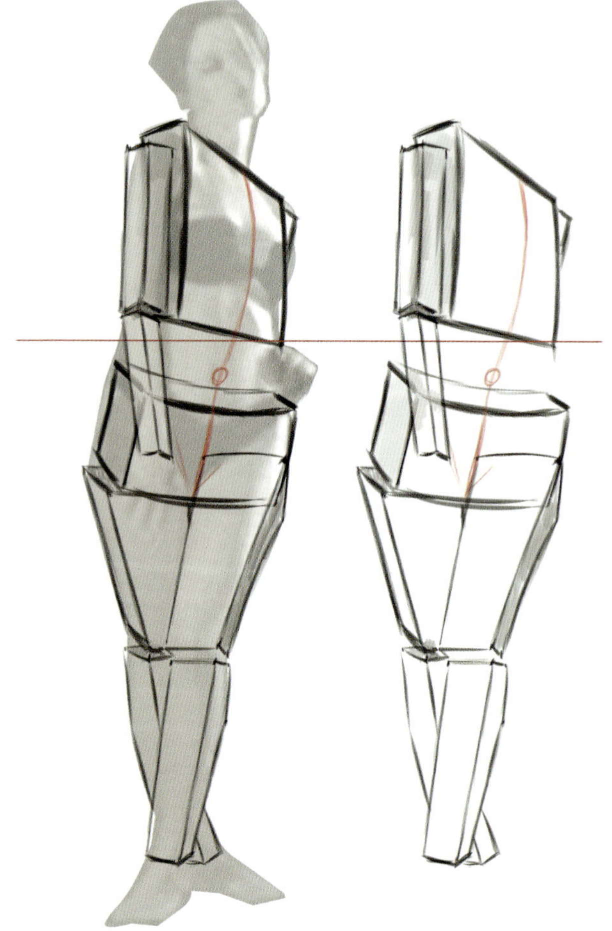

Adding the lower boxes of each limb. Remember to taper these boxes both at the ankle and at the wrist. If you want to approximate the calf muscle, it isn't a big stretch to shape that lower box a little.

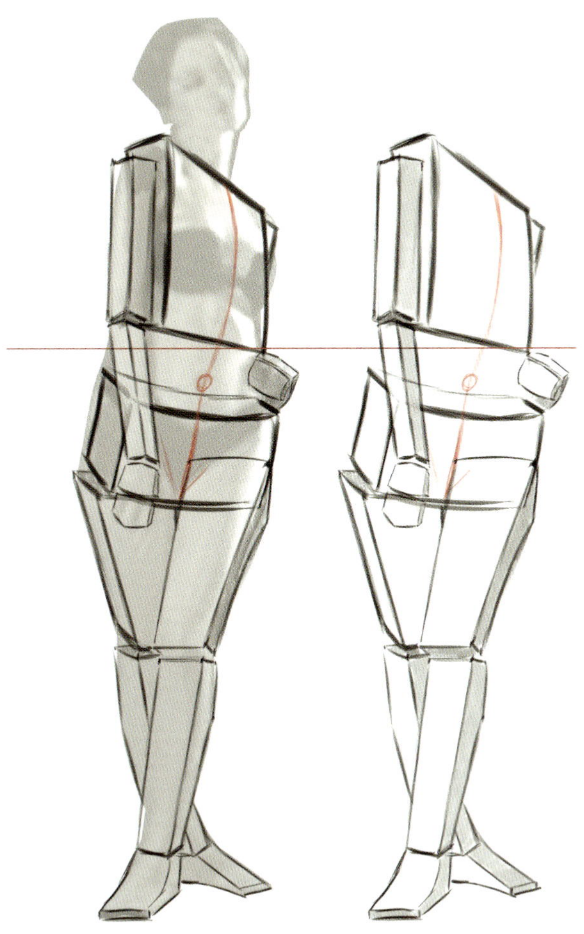

Adding the hands and feet forms. Make sure the chosen planes to shade are consistent.

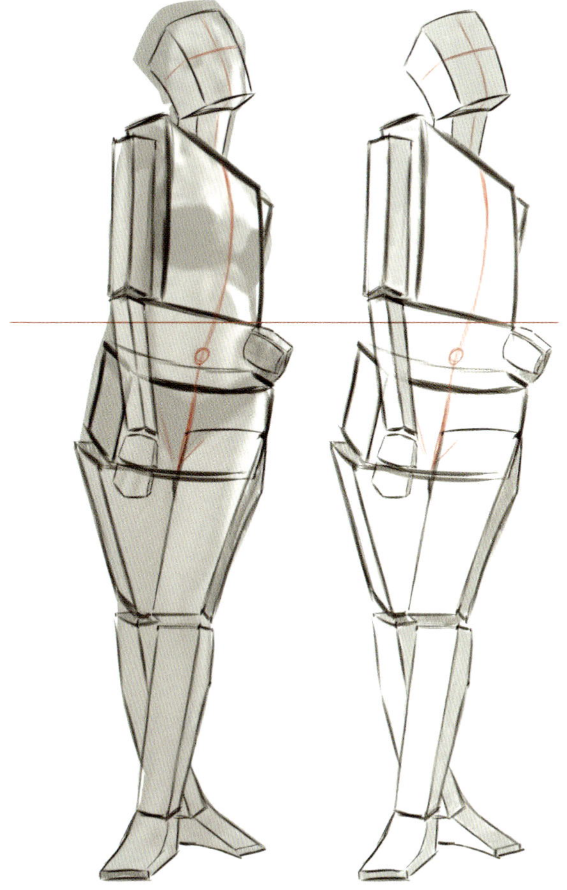

Adding the head and neck, which, surprise, surprise, are also boxes!

Figure Construction Studies

You may be wondering why I'm not interested in starting with the head when in the gesture drawing chapter, I was all gung-ho on that. It's because we're looking for different things in this phase of study. We're looking to capture the most important elements of structure first, which typically exists with the shoulders, torso, and hips. For now, try these drawings without a gesture. You can try a whole series of drawings where the only goal is to capture this area, hinting at where the arms and legs are.

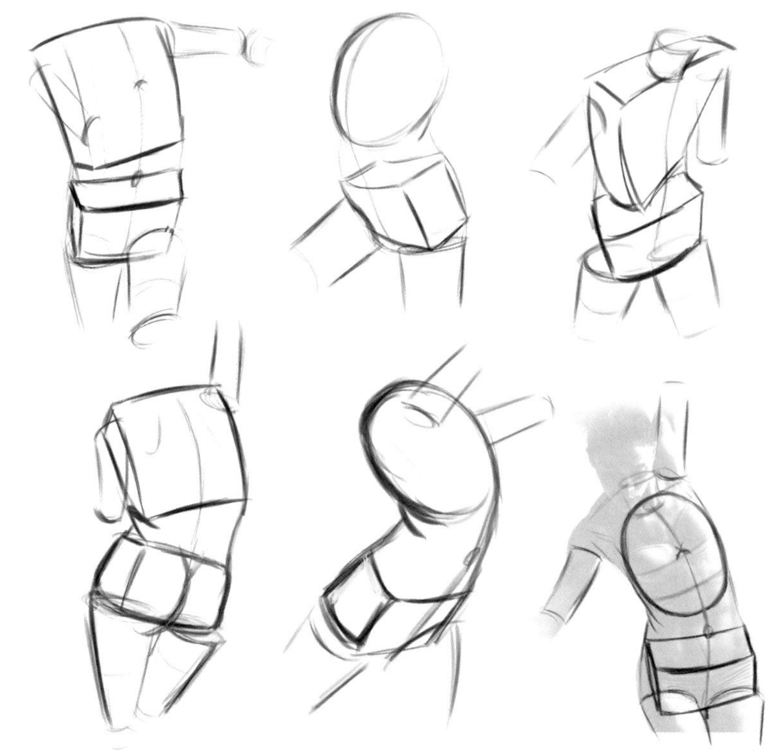

Try using boxes, cylinders, spheres. Mix and match them to find what works best for you! Remember, this is a visualization tool, and nothing more.

When you use spherical forms to represent the torso and hips, you are looking for this relationship (the left form). The spherical form is closer to real anatomy, but the box may be more visually friendly. Note that the top of the spherical form is a little higher than the top of the box form.

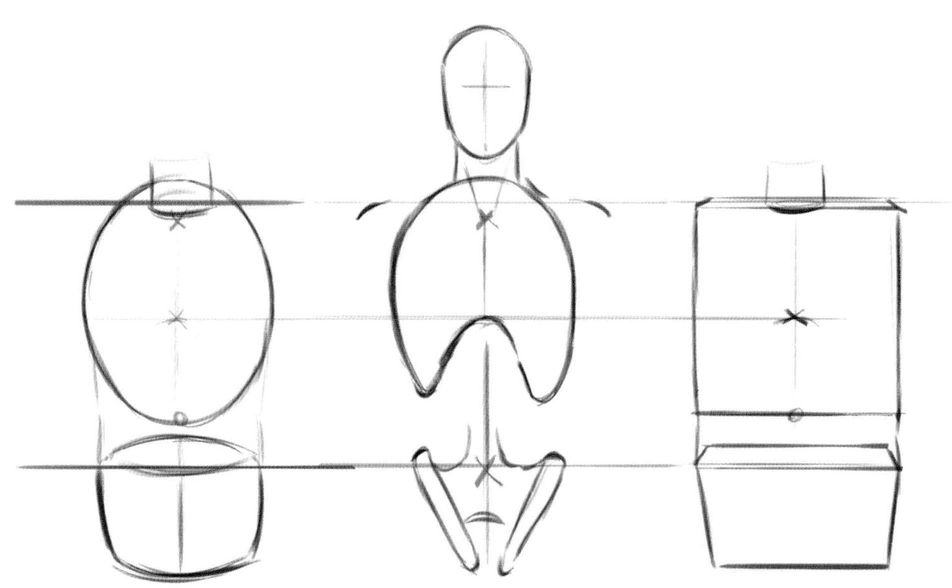

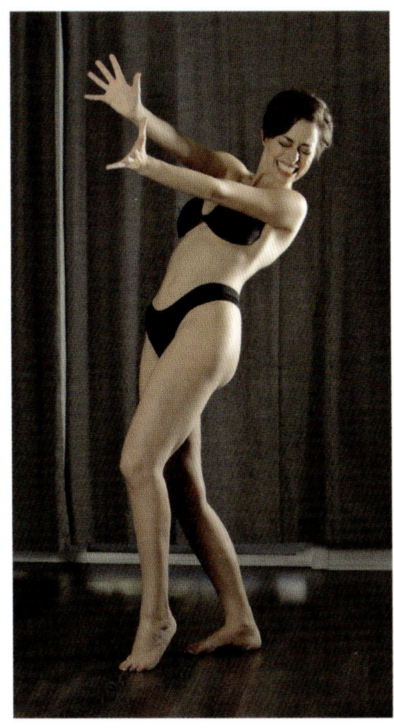

The reference photo, and our previous gesture drawing from it. We'll now build the forms on top of this framework.

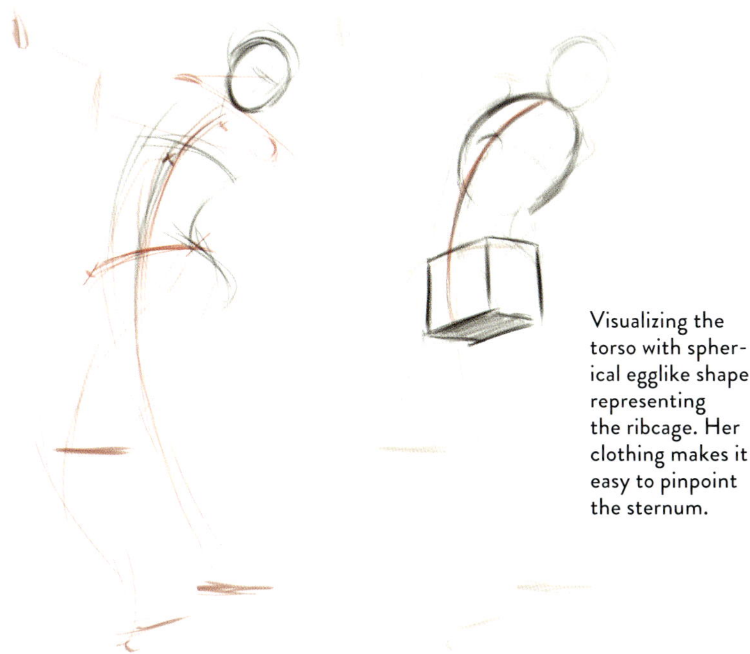

Visualizing the torso with spherical egglike shape representing the ribcage. Her clothing makes it easy to pinpoint the sternum.

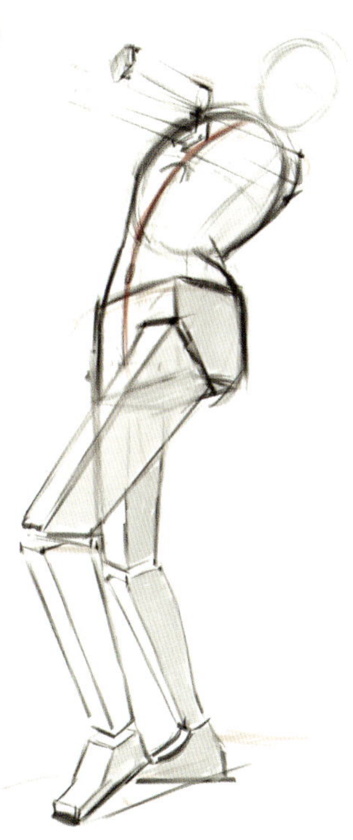

Being more careful with my landmarks and building out my box forms. I constantly refer back to the model to compare the direction that planes are facing to ensure my boxes have the correct orientation. Remember to draw through the model as though you have x-ray vision.

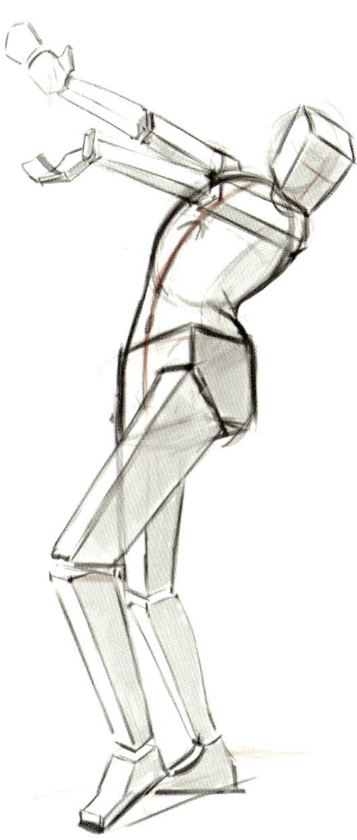

The finished simplified form study. Don't give yourself time limits on these. The figure is complicated! Let the drawing take however long you need to fill out the geometry and find the form. If you compare my own progress here, you'll find small corrections and fixes along the way. This is normal, and you shouldn't expect yourself to get every mark and placement correct the first time.

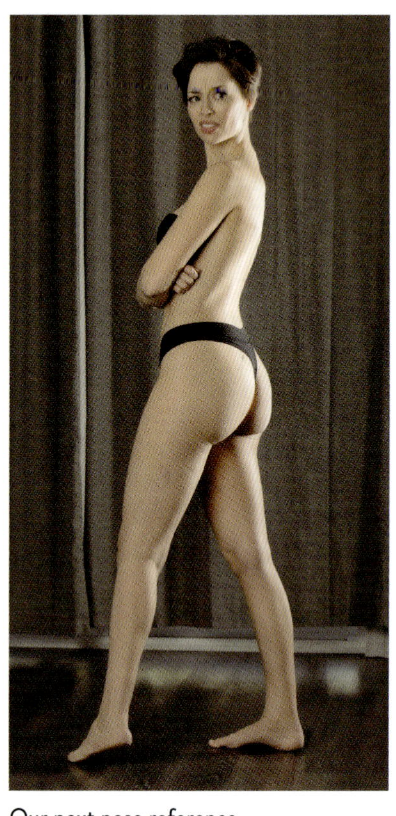

Our next pose reference.

Scan to watch a tutorial.

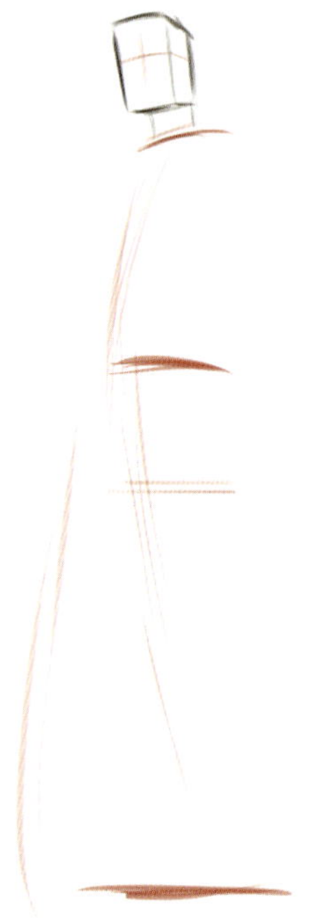

The goal isn't perfection but sharpening our observational skills and the ability to put down information in the right order. We begin here with a quick gesture that captures basic landmarks, the horizon line, and the movement in the pose.

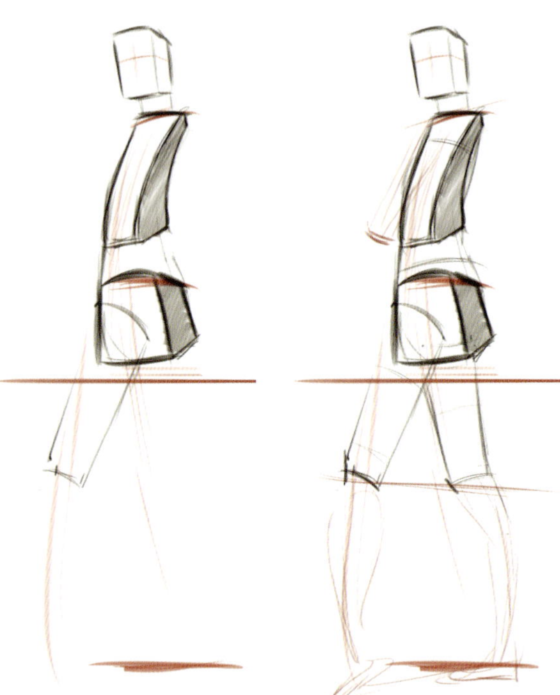

This may be the toughest part of this pose, figuring out that subtle twist right at the shoulders. Don't forget to identify that horizon line!

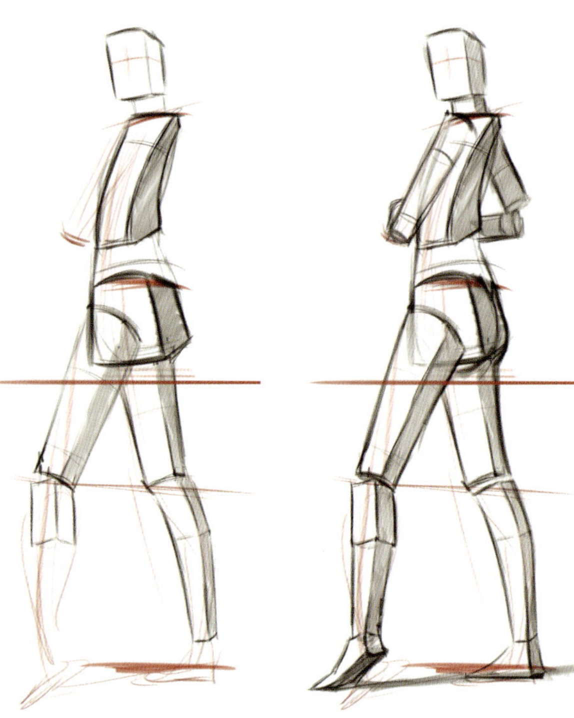

Finishing off the drawing. I added the far arm because the drawing looked strange without it.

It's okay to be frustrated when you experience incorrect pro-portions, wobbly dimensions, and uncertain angles. You can go back to tracing studies to refresh and recharge.

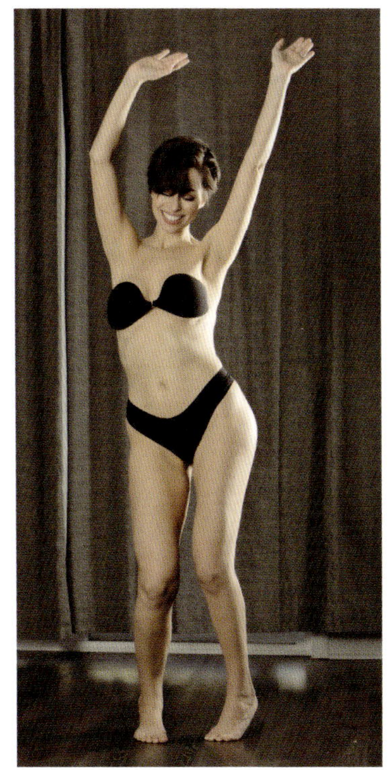

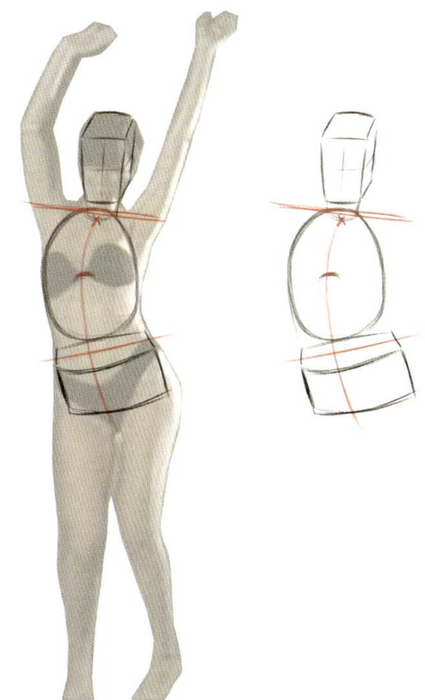

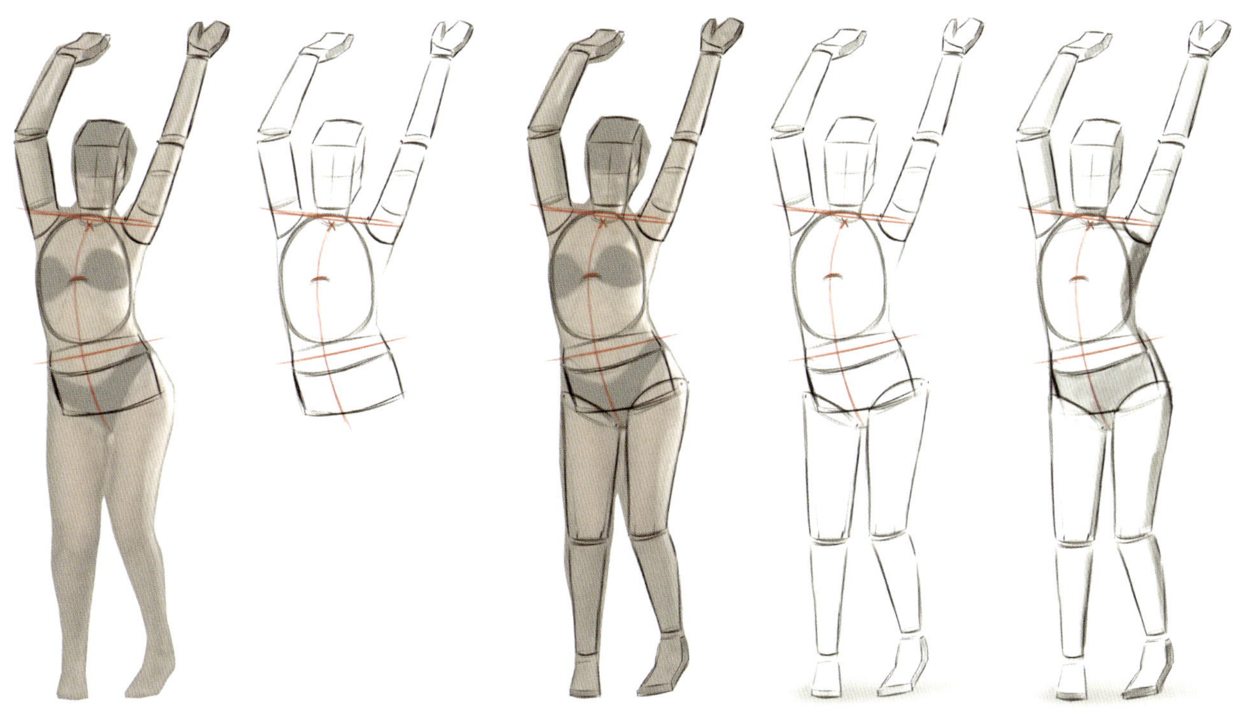

Draw, Draw, Draw

These are merely tools. You shouldn't be precious about each box having perfect perspective or every angle's precise alignment to the horizon line or vanishing point. You have huge margins of error to work within.

When you practice this, try including quicker drawings that are more freehanded, and less measured, merging the mindset of the gesture, with the accuracy of the form. Practice loosening up as much as you practice technical precision!

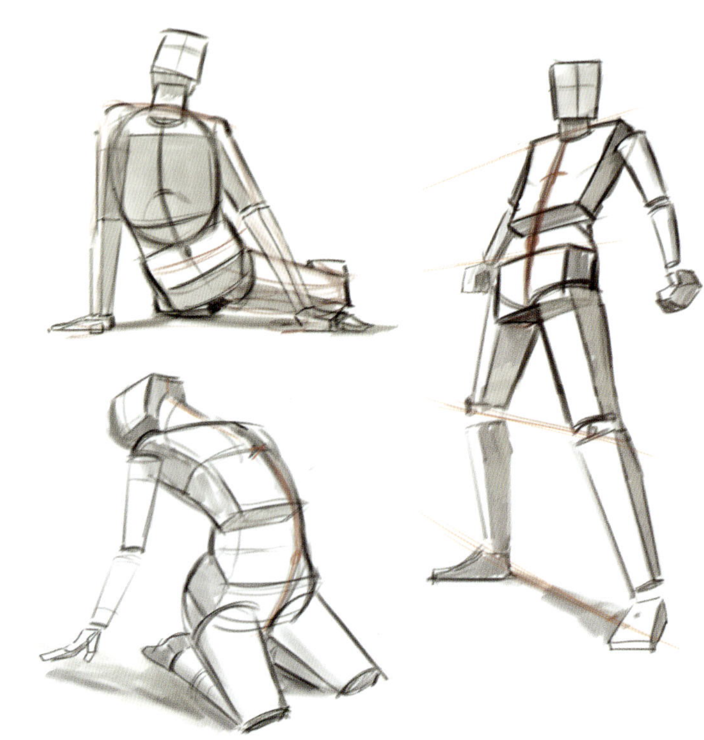

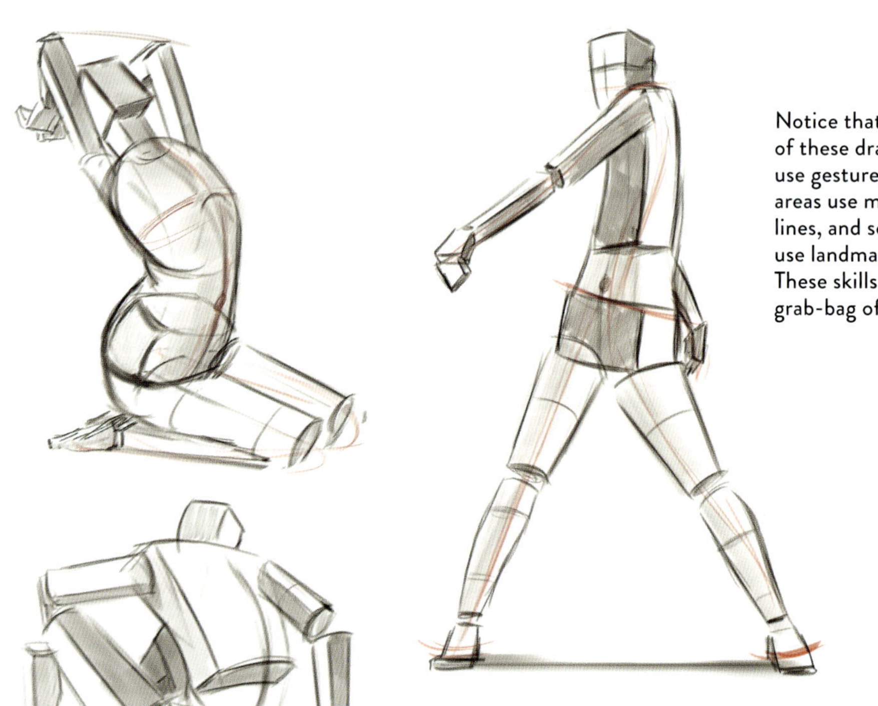

Notice that some of these drawings use gesture, some areas use mid-lines, and some use landmarks. These skills are a grab-bag of tools.

Scan to watch a tutorial.

ASSIGNMENTS

Here are several fun ways to get comfortable with building the figure. Give them a try and your drawings will definitely improve.

ASSIGNMENT #1

Using photo reference from the model, trace over it to draw two boxes representing the torso and hips. Remember that the top of the torso box should cross at the shoulders, and the top of the hips box should cross at the iliac crest. You should also leave room for the fleshy stomach area in between the ribcage and hip bone.

ASSIGNMENT #2

Draw two boxes representing the torso and hips, but from imagination this time. Remember that these boxes should still sit within a perspective grid. At this stage, however, try to draw the boxes *without* the grid. You can also try rotating and even twisting the forms to get the feel of a real torso in action. If you find your visualization skills aren't up to the task just yet, feel free to revert back to assignment #1, as well as more assignments and practice from Chapter 3!

ASSIGNMENT #3

Working from the model reference, and using the vellum techniques from the previous assignments, construct a box-drawing over the photograph. Use a box to correspond with each major form, as outlined in the chapter. Remember that it's okay to trace in your studies, so long as you're working on reducing the pose to its basic construction. In fact, tracing is often a good way of noticing where you may be making repetitive or habitual errors.

ASSIGNMENT #4

Construct poses using any of the simplification tools in this chapter—boxes, cylinders, or combinations of both. Work from photographs of the model, but this time do not trace them. Try to work small and fast. Remember that quantity and repetition is an important part of learning to draw—much better than laboring for hours over one drawing. If you notice yourself making the same mistake over and over, go back to assignment #3!

5

Capturing Poses, Shapes, and **Character**

Judging people by what they do, rather than what they say or how they look, is a life lesson we learn early. Actions reveal character. Any action can have character, whether it be a person dancing on stage or waiting in line for their morning coffee. There will always be some kind of body language in the way they pose. We want to communicate that sense of character in our drawings.

It may be tempting to draw a person or character in a static pose. But in doing so, you've already got three strikes against you:

Strike 1 - Without any movement, the pose reveals little of the subject's physicality.

Strike 2 - The audience has no way to visualize how the subject might behave.

Strike 3 - The audience has no way of engaging with the story your subject is participating in.

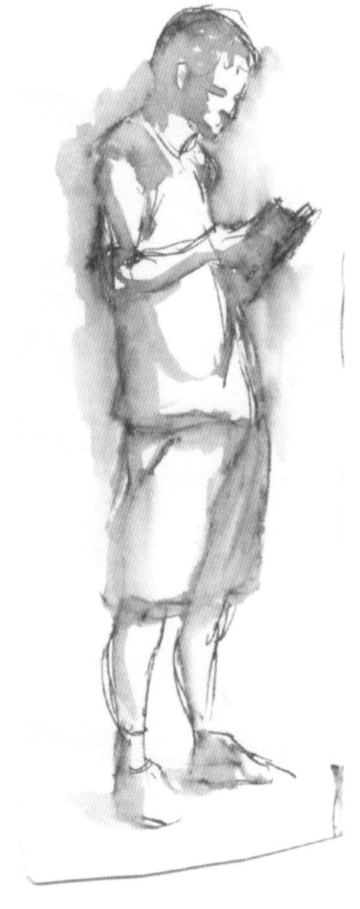

There were several years where I had my sketchbook and a pen in hand on a daily basis. These are people I observed and drew directly from life. My goal was to capture their poses in action. Of course, nobody stood still for me, so I learned to get straight to the point and draw quickly, only capturing what's essential to the pose and character. I found if I got enough information down early, even if the person moved away, I could continue the drawing. I used every tool we've discussed so far: gesture, shape, and simple forms. Some of these use basic shading, which will be discussed in a later chapter.

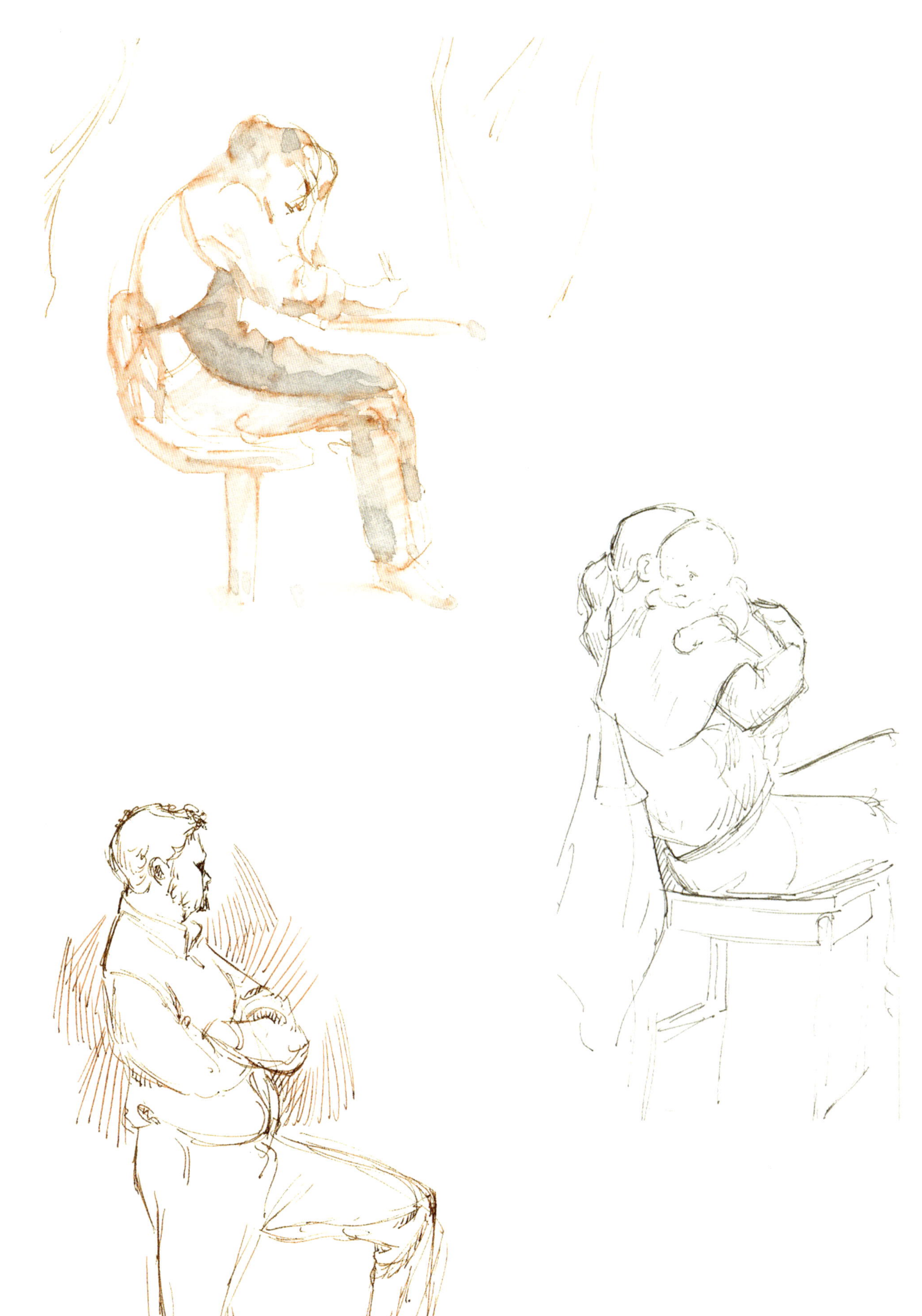

"Character" Is the Key Word

If you look at character explorations for animated films, you'll see artists find the characters through posing them in their drawings. Poses and acting are much higher priorities in communicating character than, say, getting the head shape right.

When you draw somebody, ask yourself what they might be doing in any given part of the story. Picking flowers? Delivering a pizza? Celebrating a win? Mourning a loss? The "size" of the action doesn't matter. What matters is that there is something *causing* the action.

To get started with this, try simply eliminating the option of drawing a "straight up and down" pose. Find some rhythms, tilt some shoulders, wiggle some hips, and offset some shapes!

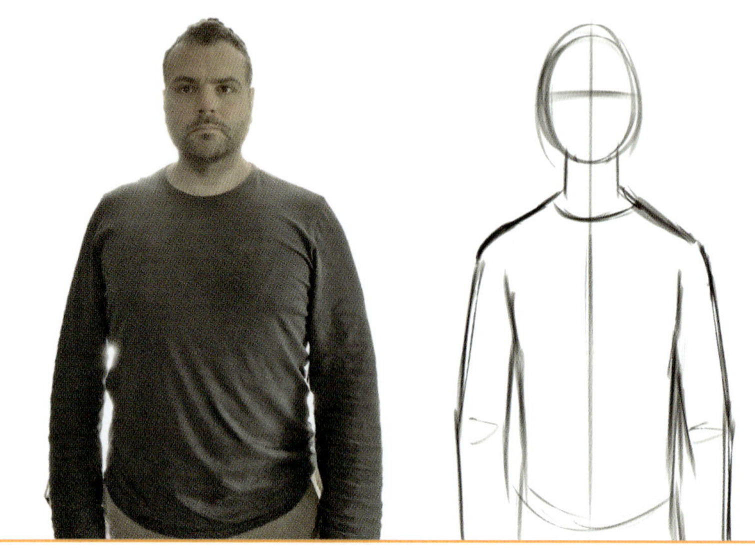

Nothing interesting is revealed in this drawing.

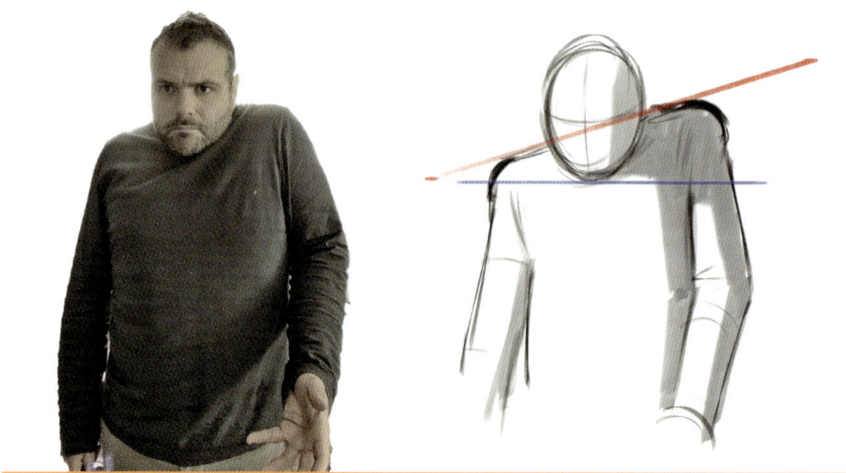

Raising or offsetting the shoulder line works wonders.

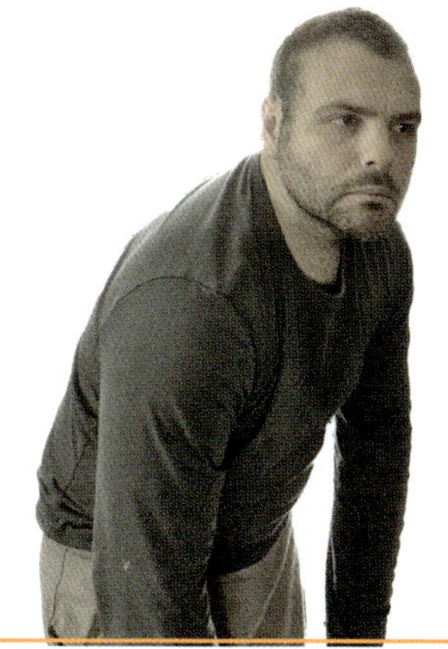

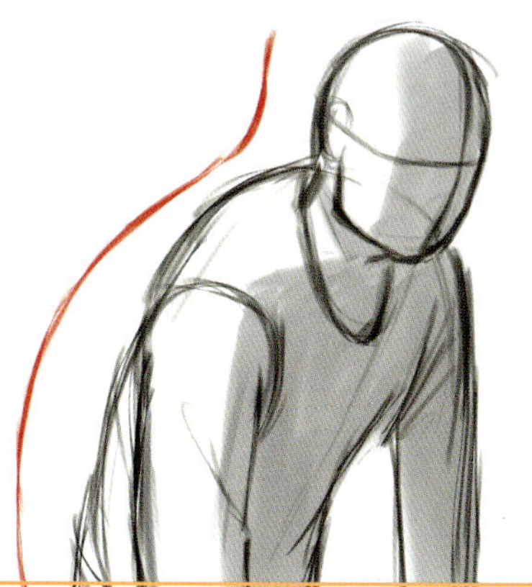

What might this character be doing, or have done, to be in this pose?

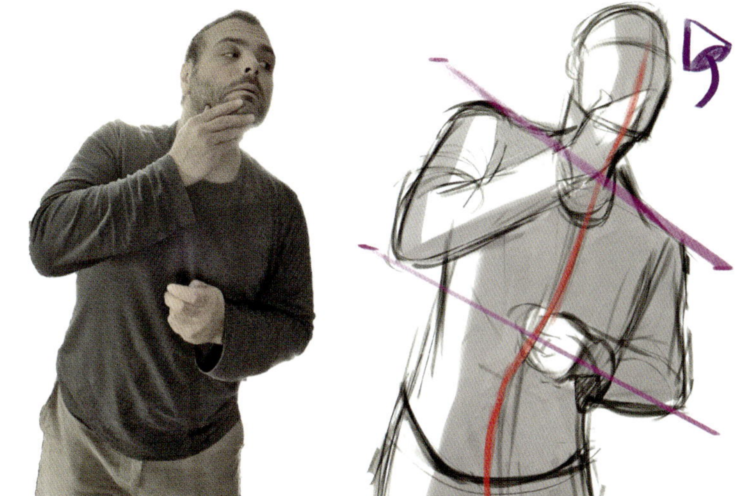

Tilting the head is another option. Try coupling it with offset shoulders!

A character I created for my YouTube videos. I'll bet you can fill in what he's saying and even imagine his next movement!

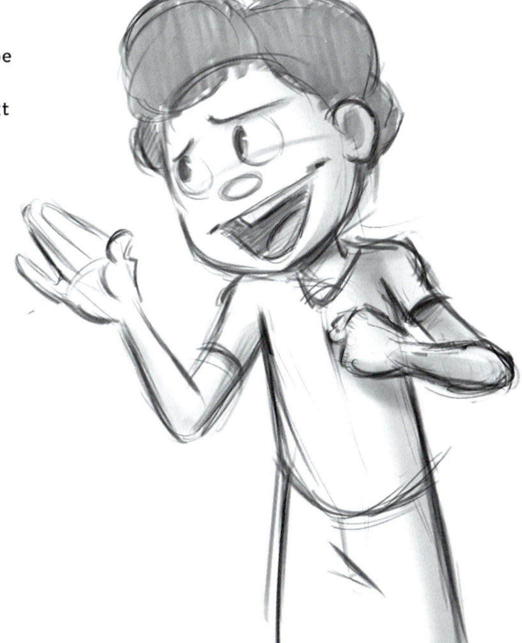

Silhouette

The silhouette is a collection of positive and negative space that makes up your subject. The golden principle behind silhouettes is that they should communicate the pose alone, without the need for any inside detail.

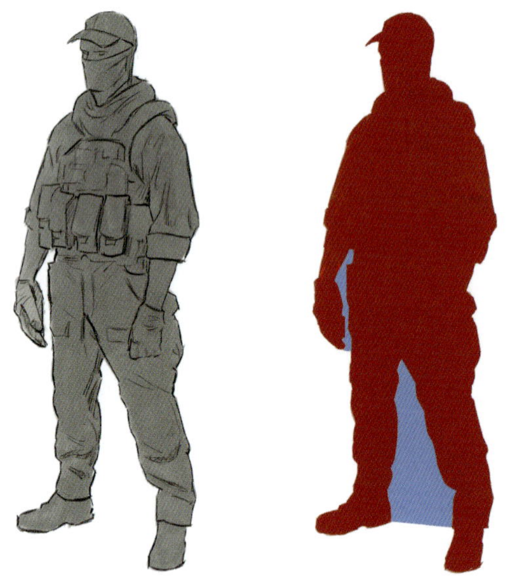

Positive space (red), versus negative space (blue). The pose of this person is clear, without the need for any of the various accouterments.

Positive and negative space are both made of shapes, and those shapes must be equally well designed, as we discussed in Chapter 1. Positive and negative shapes feed off each other. A well-designed negative space can boost the impact of a positive shape.

If there is anything resembling a rule in art, it's that your shapes must always be well thought out and easy to read. Silhouettes are a great place to maximize that discipline.

USING REFERENCE (THE RIGHT WAY)

Not every photograph you look at will be optimized for silhouette, and sometimes you will have to make editorial decisions. Take this photo, for instance:

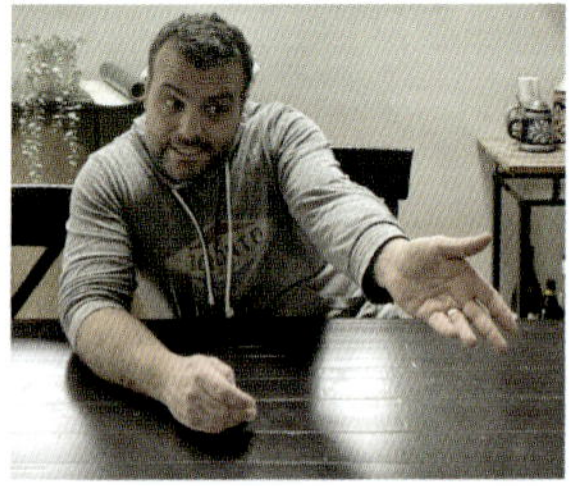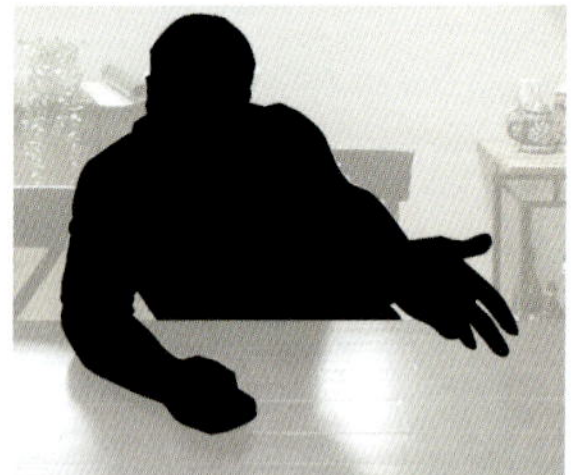

The photo, and the isolated silhouette.

One edit I commonly make to photo references is to maximize the utility of the negative space. This pose has character, but the silhouette could be clearer and quickly readable with a small tweak to the subject's left arm, namely adding a negative shape there.

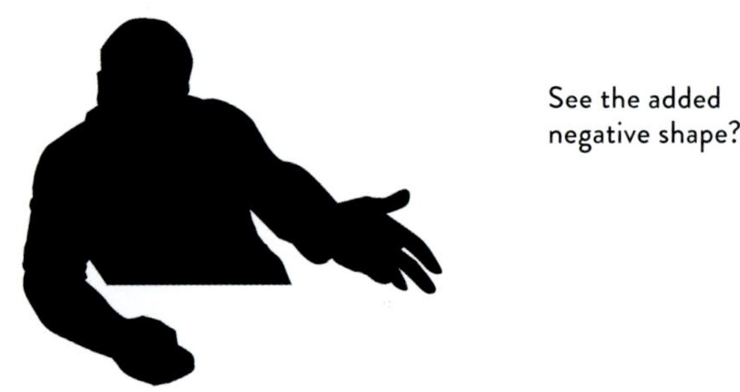

See the added negative shape?

Let's try drawing this pose. We'll use all the tools we've learned, but this time we'll complete the drawing by using shapes for the final statement.

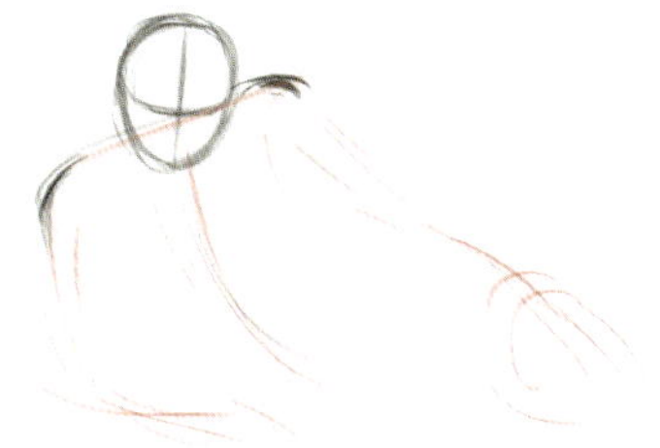

Don't be intimidated by clothing! Look for the gestural rhythms that flow through the pose.

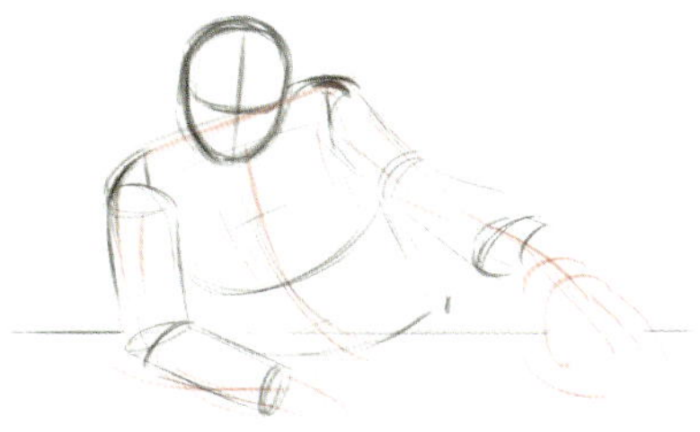

Now we build out the figure with basic box and cylinder 3D forms like we did in the last chapter. Again, try to see the basic forms through the clothing.

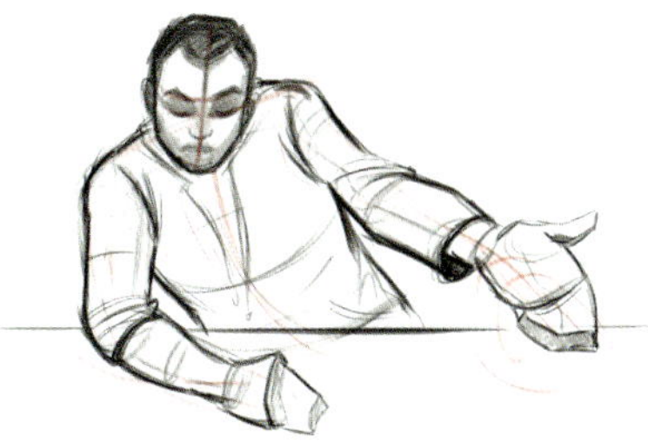

Ignore the face for now. Feel free to leave it as just a box, like we did in the last chapter. Another option is to close the eyes like I did here, which makes them easier to draw. In Chapter 6 we will go over constructing the head and facial features in detail.

This is an important moment! We're finally laying shapes over the gesture and form, taking the drawing to a more finished level. When drawing clothes the most important things to focus on are the areas that reveal basic forms. In this case, it's the ends of the sleeves, which act as ellipses, wrapping around the arm and describing its form.

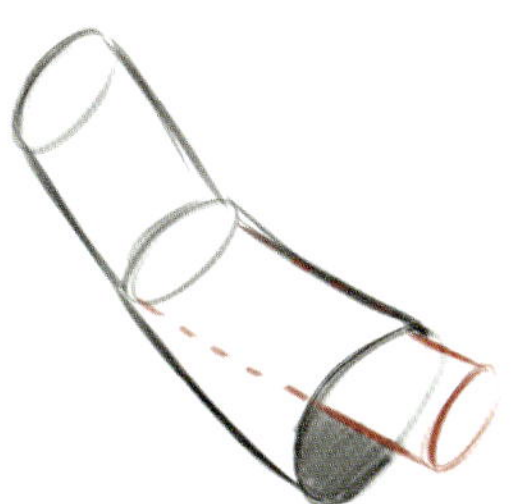

The openings of sleeves (and pants) can be thought of as the ellipses at the ends of cylinders. Visualize the arm itself (red) as a cylinder inside the sleeve-cylinder.

SHADING IS EASY NOW!

If you're constructing with basic forms, adding some shading is simple! You don't have to replicate the lighting in the photograph. Here, I've identified planes that face downward or toward the trunk of the body and applied a single tone to them.

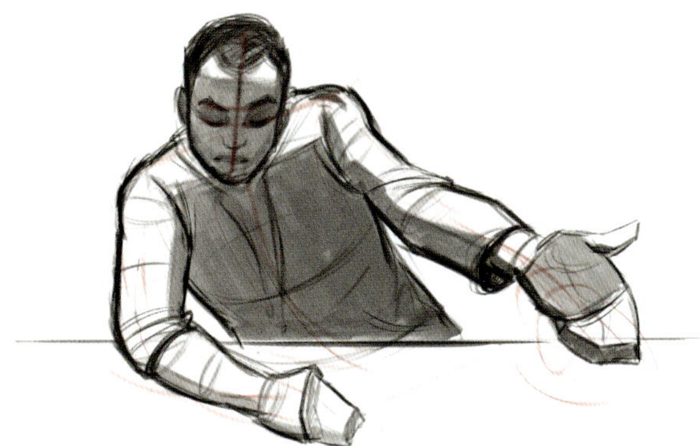

The finished study.

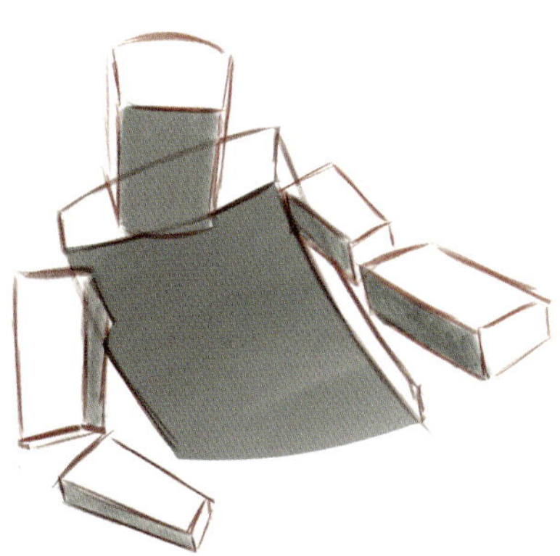

TIP: Try to keep this tone as even as possible. If working with traditional tools, I recommend using a medium-gray marker with a thick tip.

FORESHORTENING IS EASY NOW, TOO!

Foreshortening has a reputation for being difficult, and it is if you're only considering shape. If you are adept with drawing underlying forms, however, foreshortening becomes an easily solved puzzle.

Start with a cylinder. There is no foreshortening in this view, as both ends of the form are the same distance from the viewer.

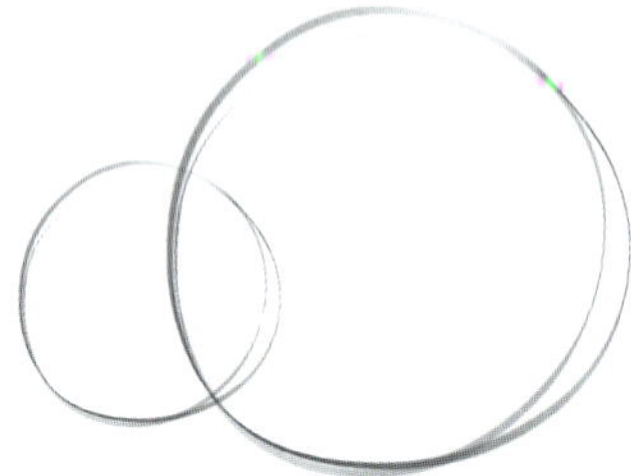

To make it foreshortened, we need to look more directly down the barrel at this object which means the ellipses will look more circular. After that, move the two end-caps closer together and make the closer end of the cylinder much larger than the further end.

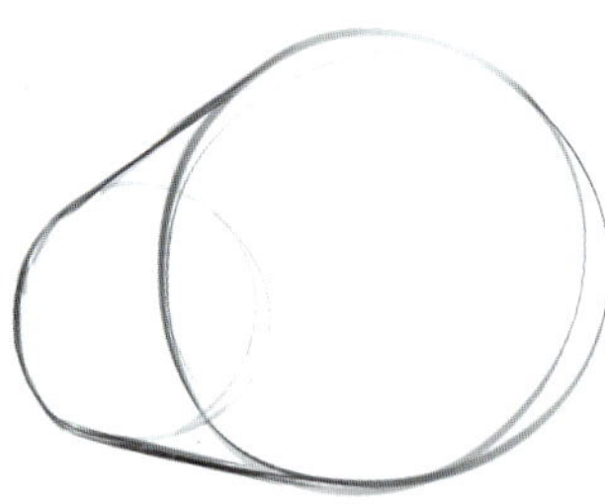

Connect the contour lines.

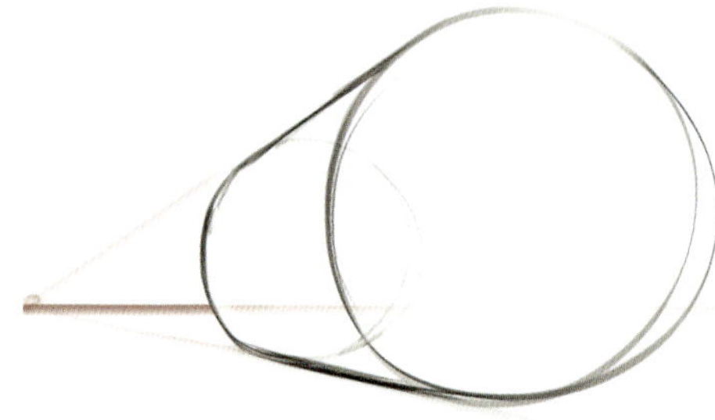

A foreshortened object is easily mappable with a simple vanishing point and a few perspective lines.

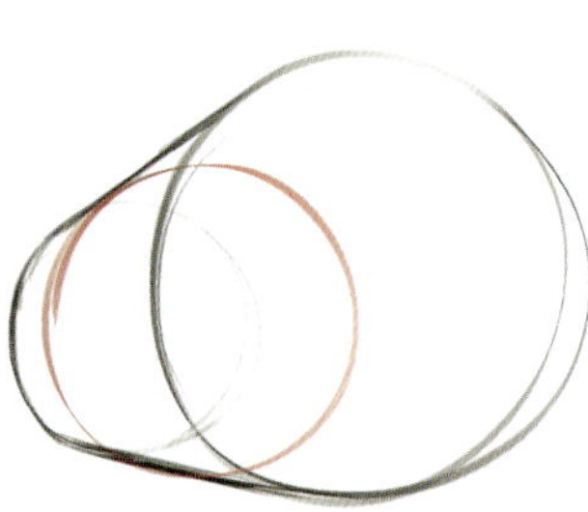

Finding the middle of a foreshortened object can be tricky. It favors the far end.

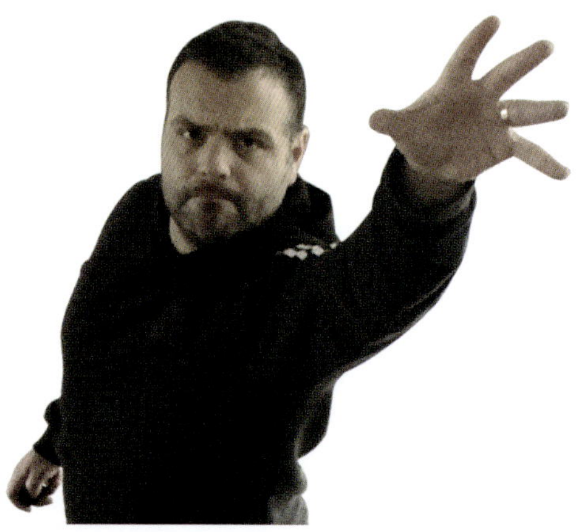

A pose with a foreshortened arm. Superheroes are often depicted this way, due to the visual drama that foreshortening brings.

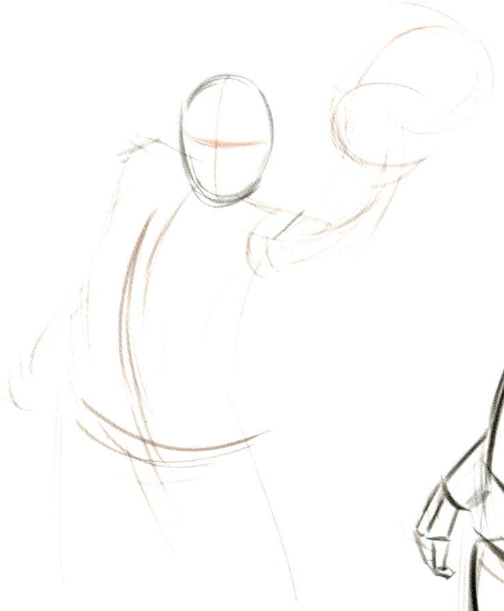

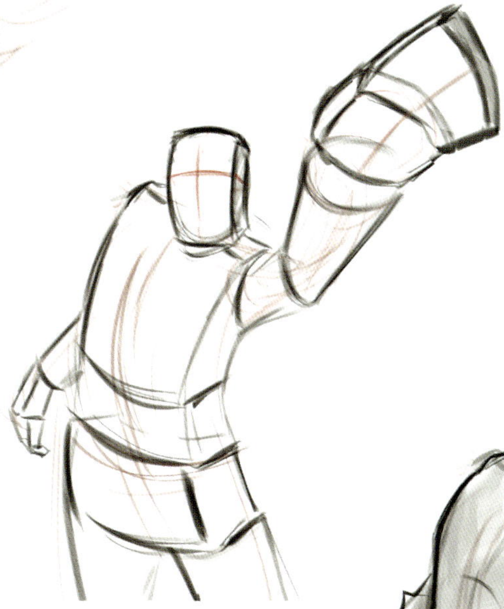

Build the figure with boxes and cylinders. Apply the cylinder example from the previous page to map out the foreshortening on the left arm. Also notice I've completed the hips and added part of the legs, which the reference does not show. It is a good habit to do this, thinking literally outside the box.

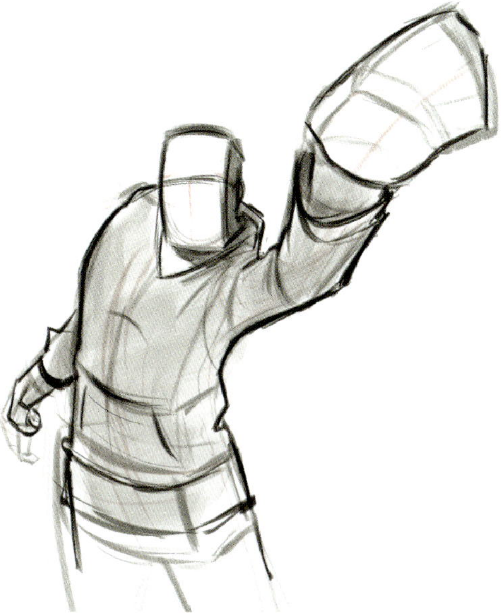

As usual, begin with a gesture. Gesture is not the tool most suited to capturing foreshortening, but you can landmark the different sizes of the cylinder's end-caps as well as estimate the size of the close hand compared to, say, the head, which is what I'm doing here.

Lay shapes over the top to complete the drawing. Notice the minor positional changes made to the gesture drawing. The addition of the sternum helps establish the center of the torso. Keep the head and hands as boxes, as to not allow their inherent challenges to enter at this stage of your study. Lastly, the tone is only there to separate the overall dark shape of the sweater.

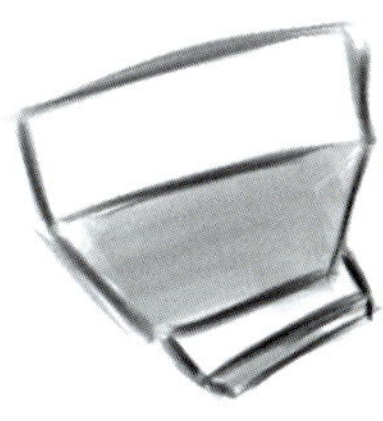

You can use basic forms to invent dynamic, foreshortened poses that would have been previously impossible.

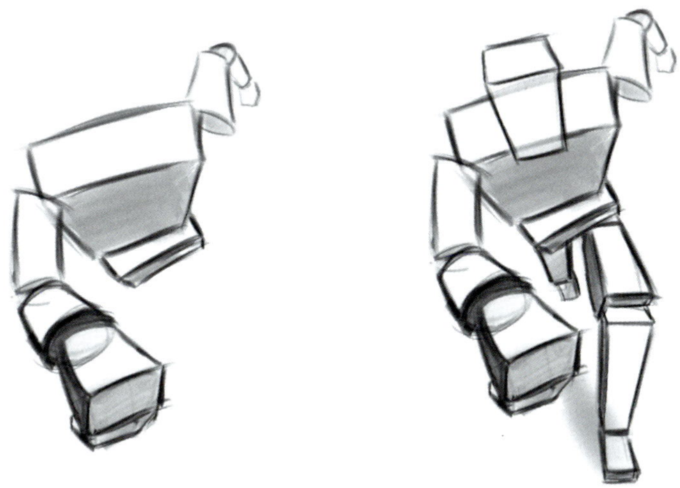

Guide to Thoughtful Shape Design, **Part II**

Now that we're *circling* back to shapes (pun intended!), let's add to our list of things that will help them look interesting. Remember, "interesting" is not the same as more complicated. Often what we're looking to do is keep our shapes as simple while finding ways to make their *contours* feel unexpected.

COMPLEX VERSUS SIMPLE

Let's look at the foreshortened arm shape from the drawing on the previous page.

Notice how the top side of the shape can be considered more complex than the bottom side.

That's another shape design principle that helps keep your shapes simple and increase their interest enough to satisfy the subject matter. It's the same relationship as squash and stretch. One side does one thing forcing the other side to do the opposite. Find this over and over in good drawings!

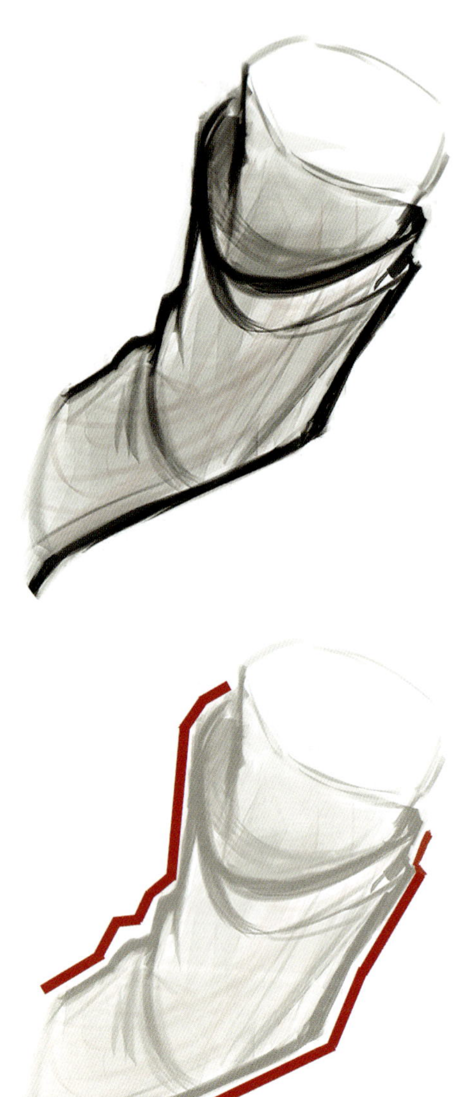

There are more lines and changes of direction to the top side of the shape, versus fewer at the bottom side.

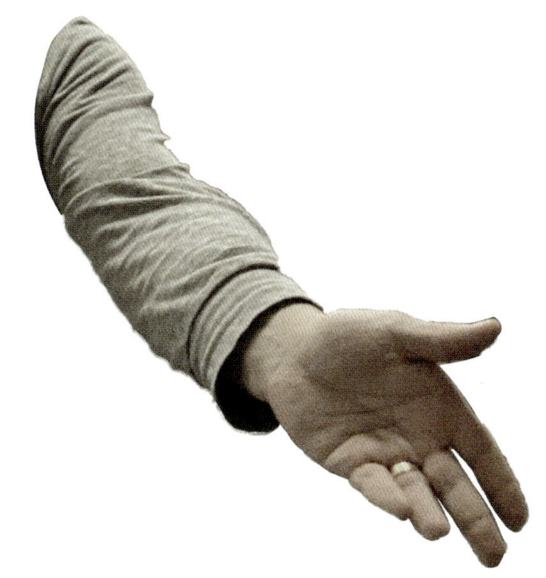

OFFSET SYMMETRY

We discussed this before, but now we see where it's used. The first step is to look for it in nature as it's all over human anatomy.

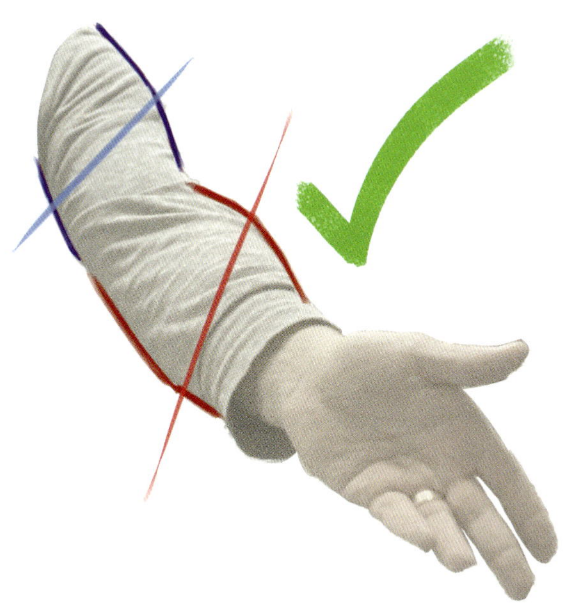

Draw a straight line connecting the widest points of each section. These lines will almost always make interesting offset angles rather than parallel ones.

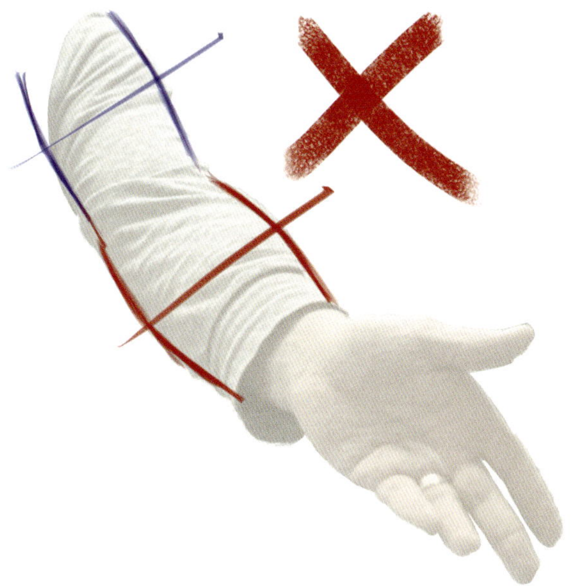

Not like this!

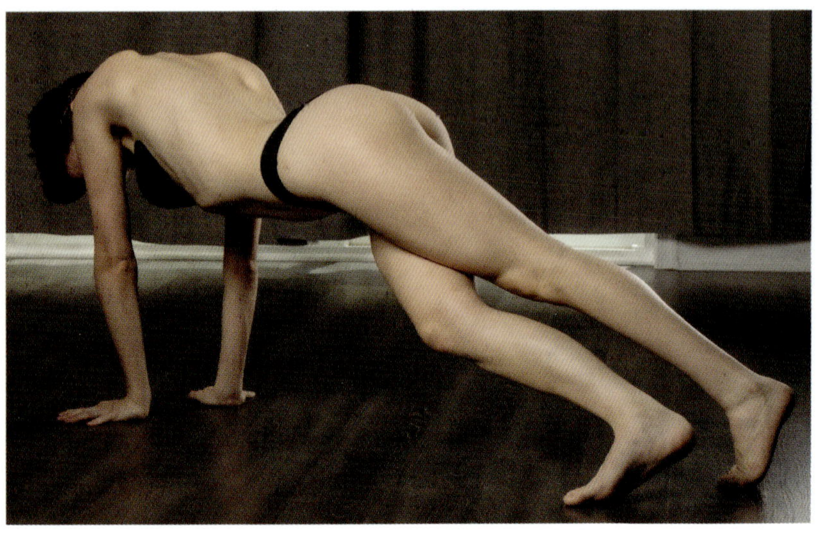

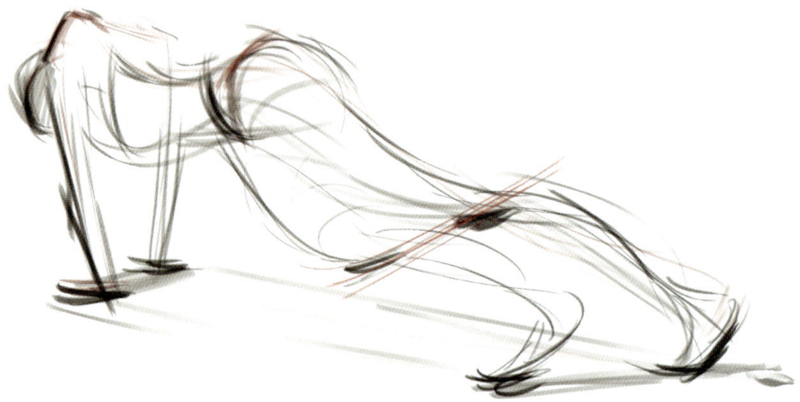

Let's revisit this pose and begin where we left off with the gesture drawing.

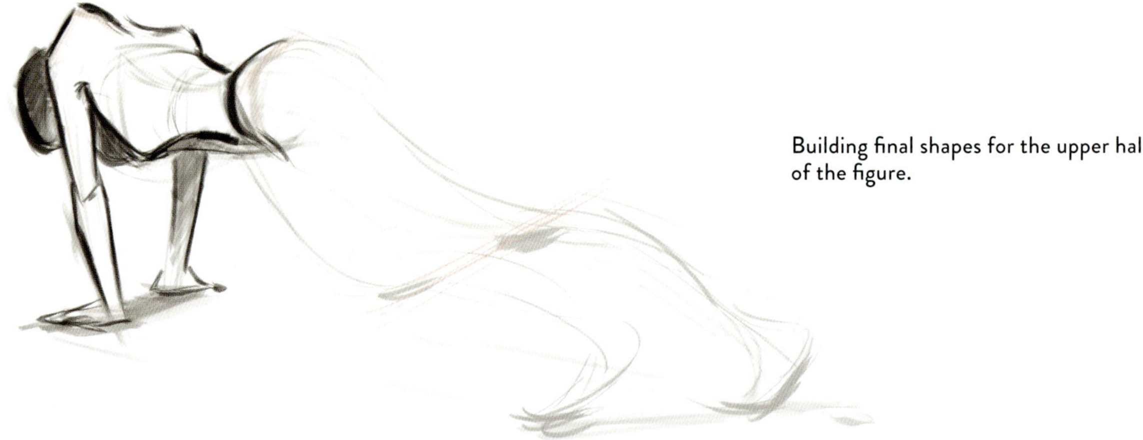

Building final shapes for the upper half of the figure.

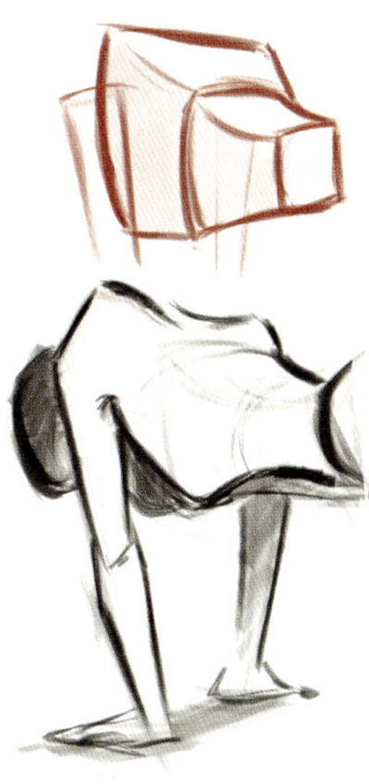

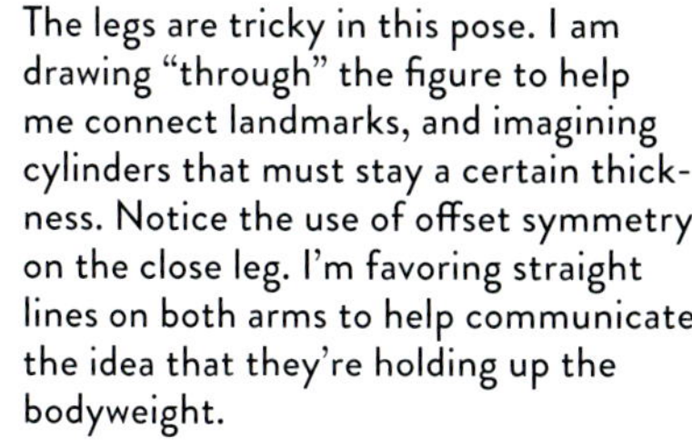

The legs are tricky in this pose. I am drawing "through" the figure to help me connect landmarks, and imagining cylinders that must stay a certain thickness. Notice the use of offset symmetry on the close leg. I'm favoring straight lines on both arms to help communicate the idea that they're holding up the bodyweight.

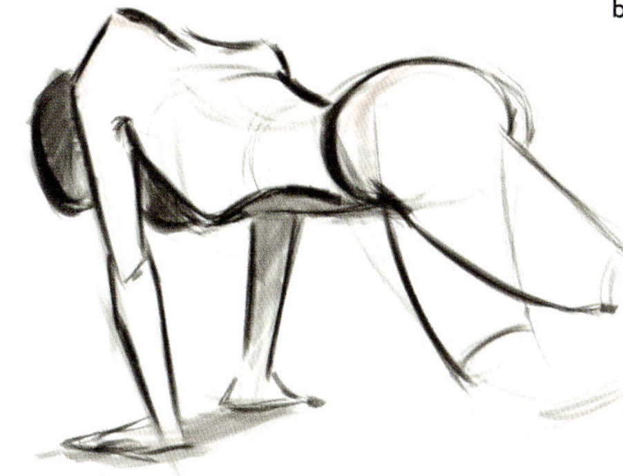

A shape is two-dimensional, but you're using simplified forms to help visualize space. In this case, I'm imagining these tapered boxes fitting into each other to form the rib cage and waist.

Using negative space (blue) to help map out the position of the legs. My gesture drawing was not accurate here, though I do want to maintain the nice flow my gesture had!

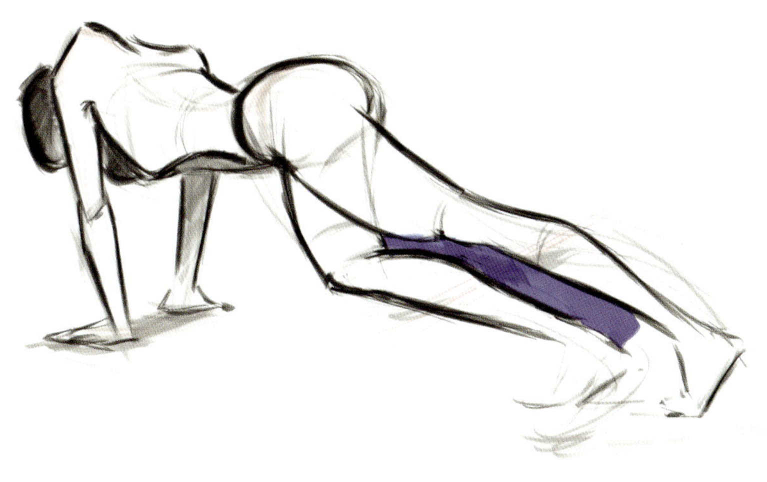

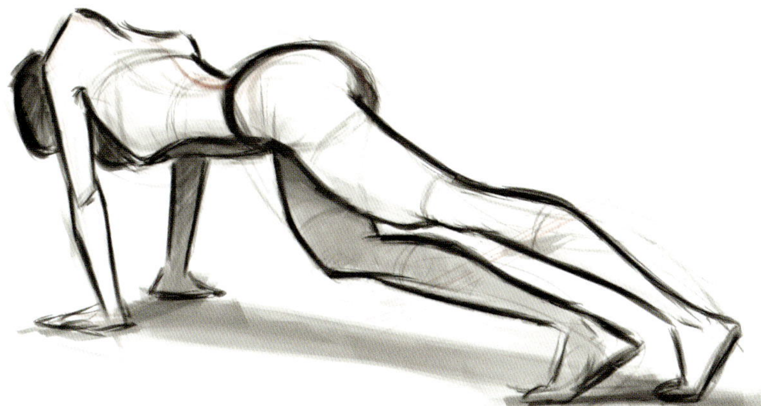

The finished figure drawing. Notice the flowy, almost unbroken gestural rhythms using C-curves, S-curves, and Straights for the legs' contours, to help maintain the flow from the gesture drawing. Another shading trick is to throw a quick tone over the far limb.

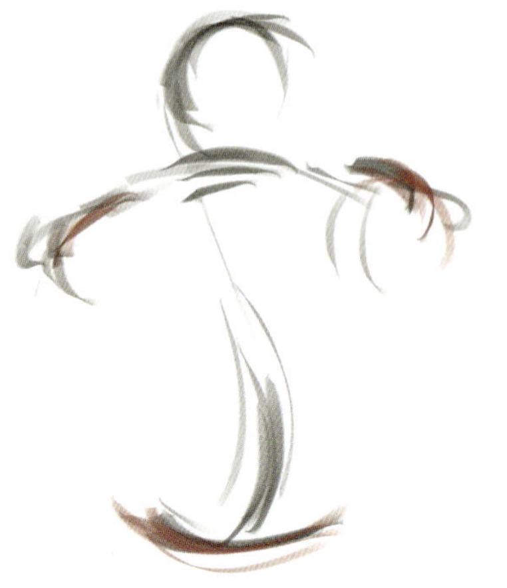

The more poses you draw from reference, the more of a mental library you'll build up. Once you've seen and studied enough angles and poses, you'll be able to begin inventing the figure from imagination. The process you follow should be the same.

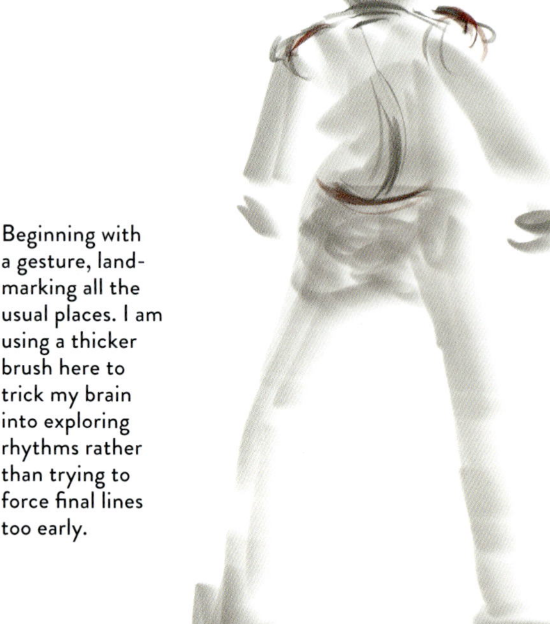

Beginning with a gesture, land-marking all the usual places. I am using a thicker brush here to trick my brain into exploring rhythms rather than trying to force final lines too early.

Using the gesture drawing to carry through to some box and cylinder forms. Having some fun playing with proportion here.

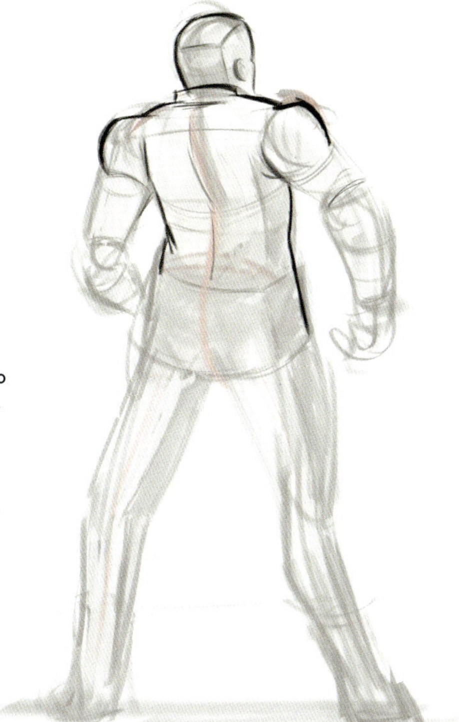

Fading the gesture back into the white canvas to help add the shapes over top. If working traditionally, this can be done with a sheet of vellum.

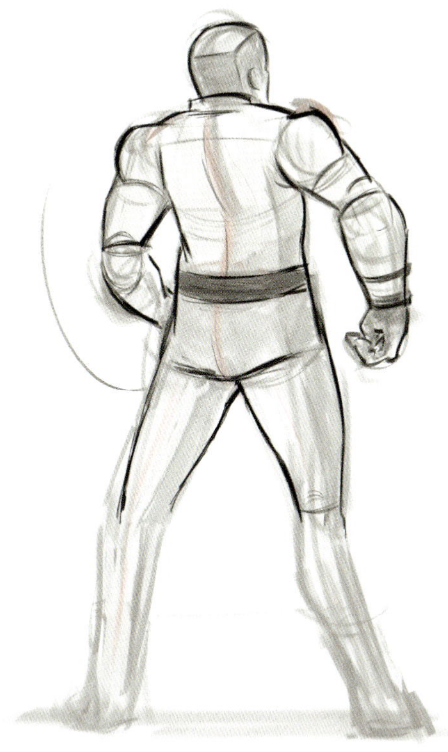

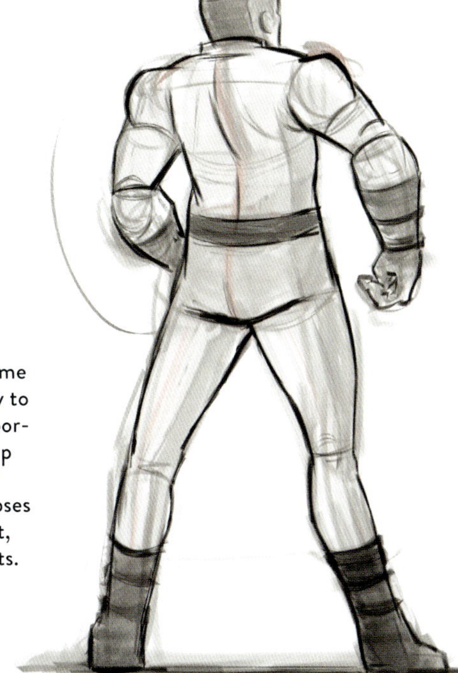

Deciding on shapes. If adding costume elements, try to seize the opportunity to wrap them around forms as ellipses such as a belt, cuffs, or boots.

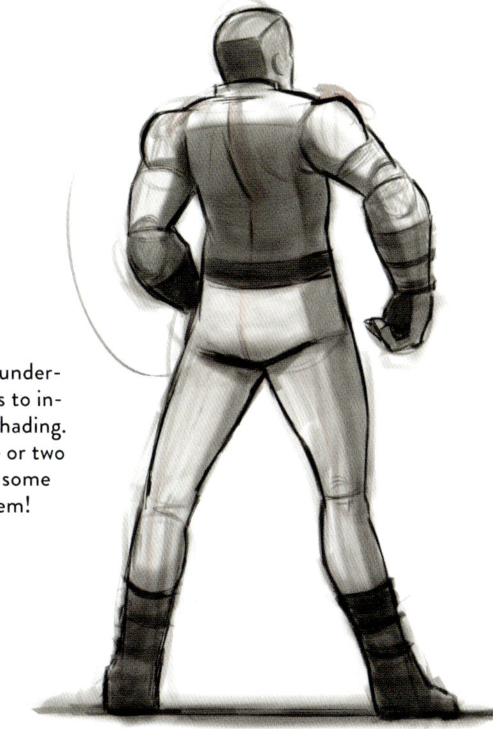

Using the underlying boxes to inform the shading. Pick a side or two and throw some shade on 'em!

Weight, **Balance,** and Movement

We've all seen babies fall over because their heads are so heavy in comparison to their body. Adults need to control their mass or else they'll begin to topple, too. Because the head is connected to the spine, I like to think of the head as the leader of the body's mass. Where it goes, the momentum goes.

A pose that is in balance almost always has a head positioned somewhere in between the two feet . . .

. . . or the head is off-center, but there is a limb in place to catch the falling weight.

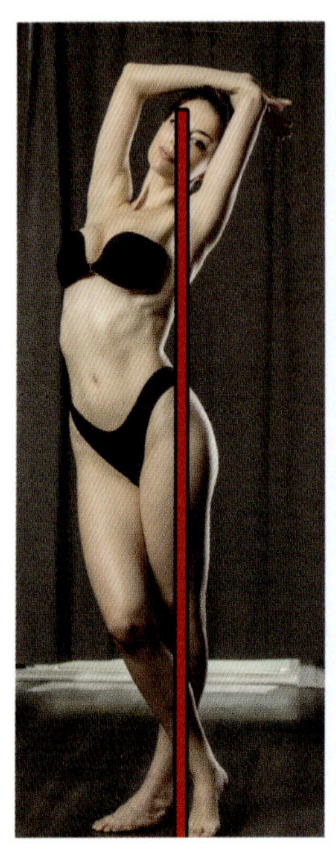
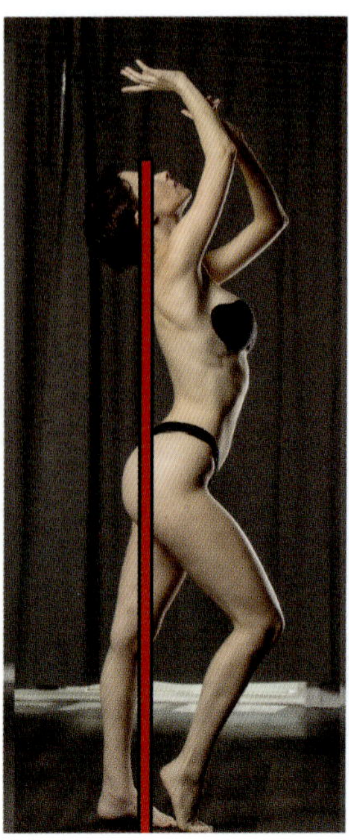
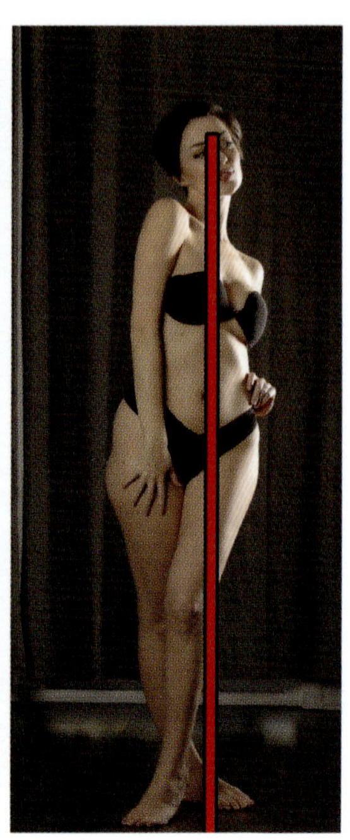

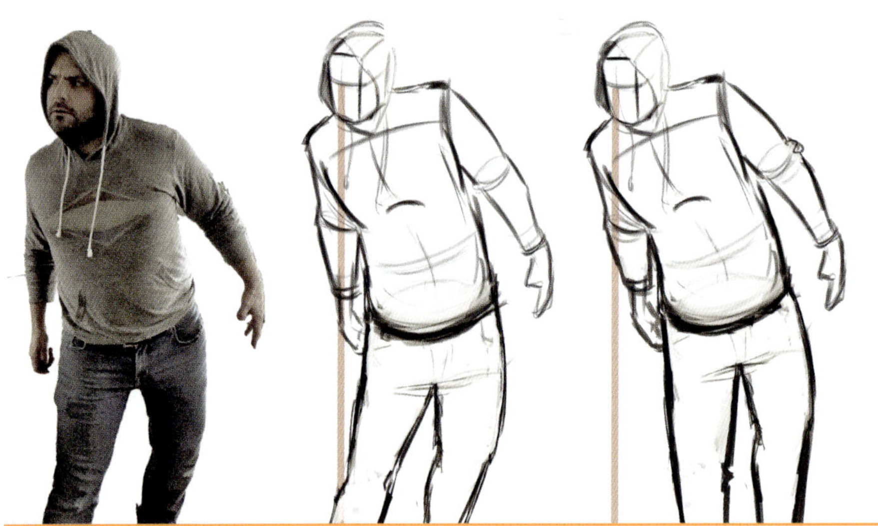

In this series, the first drawing replicates the reference, and is in balance, as the head lies just inside the right foot which I've intentionally left out of frame because I want you to imagine it! The subject can stand there indefinitely.

The second drawing pushes the head farther away from the center of mass, which disrupts the balance and makes that pose look like it's in motion. The drawing captures what it feels like a brief moment in time.

Designing Your Drawing

I'm proud to show you a series of drawings by my friend Brian Wong. If there was an award given to the person who draws more than anyone else, Brain would be a top consideration. He starts his day drawing a page of characters in different poses.

I always enjoy looking at Brian's drawings and his gestures and shape choices. You can count the number of line changes he uses in any given shape and they seem to never repeat.

It's worthwhile to study from cartoony work as much as the human figure.

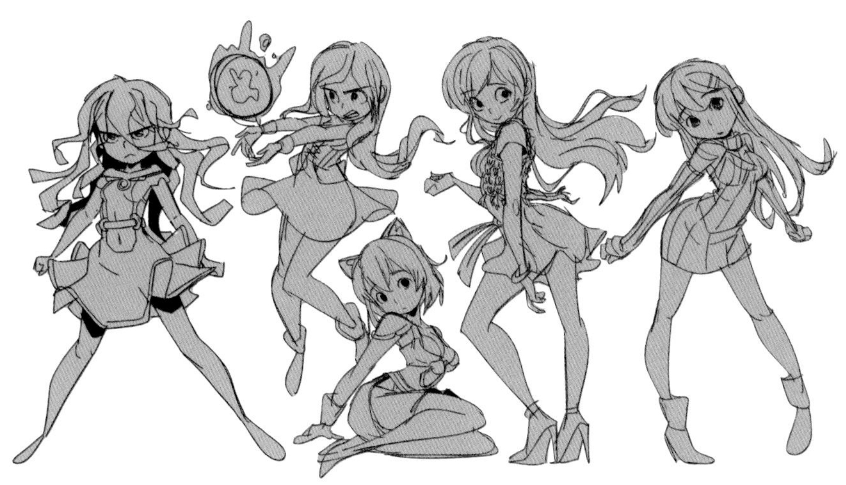

At his storyboarding work, Brian Wong probably draws a hundred pictures daily!

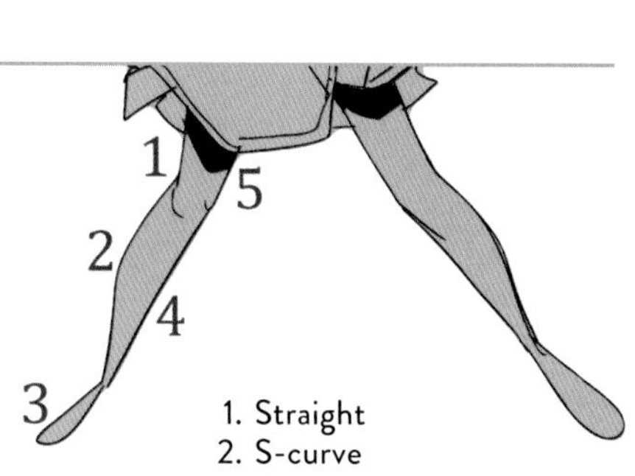

1. Straight
2. S-curve
3. C-curve
4. Straight (long)
5. Straight (short)

Working out the gesture. If there are major clothing elements, like the skirt, I'll usually include those in the landmarking process.

When you study this drawing and draw these shapes one by one, you'll see how every shape is maximized. There's no default symmetry and no changes in direction of line that doesn't add something to the design or interest of a shape. There's no repetition, and yet everything feels like it flows. That is the mark of professional work.

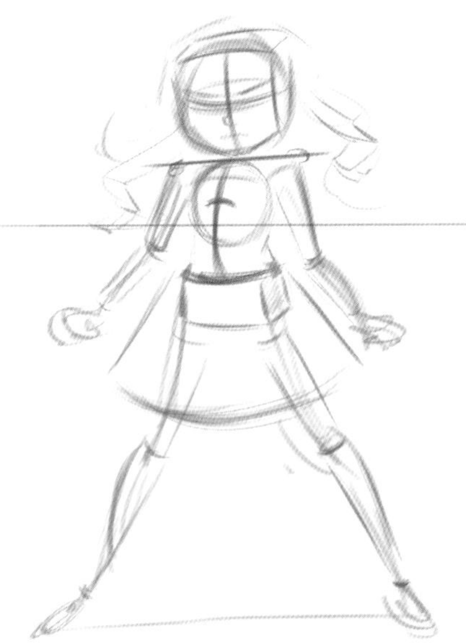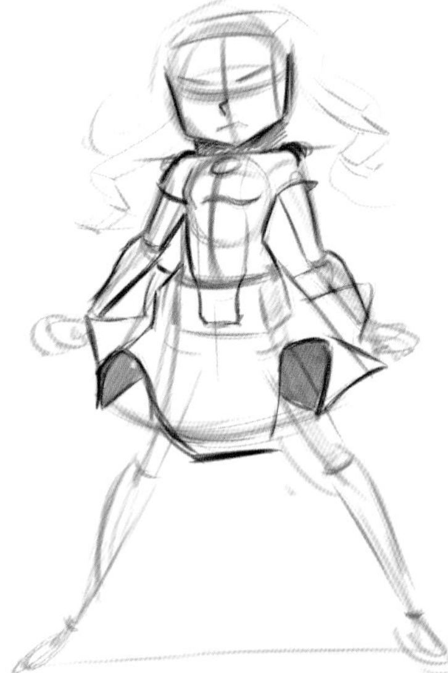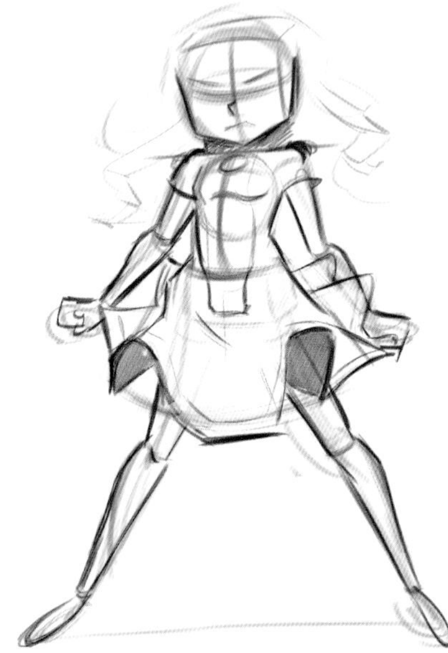

Building the 3D forms. Notice I'm not concerned with the motions of the skirt here. That would be too big a jump in complexity. I work my way there with shorter steps.

It's helpful to draw underneath everything, because now I can focus on simple shape design. See how Brian uses T-connections and cleverly avoids tangents.

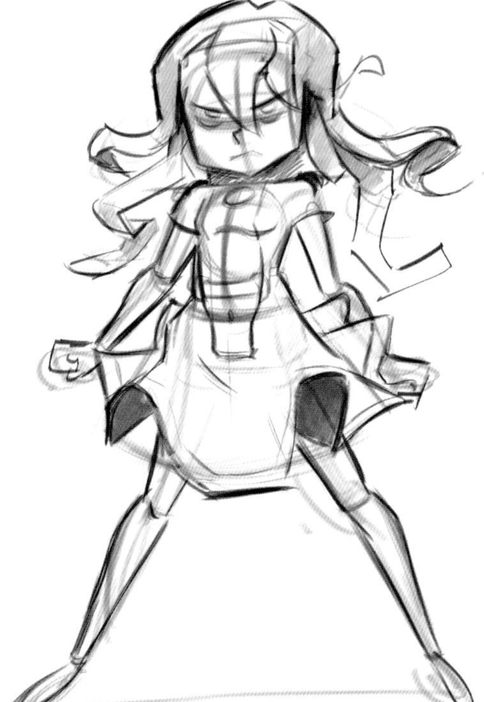

My finished study of Brian Wong's drawing.

Scan to watch a tutorial.

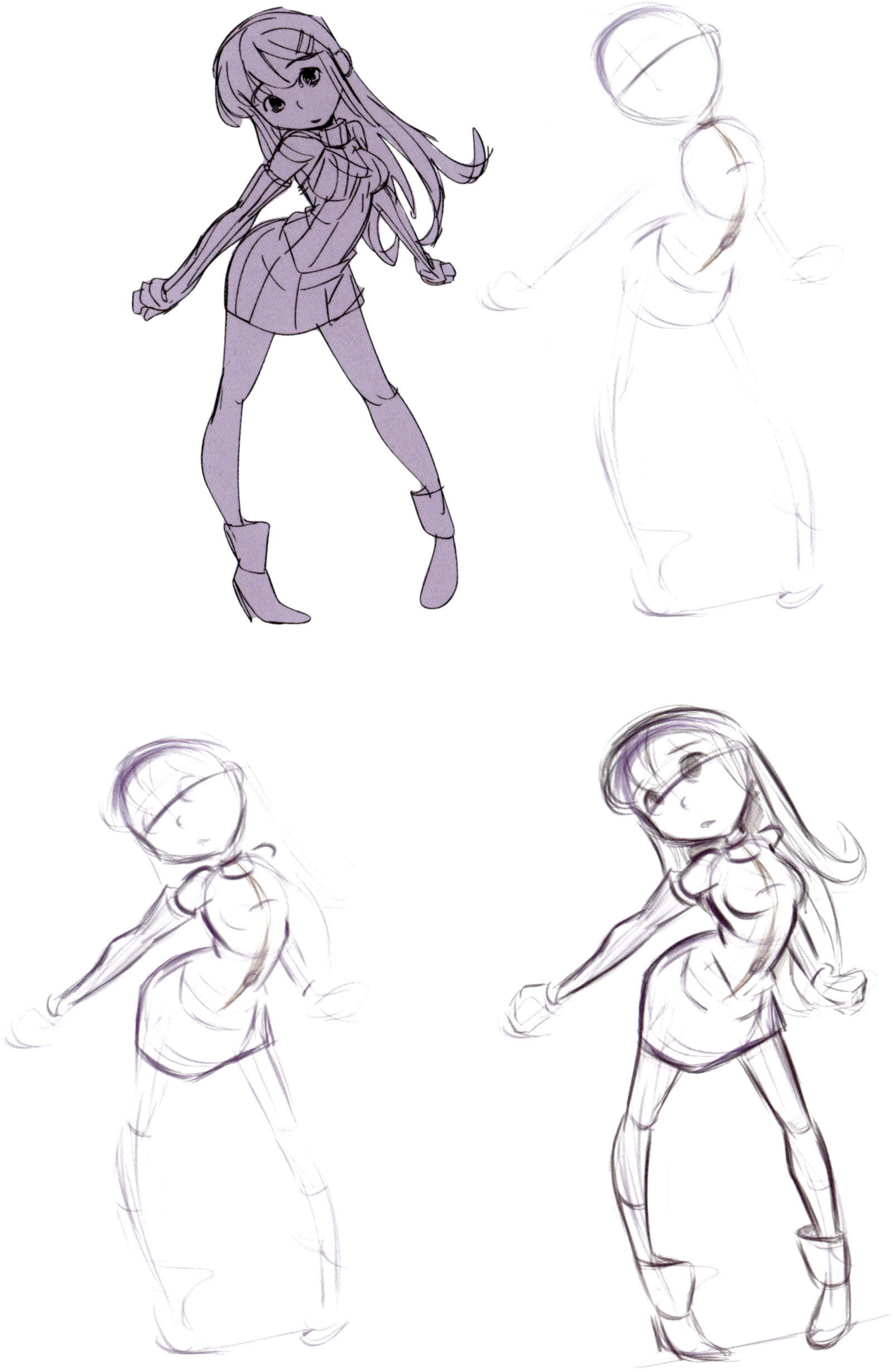

Trying another one.

REFERENCE MEETS INVENTION

Another great way to bridge the gap into character work is doing your study from the model but changing the proportions and shapes to be more caricatured. Caricature is when you take the characteristics of your subject and exaggerate them. If a shape is thin? Make it thinner. Long? Make it longer. Wide? Make it wider, and so on! Let's try it.

Scan to watch a tutorial.

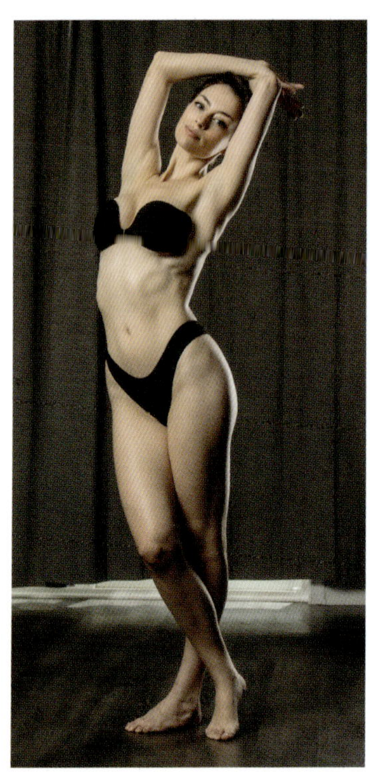

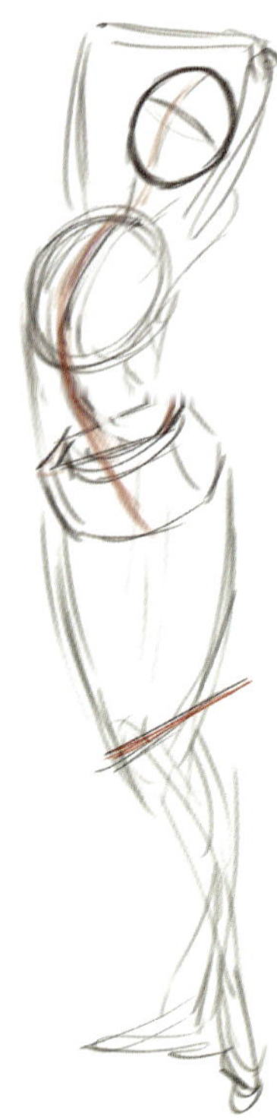

Push the gesture. Make the C-curve wider, make the rib cage mass smaller, bring the hips closer, make the legs longer. Test your ideas in the gesture stage!

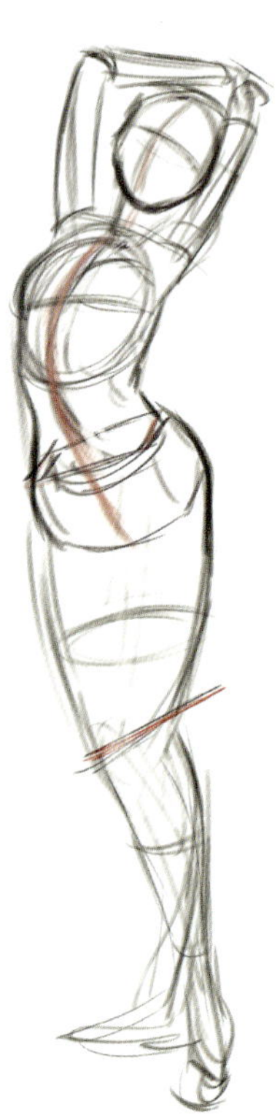

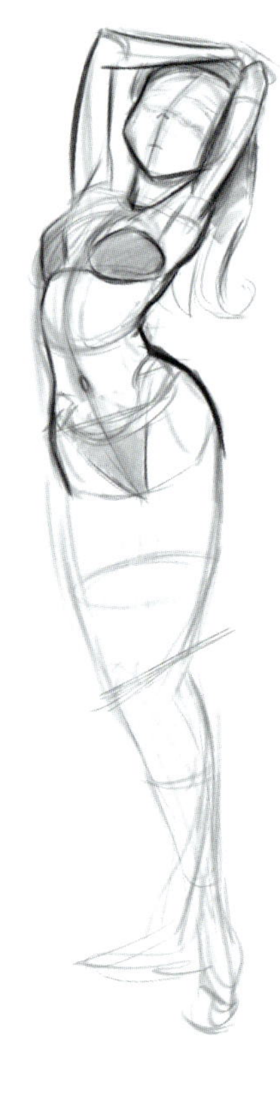

Adding the geometry. I'm simplifying both legs into one mermaidlike form to design the figure.

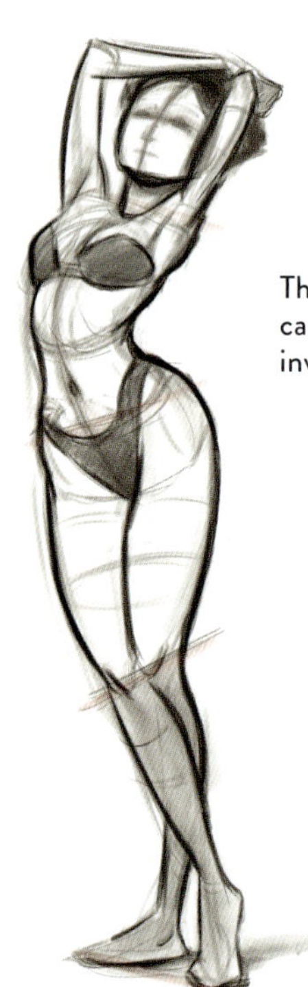

The finished caricatured figure invention.

ASSIGNMENTS

In these assignments you'll be working with images you like. You can collect them in an app like Pinterest, in a folder on your computer, or in a paper folder.

ASSIGNMENT #1

This is where we begin to apply what we've learned so far to art we like … so first, go find some art you like! The pieces can be in any style. Save them into a big "inspiration" folder that you'll always add to.

ASSIGNMENT #2

Using your inspiration art samples and working with the usual vellum-style tracing method, accurately trace out the silhouette of a character drawing you like. Fill it in with a Sharpie or uniform digital brush. Analyze what kind of shape decisions the artist has made and how shapes have been designed to be interesting.

ASSIGNMENT #3

Pick out some drawings of characters that really display an attitude. Using all the tools and procedures we've learned so far, try to imagine yourself as the original artist, and how you would go about mapping out such a drawing. Remember that what we're learning in this book are simply tools, which means you pull them out when you need them—you don't always have to follow the same process!

ASSIGNMENT #4

Find a photo or drawing of a character in a pose and try to find ways of pushing that pose to be even more dramatic. This usually involves noticing the "direction" the pose is headed and continuing on that path; for example, a lean becomes a more angled lean, a subtle tilt of the head becomes a more pronounced one. Note that it's totally ok to change the overall body language the pose communicates. In fact, you probably will do this naturally, as people are very sensitive to the most minor adjustments of body language. Complete this assignment in gesture form, as well as a more fully fleshed-out or constructed drawing.

6 Constructing the Head

We're going to take a break from the full body for a moment and focus on the head. There may be nothing more exhilarating than drawing the head, be it for a portrait, a character design, a caricature, or anything in between. The human head may be the most beloved to many artists because, well, we're all human.

The head is also a dastardly difficult form to understand. Thankfully, artists before us have taken it upon themselves to create accurate, simplified proxies for study. I've found it most helpful to study the head and facial features as a series of flat planes.

Planes make plain (no pun intended) the changes in direction of form.

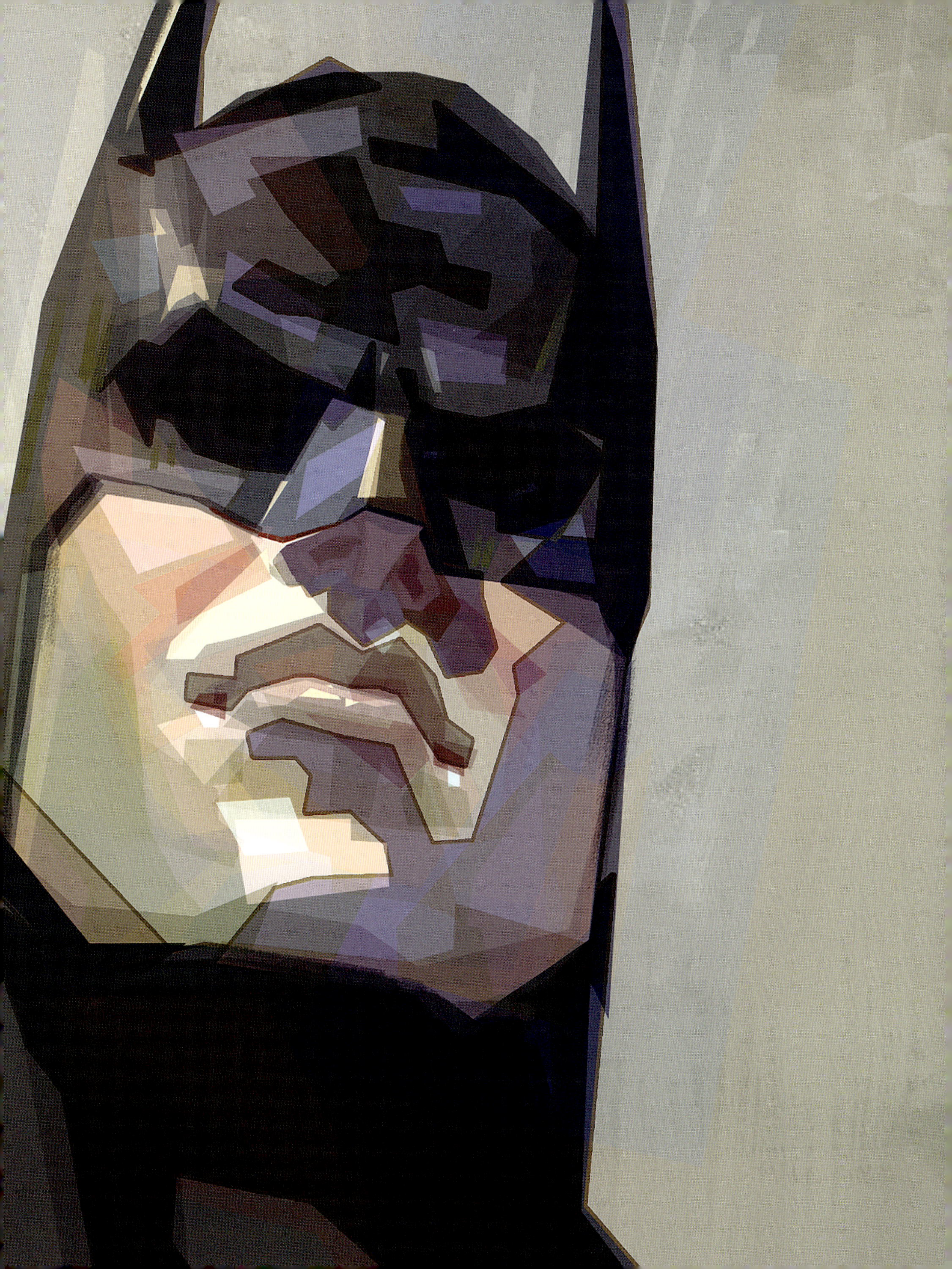

The **Head** Is a Box

To begin with, the head is essentially a box. A box has clear planes including a front, sides, back, top, and bottom, where each plane change is distinct.

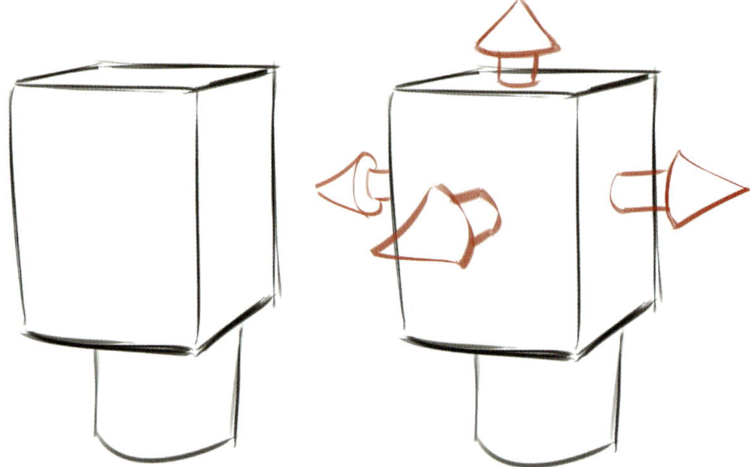

The key idea with the box is to understand the concept of orientation of planes.

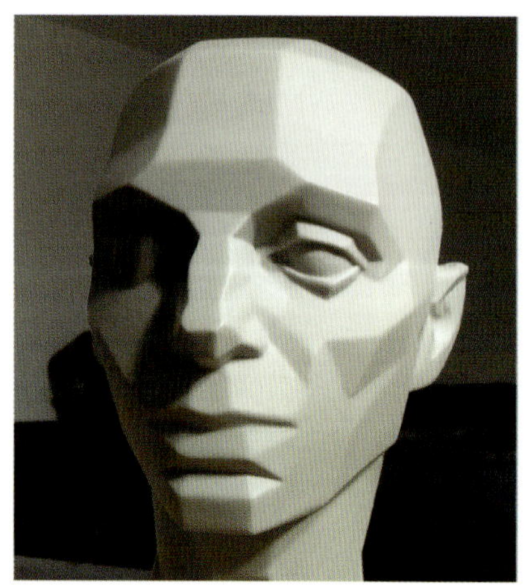

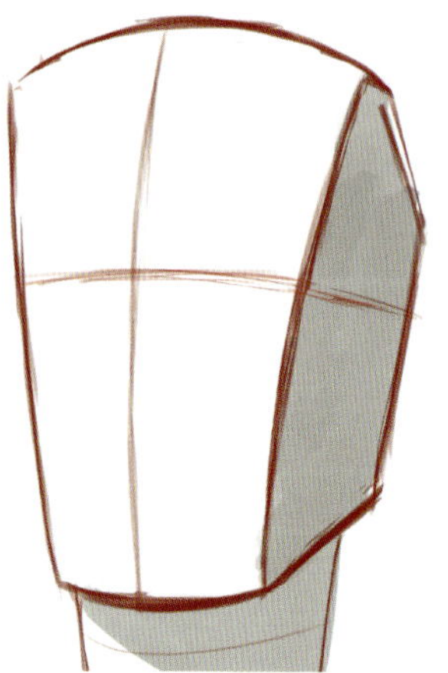

If we taper that box a bit, so it is wider at the top, narrower at the bottom, we get a step closer to the human head.

Scan to watch a tutorial.

Next, notch out a little shelf around the middle of the front face. The plane cuts inward dramatically, then rolls back out smoothly. This relatively simple form change accomplishes the protruding brow, the inset eye sockets, and the cheekbones. I also adjusted the angle of the upper-left contour to taper the forehead inward as it moves toward the top of the head.

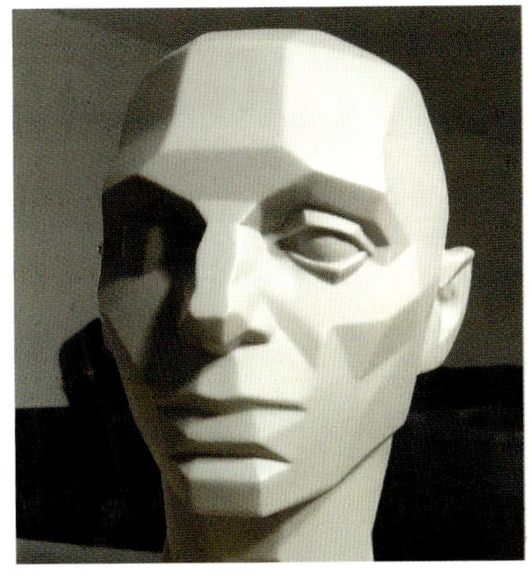

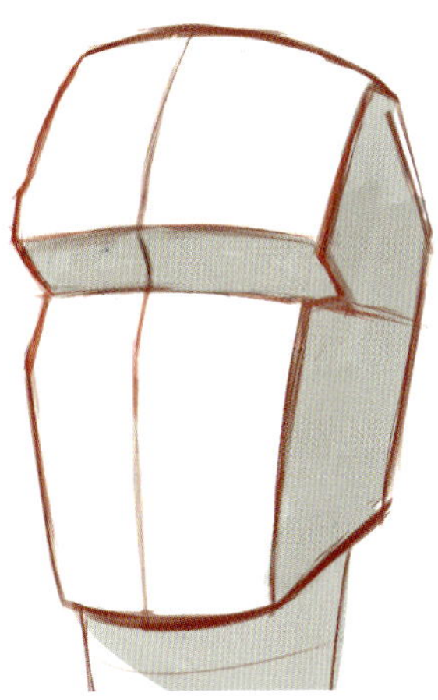

The head immediately takes shape! Notice our plane changes are starting to get more intricate than those of a simple box.

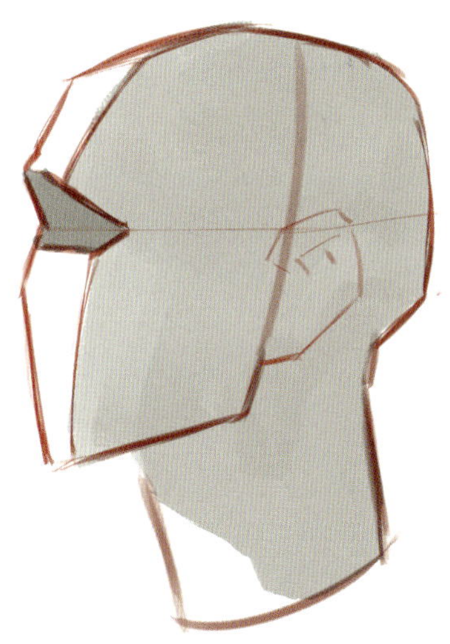

It is a very common mistake to not extend the cranium back far enough. Remember: The cranium houses the brain!

From the side, the form looks like this. Note that the jawline is roughly halfway to the back of the cranium, and the ear sits just behind the jaw.

Practice drawing this form from various angles. Keep it boxlike, overall.

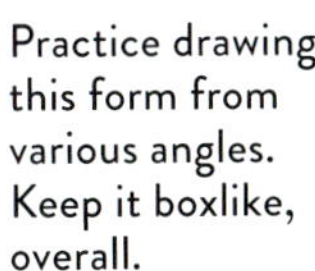

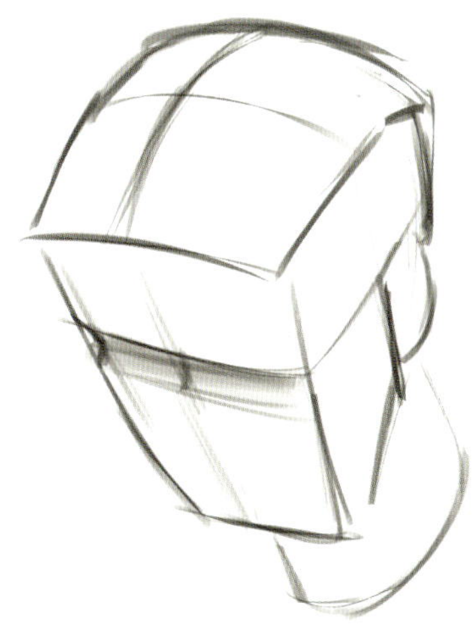

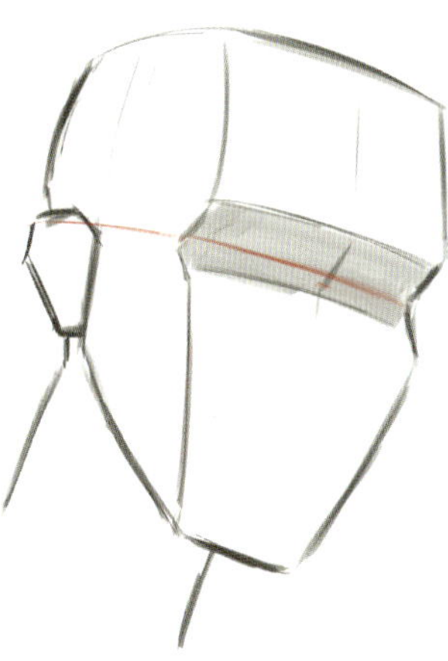

Building the **Facial Features**

Drawing facial features is an area that beginner artists tend to struggle with. It's easy to make features look flat, or like they're "pasted" onto the head instead of a natural part of its structure.

The secret is to treat the facial features as a series of boxlike planes. Understanding the orientation of planes is the key to getting a believable sense of dimension and maintaining a sense of solid structure throughout. Only *after* that are we able to apply shapes and design!

THE BROW, EYE SOCKETS, AND CHEEKBONES

This three-way combo makes for intricate form. The planes all point in distinctly different directions: The cheekbone planes point *upward*, contrasting the brow's planes which point *frontward*, the side of the head (turning at the temple) which points to the *side*, and the eye sockets, which point *inward*.

Practice drawing this form from various angles. For now, allow the cheekbones to gradually taper downward toward the chin.

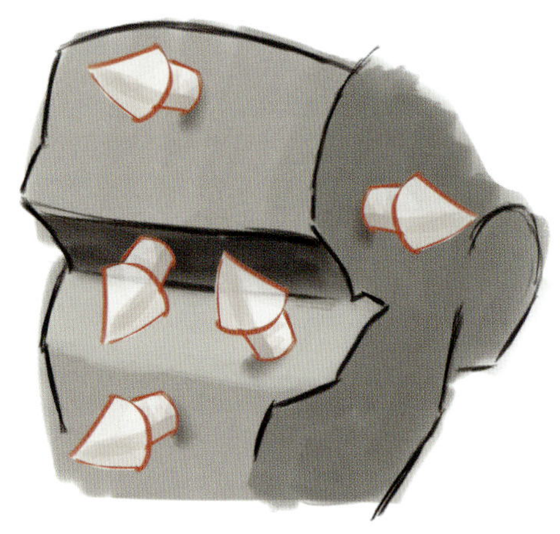

Various angles of these three key components of the head. The goal is to be fully aware of the planes' orientation in space from feature to feature.

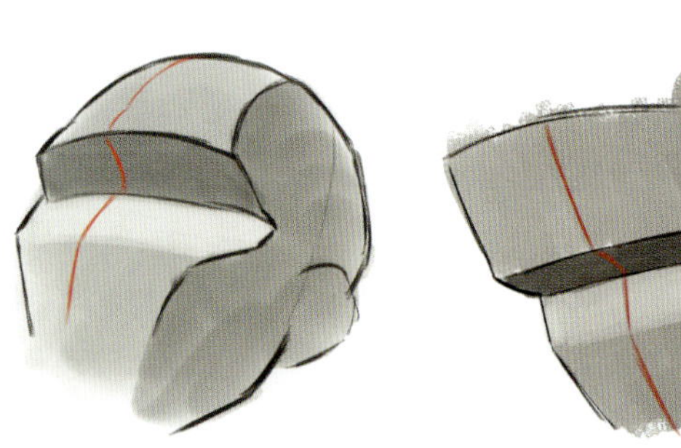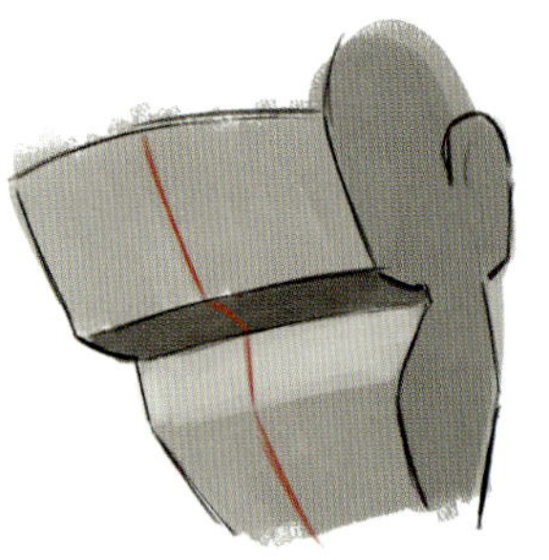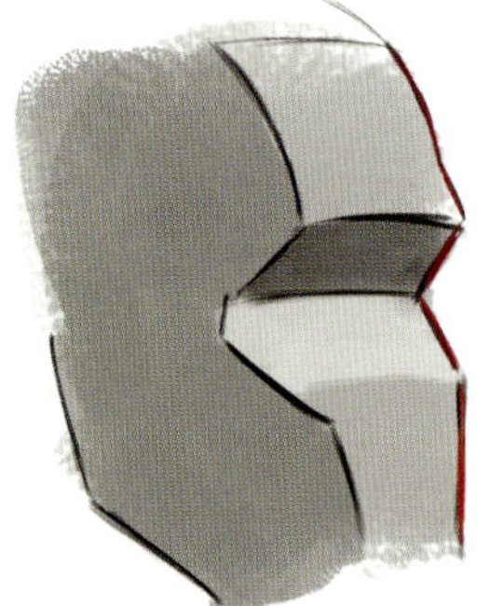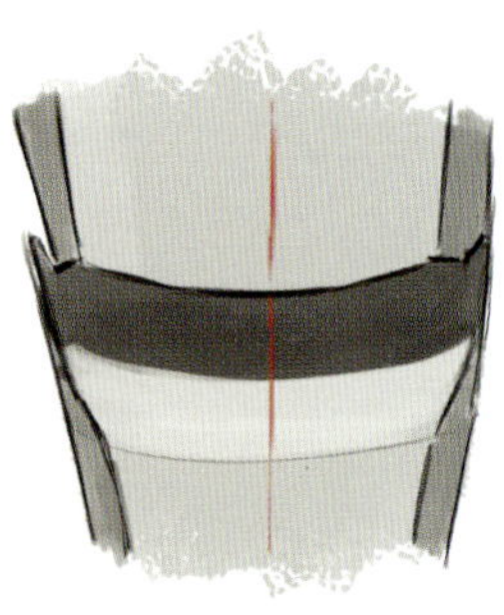

It's always good to include a midline cross-contour (shown in red) which ensures you're understanding the form's topology and perspective. Note that in a profile view, the red line doubles as the contour!

THE NOSE

The nose is a deceptively complex form with lots of little planes. Similarly to the head, the nose is best learned by working from a boxy structure.

Now we add resolution, primarily to the underside of the nose. This involves a gradually tapering form, as the ball of the nose turns. We also balloon out the side plane, which creates room for the "wing" of the nose.

Adding more resolution to our form. Note the addition of the *glabella*, the wedgelike piece at the top of the nose, which interfaces with the brow.

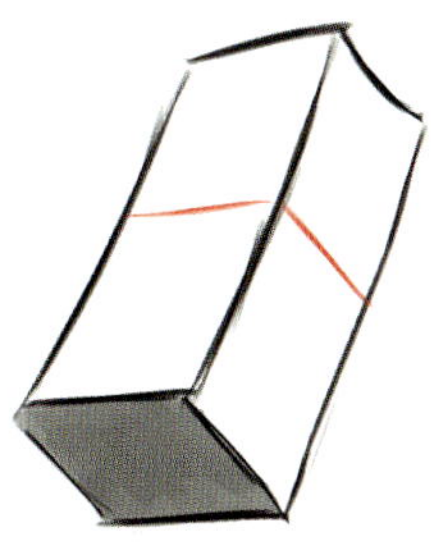

An elongated box to start with.

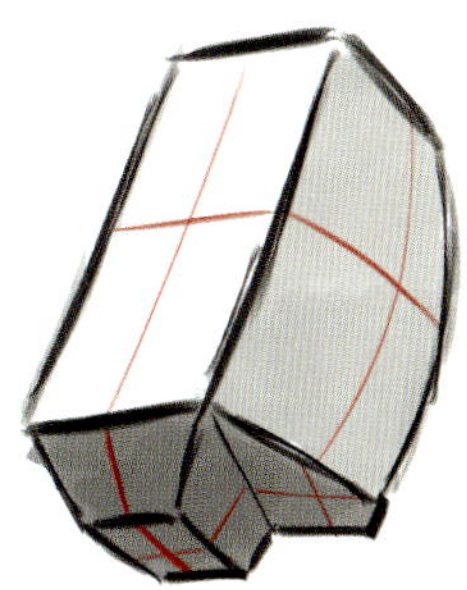

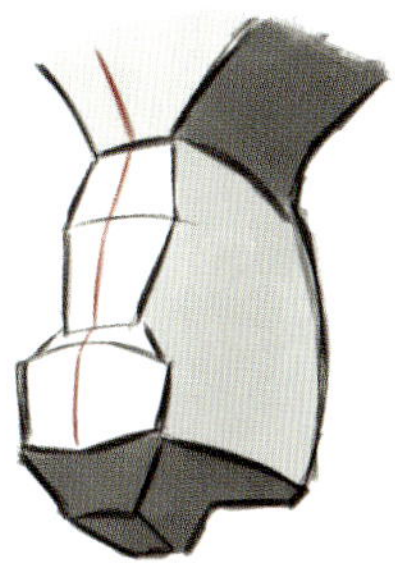

This diagram also shows the arrangement of Average Light, Halftone, and Average Shadow. (See Chapter 7 for more information.)

Adding the final information, the planes of the nose look like this.

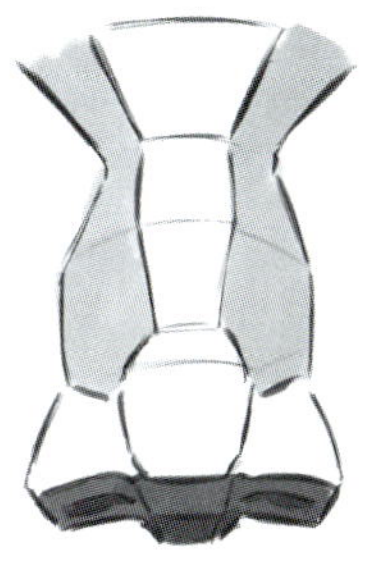

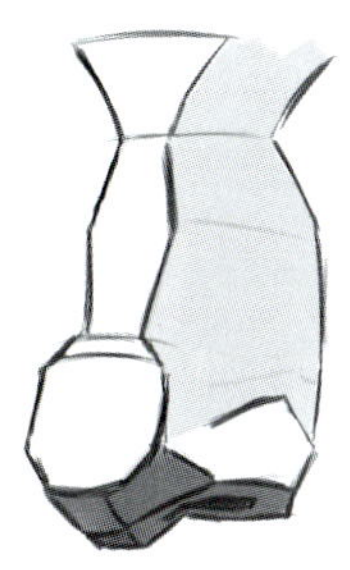

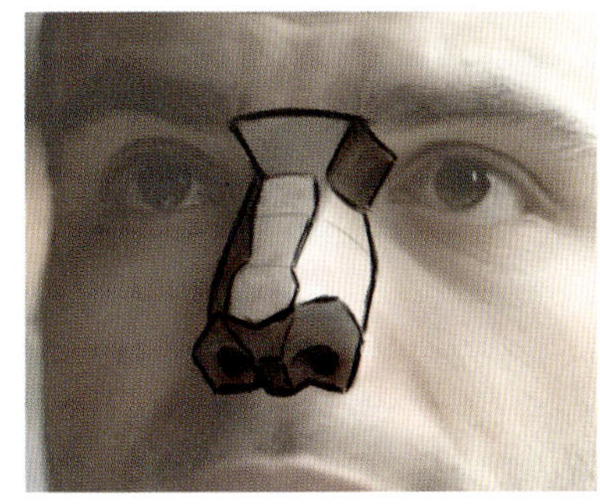

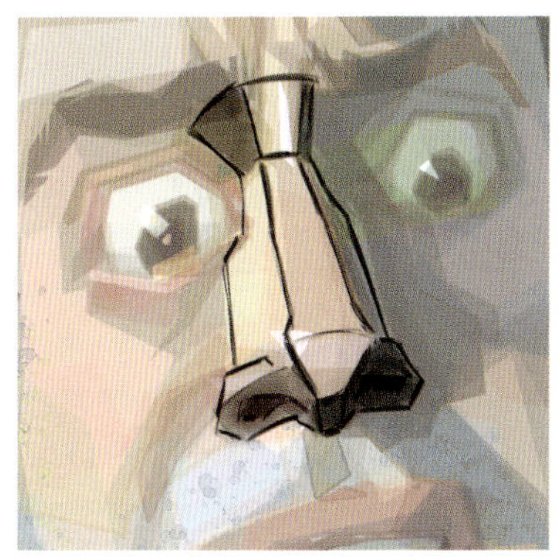

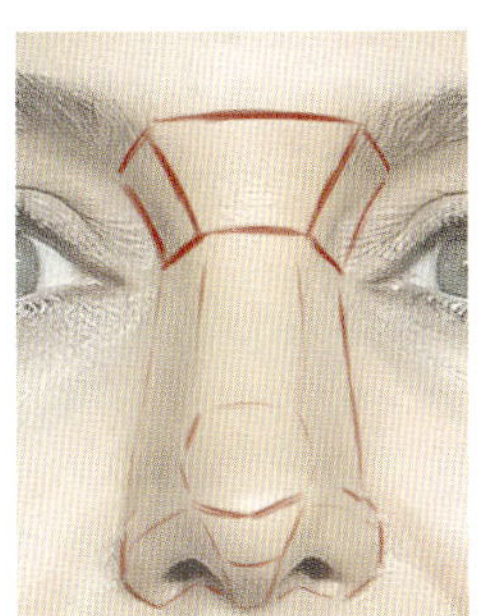

The glabella locking the nose in place in the middle of the brow.

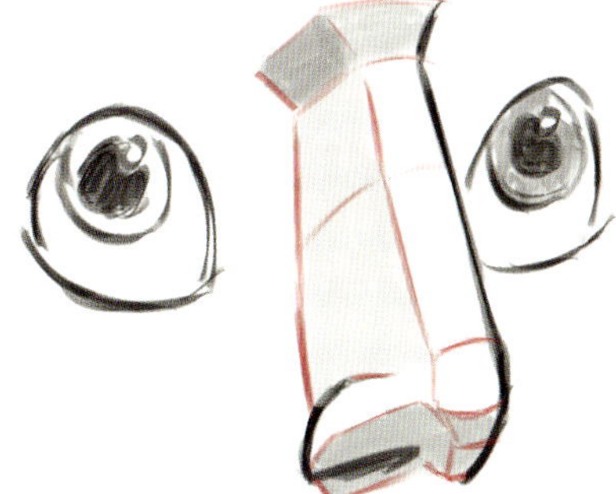

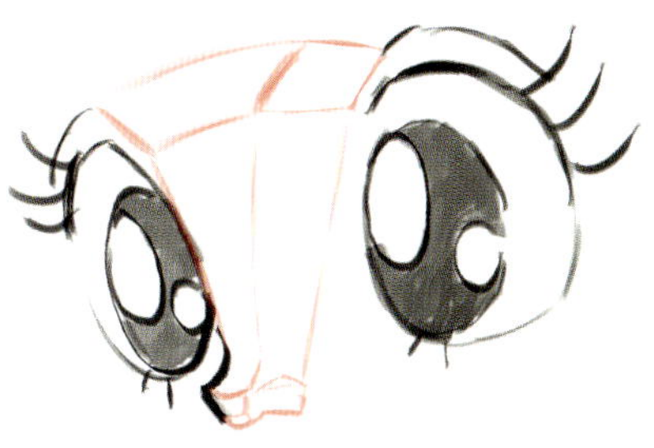

Noses in various styles. The planes are always spatially present even if the lines themselves are aesthetically or stylistically omitted.

THE MOUTH IS EASY AS 1-2-3

It's a common error to draw the mouth as a flat plane on the head.
But if you imagine a set of dentures, or perhaps your old retainer,
you know how cylinderlike the form actually is.

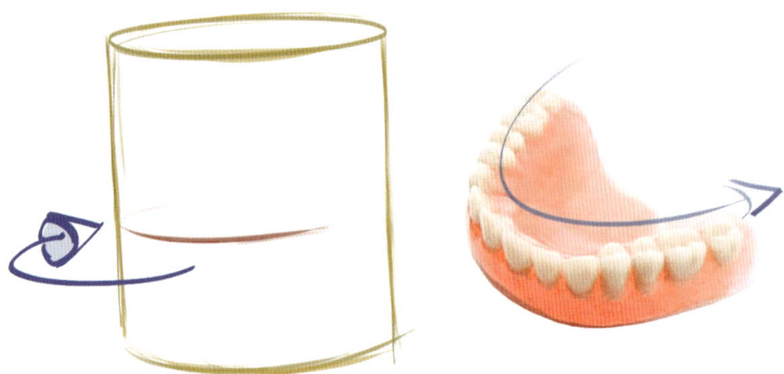

Keep in mind that the mouth isn't only lips! Anatomically, it's the
whole "muzzle" area of the face including the space above the lips,
the lips themselves, and the area below the lips above the chin.
These areas are structurally connected via the overall cylindrical
form they're built on, as well as a sequence of three planes.

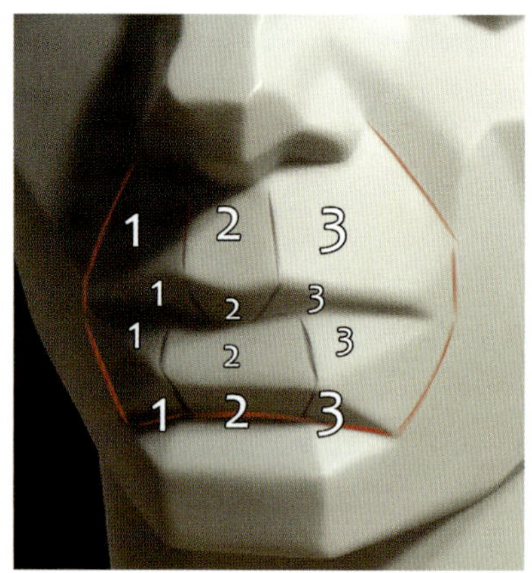

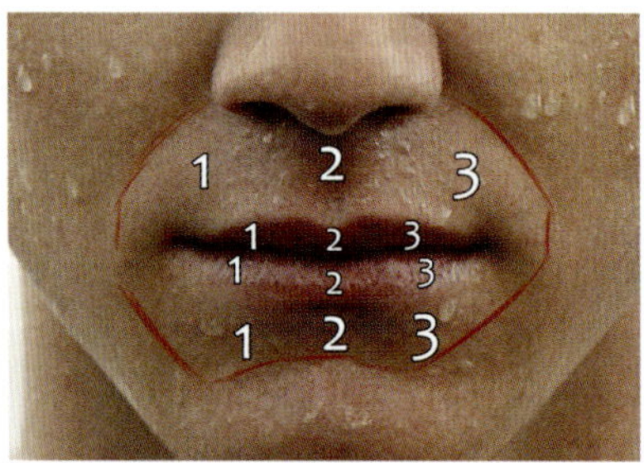

The red outline represents the perimeter
of the mouth area.

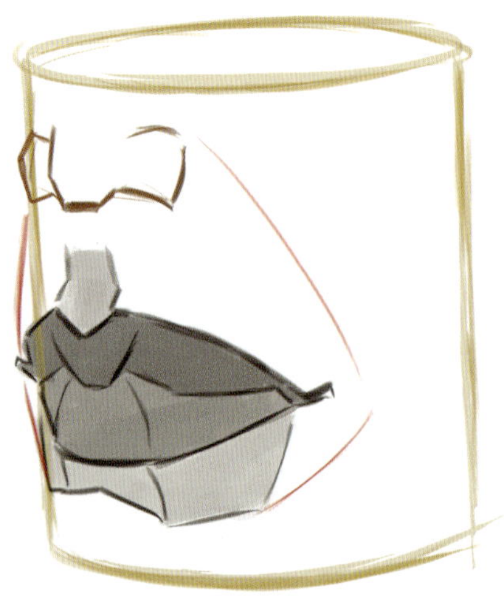

The mouth,
wrapping around
an underlying
cylinder form.
Note the fore-
shortening on the
1 planes, whereas
the 3 planes are
front-on.

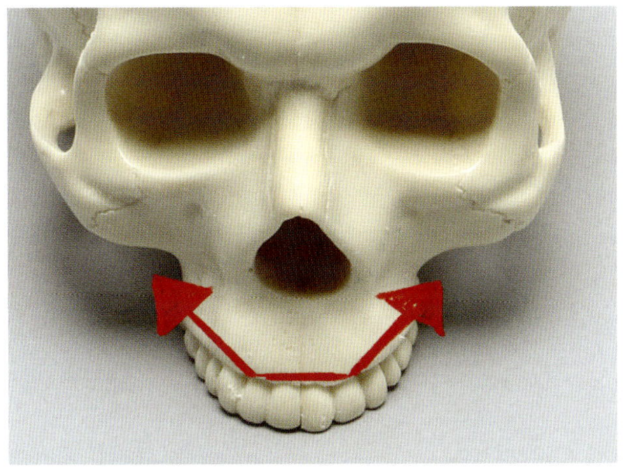

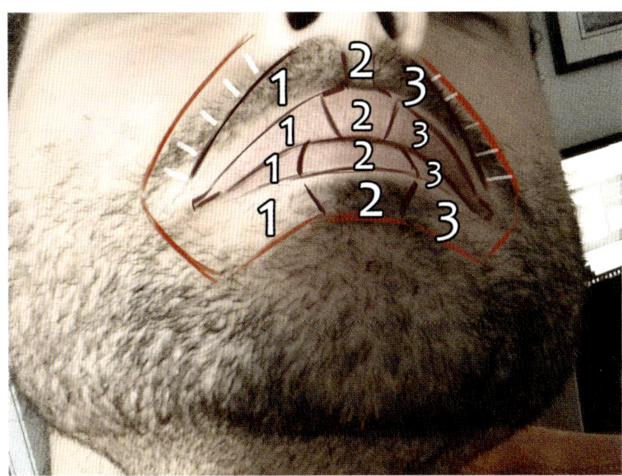

From extreme views you can gain a better appreciation of just how curved the mouth is.

In a profile view, the mouth takes on a saw blade-like progression, as each major section steps both downward and inward.

The mouth's planes do not change orientation as abruptly as the nose, cheekbone, and brow planes. The mouth planes change direction more gradually because it wraps around a round form. The

only hard plane changes are the upper lip, which dramatically points downward, contrasting with the area above the upper lip, which points slightly upward and the 2 plane just below the lower lip. I can show this with a bit of shading.

In an extreme close-up like this, I split the upper lip and lower lip into two sets of 1-2-3. This is generally a detail only worth considering when you're this zoomed in.

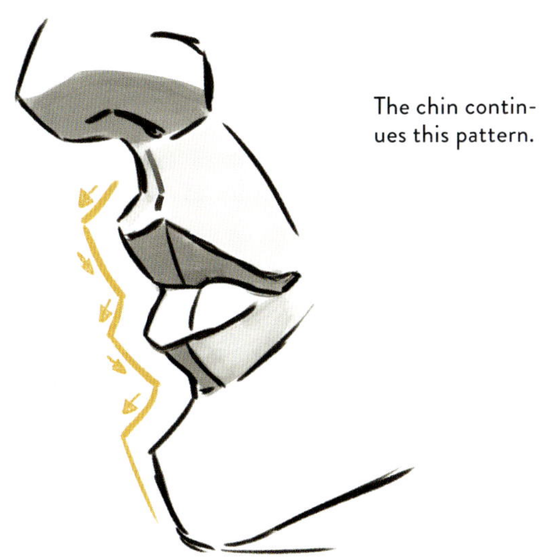

The chin continues this pattern.

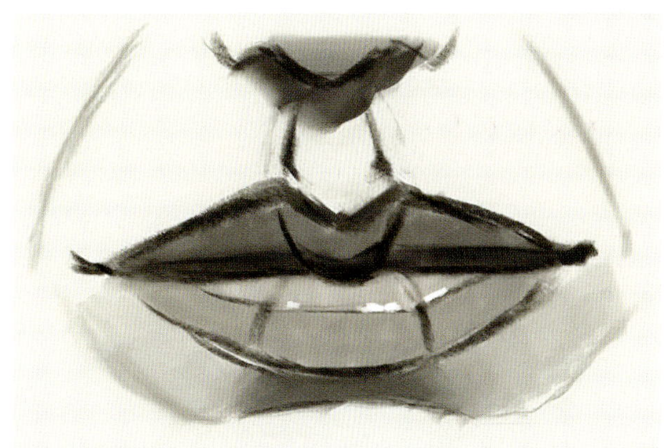

See the next chapter for more about shading and lighting!

THE EYE

The eye is a beautifully intricate form with many variations and deserves its general regard as the most visually attractive facial feature. The eye is built around a literal ball and has a three-plane construction so it's a lot like the mouth!

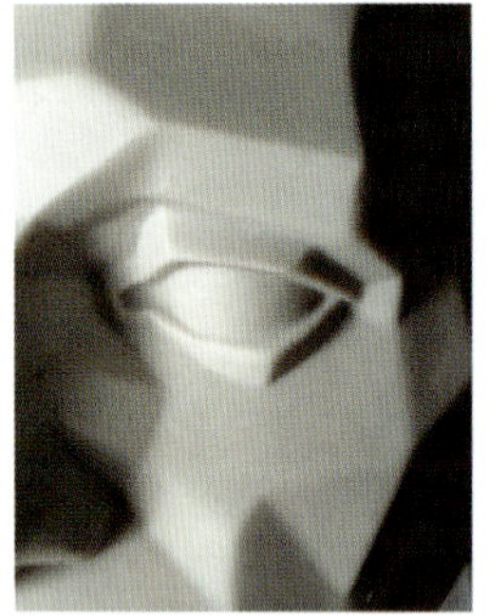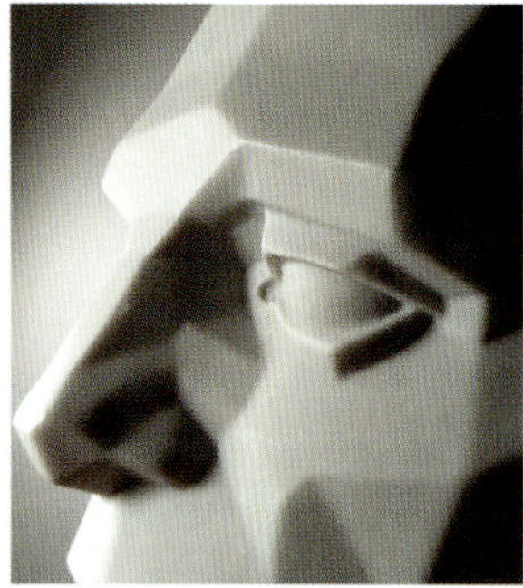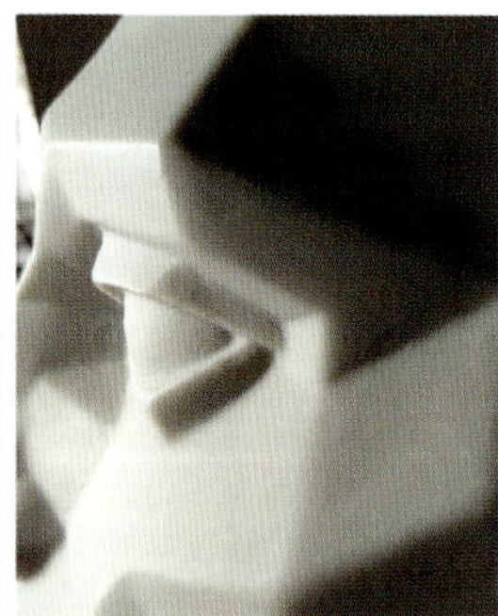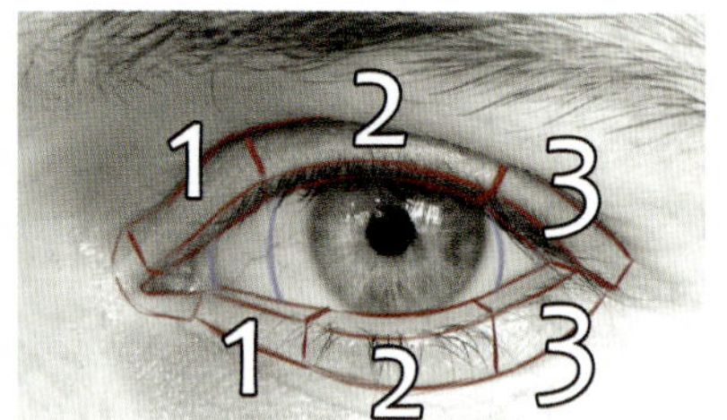

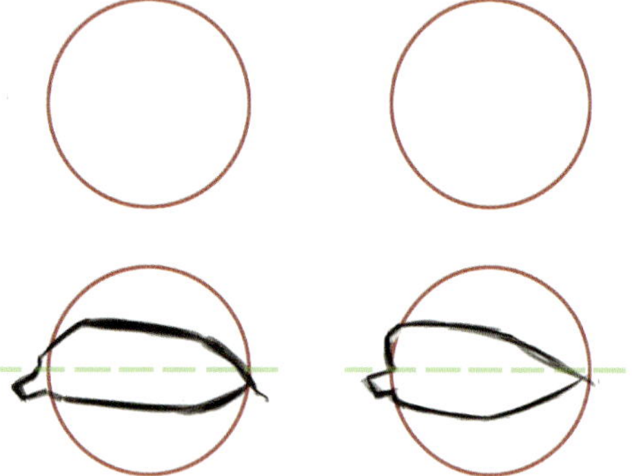

The green line shows that the tear duct corner of the eye sits just a little higher than the outer corner. Also note that the eyeball ends before the tear duct starts.

To construct the eye, first visualize a ball. We will build our planes on top of this. I'll draw two eyes here. One from the front, and one in a three-quarter perspective.

I like to start by drawing the opening of the eye. It's critical that this goes *around* the ball.

Reducing the eye to just four lines looks like this:

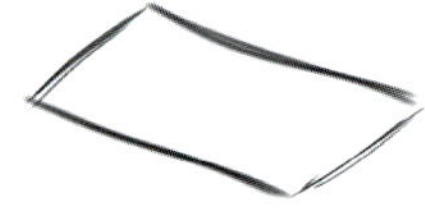

Think of a parallelogram.

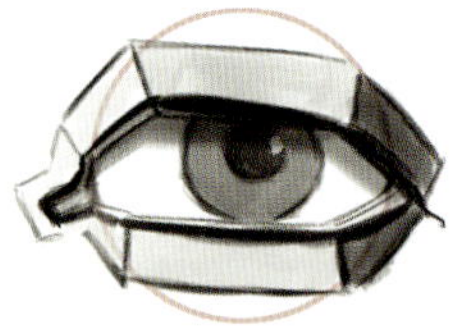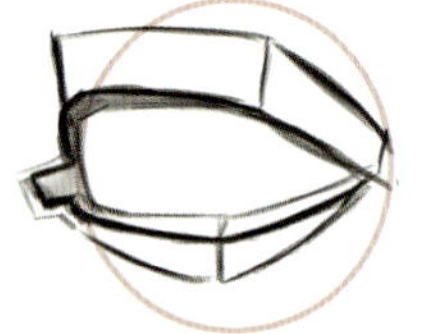

The eye on the left is shown at a more completed state, whereas the eye on the right is in a middle phase. Notice the cast shadow on the upper part of the left eyeball, which helps show the thickness of the eyelid.

Now comes the addition of the upper and lower eyelid, which adds depth to the eye. Note both the vertical height of the eyelids, as well as their inherent *thickness*.

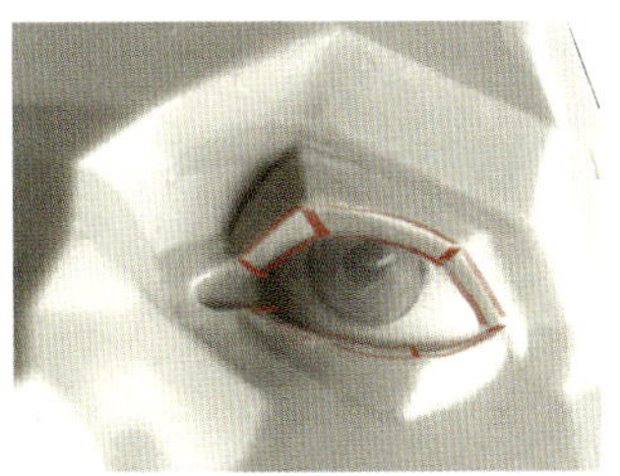

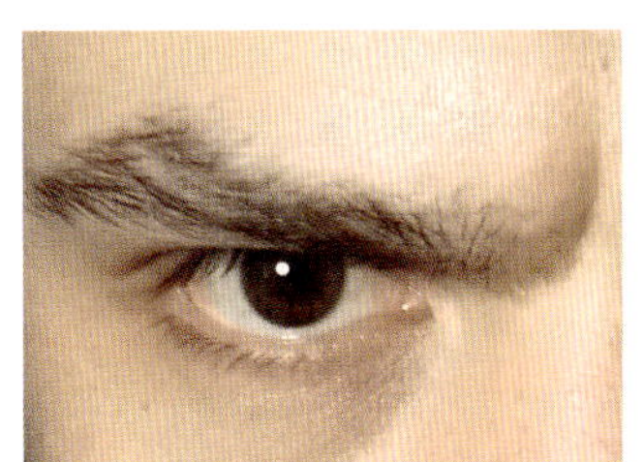

Red lines show the eye-
lids' thickness as they sit
on top of the eyeball.

The thickness of the eyelids is very easy to miss.
I've seen this aspect overlooked more times than
anything else in student work.

There is a considerable overlap of the brow over
the eye, covering a significant portion of the
upper eyelid. I think of it as a shelf. Even the
slightest downturn of the head will result in the
upper eyelid being almost completely overlapped
by the shelf.

Let's start this drawing with the curvature of the
eyebrow and the fleshy shelf beneath it.

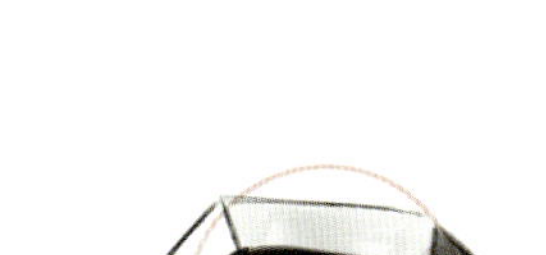

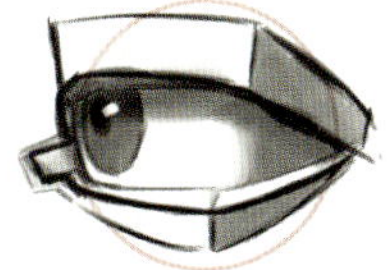

The completed studies.

The next obstacle with the eye is that its surroundings play a large role in its appearance. Particularly the brow. The brow sits far in front of the
eye, as well as above it and there is a significant,
fleshy plane change between the two.

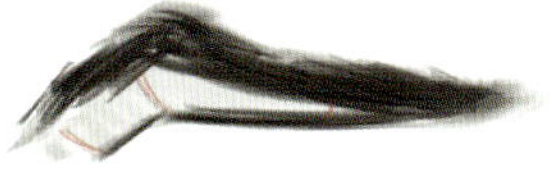

Then we'll add the opening of the eye, making sure
that the upper eyelid comes out from *underneath*
the shelf.

We can now complete the lower eyelid, whose
thickness is like a mini shelf of its own, as well as
the circular iris. Also note that the eyelashes grow
from the outermost edge of the eyelids.

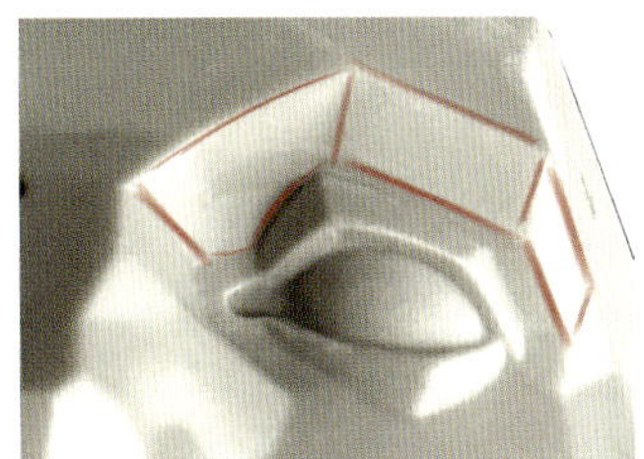

The transition planes
between the brow and
the eye are larger than
the upper eyelid.

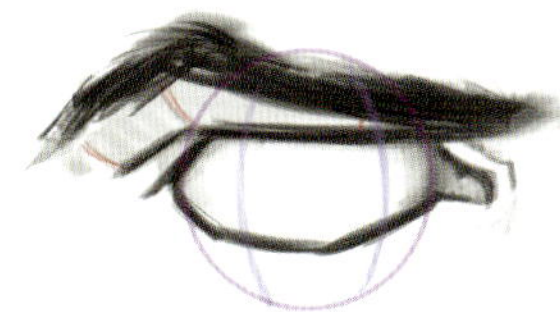

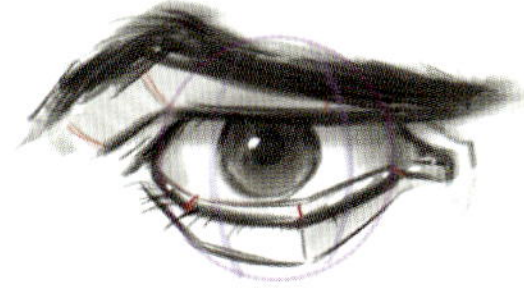

Another reminder that the eyeball ends before the tear duct
starts!

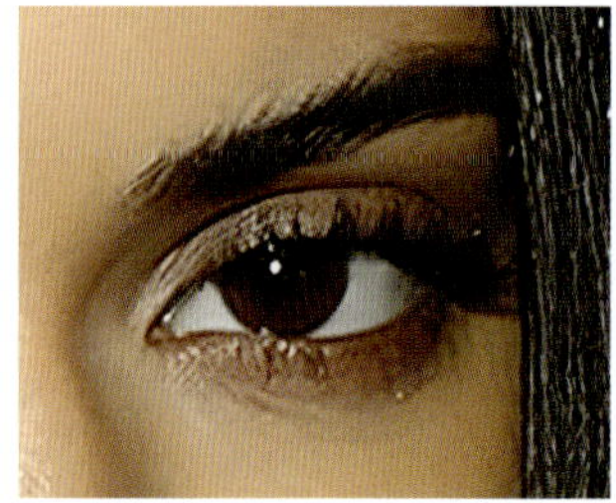

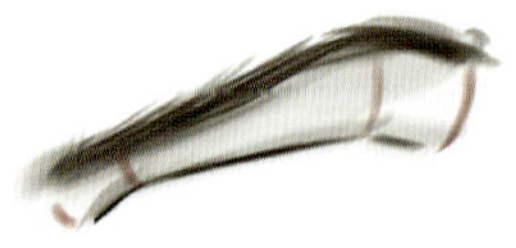

Volume shown
with red lines.

This fleshy shelf we're talking about can have various degrees of overhang. On a younger person, it can have enough tautness to reveal the upper eyelid. Even in this case, you need to take its volume into consideration.

When filling out the planes, notice that I am consistent about showing where the eyeball itself lies, particularly where it meets the tear duct.

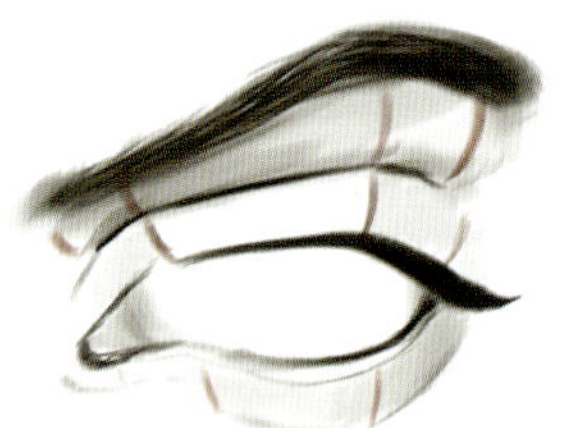

You can use thicker line weights to indicate the presence of eyelashes. Thinner line weights can help with smaller planes, like the thickness of the lower eyelid.

Finishing off the drawing becomes a straightforward process when the structure is laid in properly. Typically, you can find those classic highlights on the iris overlapping the pupil as well as on the upper plane of the lower eyelid, and on the tear duct.

On a so-called hooded eye, the full contour of the upper eyelid is visible and unaffected by the brow's overhang.

An older eye commonly has a droopier brow-shelf, which can overlap the eye significantly. Also note the pronounced bag under the eye, which is the less-elastic skin sunken into the eye socket cavity, revealing the eyeball form underneath.

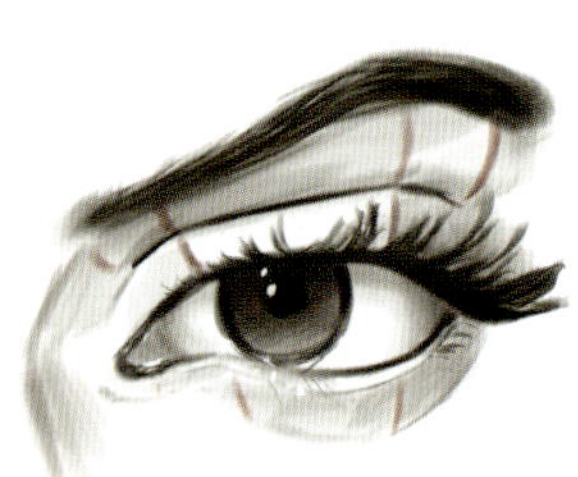

I also included the edge of the glabella, and an indication of the ridge (or front plane) of the nose.

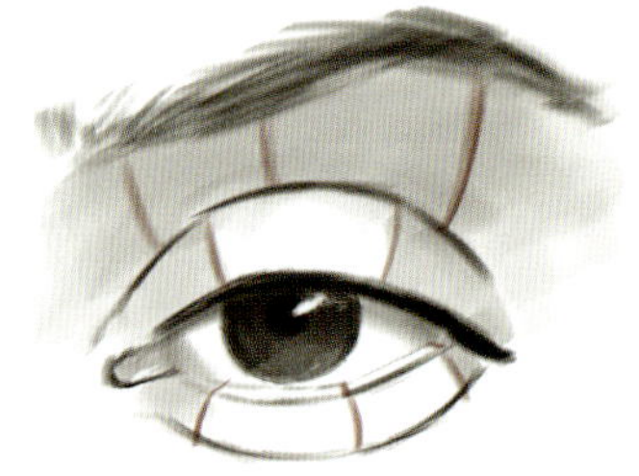

Adding to the appearance of a hooded eye, the upper eyelid can overlap a little more of the iris.

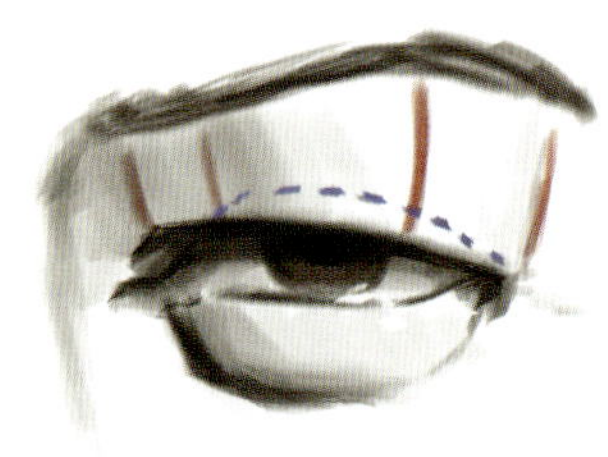

Blue dotted line shows where the top of the eye-opening would be.

The Epicanthic Fold

A distinct piece of anatomy to be aware of sur-
rounding the eye is the epicanthic fold. It's a skin
fold that traverses the inner corner of the eye. The
epicanthic fold produces the shape characteristics
of the Asian eye.

You can think of a prominent epicanthic fold as
the brow-shelf extending downward, creating further interaction with the shape of the eye itself.

It's important to note that the anatomy of the
eye itself does not change at all. It's just that the
epicanthic fold *overlaps* the eye, and in doing so,
becomes part of the shape. To draw it, I like to first
plot the epicanthic fold to construct around.

Now we add the upper eyelid, which comes out
from behind the epicanthic fold on the right side.
The eyelashes grow from this part of the eye, not
from the epicanthic fold.

Also here is the lower eyelid, including its top-
facing plane to indicate the thickness of the form.

The red lines indicate the brow-shelf form, which
tends to be more prominent. Also, because the
eyeball is behind an additional layer of skin, the
epicanthic fold, there tends to be a darker shadow
cast on the eyeball form.

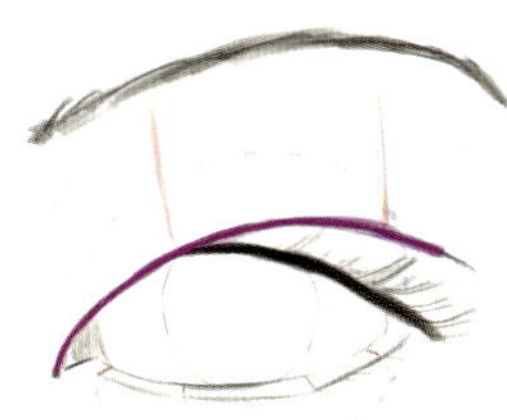

The purple line
is the epicanthic
fold. Blue dotted
line is the eyeball
underneath.

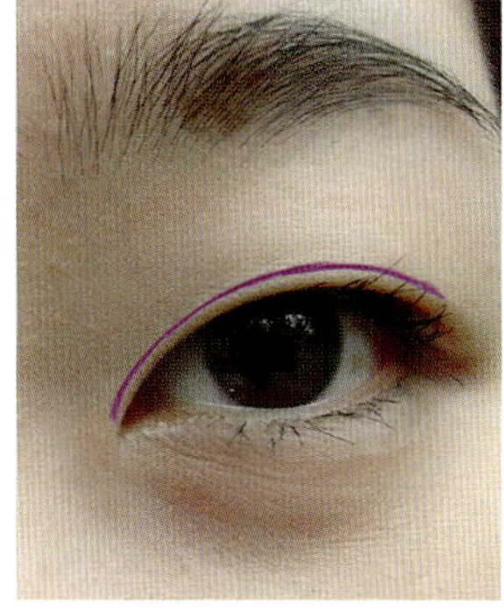

Purple line runs
parallel with the
epicanthic fold.
The actual fold on
the model is just
below it.

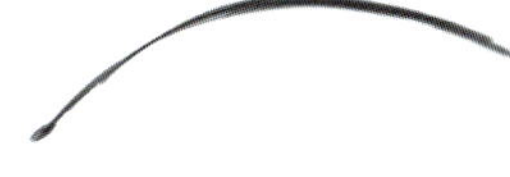

The epicanthic
fold by itself.
A nice, graceful
curve.

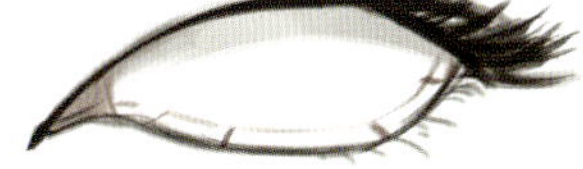

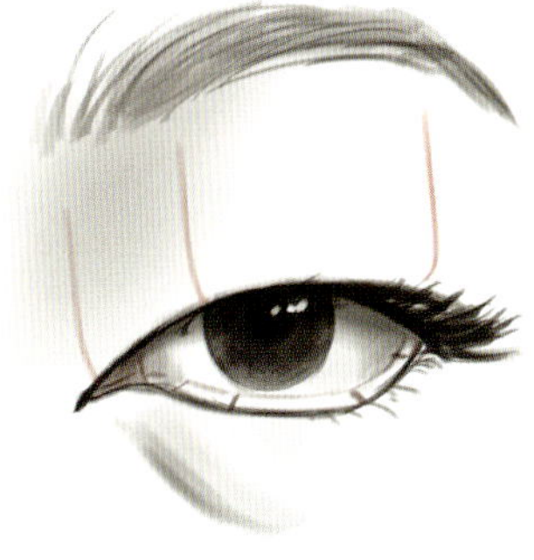

Note that a highlight will still be equally bright, even if it exists
inside a shadowed area. This is because a highlight reflects the
light source, or light parts of the environment. (See Chapter 7
for more on lighting and shading!)

THE EAR

I like to joke that the ear has no right to be as complex as it is. It occupies a sort of no-man's-land area of the head, and unless you're a doctor, there's rarely a time when we want to focus on someone's ear. Yet there it is, in all its undulating topology! Let's quickly go over its construction.

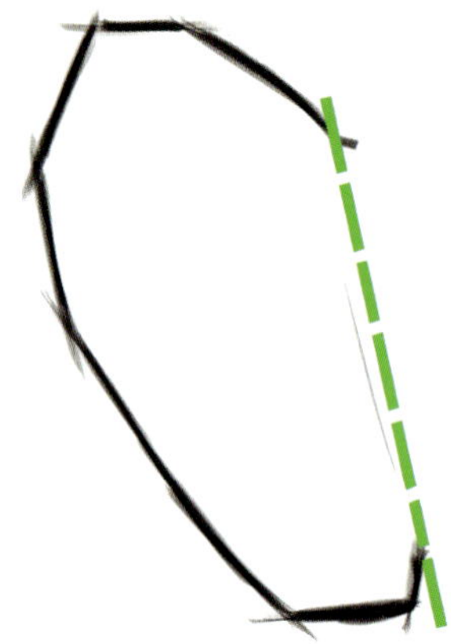

Dotted green line indicates the ear's offset angle, which follows the jawline.

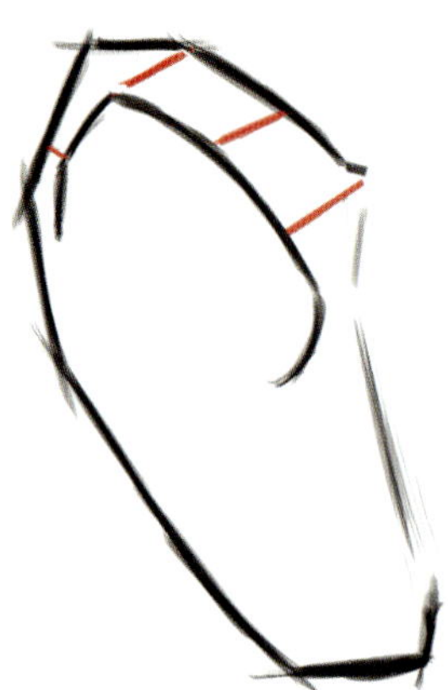

Red lines indicate the tapering width of the form. Note that the back of the ear is called the helix which will become helpful on the next page.

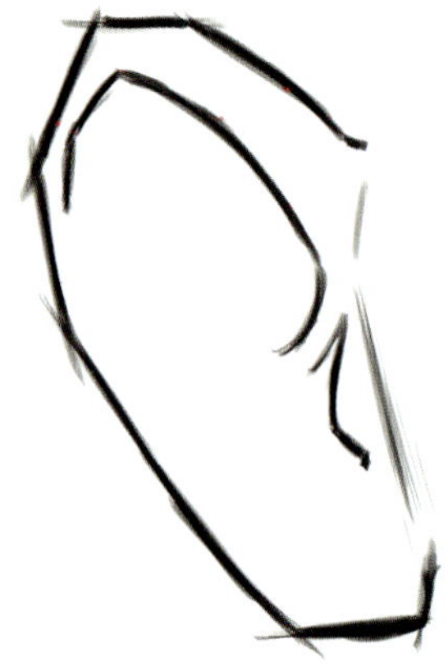

I've always remembered the tragus because it's a popular place for piercings.

First, think of the silhouette of the ear as a series of seven straight lines.

Next, add a kind of upside-down, flattened U shape. Make sure the form is widest near the front of the ear, close to the jaw, and narrower at the back.

Now add the *tragus*, which is the little nib or flap overhanging the ear canal.

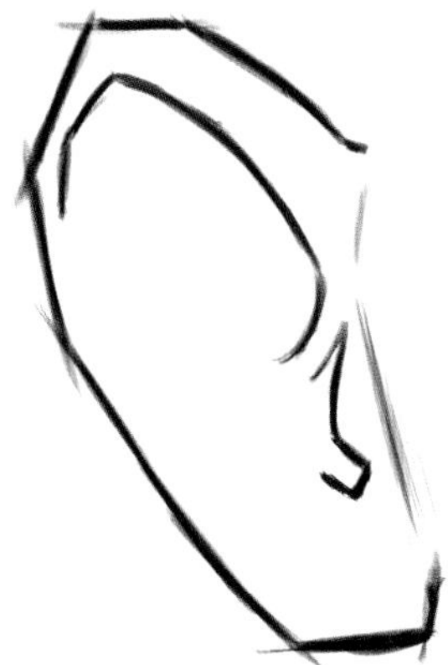 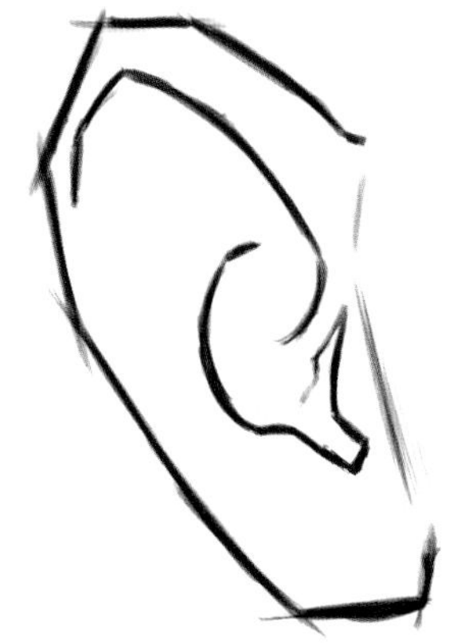 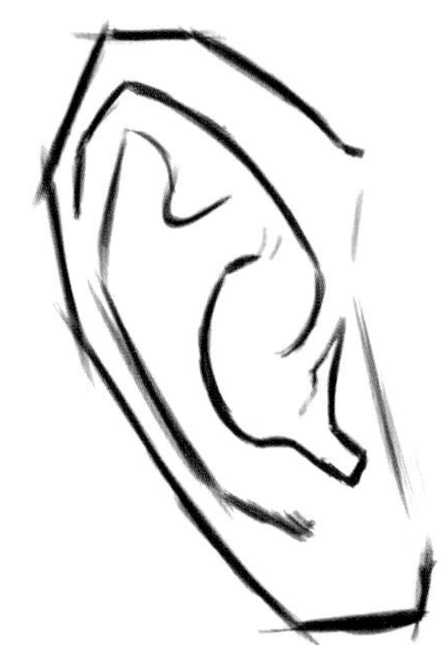

The antitragus area resembles a back-ward question mark.

It may not look like much has changed in this next image. But I've added the little notch that connects the *tragus* with the *antitragus*. Sometimes you'll see this called the intertragic notch.

The antitragus has a similar nib form and is another common area for piercings, though it's inverted from the tragus. It makes a C-curve, which grace-fully spirals into the ear cavity.

Now we add a larger form that resides inside the ear, the *antihelix*. The outer edge of this form runs parallel with the *helix*.

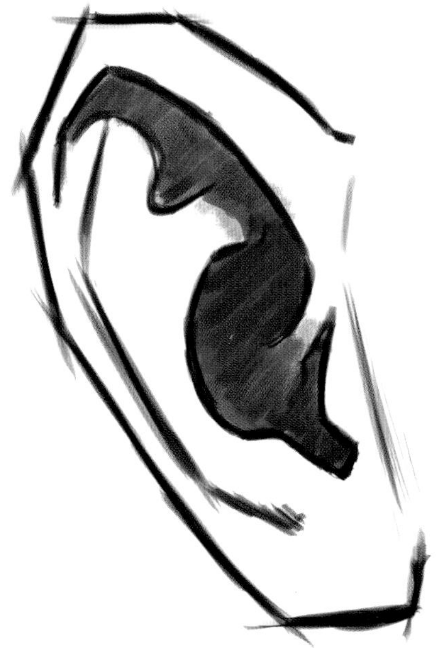

To finalize our ear, it's common to throw in a single shape of shading, as that's the most use-ful way to show the viewer that there's a deep cavity present.

Just use one tone here and keep the shape nice and simple. Yes, the shape design fundamentals transfer right over to tones and shading!

General **Proportions**

Let's zoom back out to the head at large and finalize its overall construction before inserting the features.

Finally, we see how the planes of the lower third of the face connect with the upper planes. Notice that from the top of the brow to the bottom of the chin is essentially one large plane that tapers from widest at the top, to narrowest at the bottom.

It may initially seem like the front plane tapers too narrow at the chin. A quick look at the skull explains it.

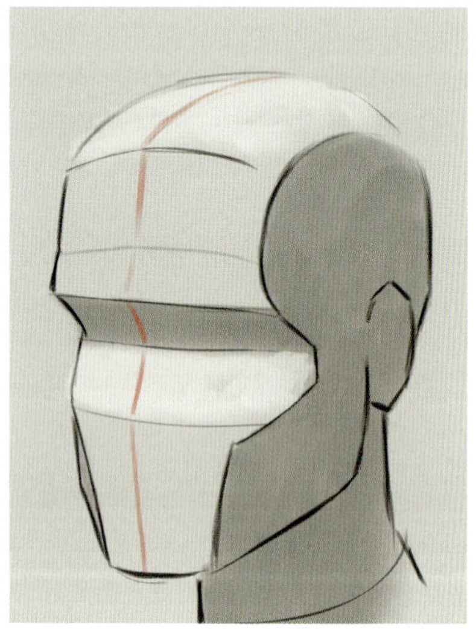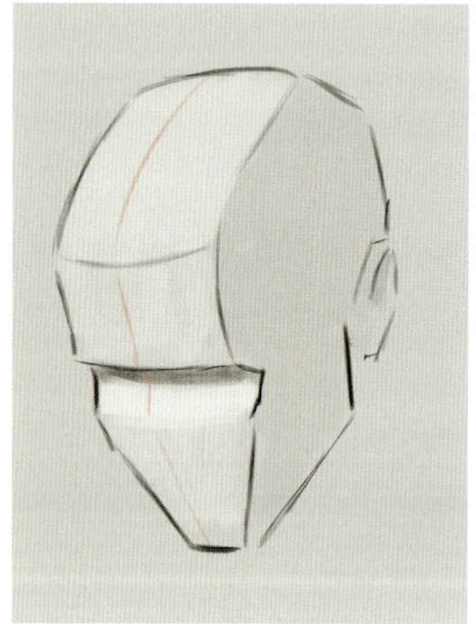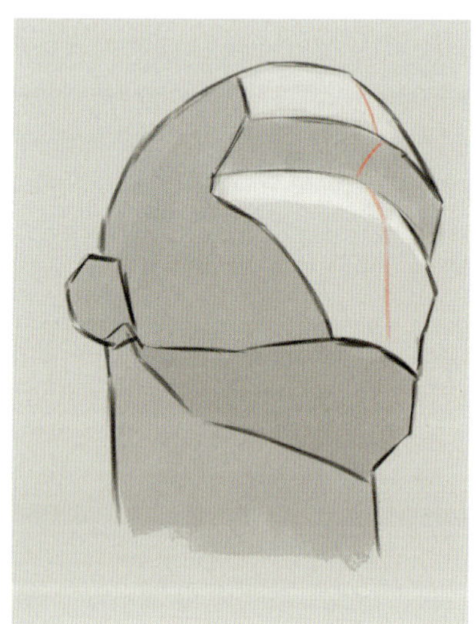

As always, practice these forms by drawing them from various angles.

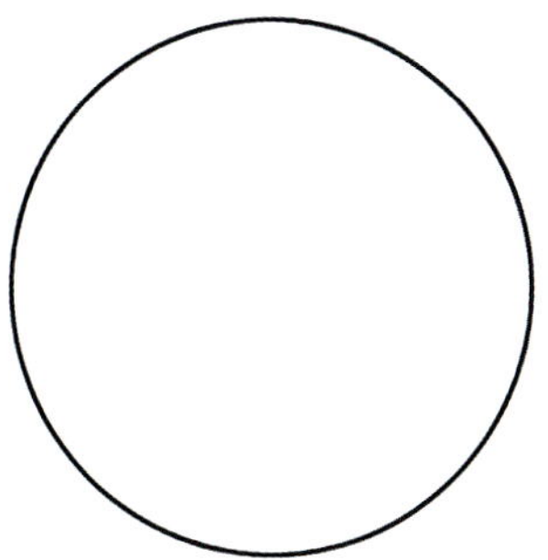

Step 1: First, take a circle. This represents the upper half of the head, all the way to the back of the cranium.

Now that we know how each part is constructed, we need an overall framework for their placement and proportion. There are many ways to go about this but what they have in common is that each takes common measurements and plots out easy-to-follow steps to make sure you get them right before diving into the smaller facial features.

Perhaps the most popular framework is the Loomis method, named after famed artist and instructor Andrew Loomis.

Step 2: Cut a flat section of the circle where the plane for the temple is. Identify its center and middle lines to make a crosshair.

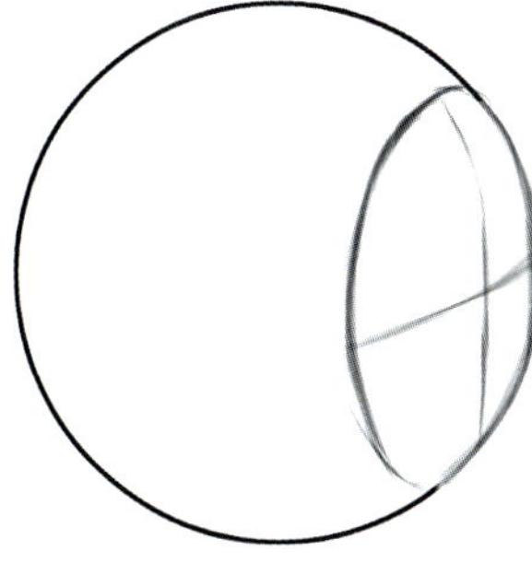

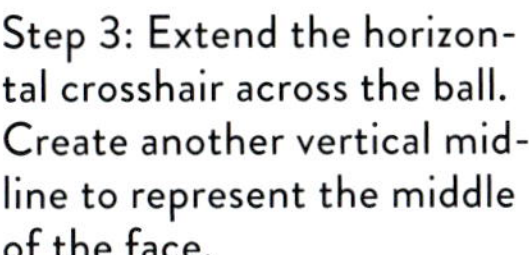

This is what we're representing on the skull.

Step 3: Extend the horizontal crosshair across the ball. Create another vertical midline to represent the middle of the face.

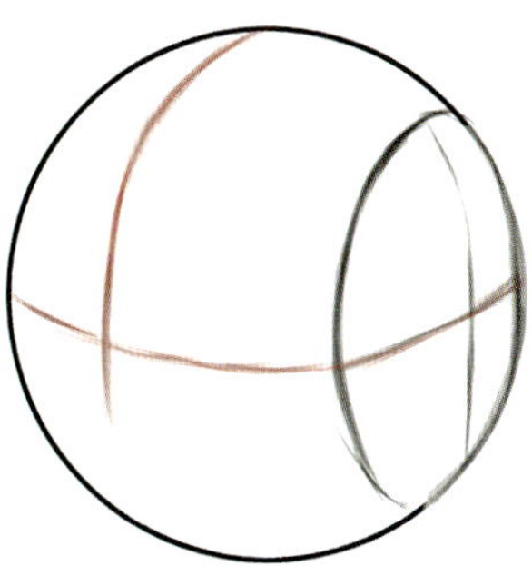

Scan to watch a tutorial.

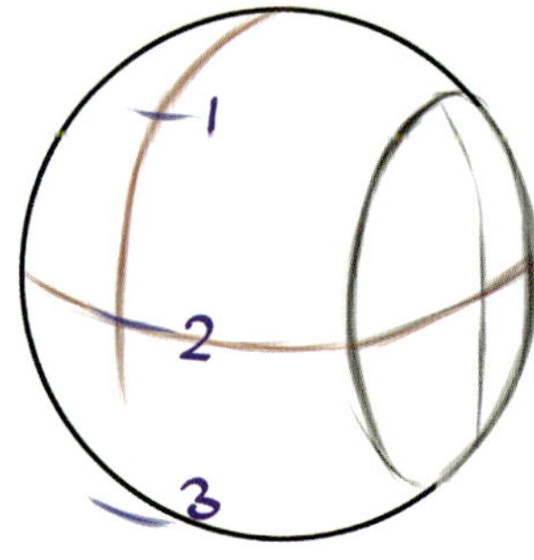

Step 4: Make four equally spaced marks. Number one is the hairline, number two is the brow line, number three is the bottom of the nose, and number four is the bottom of the chin.

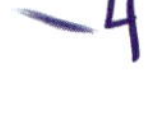

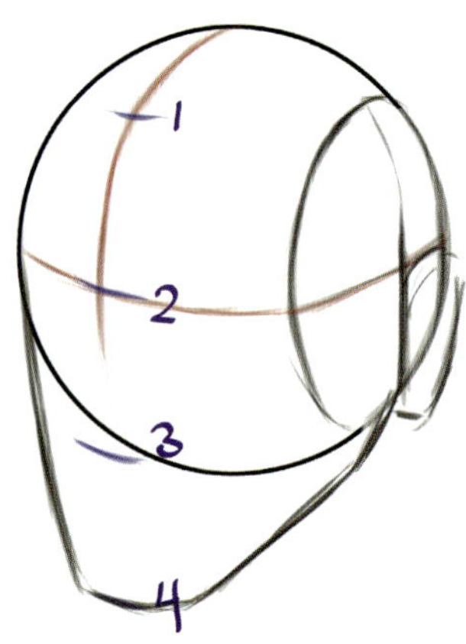

Step 5: Extend a line downward at an angle, following the ball's trajectory, to meet the chin. Bring this line upward at an angle toward the sliced-off center line. This forms the lower half of the head. Note that the top of the ear aligns with the brow line, and the bottom aligns with the base of the nose.

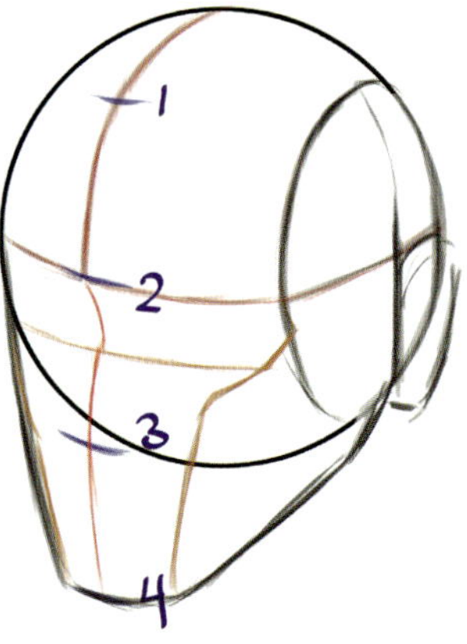

Step 6: Now you can complete the front of the face box form, as seen previously in this chapter. The difference with this method is we have some nice assurance that we're staying in proportion.

I recommend stopping right here, and filling many, many pages with these. Be sure to practice this framework from different angles, favoring the most common angles. After some repetition, you will be able to frame the head without needing to go through each step.

PROPORTIONS CHEAT SHEET

Here are the basic proportions of a head. Not every head will follow this but as a starting point it will apply to basically any head you draw assuming you're looking for human proportions. It's easy enough to memorize, but there are a few intricacies that can trip you up!

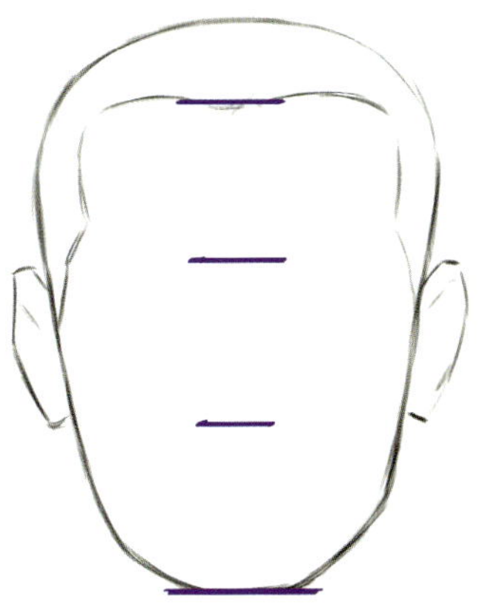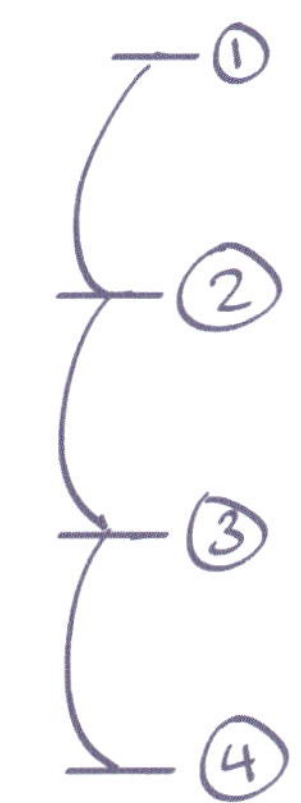

The placement of four equal marks, moving vertically down the head. Note that the top mark is the hairline, *not* the top of the head.

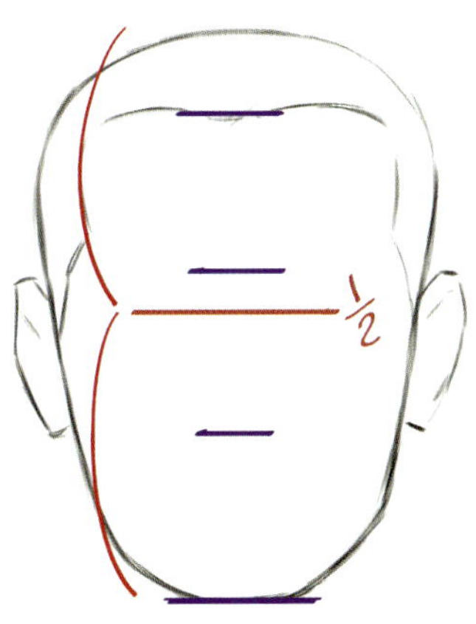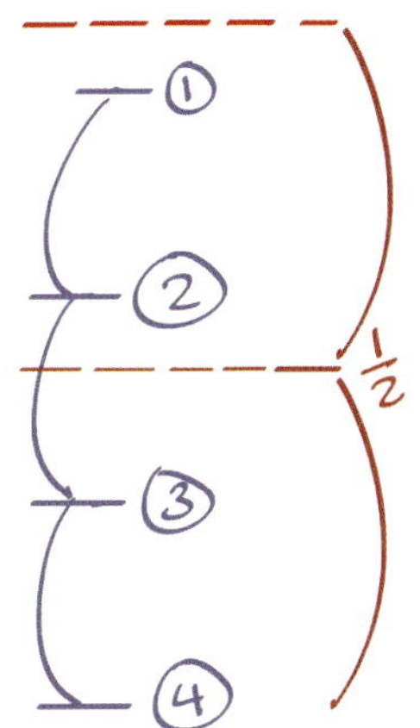

Now place a mark halfway between the top of the head and the chin. That's the *top of the head* this time, not the brow line! This is the midpoint of the eyes.

First the green mark gets placed halfway between the bottom of the nose and the chin. This is the bottom of the lower lip. Do not confuse this with the line in between the lips!

The line in between the lips is indicated by the yellow line, which lies halfway between the green line, and the bottom of the nose. Phew!

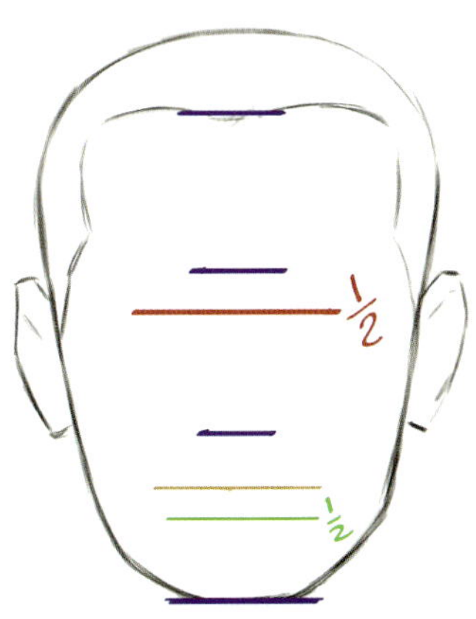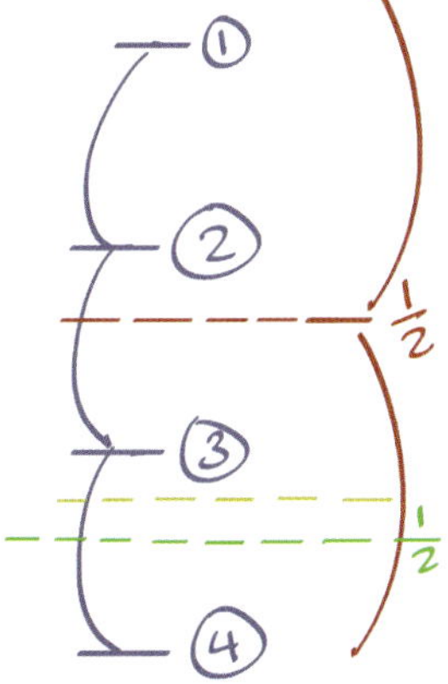

Here it is, from a tough angle, overlaid on the Asaro Head model.

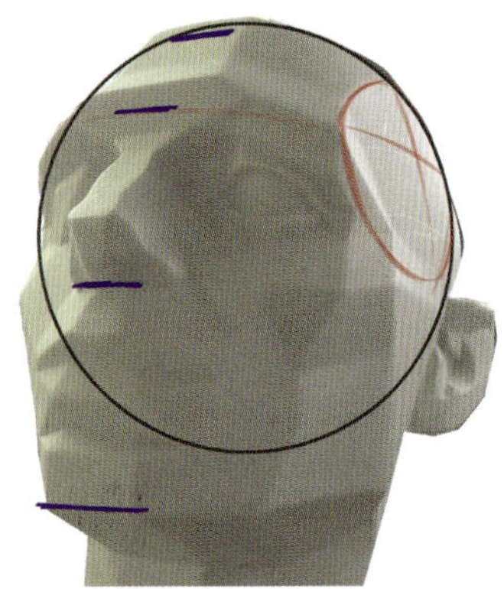

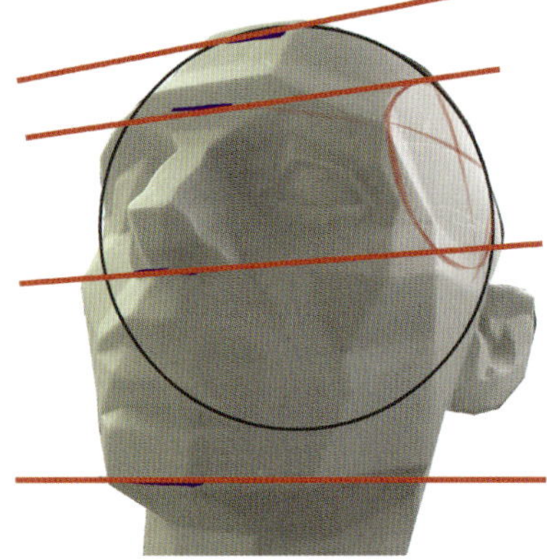

Due to the foreshortened perspective, the marks taper in apparent distance.

Remember that the head follows a perspective grid too!

Note that from certain angles the protruding cheekbone plane can jut out from the ball.

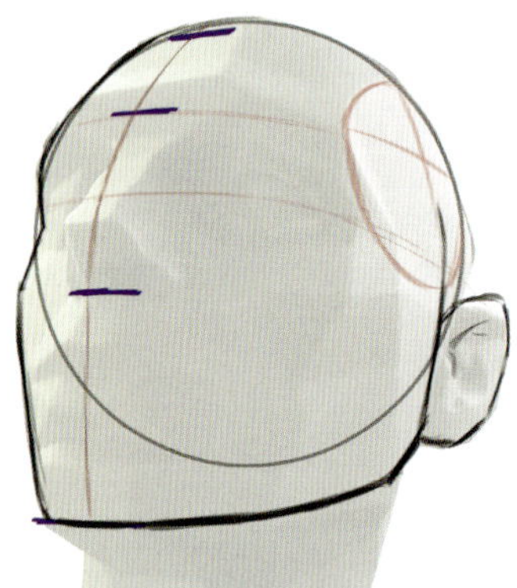

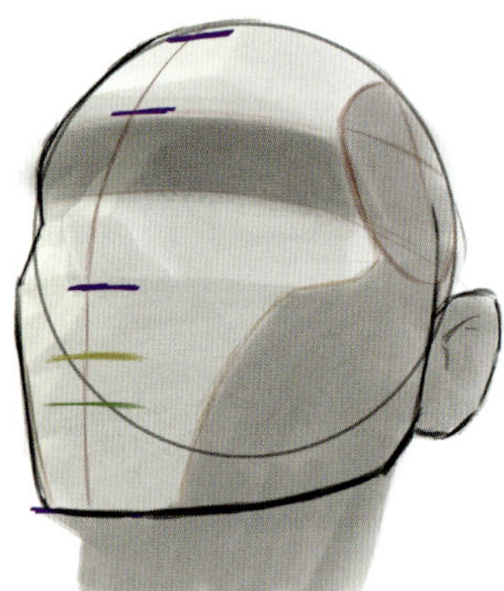

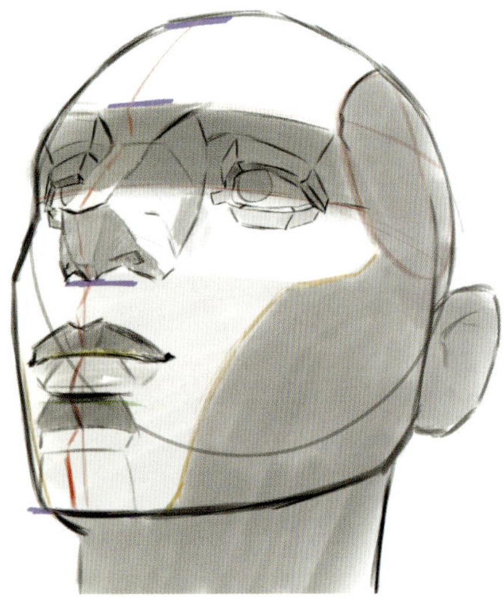

The finished facial features. A difficult, yet common, view for your reference.

Adding **Features** onto Framework

The framework is a safety net for adding features. We don't have to fear losing proportions anymore. We'll resume here with the boxy head we had a few pages ago.

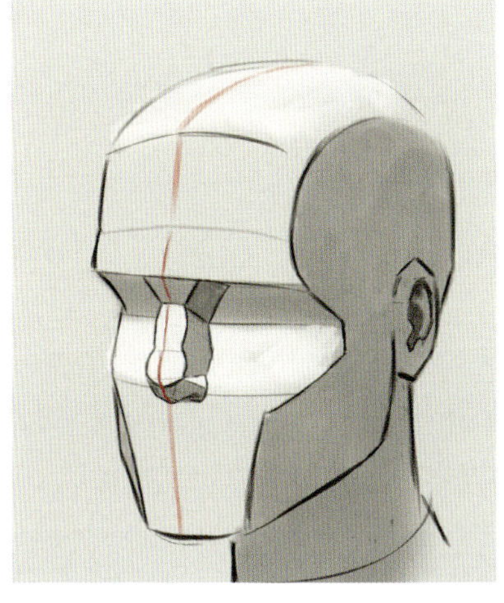

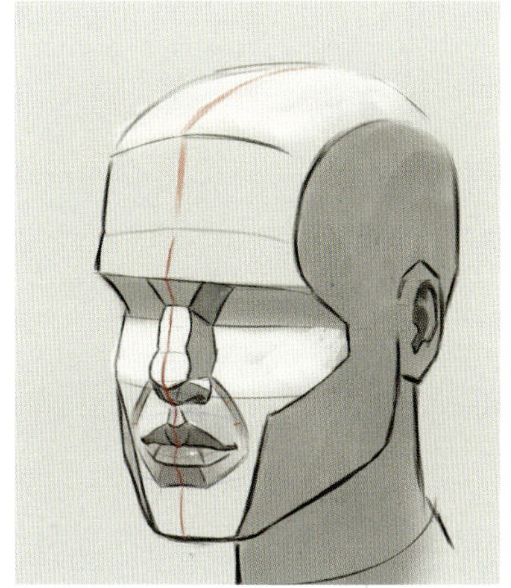

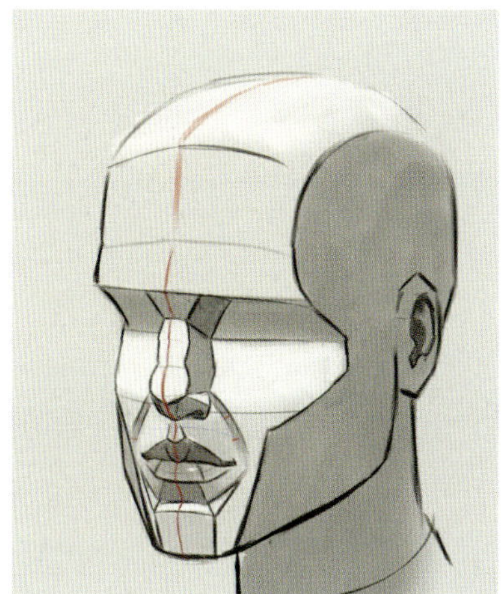

Adding the nose planes. Notice the red cross-contour line, which has also been updated from earlier to now travel over the new topology.

Adding the mouth construction. Remember that the middle of the lips is one-third of the distance from the bottom of the nose to the bottom of the chin. We also now see that the outer perimeter of our mouth construction are the nasolabial folds, or laugh lines.

The chin is the easiest feature. It's another three-plane construction. And we've already seen the stair-step pattern that the middle line takes as it progresses down the lower third of the face.

Even though we've drawn some eyebrows, we haven't seen where exactly they lay on the overall construction of the brow. Probably the most important aspect of the eyebrows is where the direction breaks which is exactly at the temple plane. In this way, the eyebrows describe the planar nature of the head, and are a great tool to add depth to your head drawings.

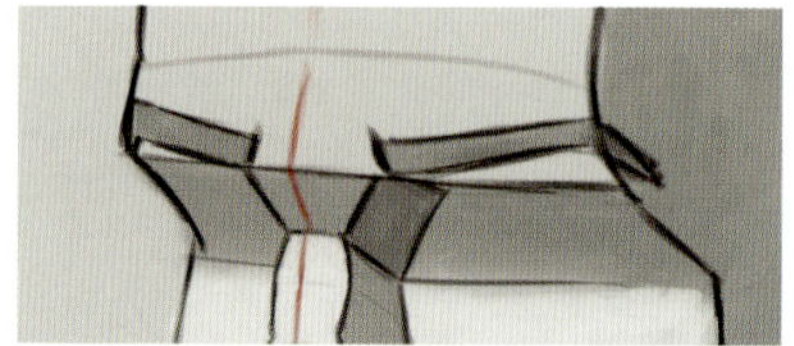

The far eyebrow in this drawing isn't fully visible. It is wrapping around to the other side of the head.

Finally, we add the eyes, and arrive at our final construction. I've intentionally kept this head as generic as possible, even to the point of being less than interesting design-wise. These base foundations open the lane for stylization which we will see in the next chapter!

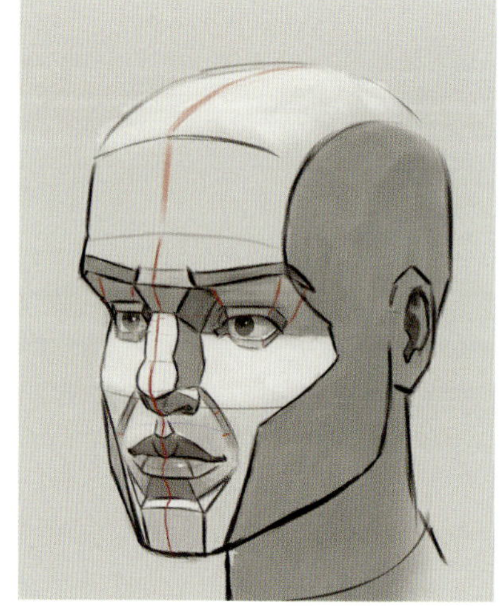

Here is the head construction from the profile view. I've added more resolution in the jaw and cheek area. The narrow plane that drives back to the ear is called the zygomatic arch, which is part of the cheekbone. It is a superficial bone in the skull meaning it sits just underneath the skin. Feel it on your own face!

Secondly, look at the underside of the jaw. There is a noticeable plane there. From a front and three-quarter view, the jaw makes up the profile. But the closer you move to the profile view, the more exposed that under-plane will be.

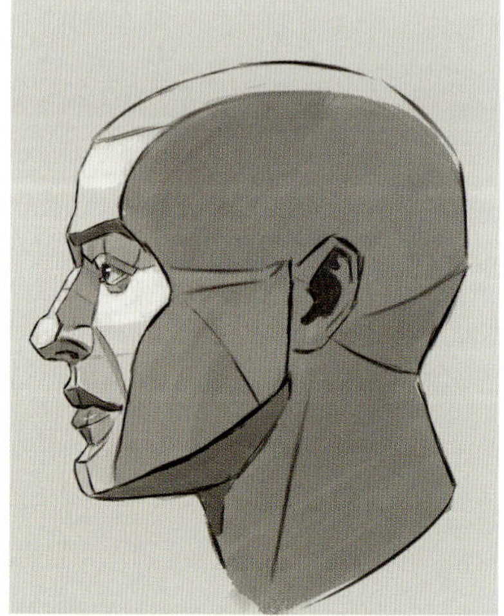

There is no red line running down the middle of the form here, because in profile, the contour and silhouette serves that purpose!

ASSIGNMENTS

Drawing the face and head can be intimidating, but looking at how they're built and practicing drawing them with different approaches will give you the confidence you need!

ASSIGNMENT #1

Start by practicing how the basic box becomes a head-form. Remember to draw cross-contours and midlines to help indicate direction and orientation. For additional information, chop out the brow plane cutting into the head, and make sure it is equaled by a simplified cheekbone plane jutting back out. Draw these from many angles. Feel free to use photo reference to help with these, even using the vellum/tracing method, if needed!

ASSIGNMENT #2

Get a sense of the overall head proportions using the method shown at the end of this chapter. Keep these drawings at either a three-quarter angle or a front view at first, to build confidence in your proportions and process.

ASSIGNMENT #3

Study the construction of the facial features individually, using the planes and methods shown in this chapter. Remember that each facial feature is a landscape unto itself and needs to be understood before you can place it onto the overall head construction! Feel free to mark up photos as well, if you need help identifying and/or seeing the planes.

ASSIGNMENT #4

Finalize a head construction using the lessons in this chapter. Remember that it's totally OK if your character design isn't great yet. The goal is to get the head working in three dimensions, with all the features rigidly built onto it. I recommend working with a three-quarter view at first, and only changing angles once you feel ready to move on.

7

Shading and Lighting

Here, I am happy to report, is where we begin achieving that *wow* factor in our art.

For some reason (at least, in my experience), depicting a convincing sense of light and shadow impresses people more than, say, shape design or gesture does. I'm not totally sure why. Perhaps it's because adding shading and lighting to a drawing is the closest we get to mimicking how we actually perceive real life.

It doesn't matter what the medium is, pencil, pen, paint, traditional, or digital, everything in this chapter applies. The only thing that will change is the application of technique based on the tools you're using. Let's dive in!

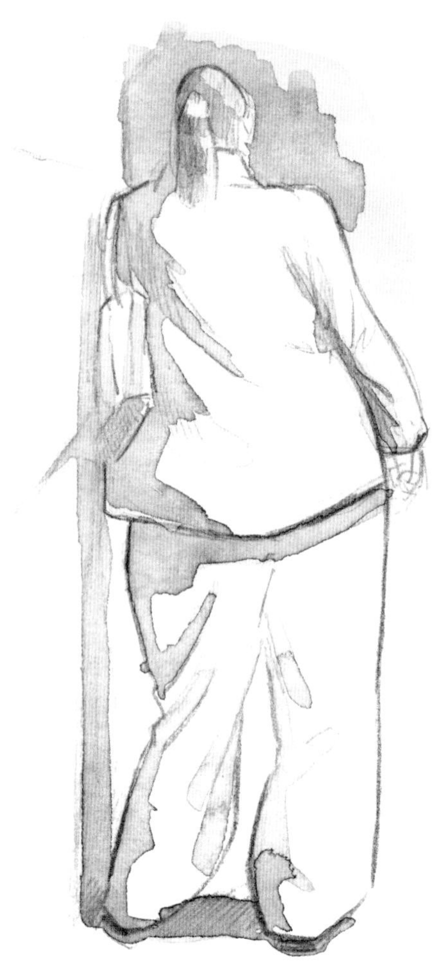

In these quick life drawings I only used two tones: the white of the page, and a darker marker or brush-pen. The lines are still needed in these faster drawings to help show form.

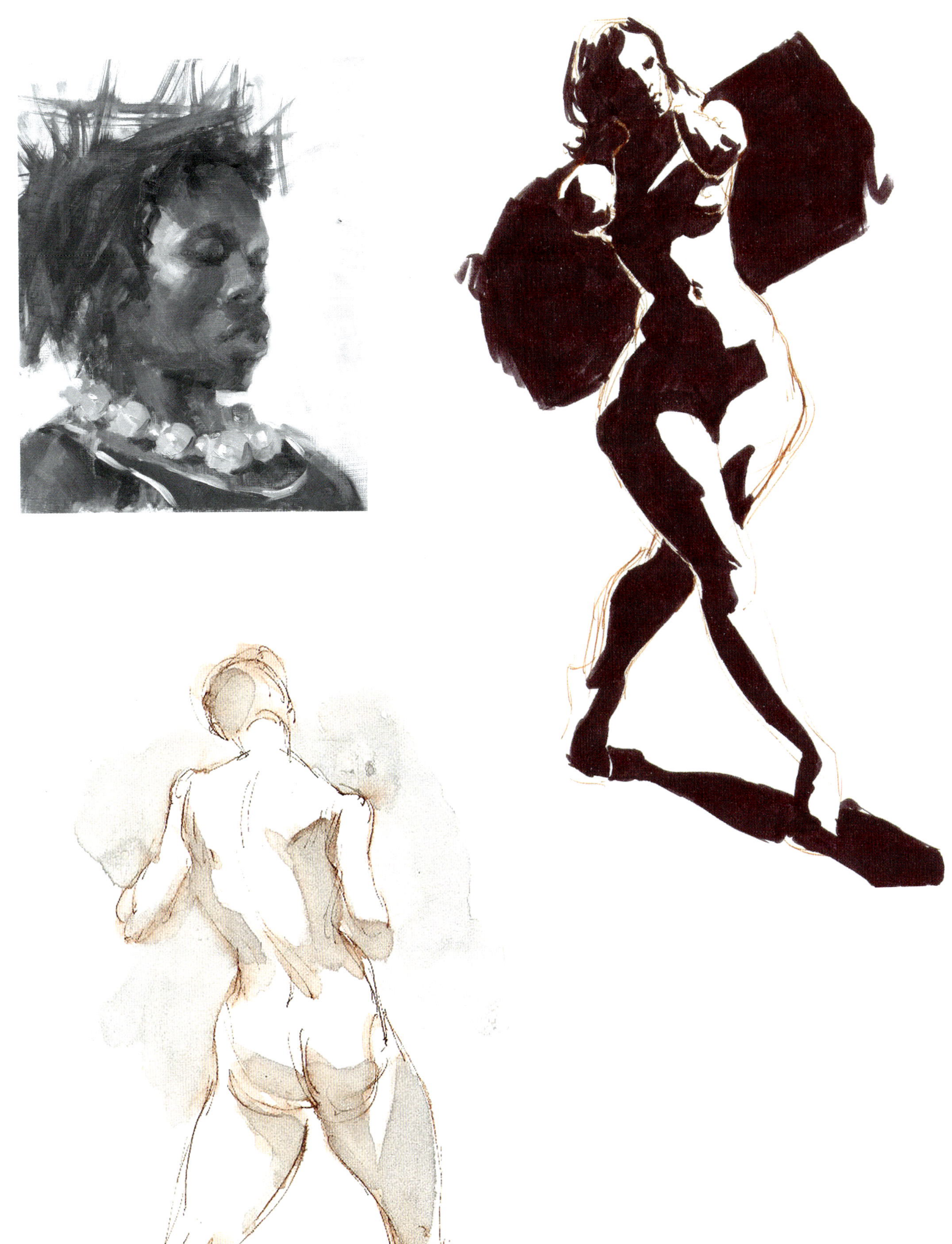

Light and Shadow: Neighbors That Don't Get Along

The good news is that we artists don't have to understand light at a scientific level. We just need to understand how it behaves visually.

IT STARTS WITH THE LIGHT SOURCE

The light source refers to where the strongest light in the scene is coming from. It could be the sun, a light bulb, a lamp, a candle, moonlight, skylight, or even through a window. Because light traveling through air does not bend, rays of light fall in straight lines.

A good analogy is jets of water spraying out of a shower fixture. Light rays collide with whatever happens to be in their way and facing it, a person's face, a building, or a tree. Though that isn't exactly right. For instance, if you stand facing the shower head your face will get wet but not the back of your head. Here are a few simple examples.

ARE SHADOWS THE ABSENCE OF LIGHT?

No! Shadows in the real world have lots of light illuminating them, which is why we can still see things that are in shadow. Shadows are areas that don't receive their light from the light source directly. By the time light rays from the light source find their way to the shadow areas by bouncing around nearby objects, their strength, or brightness, dwindles significantly.

Light versus Shadow

We're left with a clear visual delineation. Either an area is hit directly by the light source, or it is not. That means we only need two tones or values, which is usually the preferred term, to begin a rendering. A light value for the light side, and a dark value for the shadow side. It does not matter which two values you choose for these, so long as the contrast between them is obvious. Breaking up your subject with these two tones or values is the first major task of depicting realistic light.

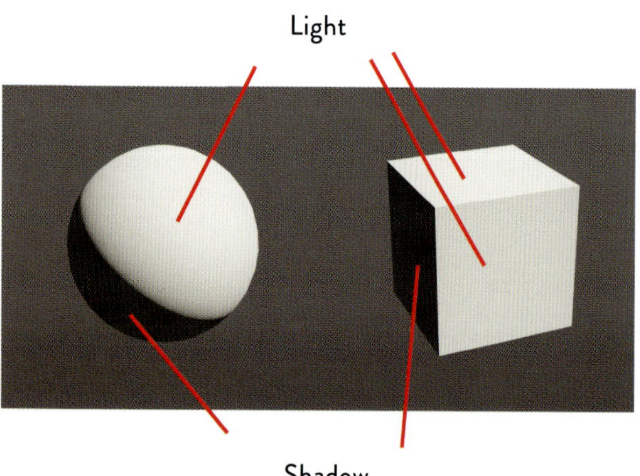

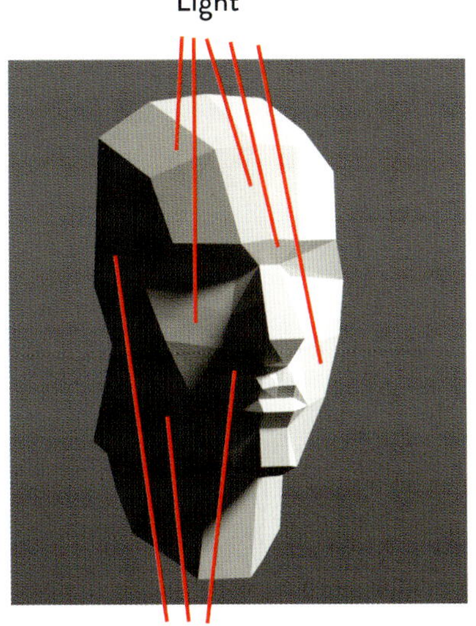

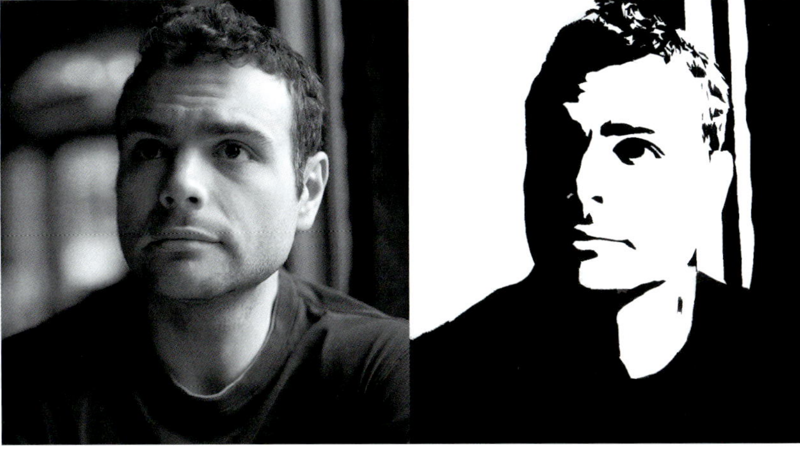

There are often multiple shades of light and shadow in any given reference, so the initial task is to group them to just *one* value per family.

THE NEIGHBORS STAY ON THEIR SIDE OF THE FENCE

I like to imagine light and shadow areas as wary neighbors. They live beside each other, but never cross the fence to visit. As an artist, you cannot put a shadow tone or value into the light side, and you cannot put a light tone or value in the shadows. If you do, you will ruin the effect of convincing light. If the neighbors cross the fence, they'll fight, and ruin your art in the process!

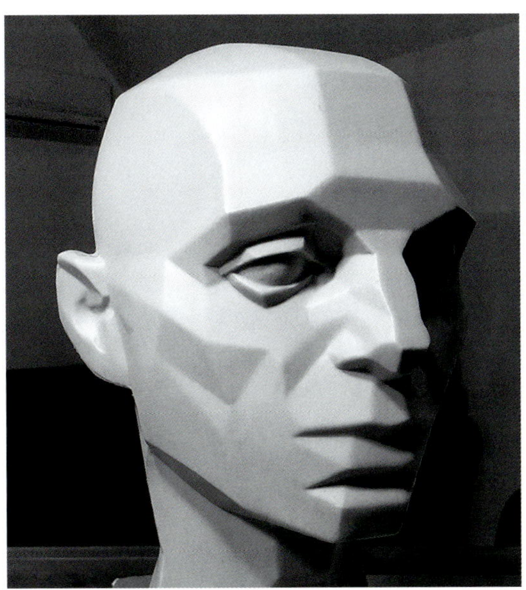

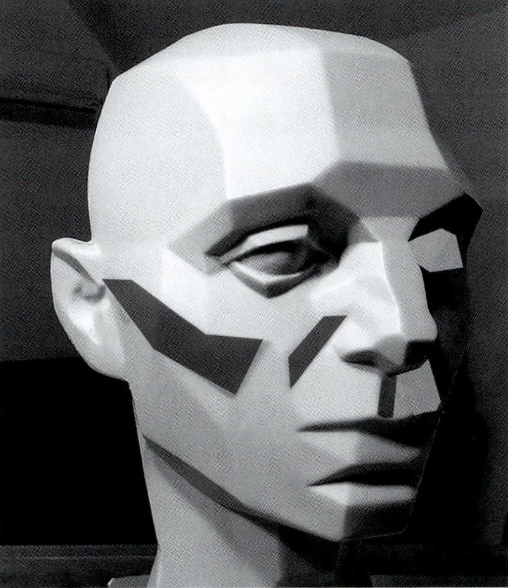

On the left is an untouched photograph of an accurate head model. On the right I've put just a few shadows into the light side, and some lights into the shadow side. See how it destroys the effect of light and form?

Good News: You Only Need to Know Six Values!

Every tone, or value, appears on basic forms. Let's get to know all six values complete with names and where you can find them. On the next page I'll show you how to use them. Think of this as a little cheat sheet you can always refer to when things get more complex later.

VALUES IN THE LIGHT FAMILY

Average Light (1)

This value is a great one to start with, especially when it's paired with Average Shadow. You take all the light tones and values that exist on your subject and average them together. This value needs to leave darker space for Halftone, and lighter space for Highlight.

Halftone (2)

This value is where the form is turning away from the light source and toward shadow but not enough to *be* fully in shadow. It's darker than Average Light, but not by much. Halftone should still be noticeably lighter than Reflected Light.

Highlight (3)

A highlight is a direct reflection of the light source. Highlights will always be your lightest value. A helpful rule of thumb: The shinier the surface, such as a billiard ball, or the wetter, like lips, the tighter and sharper the highlight. The highlight on rougher surfaces like skin and clothing will have softer, more diffuse edges. On very rough surfaces like rubber or sweaters, you won't see highlights at all because they are so diffused.

VALUES IN THE SHADOW FAMILY

Average Shadow (4)

This is often paired with Average Light to create a two-tone drawing. It's the same as Average Light, only for shadow. Average out every value or tone inside the shadow family, and you've got it. This value should be much darker than Average Light, so that you can make it a little lighter for Reflected Light without crossing that fence!

Reflected Light (5)

Also known as bounced light or ambient light. Because light bounces or reflects off objects, shadows almost always receive soft, diffuse illumination from their surroundings. This value is a touch lighter than Average Shadow but should not come close to crossing the fence over to the light family. Never make this value the same as Halftone. It should be noticeably darker! You often find this value in areas of the form that are exposed to the environment, making it more likely that bounced light rays will land there.

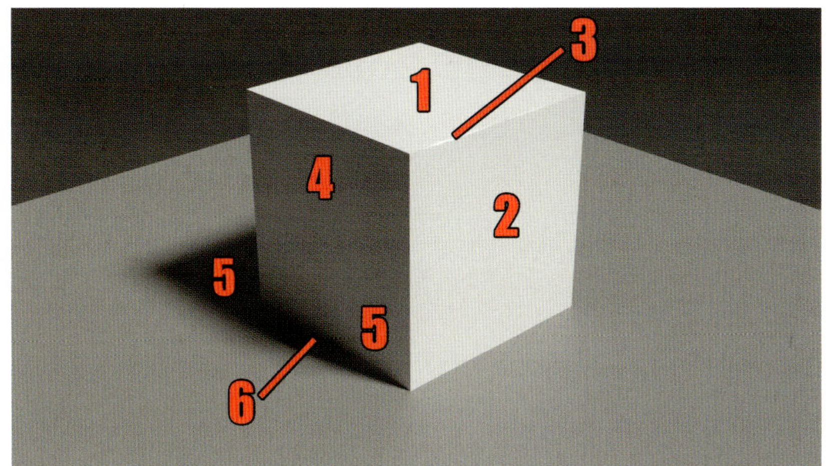

Ambient Occlusion (6)

Think of this value as the opposite of Reflected Light. It's where the Reflected Light cannot get to, making it the darkest part of the shadow. You'll find it in tight spaces, crevices, or overhangs. You will generally see this value where two objects touch, like a ball sitting on a table causing a tight space at the intersection, or where one object overhangs another, like the eaves of a roof, the jaw overhanging the neck, or the nose overhanging the upper lip.

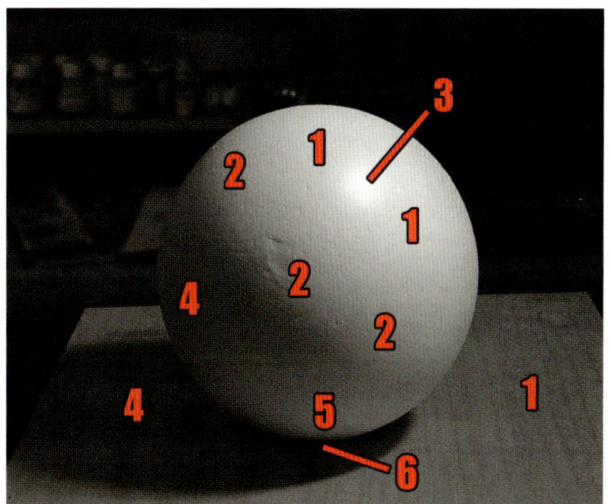

Spend some time on this spread, memorize this list!

THE VALUE SCALE

Rendering simple forms value by value is a great way to get to know the value scale. We'll see how and when each value is used, and in what order to work with them. Let's get acquainted with it!

The value scale is a full range of white to black tones.

Our First Two Tones: Average **Light** and Average **Shadow**

We can't start with just one value, or tone, we need to start with two. That's because light cannot look like light *without* shadow. I'll show you what I mean.

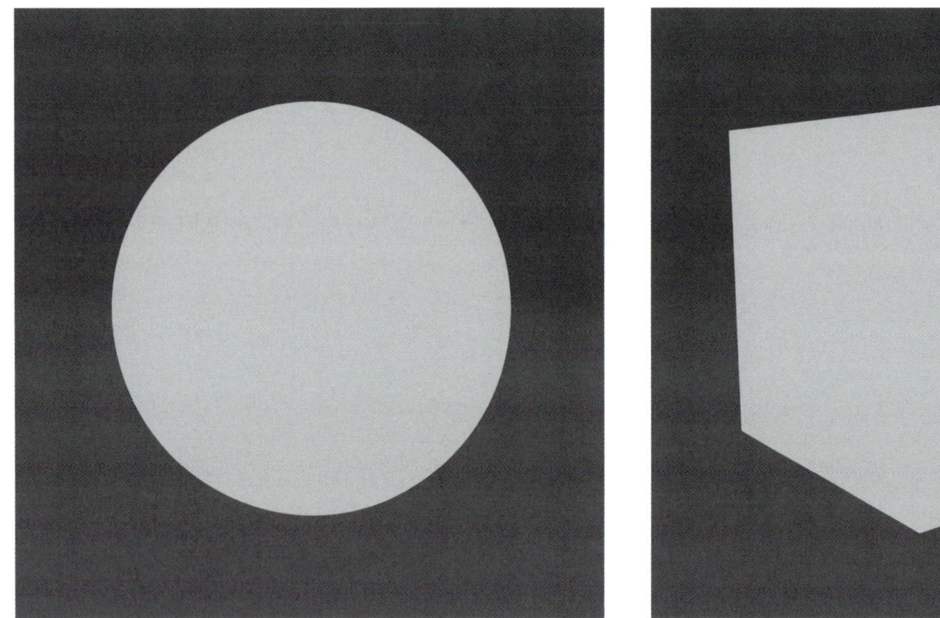

A sphere and a box, with only Average Light, but there is no dimensionality yet with just one value.

Choosing an Average Light value, or tone, is easy. Pick anything that leaves lots of room for the shadow family. I've chosen this value on the value scale:

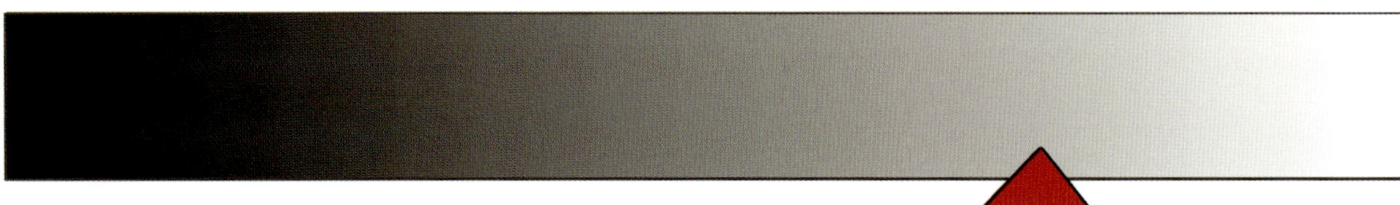

Generally a good safe spot for Average Light.

Before we apply Average Shadow, we need to know where to put it depending on the location of the light source. I'll imagine a light source coming in from the upper-right. Remember that you are saying something very important with your shadows. You're telling the viewer that the form has turned away from the light source enough that it no longer gets hit by light directly. Think of the shower analogy and what gets wet and what *doesn't*!

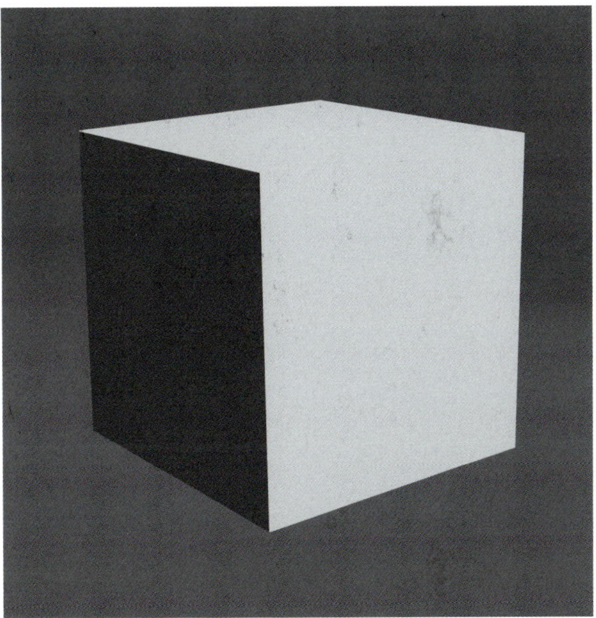

Depending on your medium, sometimes you simply let the white of the page be your Average Light, and therefore Average Shadow is the first value you physically apply.

We now have some dimensionality starting to appear! Also, notice that the edge of my shadow shape is dictated by the roundness of the form. The round ball gets a softer edge, the planar box gets a harder edge.

Here's the value I chose for my Average Shadow (blue). It's nice and dark and far from Average Light (red).

Form **Shadows** and Cast Shadows Act Together

The shadows that exist on the objects are called form shadows. But, as I'm sure you're aware, objects cast shadows onto other objects, too! In this case, our object will cast a shadow onto the floor it's sitting on. For the purposes of learning, I highly recommend you keep your cast shadows grouped in with whatever value you've chosen for your Average Shadow, like this:

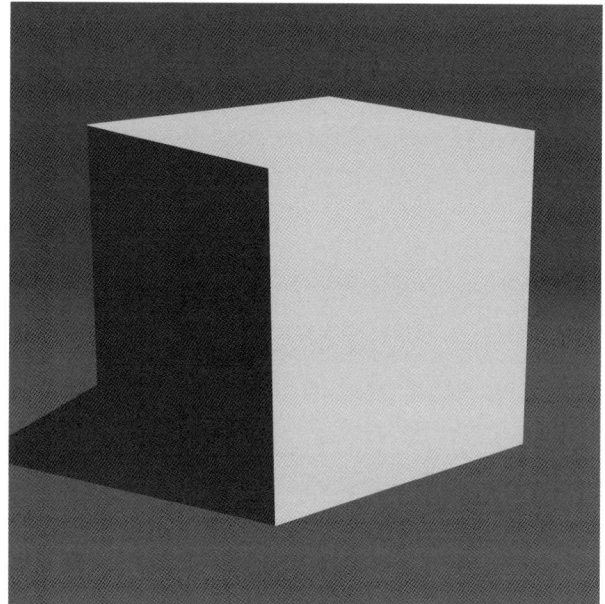

We now have form shadows as well as cast shadows.

Don't worry if you lose the edge between the object and the floor. This happens in real life all the time. But don't worry, we'll get some of that information back as we add more values.

Halftone: The Bridge between Light and Shadow

Even though I told you about this a few pages ago, it bears repeating: Halftone is part of the light family. It goes where the object is turning away from the light but *hasn't* turned away enough to be in shadow. I emphasize this because many, many people get this wrong! Here is the addition of Halftone on our sphere and cube:

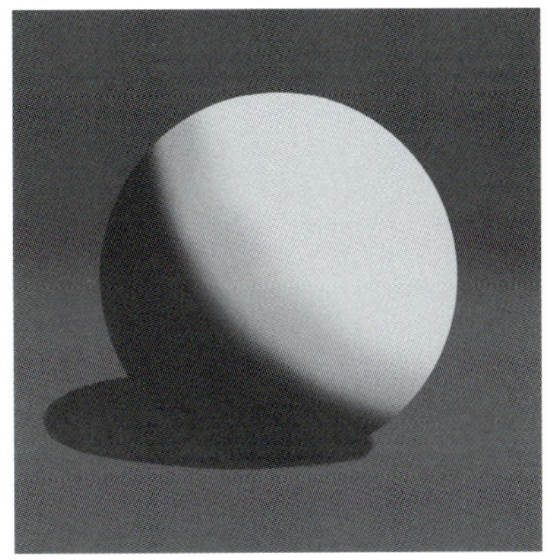

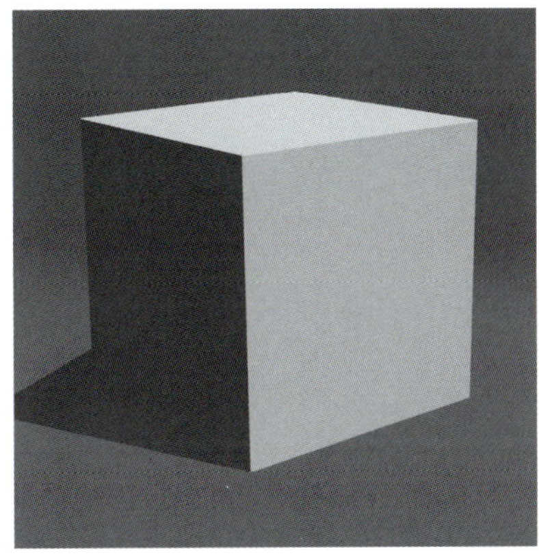

Halftone adds three-dimensionality because you are giving the viewer more detailed information about how the form interacts with the light source.

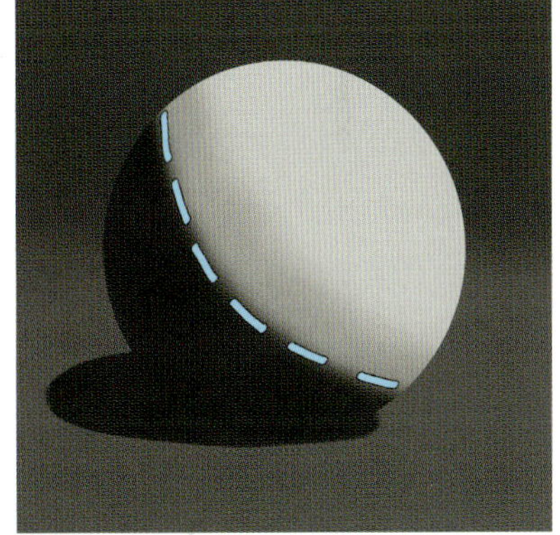

The all-important fence that separates the light and shadow families!

Notice how the shape of Halftone stays in the light family and does not cross the fence over to the shadow family.

And now for an updated look at our value scale:

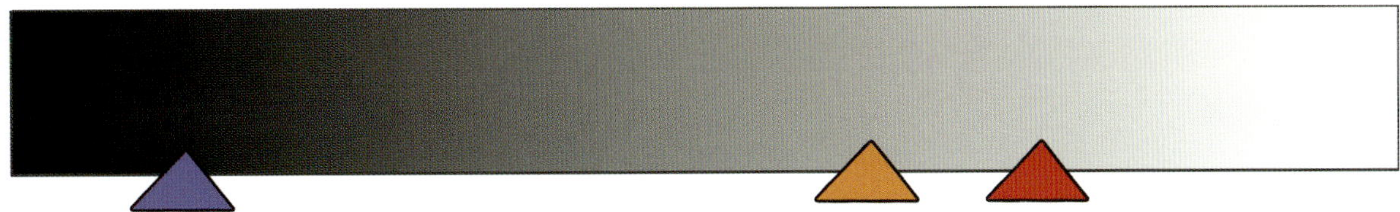

Halftone (orange) is darker than Average Light, but not by much.

Reflected Light
Illuminates the Shadows

Reflected Light is like the Halftone of the shadow family. It's caused by direct light hitting something nearby and bouncing or reflecting up into the shadows. At right is a diagram to demonstrate the concept.

Because surfaces in real life are rough and irregular on a microscopic level, when light rays bounce off them, they scatter in all directions. This has the practical effect of softening the edge of your Reflected Light value, making for a more subtle statement.

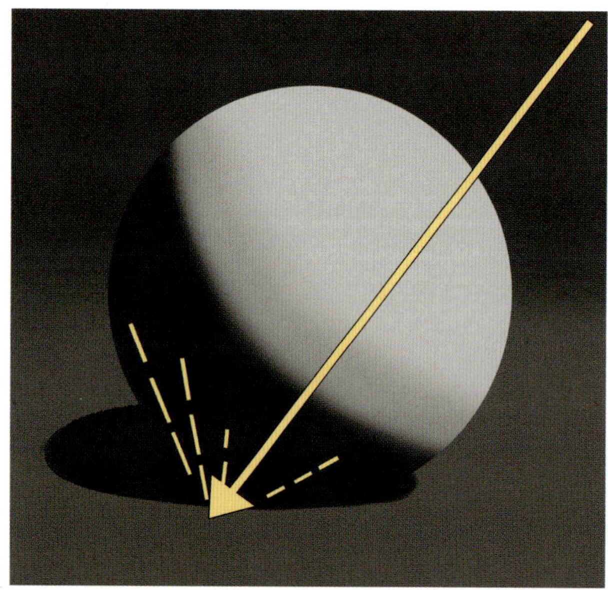

Direct light rays are bounced or reflected off the floor, and back up into the shadows.

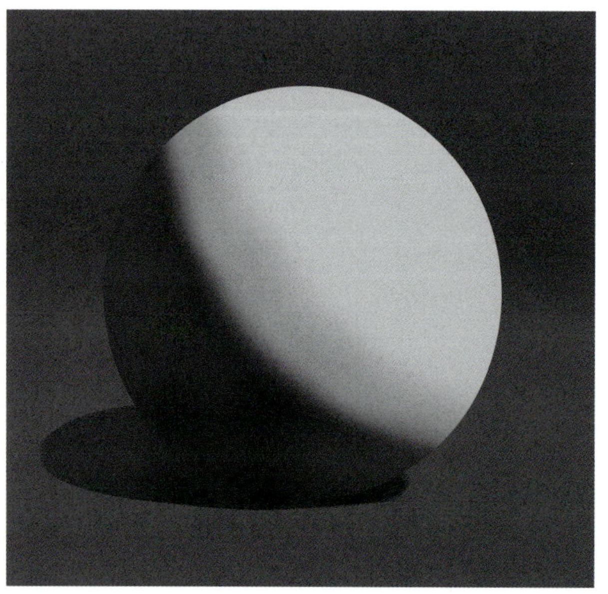

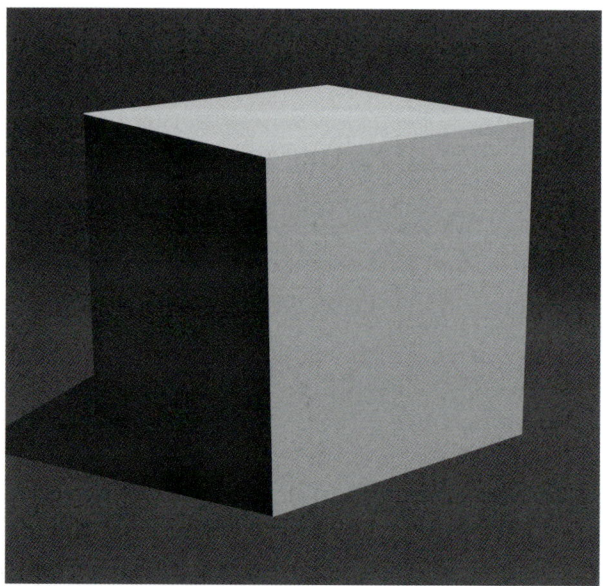

Cast shadows receive Reflected Light, too! Like Reflected Light on form shadows, typically you'll find it where the cast shadow is most exposed to the environment (i.e. farther away from the object casting it).

Let's circle back to our value scale. Things are filling up around here.

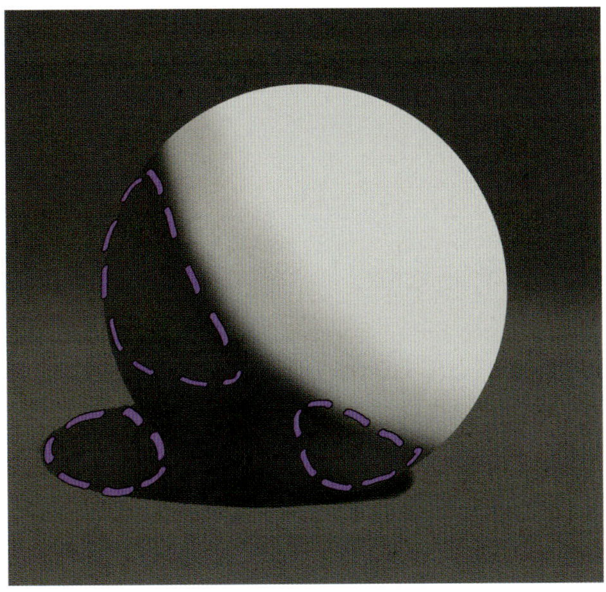

Areas of Reflected Light.

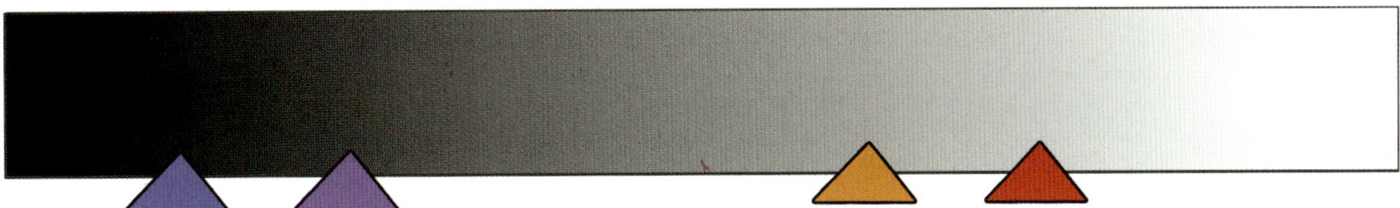

Can you see how Reflected Light (purple) has a similar relationship to Average Shadow as Halftone (orange) to Average Light?

You should also now be able to see the clear demarcation of a fence between light and shadow families, and how those two families strictly stay on their side.

Practically speaking, leaving a large gap between the light and shadow families like this will help the clarity of your lighting and shading. It's an especially useful idea for beginners because it helps ensure nobody crosses the fence. As a bonus, it also ensures that you're using a lot of contrast, which always helps pack a punch!

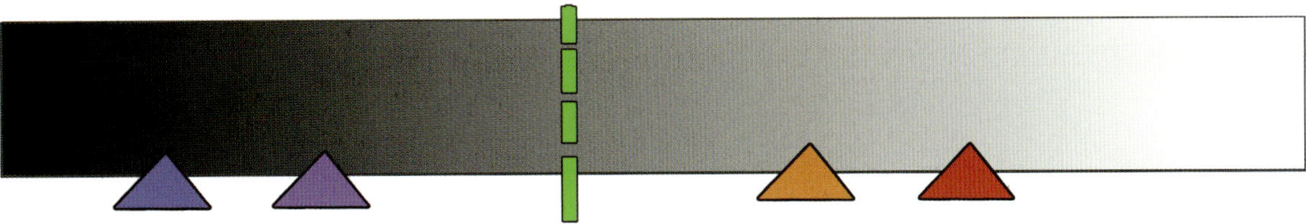

Fenceline shown in green.

Highlights: Your Lightest Value

All the values we've looked at so far will stay in place on an object, no matter which angle we observe it from. A highlight doesn't. It moves along *with* the viewing angle. That's because a highlight is a literal reflection of the light source itself, and re-flections are view dependent.

Here I used a 3D program to show how a highlight is part of an object aligned to reflect the light source. The yellow dot is the light source location.

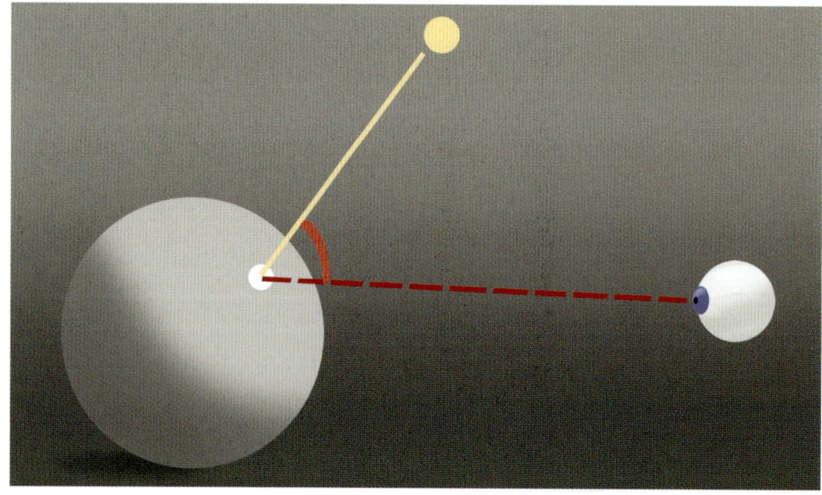

A schematic-style diagram of how a Highlight works.

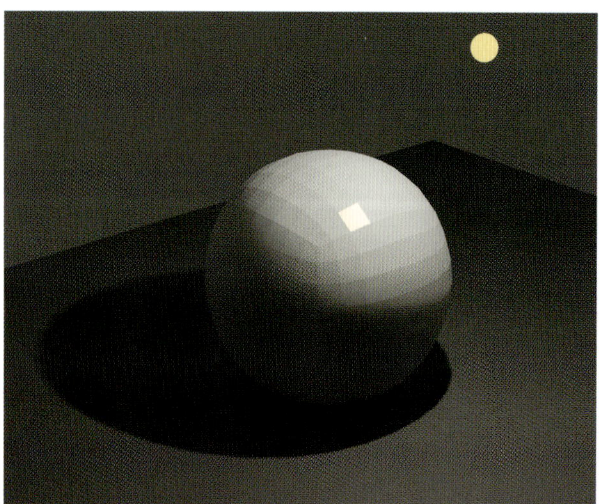

TIP: It helps to think of round objects as a series of flat planes.

Here are the highlights placed on our two objects. The sphere seems straightforward, but you might be wondering why there is a highlight on a box. That's because an abrupt plane change, like you see on a box, is never perfectly abrupt. There will almost always be a small beveled or curved edge that presents many possible reflection angles. So, when plane changes are boxy, look for a highlight running right along the edge! You won't always find one, of course, but it's not uncommon to spot one there.

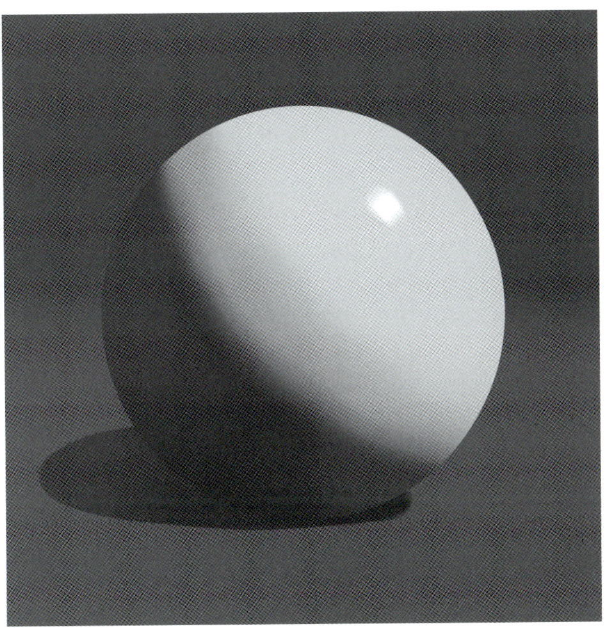
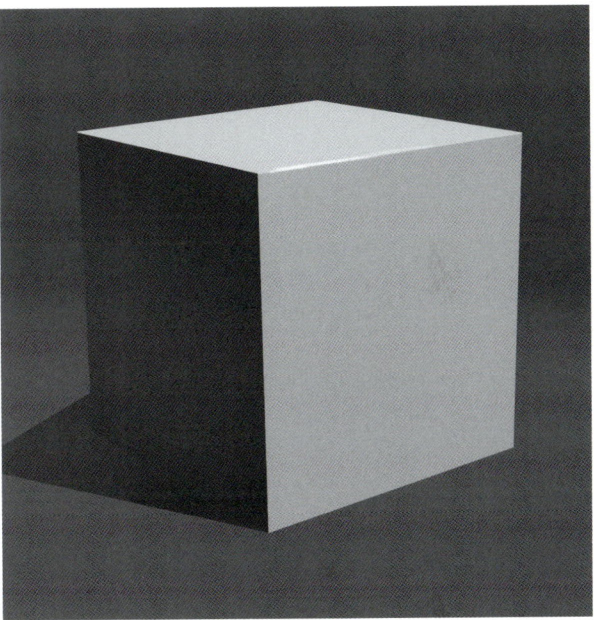

Tight highlights like these give the effect of a shiny surface. For more matte surfaces soften the hotspot.

The highlight value needs to be the lightest value on your value scale. Use pure white if you like!

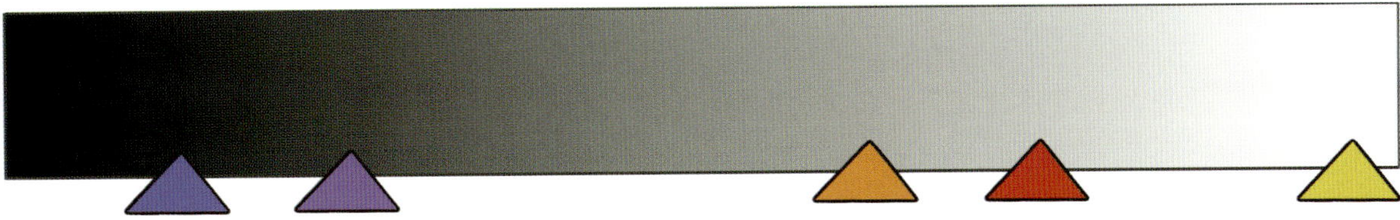

TIP: Making your highlight value lighter than Average Light by several shades will help clarity and pop.

Dark Accent/Ambient Occlusion:
The Anti-Highlight

Just as Highlight is the lightest part of the light family, so Dark Accent and Ambient Occlusion is the darkest part of the shadow family. To understand this value, let's look at a photograph of a ball sitting on a table.

There is Reflected Light on the underside of the ball caused by the light source hitting the table and bouncing back up. But look at the contact point where the ball is touching the table. See how both the ball and table darken? That's because fewer bounced light rays can find their way into that tight space. In other words, the ambient light is occluded, hence the term Ambient Occlusion. Less technically-minded artists often use the more visual term Dark Accent.

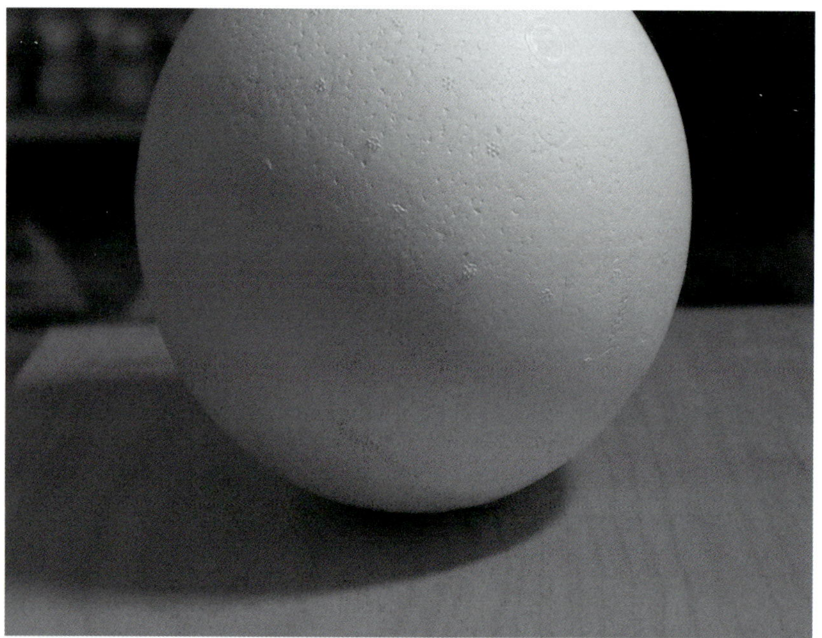

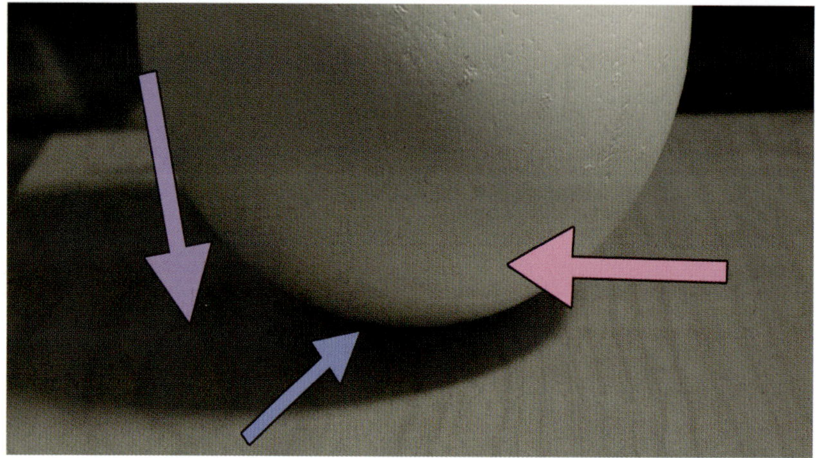

Blue: Dark Accent or Ambient Occlusion.
Purple: Average Shadow.
Pink: Reflected Light.

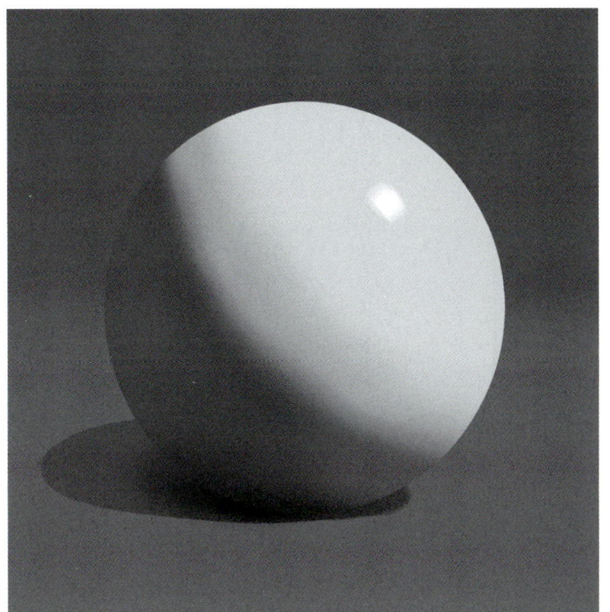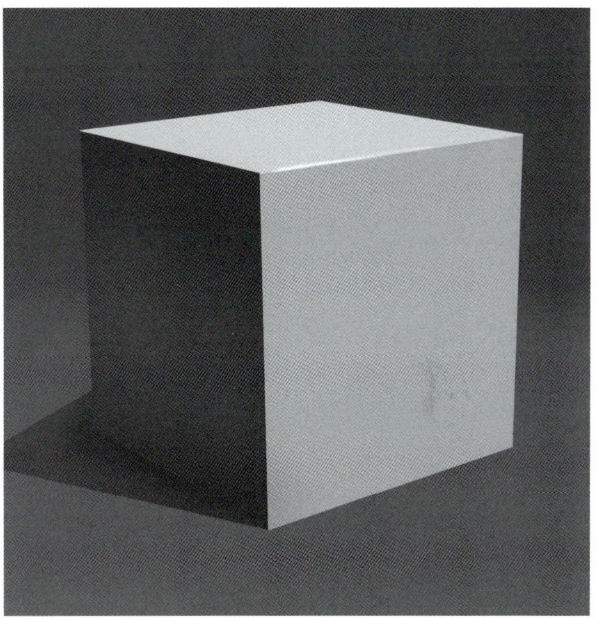

TIP: Much like Reflected Light, it's generally best to keep Ambient Occlusion or Dark Accent soft.

Much like a highlight, this value is generally applied in small areas, and makes for a big pop!

Two families and six values are all you'll ever need!

You can render anything with this system!

Applying the **Value System** to More Complex Subjects

Even with more complex subjects like people or characters, you still only need the six values we've just learned. Let's try it out. Below is a finished rendering of an elf character.

DRAWING: NOT ALWAYS DONE WITH LINES!

This is the first step I took in creating this character. I consider this my primary drawing stage although there isn't a line in sight. Instead, I am drawing with shapes of value! Remember to keep it down to just two values at first: Average Light, Average Shadow.

Drawing with value encompasses all the fundamentals in previous chapters but adds information about how light falls on the subject. The added information makes this more difficult, like throwing a few more bowling pins at the juggler, but it only takes practice.

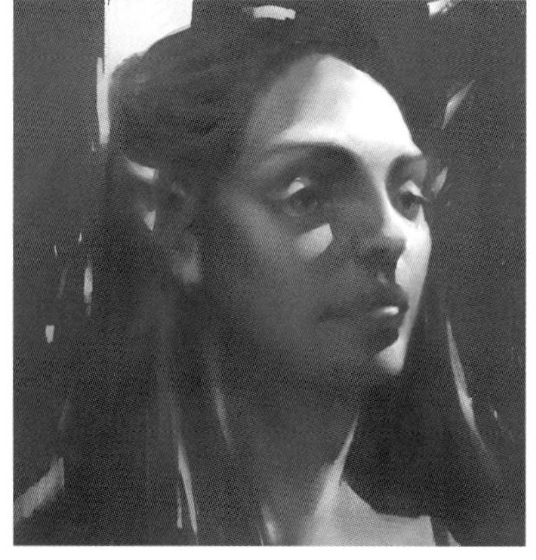

Before moving on, see if you can visually identify all six values: Average Light, Halftone, Highlight, Average Shadow, Reflected Light, Ambient Occlusion.

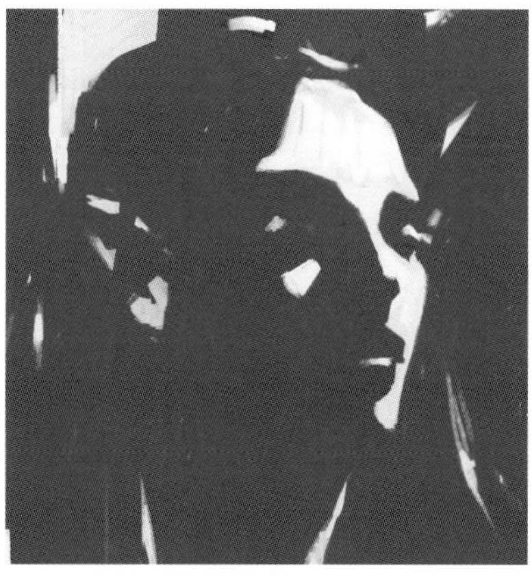

TIP: Blocking out form this way can be much faster than drawing with lines once you're comfortable with the process!

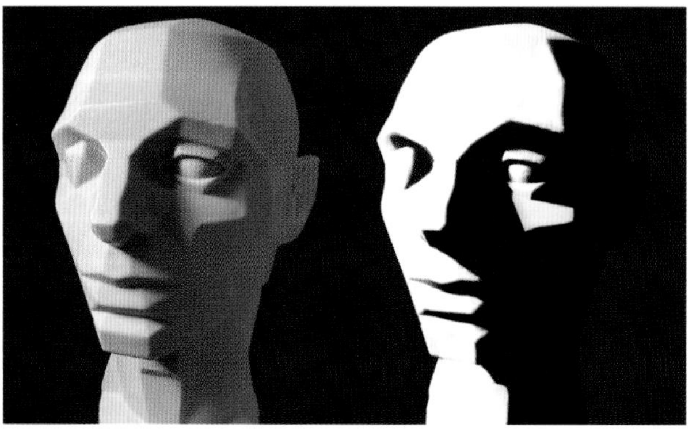

Raw reference on left. Light versus Shadow families isolated on right.

MEMORIZING LIGHT PATTERNS

Without reference, you may be wondering how I knew where to put my light and shadow shapes. This is something I can tell you but can't necessarily *teach* you. I've memorized the shapes and patterns that occur when light falls on the head from different angles. It's a skill set I've built over many years and reference-studies.

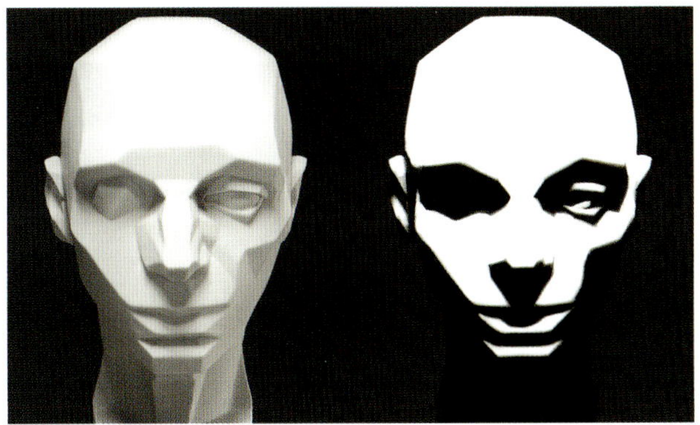

The head model pictured here is called the Asaro Head. (Dollar for dollar, this is probably the most impactful purchase I have made in my art career.)

A SERIES OF 2D SHAPES

Ironically, even though rendering can produce a powerful 3D illusion, what we're actually working with is a series of 2D shapes. Being shapes, they need to be kept simple and well-designed for optimal clarity (see Chapter 1)!

Sometimes nature will give you a clean, well-designed shape, and sometimes not. It's up to you to sort through it and decide what can be copied and what needs to be redesigned. This takes time and practice!

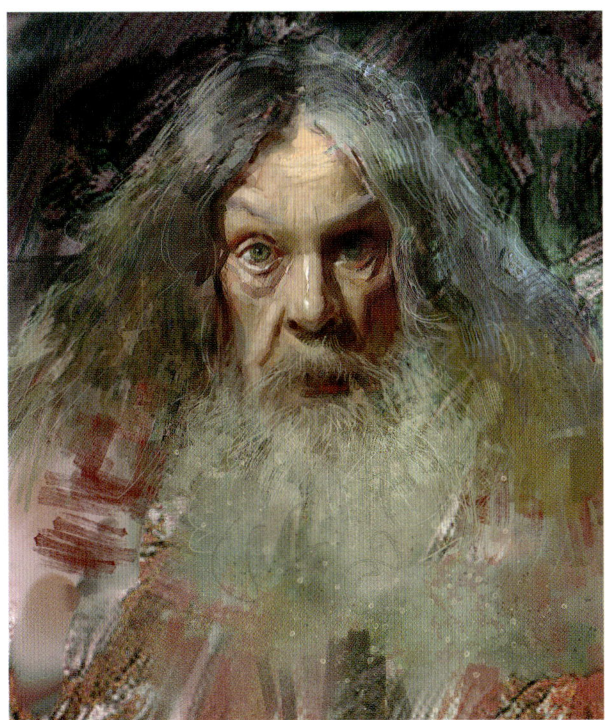

A portrait of Alan Moore, digital. Done from photo reference.

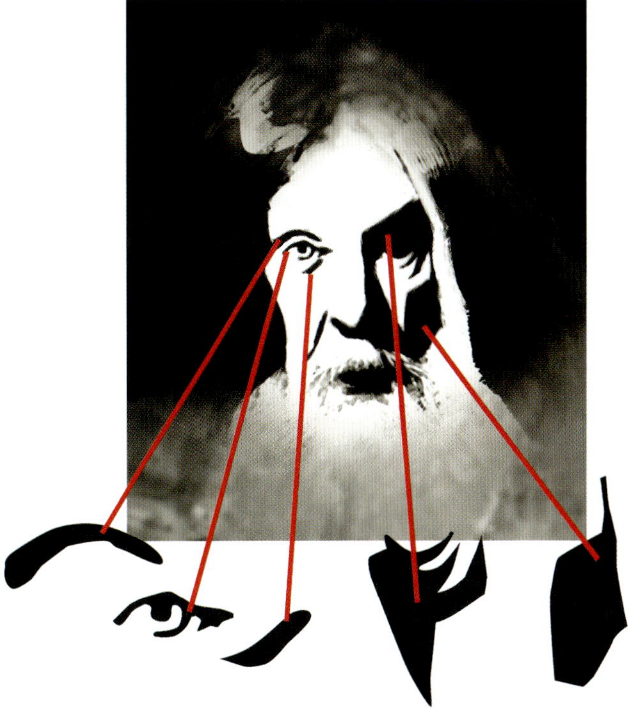

Some of the designs I came up with for the various shadow shapes.

Okay, back to our elf character. The addition of Halftone adds interest to the form.

A reminder to always keep your shapes in check!

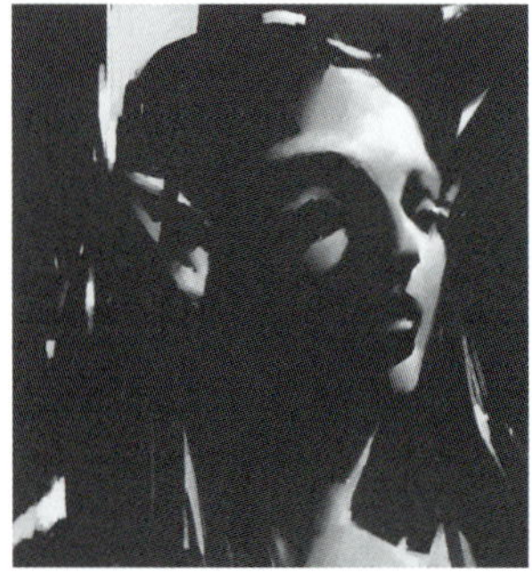

Remember that the hardness or softness of the edge varies along with the roundness or firmness of the form itself.

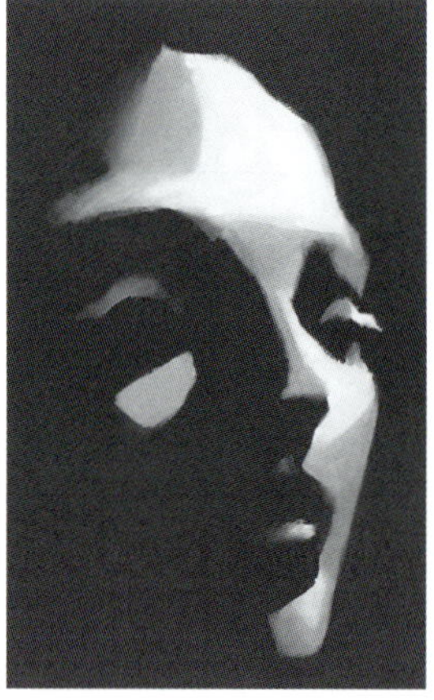

I made the halftones hard.

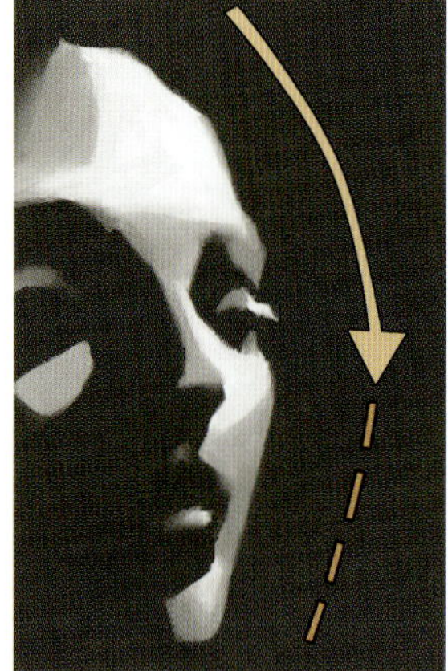

The head is an overall-round form. When edged to reveal their shape design, the form begins turning away from the light (dotted line) that's where you'll begin to see halftones.

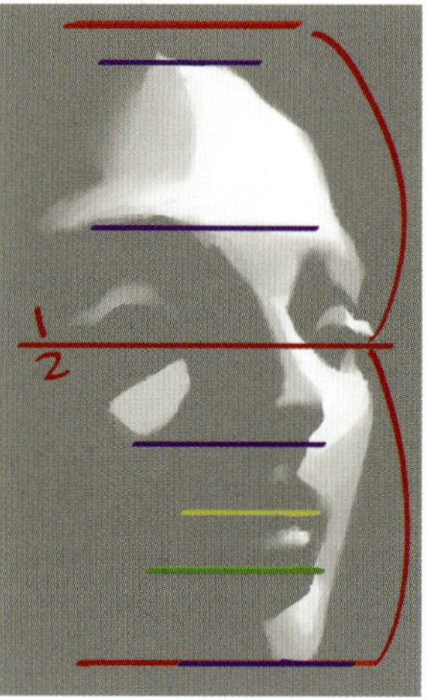

Remember the proportions from Chapter 6! I am keeping them in the back of my mind here to check my work as I go. Notice I have subtly altered the proportions to suit this design, but the overall framework is intact.

I've jumped back into the shadow family now, to add Reflected Light. In this case I'm adding it to areas of the form that are freely accessed by the environment at large.

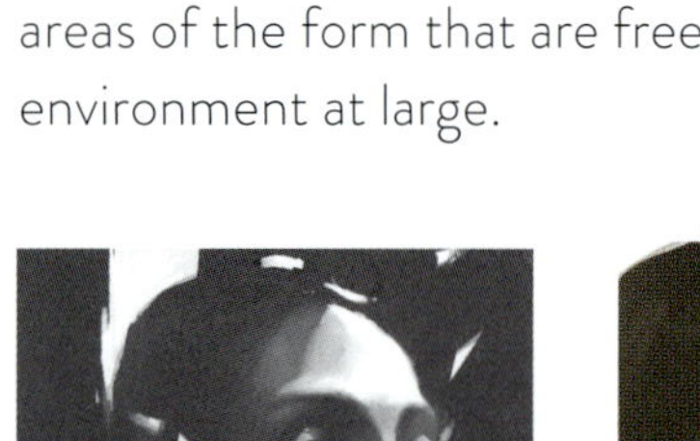

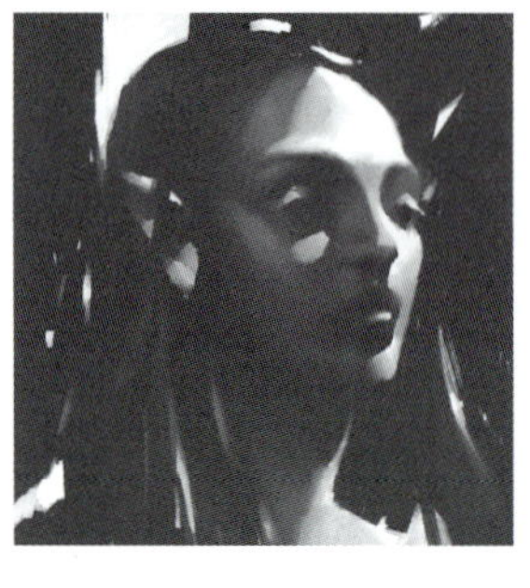

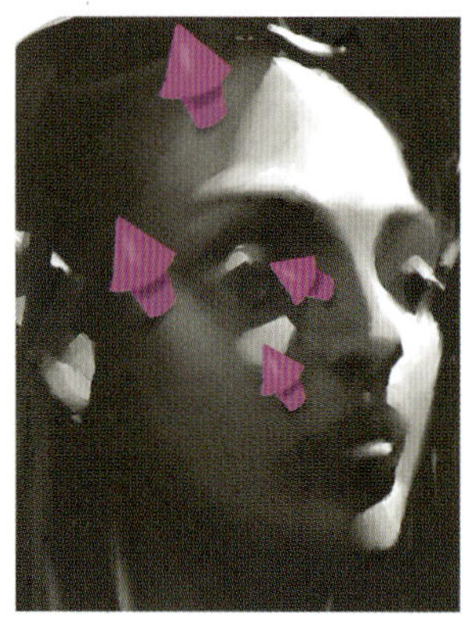

TIP: Reflected Light is often soft-edged, due to its diffuse nature.

I like to add Dark Accent or Ambient Occlusion in the same pass, since it's also caused by the Reflected or ambient light. This time a *lack* of it. It goes in those tight spaces or under overhanging areas. You'll find it all over the place on more complex forms.

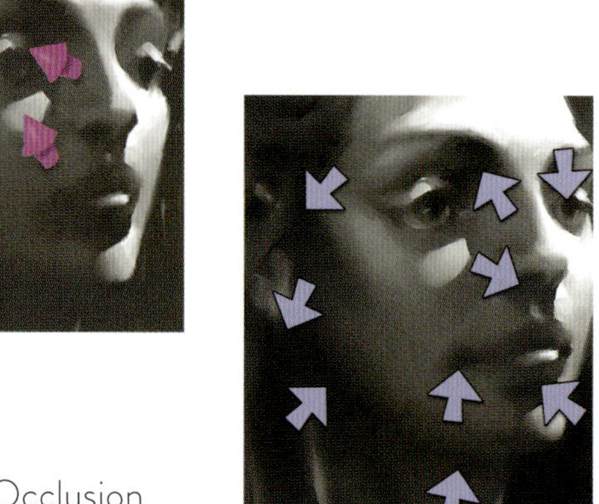

Sometimes the features themselves can be defined with Dark Accent. Here, the iris and upper eyelid are defined by one passage of Dark Accent. Same with the nostrils and nose-overhang.

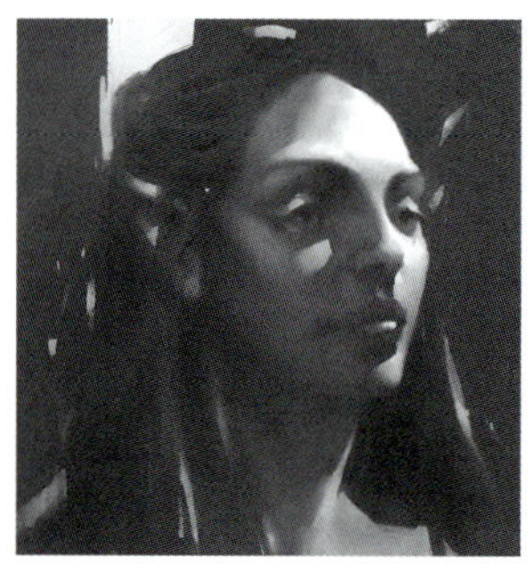

Another look at the final. I didn't even use any highlights on this one!

ASSIGNMENTS

Don't skip over studying and practicing value to get to color. Having a firm foundation of light and shadow will make adding color much easier and more effective.

ASSIGNMENT #1

Using your medium of choice, create your own value scale. It's a helpful exercise and you can use it as a tool when shading your drawings.

ASSIGNMENT #2

Using the process shown in this chapter, render a sphere and a box form. You can use any medium you like, be it traditional or digital. It may be helpful to use a value scale alongside your work, placing the values you are using on that chart as you go. This will help you stay in control with regards to which family you're working in, and how each value relates within each family.

ASSIGNMENT #3

Using a reference taken with a single light source, separate the reference into a single light shape and a single shadow shape. This can be done across an entire pose, the head, or any type of character. Remember to think about your form as a series of planes, as well as how those planes relate to the light's position in space (also recall the shower analogy, if it helps!) .

ASSIGNMENT #4

Look back at a few of the images you gathered for the assignments in Chapter 5. Using your photo-editing app of choice, convert them to black and white. Compare the black-and-white images to the color to see the corresponding values.

8

Color Doesn't Have to Be **Scary**!

Ask a hundred students what the hardest part of art is, and I'll bet at least eighty of them will say it's color. I would've been one of them, back when I first started! While many artists do struggle with color, the trouble mostly happens when you make color a priority too soon, because that is sure to muddy up your other fundamentals, which are, to be sure, far more important. There is a reason color comes last in this book!

Here's a quick insight as to why. Let's say you have something in your painting that you want to make purple. Great! But there are a thousand shades of purple. How light or how dark should the purple be? Well, that right there is not a color decision, it's a *value* decision. Value, therefore, is a fundamental that must come before color.

Okay, so you choose a value for the purple. Now you must decide what *shape* it fits into on your painting. That isn't a color decision. It's a drawing decision. See what I'm getting at?

For some reason artists let their lust for pretty colors override decisions of drawing, shapes, and value. That leaves color to lift far too much of the load.

Let's put it this way: Color cannot save a picture. It can only enhance a picture that is already working.

Sure, color is nice . . . but can you spot the fundamentals underneath?

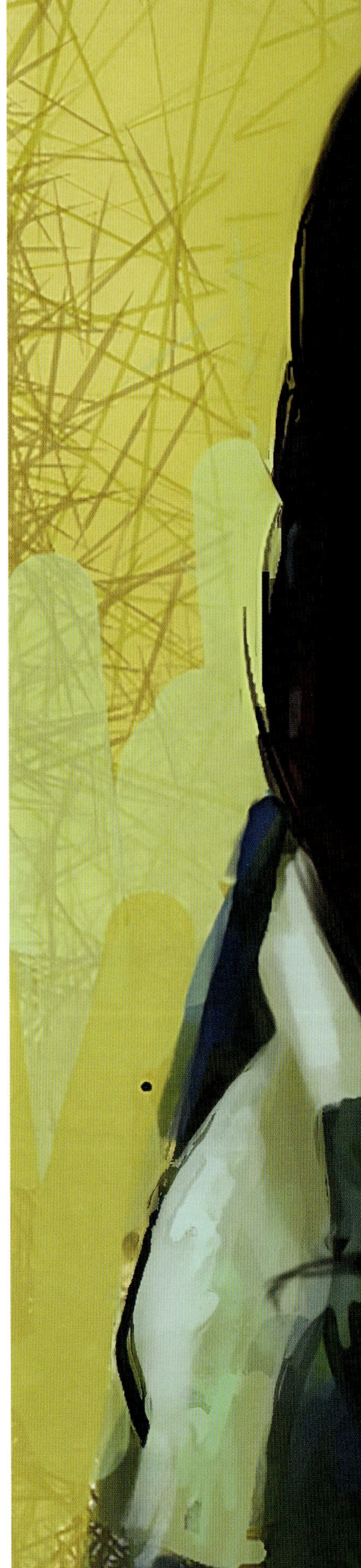

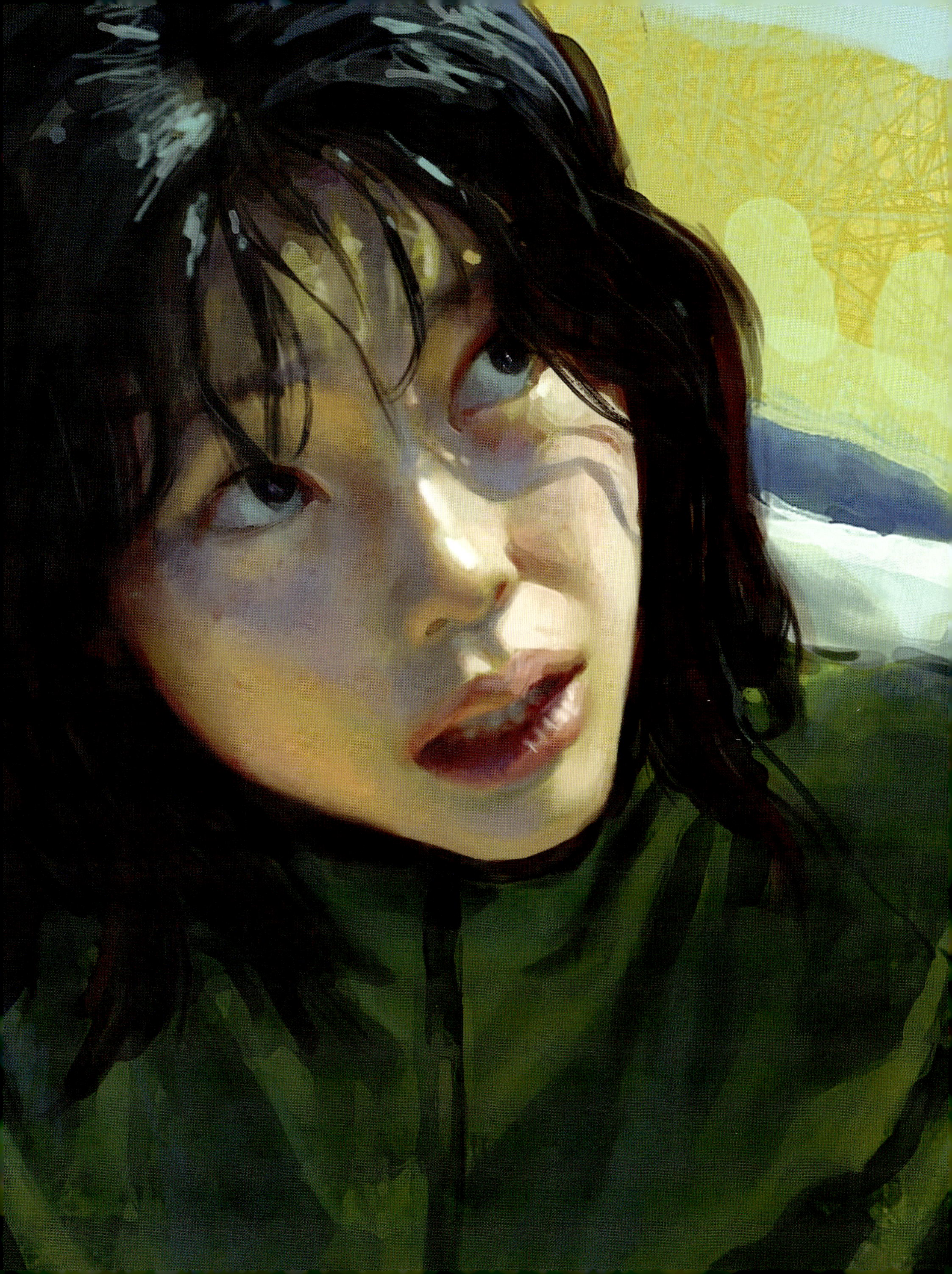

Color Temperature:
The All-in-One Color Theory

I can boil all this down to three words: warm versus cool. To me, this is the holy grail of color, and understanding it has underpinned my fifteen-plus-year career as a professional artist who often specializes in color work!

First, the all-important color wheel.

It's a series of hues. Hue is simply the color name. Think, red, yellow, green, or blue. We'll constantly refer back to this. Now let's break this warm versus cool theory down on a broad level.

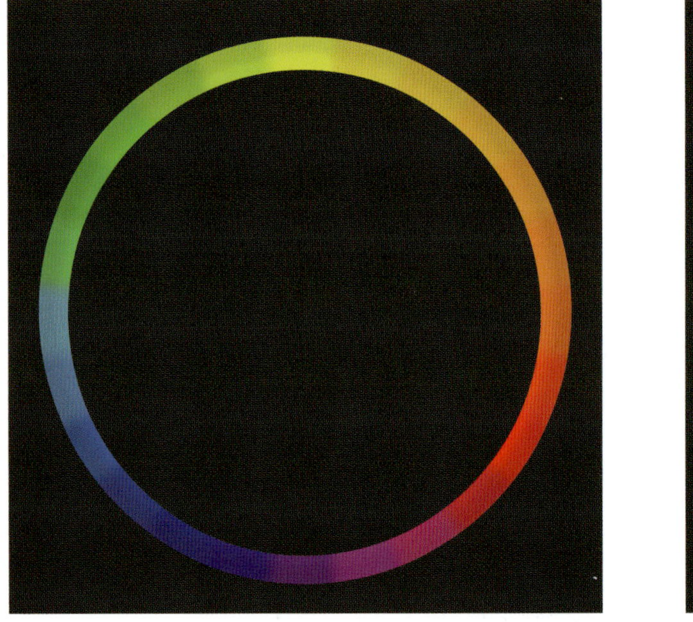

Take note of the sequence of hues. Yellow to orange, to red, to magenta, to purple, and so on. Note: Sometimes you'll see this as a vertical strip.

WARM COLORS

I remember being taught in elementary school that warm colors were anything in the realm of reds, oranges, and yellows. While simplistic, this is indeed a good place to start! I've painted a swatch of these colors at right. Notice how they feel cohesive together. This makes sense, as those colors are also direct neighbors on the color wheel.

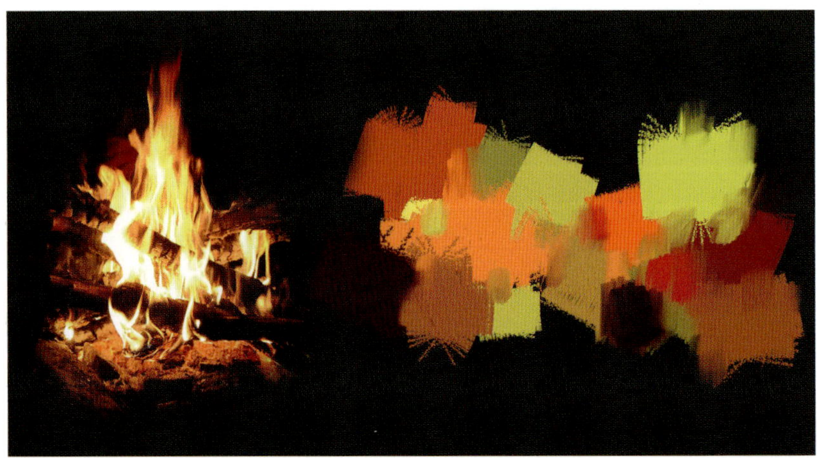

Think of warm colors overall as the colors of a campfire.

COOL COLORS

Keeping it simple, cold colors are on the opposite side of the color wheel. Think blues, primarily. Blues have quite the range, from cyan, to royal, to ultramarine. I also like to group blue's direct neighbors in with the cold colors. Think turquoisey greens and deep violets.

Due to the terms warm and cool, we refer to this type of description as *color temperature*.

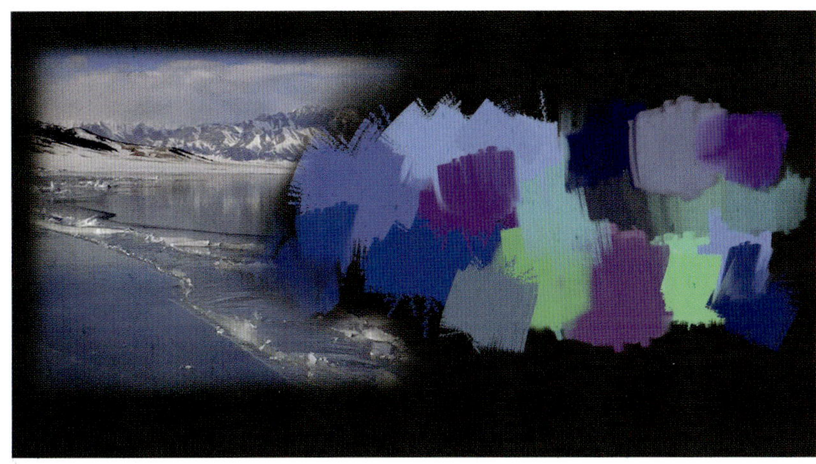

Think of cool colors as snowy mountains and icy waters.

THE TWO FAMILIES COMPLEMENT EACH OTHER

Much like how light needs shadow to communicate, colors need their opposites. There is an official art term for this: *complementary*. When looking at the color wheel, the warm section of colors and the cool section are opposite each other.

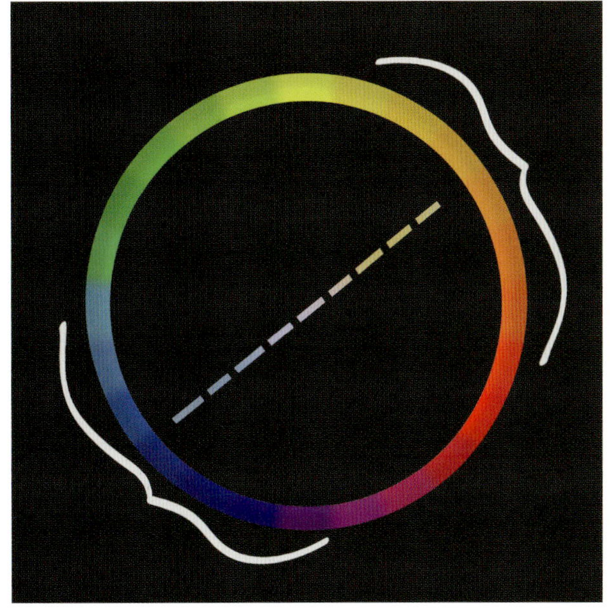

The Easiest Way to Move from
Warm to **Cool** and **Back**

This sets us up for the most important concept to understand about color: movement. Unlike values, where we had to maintain that fence to clearly separate families, colors are much freer to mingle with one another. But their mingling isn't aimless. There's a path from warm to cool and from cool to warm. Every color can go on this journey. The easiest way to do it is by following the hues on the color wheel.

This chart illustrates how any hue can travel warmer or cooler. In the middle is the starting hue. Running to the left, the color gets (or stays) warmer. To the right, it gets (or stays) cooler.

How do you know which direction on the color wheel to move? Take the shortest route to the desired overall destination.

Let's take a purple. Because the closest members of the warm family are to the right of that initial swatch, we move that hue around the color wheel counterclockwise to make it warmer.

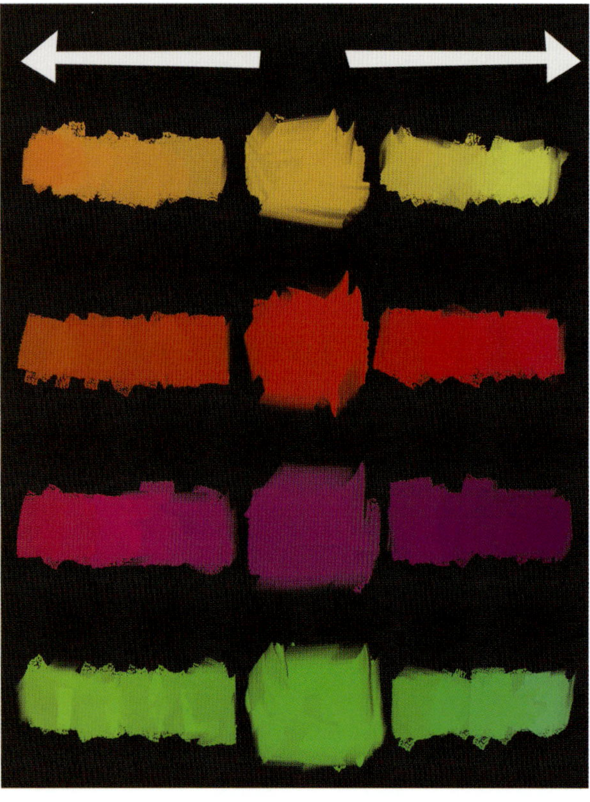

I am trying not to deviate outside of the particular hue in question. For example, I want all those reds to still be identifiable as red if the color were to be seen alone.

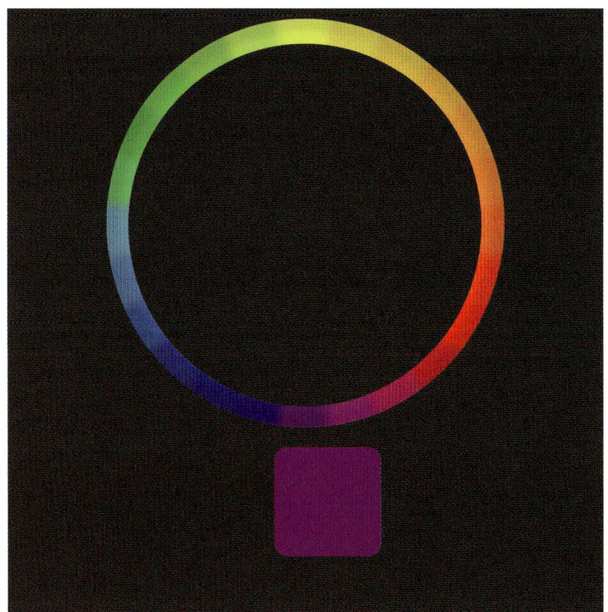

Our starting color.

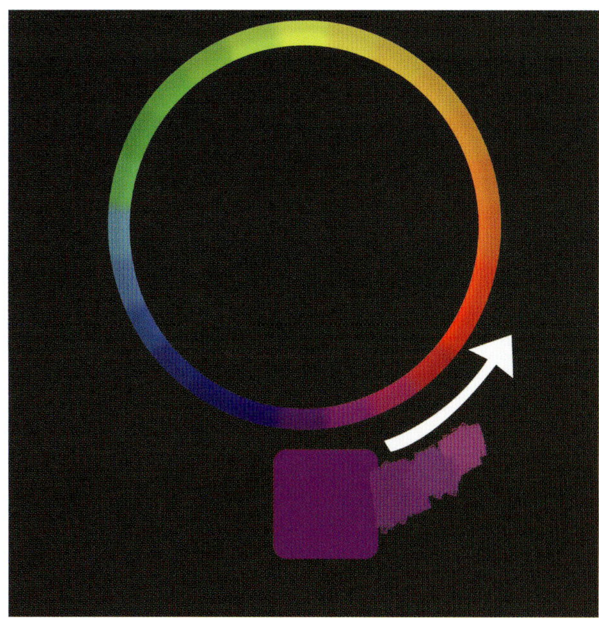

Move the color this way, toward the nearest end of the warm overall family of colors.

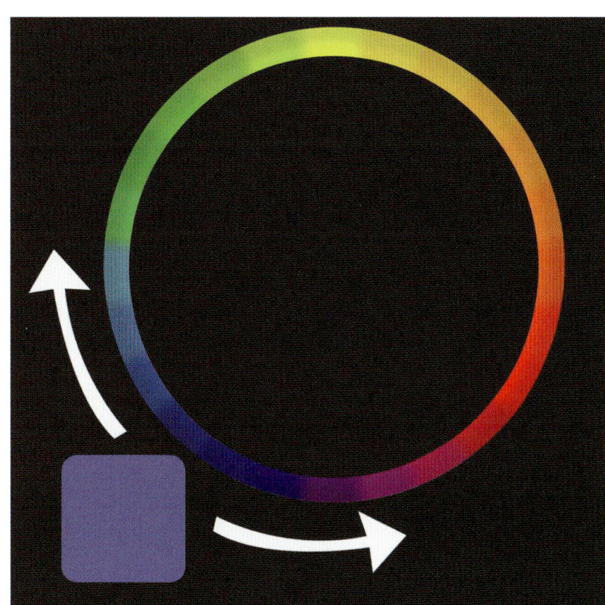

Which way should this color move to get warmer?

How about a royal blue, though? This is in the middle of the cool colors.

The blue from right, moving toward the warm hues. Note that on the right we're into violet so I stopped there.

There is no objectively correct answer to this question. I would move it counterclockwise. Why? Because we hit magenta and red sooner than we hit yellow. My swatch is shown above.

Why didn't I go the other way through the greens? Well, green is the hue with the most variations. As such, it takes a lot of traveling around the color wheel to finally get a green that doesn't contain blue before the yellows start taking over.

TERMINOLOGY

Before we continue, let's establish the rest of our color terminology.

Hue is the color name itself.

Saturation is the amount of chroma in a hue. It's how colorful or vibrant the color is.

Value is what we studied in Chapter 7. It's the measure of light and dark tones. Value is unique because you can use it independent of color like we did in the previous chapter. In this chapter, every color we pick will also have a corresponding value. At right is the same hue, with the same amount of saturation, shown in three different values.

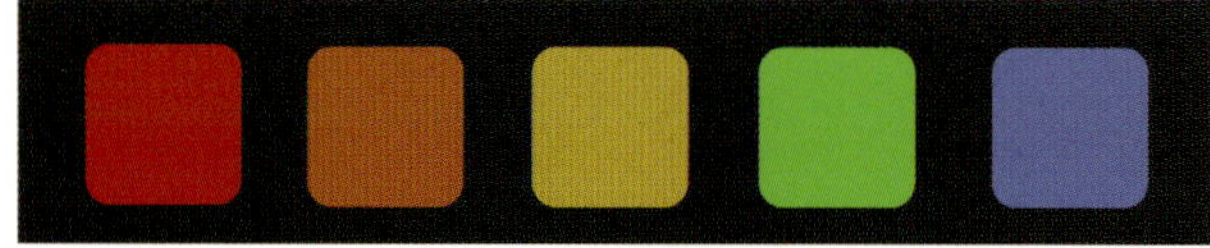

Red, Orange, Yellow, Green, and Blue hues.

A lack of saturation is pure gray (left side), and full saturation is the most colorful version of that hue (right side).

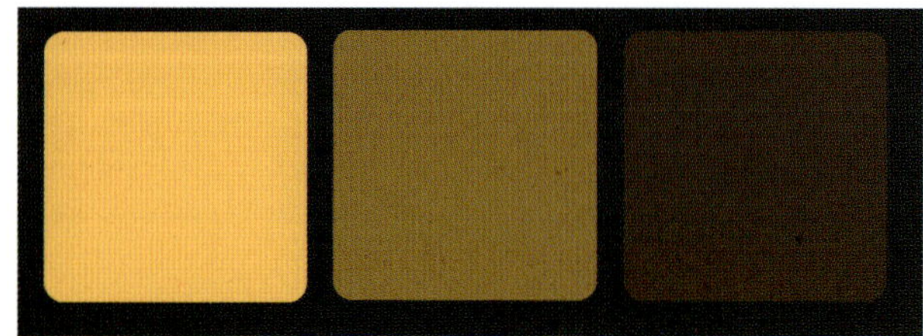

Value alone can dramatically alter the perception of a color. For example, many would call the swatch on the right brown, but you likely wouldn't give that name to the swatch on the left!

DESCRIBING COLORS

First, we can throw color names right out the window. Saying a color is "red" doesn't do an artist any good because it's too vague. In this example, I'd describe the color on the left as a warmer red as compared to the cooler red on the right.

I bet you're not a stranger to color temperature at all! It's a staple of modern life. When you buy a lightbulb, there will be a listing on the box, typically a number followed by a *k*, which stands for *Kelvin*, indicating its color temperature.

A reading lamp might be 2700k and aptly called yellow light. A pot-light might be 4000k, which is often branded cool white. You might see 3000k

Both of these, seen in isolation, would likely be described as red.

called warm white. If you've done any kind of home decoration, you're probably familiar with how different color temperatures affect a room's lighting and mood!

Light and Shadow Colors:
The Bully Principle

The only reason we see any color at all is because of light. While we don't really measure color temperatures with the Kelvin scale in art, we do keep track of a color's temperature visually. This is where we bring back our friends, light and shadow. They hold the first key to unlocking an understanding of color temperature. Consider the photograph at right.

Here's the exercise. What I am doing is using a digital color picker (or sample tool) to select colors that exist in either the light or shadow family. Then I'll paint a swatch of it below, in its appropriate category.

What I want you to notice here is that the hues of the light colors are all quite close together. They seem to be pinned together with the center point yellowy-orange. This is across multiple objects: trees, roofs, rock, bushes, and walls.

This demonstrates what I call the *Bully Principle*. The light source is the strongest influence of color in the scene, so much so that it *bullies* the colors of what it hits to be like it.

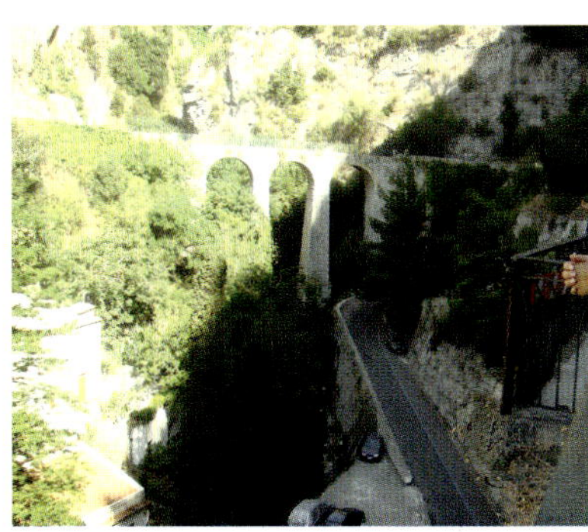

This photo (which I took during a trip to Italy in 2004) was instrumental in building my own understanding of color.

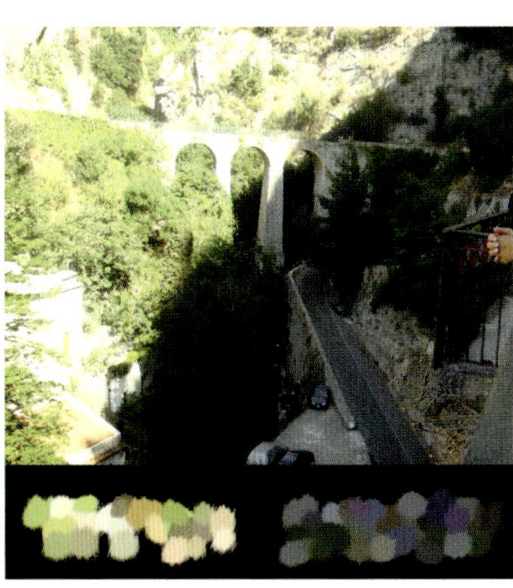

Light-color swatches on left, shadow-color swatches on right.

In this case, the light source is the warm afternoon sun, which has some yellow and orange in it. That explains why that hue is at the epicenter of the light's colors in the photo. Even where it's allowing other colors to exist, like the red rooftops, it is still forcing its warm color temperature onto these objects.

Okay, let's look at the shadow colors now. Do you notice a difference in their overall characteristics?

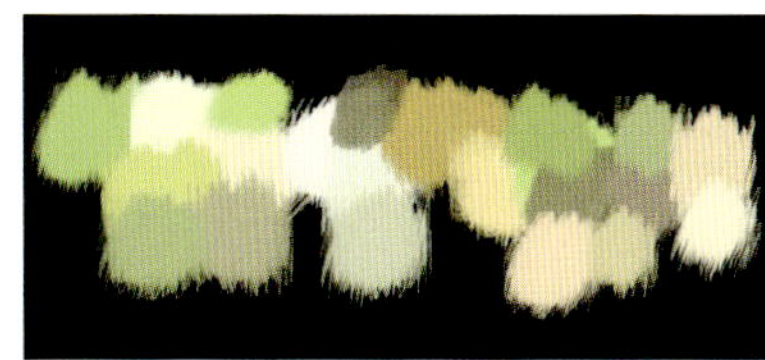

The colors in light.

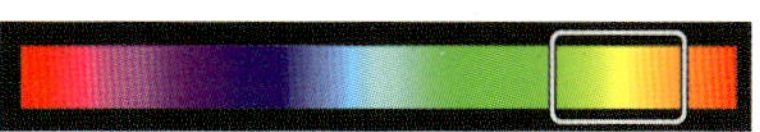

Here they are on the hue strip.

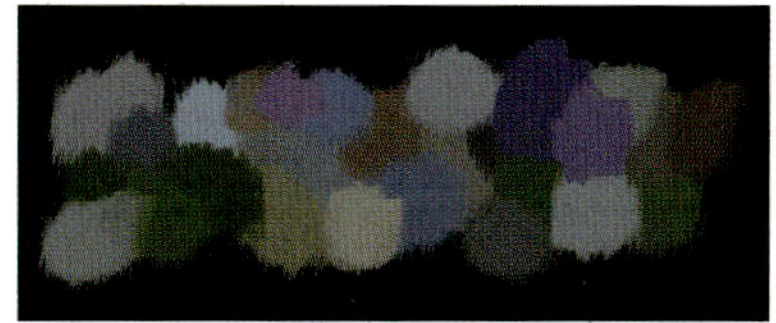

The color samples in shadow.

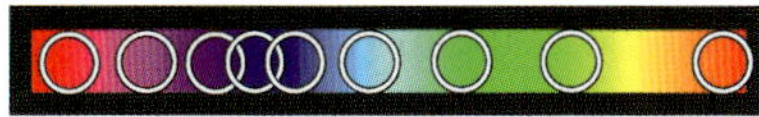

Shadow hues located on the hue strip.

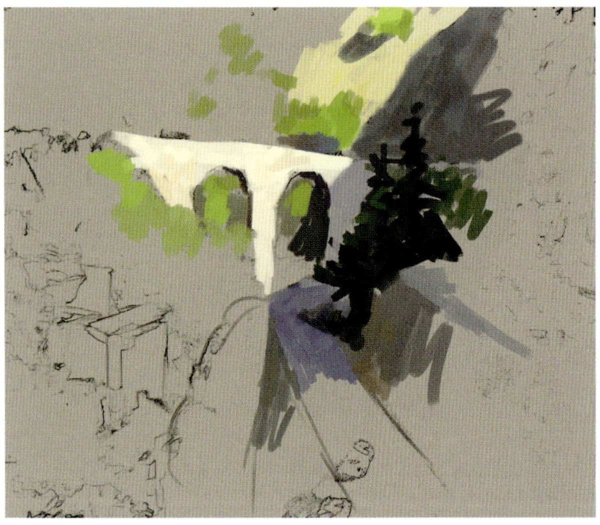

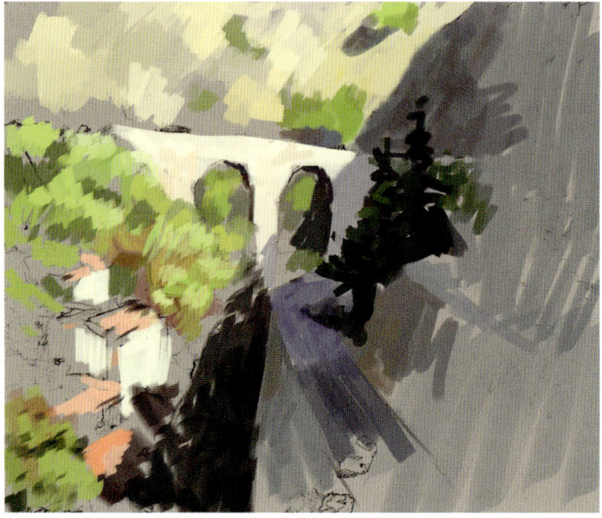

I get the overall color relationships going by working the areas where light and shadow touch. In this case it's down the middle of the picture.

TIP: Keep your canvas, digital or traditional, small for these quick studies.

Expanding out toward the edges of the frame.

TIP: If you're struggling, compare the color you've chosen with the colors in your swatch study. Try to not sample colors from the swatch study or photograph itself, as this works against your learning.

The shadow colors are all over the place! There's a reason for that. The shadows are areas *not* hit directly by the light so they are free of the bully! As such, they're influenced by many other factors, for example, skylight, bounced or reflected light, and local color. The colors can slide around more in shadow and there's a broader mix of color temperature.

We have two very different ecosystems of color. The bullied colors in light and the free-roaming colors in shadow.

At this stage we can try a little painted study of what we've learned! Notice how coarse and unrefined the drawing is. That doesn't matter. Get the color relationships right, and it will still read as believable light.

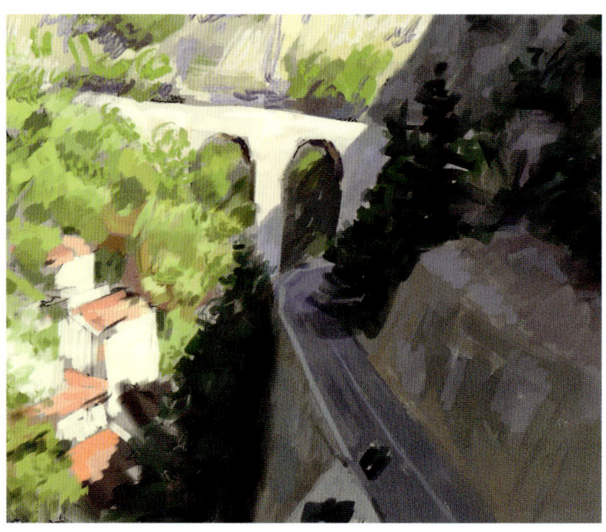

Finished light and color study. Working quickly on these allows you to do many of them and sharpens your decision making.

The illustration at right (2010, digital) was directly inspired by the previous photograph and color exercise. The only difference is I spent many more hours refining the shapes and fantasy design in this piece.

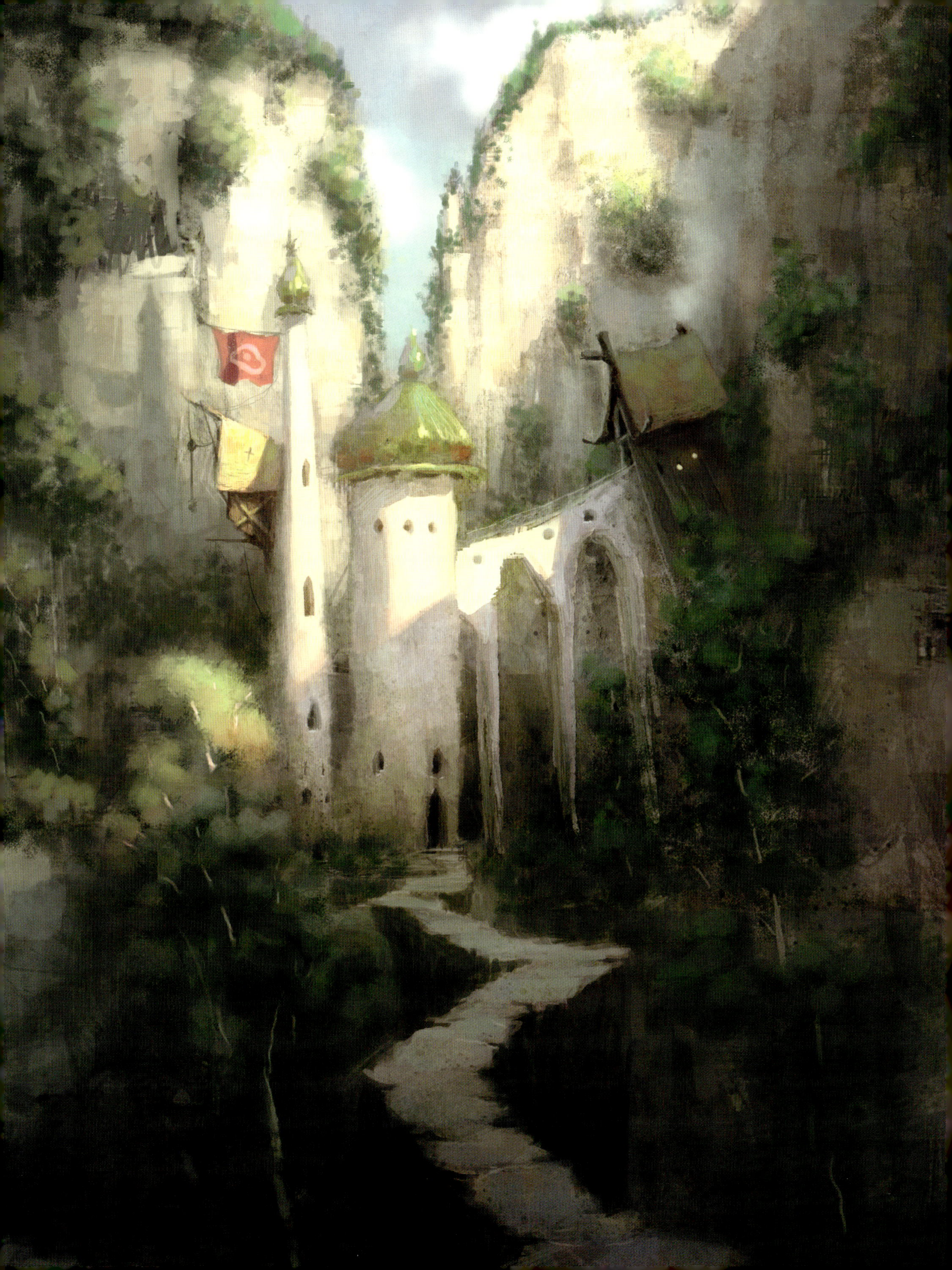

Grays Are Powerful
(And Another Way to Shift Temperature)

You may notice from the various paintings so far that colors have very different levels of saturation. In fact, upon closer inspection, many colors are quite *desaturated*, or close to gray. What's with that?

There is another way to shift color temperature. Consider the chart below. The top row of color uses only hue to shift while the bottom row achieves the same thing, but in a more subtle way.

The colors on the bottom row are moving through the gray. Gray is an extremely powerful aspect of color theory. Every hue has pure gray in common.

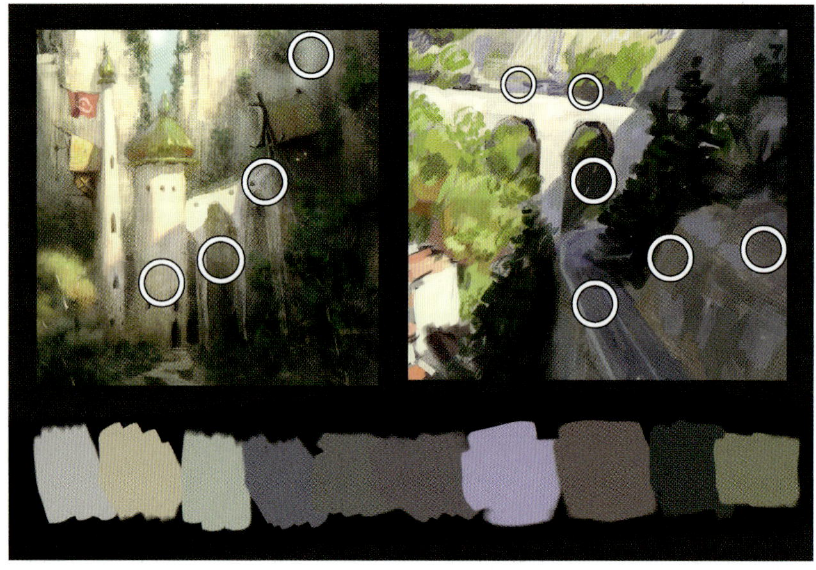

Many colors used in these paintings are fairly desaturated, despite an overall colorful vibe to the final pieces.

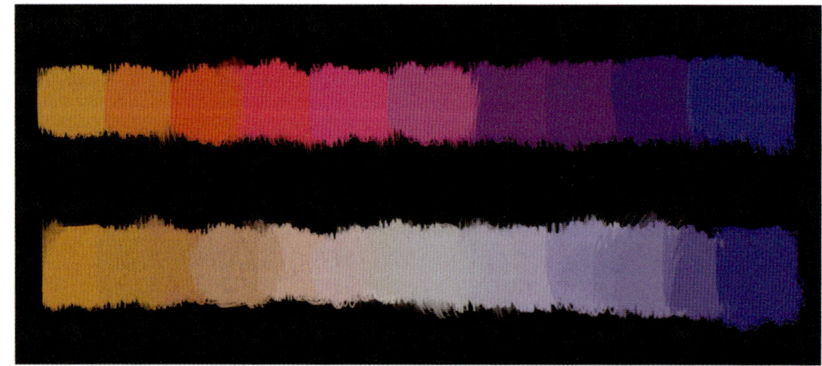

I like to think of gray as a global passport for color. Because all the colors meet at gray, you may use gray to travel from any one color to any other color. You can also use gray as a verb. *Graying down* a color, or desaturating it to some degree, causes something pretty magical to happen: *color harmony*. Let's think of color harmony as a pleasing passage between various color temperatures like warms to cools.

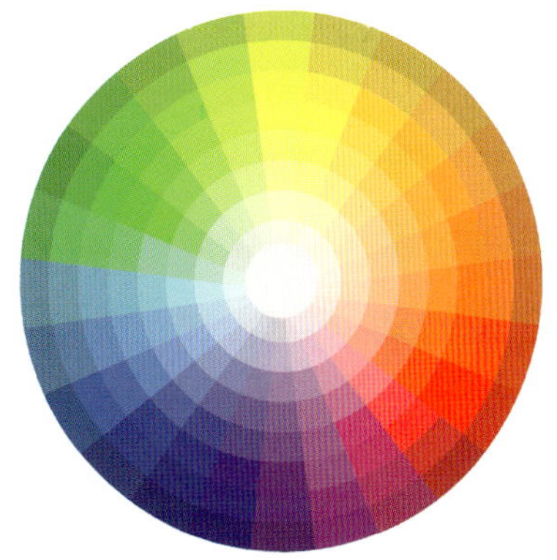

This color wheel includes a saturation chart within each hue. Notice how every color (or hue) ultimately leads back to a gray or a color with no saturation whatsoever.

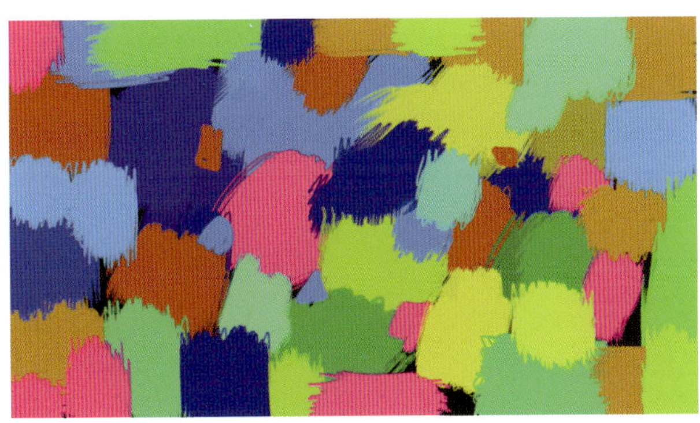

Every color is very saturated, resulting in a chaotic, almost loud, feeling like every color is shouting for attention. This is generally not pleasing to the viewer, because one color has nothing to do with the next.

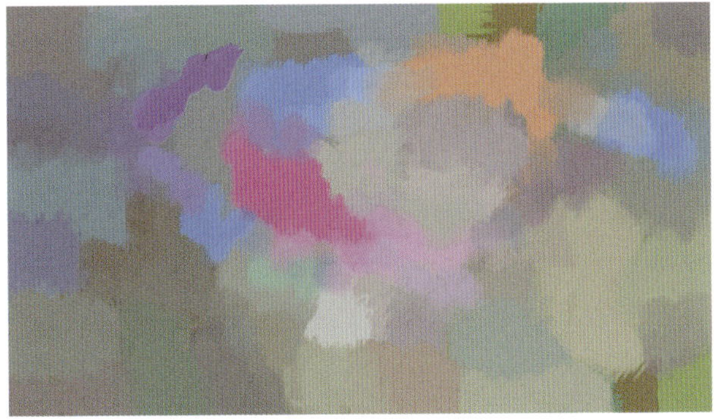

Graying down the colors allows various color temperatures to merge in a more natural and pleasing way. In the middle you'll find a few saturated colors which can grab your attention much more effectively because they are lifted by the grays.

Thinking about gray can provide you a good starting point for selecting multiple colors within a palette. Let's say you're working on a painting that features these three colors:

You could move between them like this, and end up with these colors in your painting:

But then you'll more than likely encounter the loud-voices problem, where no one color really matters, because they're *all* clamoring for attention.

Instead, try moving from color to color through the gray, like this:

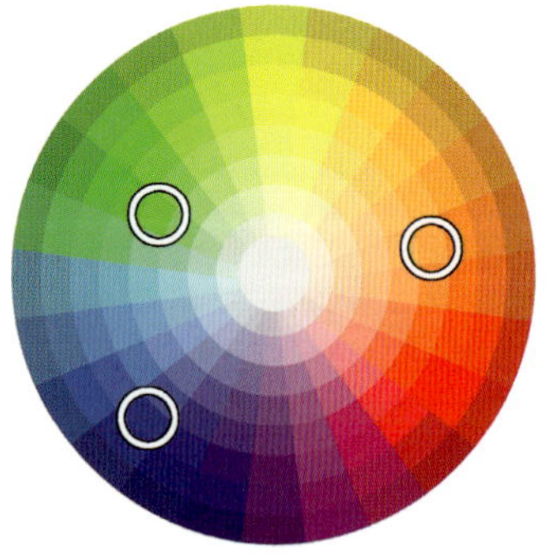

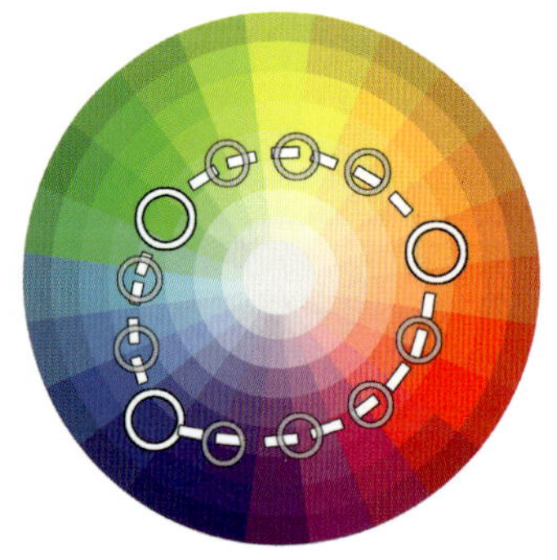

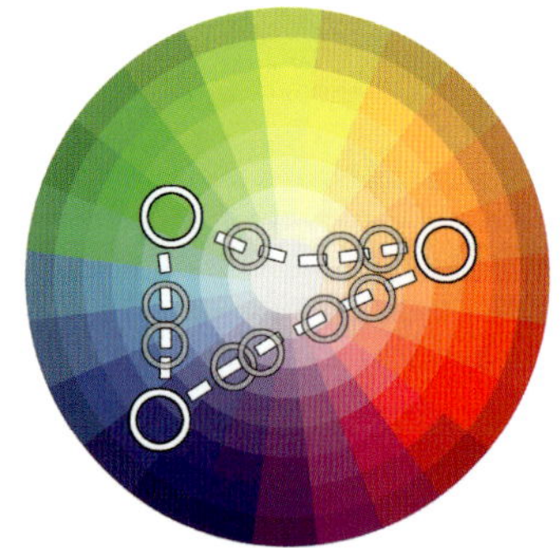

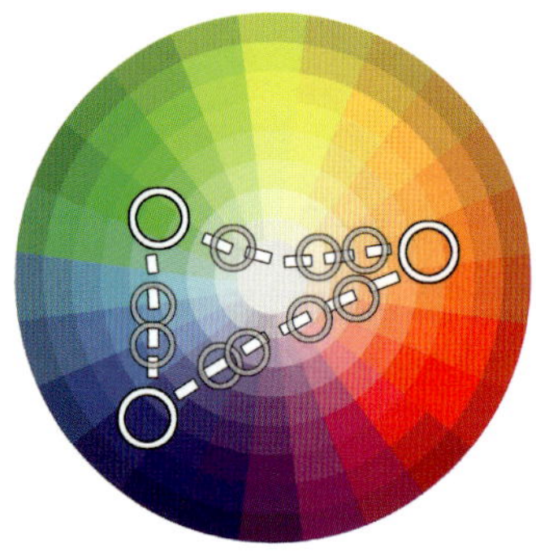

The intermediate circles represent colors that could appear in your painting.

Notice that the more opposite the color is, or the closer it is to complementary, the more that gray will influence its path as it passes through. I like to think of this as gravitational pull. The blue and green above are basically next-door neighbors so their path may maintain more saturation.

Then you're free to choose colors anywhere along that path. Your color choices could be like this (at right):

Or like this (at right) . . .

. . . or anything else. So long as you pick a few colors along the path, the viewer will intuitively understand what you're doing, because we're so intimately familiar with seeing color shifts in nature.

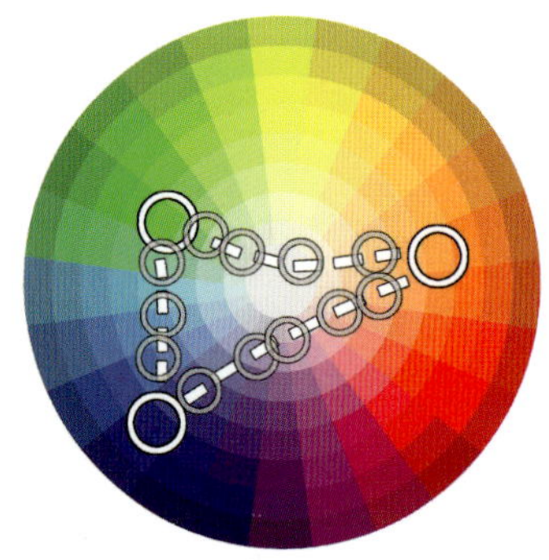

HOW DO YOU WARM UP A BLUE?

There's more! This path idea is how you determine whether you are moving warmer or cooler, and it works on very subtle levels. We need this in our color arsenal, because often you will need to compare the temperatures of two very similar colors.

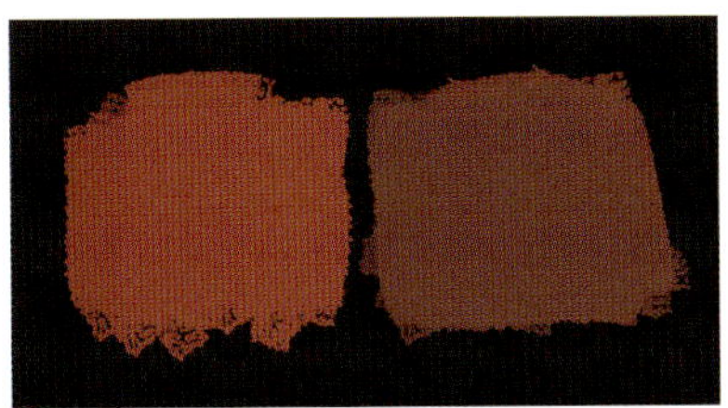

Which is warmer, which is cooler?

Not only that, but the context is always changing! For example, I'm going to say the swatch on the right is the cooler color. But now here's that same color up against a slightly different one:

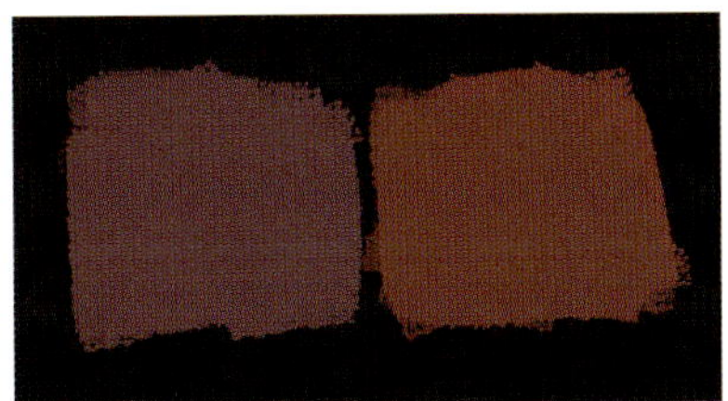

Now the swatch on the right is warmer. The conclusion? Colors can have multiple identities, depending on the colors they're seen against. To make sense of all this, you need to visualize the path the color is on. The colors above were taking this path on the color wheel:

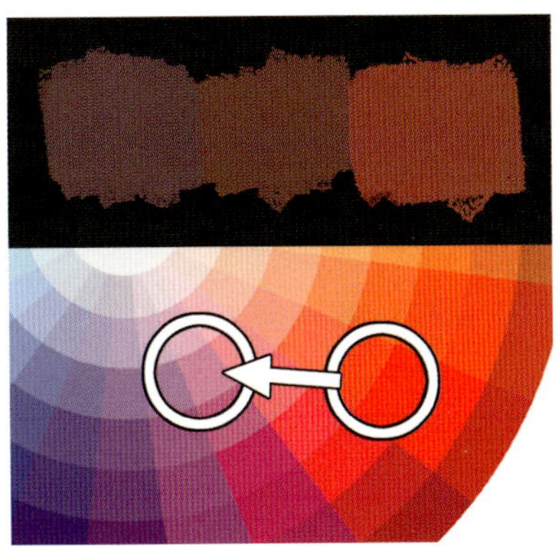

The red (right circle) is getting cooler in two ways. Its hue is moving toward violet (left circle), and it is losing saturation while doing so. Remember how every color has gray in common? That means that if a color in the warm family (red, orange, yellow) loses saturation, it is getting cooler simply because, by getting closer to gray, it is gaining something in common with the cooler family of colors.

The inverse is true as well. Consider this path:

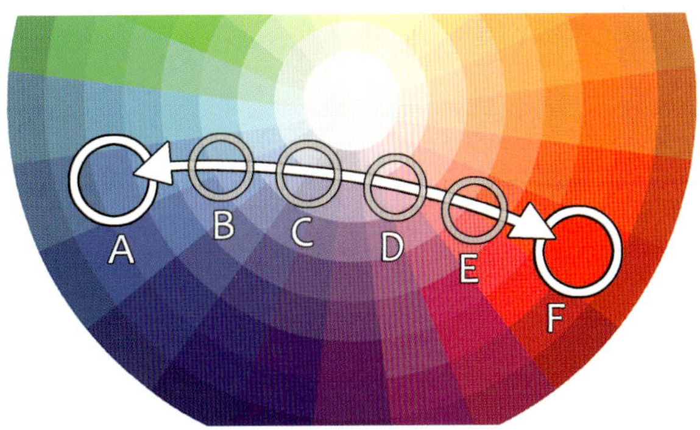

The path (shown in white) looks like this because of gray's gravitational pull that commonly occurs when two colors have gray in between them.

This shows how you could warm up a blue, or cool down a red. B is warmer than A. D is cooler than F, but warmer than C. C is a little warmer than B, but much warmer than A.

The idea is that you'd show multiple selections along this path in your painting to give the viewer the context they need to decipher it.

ASSIGNMENTS

For these last assignments, it's easiest to work digitally, but you can approximate the exercise with traditional painting tools.

ASSIGNMENT #1

Probably the most important aspect of understanding color is getting acquainted with that *bully principle*. Digital tools are best for this. Simply bring in a photograph and give yourself some room off to the side or below to paint swatches of color. Clear sunlit photos will give you the most obvious delineations of light and shadow, and the clearest shapes. Using simple swatches, paint in any and all light colors that you can sample from the photo. Once done, put your color picker close to your swatches (even placing it over the photograph itself), and sample your swatches with rapid clicks. Try to see how the colors are "pinned" on the hue strip or color wheel, toward a single hue.

ASSIGNMENT #2

Advance assignment #1 by sampling and painting swatches for any and all shadow colors in the photograph. Keep these two families separated in your swatch area. Repeat assignments #1 and #2 over several photos featuring different subject matter—from open landscapes to buildings and structures. The goal is to simply familiarize yourself with the patterns that occur in nature.

ASSIGNMENT #3

Find a painting whose palette appears to be complementary (if not complimentary, a two-color palette.) Using digital tools, make some space below the image for another swatch study. Place the warmest color on one end, and the coolest color on the other end. Using the sample tool, try to find colors in the painting that fill out the space in between, ideally being as close to gray as possible in the middle. Feel free to move colors around and repaint them in your chart as you work. What you are doing here is training your eye to respond to color temperature relationships, rather than simply looking at colors individually. Remember that very close temperature relationships can be purely subjective, and you may sort them out in a way that feels logical to you!

Final Note

As we reach the end of this book, it's my sincere hope that you have been able to find some aspect of it—something that is perhaps already in your wheelhouse or an element you feel just "clicks"— that you can use as your way into the grand world of drawing and making art. I know from experience that getting better at drawing is one of the most fulfilling personal achievements. I need to tell you, though, that the learning path is not linear. You may see real improvement one week, but then nothing the next week, maybe nothing the next several weeks. That is totally normal and destined to be part of your learning and growing. The core fundamentals and skills in this book may *appear* simple, but in reality, they can take years to master.

Improvement is simply exchanging your old set of problems for new ones. It's easy to be bright-eyed when you are actively overcoming barriers and witnessing self-improvement (and you will!). But during those inevitable times of stagnation, remember that, too, is a form of improvement. New problems are always harder than the old ones. When you level up and face new challenges, don't place the burden of expectation on yourself to solve them all right away. Bad drawings are worth their weight in gold, because eventually, and with practice, they'll point you in the right direction, clearing the way for the good stuff. You'll simply know the turns *not* to take as you navigate your way through a drawing. But the key word there is: practice!

The chapters of this book are like college semesters, each one providing enough material for several weeks, even months, of practice. I recommend doing the assignments many times over and comparing your results. Do them with not only the reference provided in this book, but find your own reference, too, and tackle the problems from many angles! Allow yourself to notice equally your improvements and your weaknesses and use that information to fuel the next round. Remember to continue to practice what you already succeed at, to refine it. But you should practice even more where you are falling short, because that's the only way to fill the gaps in your skillset.

One day you will show your drawings to someone close to you, and their jaw will drop, and they will say they had no idea you were so talented. On that day, you and I will share a knowing grin, because we can look back on all that went into it.

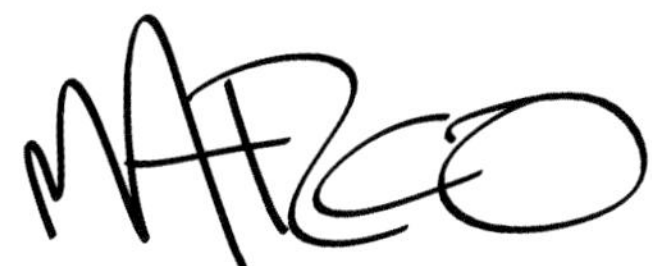

About the Author

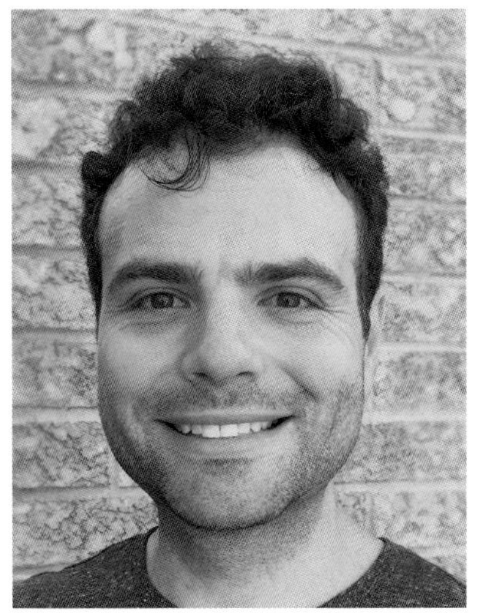

MARCO BUCCI was not artistically gifted as a child. In fact, he just plain couldn't draw. He only began his serious study of drawing at the age of 19, when he read that it's actually possible to learn. This news was a revelation, since Marco (like many people) believed one had to be born with a special talent. But through being exposed to the right kinds of information and practice, Marco now makes a living as a professional artist, working on everything from feature films, to commercials, games, book covers, children's book illustration, and television with such companies as Walt Disney Publishing Worldwide, Marvel, LEGO, LucasArts, Mattel Toys, Fisher-Price, and Hasbro. Through his YouTube channel, Marco reaches nearly 900,000 artists. He also teaches through his own platform, as well as at other online schools, such as Proko, Creature Art Teacher, Skillshare, Domestika, and CG Master Academy. He lives in Toronto, Canada.

Index

3D form and space, 56–73. *See also* Horizon line
   bending, twisting, and folding forms in, 69–72
   flour sack exercise, 72
   foreshortening and, 60–61
   perspective grids, 62–67

A
Accordion effect, 81–83
Ambient Occlusion, 143, 152–153, 156
Angles, gesture drawings in different, 50–51
Animation, 6, 72, 98
Arms
   attaching to torso, 84, 85

foreshortened, 102–103
   in gesture drawing, 42, 43, 46, 52–53
Asian eyes, 127
Asymmetry, 21
Average Light, 121, 142, 144–145
Average Shadow, 121, 142, 144–145

B
Balance, poses in, 110
Ballparking, 65, 68
Bending forms and shapes, 21, 69–72
Body language, 29
Bolded lines, gesture drawing and, 43, 44
Box(es), 76
   converting cylinder to a, 85
   draftmanship and, 76

figure, 78, 79
hands and feet, 86
the head as a, 118–119
hips, 77, 79, 80
in perspective grid, 63
torso, 77, 79, 80
Brow. *See* Eyebrows
Bully Principle, 165, 166

C
Cast shadows, 146
C-curve(s), 14, 15, 29, 40, 43, 44, 46, 47, 48, 107
Character(s), 96, 98–99
   by Brian Wong, 111–113
   caricatured figures, 114

flour sack exercise and, 72
twisting/folding forms and, 69
Cheekbone, 120, 136
Chin, the, 135
Circles
for constructing the head, 131
ellipses as foreshortened, 60–61
in perspective grid, 64
Clothing, 101, 109, 111
Color(s), 158–172
color temperature, 160–161, 164, 165
complementary, 161
describing, 164
moving from warm to cool, 162–163
shadows and, 165–166
shifting temperatures of, 168–171
terminology, 164
Color wheel, 160, 161, 162, 163, 169
Complementary colors, 161, 170
Computer animation, 6
Construction studies, of the figure,
90–93
Contour drawing, gesture drawing versus,
45
Cool colors, 161, 162, 163
Cross-contour lines, 68, 71, 120
Crosshairs, 39, 131
Curvy rhythms, 42
Cylinder(s), 76, 108
for the arms, 85
drawing, 64
foreshortened arms and, 102, 103
for the head, 79
for the mouth, 122
in perspective grid, 64

D
Dark Accent, 156
Depth
overlapping forms and, 81
perspective grid, 62
tangents of shapes and, 16
T-connections and, 18
Design
drawing as, 14
shape, 15, 19–23, 104
Draftmanship, 76
Draw, learning to, 6–7

E
Ear(s), the, 128–129
Ellipses, 60–61, 64, 79, 101
Epicanthic fold, of the eye, 127
Eyebrows, 120, 125, 126, 132, 136
Eyelashes, 125, 126, 127
Eyelids, 124–125, 126, 127
Eyes, the, 124–127, 136

F
Face, profile view of, 120, 123, 136. *See
also* Head, the
Facial features, building the, 120–129
Feet, 40, 41, 44, 86, 89
Figure, the, 74–95. *See also* Pose(s)
basic forms for, 76
building from imagination, 108–109
hands and feet for, 86
horizon line/eyeline and, 78–79
legs and arms for, 84–85
offset symmetry, 105–107
overlapping forms, 81–83
torso, shoulders, and hips for, 77, 79,
80, 90–91
tracing studies for, 87–89
Flour sack exercise, 72
Folding a form, 70
Foreshortening, 60, 102–103
Forms
of the body, 76, 77
cross-contours and midlines going
through the middle of, 68
overlapping, 81–83
twisting, bending, and folding, 69–72,
80
Form shadows, 146
Freehand, 68
Fundamentals, learning the, 8–9

G
Gesture and gesture drawings, 26–55
amount of time for, 45
caricatured figures made from, 114
creating drawings from, 106–109
examples of, 45–54
as exploration stage of drawing, 29
foreshortening and, 103
landmarking and, 38–41
multiple strokes used for, 37
rhythm and movement in, 26, 28–29,
36–37
stick figure for, 32–35
Glabella, 121, 126
Gray(s), 164, 168–171

H
Half-filled flour sack exercise, 72
Halftone(s), 121, 142, 147, 156
Hands, 41, 86, 89
Head (box), 89
Head, the, 116–137
adding features onto framework of,
135–136
as a box, 118–119
facial features on, 120–129
in gesture drawing, 39
for a pose in balance, 110

proportions on, 130–134
tilting the, 99
Helix, 129
Highlight(s), 142, 150–151
about, 142
in the eye, 126, 127
Hips
below the eyeline/horizon line, 78, 79
the figure, 90
in gesture drawing, 33–35, 39, 40, 47
relationship to torso, 77
spherical forms representing, 90
twisting and bending, 80
Horizon line
about, 58–59
ballparking, 65
the figure and, 78–79, 87
foreshortening and, 61
for one-point perspective grid, 62, 63
positioning bending and folded forms
using the, 70
vanishing points on the, 66, 67
Hue(s), 160, 162, 164, 165, 168, 169

I
Iliac crest, 33, 40, 83
Illusion. *See* 3D form and space
Iris of the eye, 125, 126
Irreducible simplicity, 12

K
Kelvin scale, 164, 165
Knees, 40, 44, 84

L
Landmarks and landmarking, 38–41, 43,
44, 80, 103, 108
Legs, 44, 48, 84, 87, 88
Life drawing(s), 6, 7, 74–75, 138–139
Light(ing) and light source, 138
about, 140
Average Light, 142, 144
Average Shadow and, 145
color and, 165
Halftone, 142, 147
Highlights, 142, 150–151
Reflected Light, 142, 148–149
shadow versus, 140
values in, 142
Light patterns, memorizing, 154
Lines. *See also* Horizon line; Midline
ballparking, 65
C-curves, 14, 15, 29, 40, 43, 44, 46,
47, 48, 107
cross-contour, 68, 71, 120
"ghosting out," 70
one-point perspective grid, 62, 64
parallel, 33

plumb, 41
S-curve, 14, 15, 29, 40, 44, 45, 46,
    107
straight, 14
three types of, 14
two-point perspective grid, 66
Loomis method, 131–132

M

Midline, 68, 94. *See also* Horizon line
changing, 76
for drawing figures, 77, 80, 87
for the face, 120, 131
folding a form and, 70
on the head, 131
Mouth, the, 122–123, 135
Movement
adding to shapes, 21
color and, 162
in the figure, 79
gesture drawing and, 26, 29, 36–37,
    42, 47

N

Neck, the, 39, 40, 43, 79, 89
Negative space, 100, 107
Nose, the, 121, 132, 133, 135

O

Offset symmetry, 19, 98, 99, 105–107
One-point perspective grid, 62–65
combining with two-point perspective
    grid, 67
Overlapping forms, 81–83

P

Parallel lines, on perspective grid, 62, 66
Perspective grid, 62–67
ballparking without a, 65
combining one-point and two-point
    grids, 67
one-point perspective grid, 62–64
two-point perspective grid, 66
Planes, 76, 78, 79, 84, 101, 116, 118,
    120–126, 130, 150
Plumb lines, 41
Pose(s). *See also* Figure, the; Gesture and
    gesture drawings
in balance, 110
with character, 98–99
foreshortened, 102–103
in silhouette, 100–101
static, 96–97
Positive space, 100
Profile view of the head, 120, 123, 136
Proportions, facial features, 130–134

R

Redundancy, 19, 20, 21
Reference photos, 100
Reflected Light, 142, 148–149, 156
Rhythm, gesture drawing and, 28, 29,
    36–37, 42–43, 48
Ribcage, 77, 80, 91
Rotating forms, 71, 80

S

Saturation, 164, 168, 169, 171
S-curve(s), 14, 15, 29, 40, 44, 45, 46,
    107
Shading, 101, 109, 138
Shadow(s), 140–141
Ambient Occlusion, 143, 152–153
Average Shadow, 142, 144–145
cast shadows, 146
color and, 165–166
form shadows, 146
light and, 144
Reflected Light, 142, 148–149
values in, 142–143
Shapes, 10. *See also* Forms; specific types
    of shapes
about, 12–13
art styles and, 24
complex versus simple, 104
fixing poorly designed, 23
overlap between two, 17–18
sprucing up boring, 19–23
tangents of, 16
types of lines for drawing, 14
understanding design of, 15
Shoulders
the figure, 90
in gesture drawing, 33–35, 39, 40,
    43, 47
horizon line/eyeline and, 78, 79
raising or offsetting, 98–99
relationship to hips, 77
rotating/twisting, 80, 92
Silhouette, the, 100–103
Sizes, varying shapes in different, 20
Skull, the, 130–131
Spheres, 76, 81, 90, 91
Square(s)
bending, folding, and twisting, 69–72
offset symmetry using, 19–20
in perspective, 61
Static pose, 96–97
Sternum, 43, 87, 91, 103
Stick figure, 32–35
Straight lines, 14, 15, 29, 41, 42, 43, 44,
    52, 107
Symmetry, shapes out of. *See* Offset
    symmetry

T

Tangents, 16–17
T-connections, 17–18
Tear ducts, 124, 125, 126
Tibia (shinbone), 41
Tone, using one or two, 101, 129, 138,
    140. *See also* Value(s)
Torso, 40, 77, 79, 80, 84–85, 87, 90
Tracing studies, 87–89
"Trending" shape, 22, 23
Twisting forms and shapes, 21, 69, 71, 80
Two-point perspective grid, 66
combining one-point perspective grid
    with, 67

V

Value(s)
color and, 158, 164
in the light family, 142, 144, 147,
    150–151
in the shadow family, 142–143, 145,
    148–149, 152–153
used with people and characters,
    154–156
Value scale, 143
Ambient Occlusion on the, 153
Average Light on the, 144
Average Shadow on the, 145
Halftone on the, 146
Reflected Light on the, 149
Vanishing point
in one-point perspective grid, 62, 63,
    64
for two-point perspective grid, 66
when combining one-point and two-
    point perspective grids, 67
Viewer eyeline, 39, 58–59, 78. *See also*
    Horizon line

W

Warm colors, 160, 161, 162, 163, 165, 171
Wong, Brian, 111–113

Z

Z axis, 62, 63
Zygomatic arch, 136